Club Management Operations

Fourth Edition

Club Management Operations

Fourth Edition

Written, edited and published under the auspices of

The Club Managers Association of America
7615 Winterberry Place
Bethesda, Maryland
20817
301-229-3600

KENDALL/HUNT PUBLISHING COMPANY
2460 Kerper Boulevard P.O. Box 539 Dubuque, Iowa 52004-0539

Library of Congress Catalog Card Number: 88–83133

ISBN 0–8403–5024–4

Printed in the United States of America
10 9 8 7 6 5 4 3

Contents

Club Managers Association of America

7615 WINTERBERRY PLACE • BETHESDA, MARYLAND 20817 • PHONE (301) 229-3600

TO THE READER

Dedicated club managers have a great desire to excel in their chosen profession. They are a proud group and a generous group. They are at their best when practicing their craft for the benefit of those enjoying the amenities, gracious service, excellent cuisine, and the "good life" of modern day clubs. Most of this book's authors are, or have been, managers of some of our country's finest clubs. The remainder are consultants, educators, or professionals with inseparable ties to private clubs.

All of these contributing authors have demonstrated their desire to share their knowledge and expertise for the reader's benefit. The student readers may use this book as a reference source. The competencies herein are proven tools and methods that are required for the efficient and professional management of a private club.

On behalf of all those who may find this book helpful, we thank the Club Managers Association of America Textbook Committee, chaired by Norman J. Spitzig, Jr., CCM; Roger Ross, CCM; Chester Beatty, Sr., CCM; John B. Hightower, CCM; Stephen A. Joyce, CCM; Donald M. Masse, CCM; and Susan Sheahan for their untiring work in completing this Fourth Edition. We also recognize the contribution of our CMAA Staff Liaison, Karen Miller.

G. Mead Grady

G. Mead Grady, CCM, President
Club Managers Association of America

Preface

In 1890, applying for a charter for the Philadelphia Country Club, John C. Bullitt made the following statement:

> Most of the subscribers are heads of families, the inducement to whom is that they, as well as their wives and sons and daughters, can visit the club for the purpose of recreation and pleasure without encountering any person or anything which will in the least degree be inconsistent with good behavior or good manners. We hope to have it conducted in so quiet and respectable a manner that ladies can go to it alone, and we hope to make it so attractive that the best people of the city will feel that it is very advantageous and desirable.

It is a statement with charm. It contains the essence of what the right of private association was—and is—all about. A club is where one may associate with one's peers, or those who have the same athletic, social, ethnic, or intellectual interests. This is good, and the right to it needs to be protected and encouraged.

However, clubs today face problems that did not exist one hundred years ago, or even yesterday. The world has changed, members have changed, and clubs have changed. Life is more complex and so are clubs and club management. The day is long past when a club can be run by a steward, or when a favorite employee on the staff can be promoted to the position of manager simply on the basis of his likeability. (Of course this has worked in the case of exceptional individuals, but even they require additional training and information.)

Back when Mr. Bullitt founded his club, the executive committee—composed of six men—did everything: renewed the lease on the rented grounds, installed a fireplug, hired and fired (right down to the locker room boys), raised salaries, and prepared financial statements. Members today do not want (or should not want) to get involved in the day-to-day management of the club. That is a job for a professional, not a committee of amateurs, and therefore, with proper management, such involvement is neither necessary nor desirable.

Furthermore, in Mr. Bullitt's time, wealthy members banded together and contributed heavily to bail clubs out of their frequent financial straits. In this age, members are not ordinarily willing to rescue a club financially. Philanthropy in most clubs is dead. The bottom line counts in today's club management, and the manager today is a businessman, a management man.

Clubs have the same purpose today as they had in the past. But they have become considerably more complex in nature and considerably more complex to manage. And so this text has been written to assist those who are in this field, or who are contemplating entering it—to help them manage, to help them achieve identity.

Donald R. Beever, CCM

In the mid 1970's several active leaders in the field of club management began to realize that there was a need for a comprehensive book covering all aspects necessary for the efficient management of a private club. This book would (ideally) spell out for the manager and prospective manager his duties and responsibilities, which would help him solve (or better yet avoid) problems which commonly arise, and which would explain some of the more complicated legal and technical problems that clubs and their managers face.

In an effort to meet this need, a committee working under the auspices of the Club Management Institute, the educational committee of the Club Managers Association of America, developed an outline for such a book with the intention of finding a teaching professional in the hospitality field to write it. This method of procedure proved unsatisfactory for a number of reasons—not the least of which was the difficulty of finding someone equally knowledgeable in all aspects of the field. The project then languished until 1978 when a Textbook Committee was appointed by George Burton CCM, then president of CMAA. The original committee members were Charles R. Walter, CCM, chairman; Donald R. Beever, CCM; Joseph Brem, CCM; E. Guenter Skole, CCM; Charles E. Smith, CCM; Horace G. Duncan, CAE, then executive director of CMAA; Arthur Gabler, then CMAA director of education; and Dr. Herman Strock, advisor.

It was obvious from the inception of the project that such a book was not going to be easy to put together. There are numerous areas of management to be covered, some relevant only to clubs. Some of the information would, of necessity, be highly technical while some could only result from years of experience. It was, therefore, the decision of the Textbook Committee to ask specially selected managers, as well as experts in relevant technical fields, to contribute individual chapters in their specific area(s) of expertise. What resulted in 1980—*Club Management Operations*—was not a be-all and end-all, but rather a compendium of the insights of people knowledgeable in the private club industry.

A second edition of this book was published in 1983, a third in 1986 and now, in 1989 the fourth edition makes its appearance. Each edition, it is fair to say, has been an improvement over its predecessor. Topics have been added or deleted, expanded or reduced and rewritten or left unchanged as required. This fourth edition was specifically prepared with varied readership in mind. Not only does it continue to function as a textbook for aspiring club managers, but it also effectively serves as an updated reference source for experienced managers as well as club directors and officers.

Fourteen chapters grace these pages, the most of any edition. Many of the chapters have been extensively rewritten to make the material more timely and more readable. For example, the chapters on "Insurance and Security Awareness" and "Taxes and Regulations" have been substantially revised to provide information meaningful to managers working in today's club environment. The various charts and exhibits throughout the book have been carefully reworked to provide more representative numbers and examples. The wealth of information on cost controls has been reorganized and expanded into two complementary chapters, one dealing specifically with food and beverage (Chapter 4) and the other with labor (Chapter 5). A new and long overdue chapter on "Clubs and Computers" has been added.

The Club Managers Association of America owes an immeasurable debt of gratitude to all those who have participated—authors, Textbook Committee members, club managers and CMAA Staff—in the ongoing success of *Club Management Operations*. I am proud and honored to have personally contributed to the advancement of the club management profession as general editor of this fourth edition and hope that you will find this book informative and useful.

Norman J. Spitzig, Jr., CCM

Contributing Authors

This book deals with the special techniques needed to successfully manage a private club. In order to provide a most comprehensive, expert and up-to-date manuscript which would be of value to the wide range of readers associated with the private club industry, the Club Managers Association of America asked top professionals to contribute. Each contributing author wrote on a specific subject area, but in order to maintain continuity of text, some of each individual's work has been integrated into other chapters as required.

The officers, directors and members of the Club Managers Association of America express their most sincere appreciation to the following authors whose work in the three previous editions of *Club Management Operations* helped lay the foundation for this most current edition: Wes Clark; Horace G. Duncan, CAE; J. Randolph Dunnavant, CPCU; A. E. "Lon" Martin, CCM; Eugene T. McSweeney, CCM; Milton E. "Bob" Meyer, Attorney; Robert R. Statham, Attorney; and Herman Strock.

The following authors directly contributed, either in the form of a new manuscript or a substantial revision of an existing chapter, to this fourth edition of *Club Management Operations*. All of us associated with the private club industry are in their debt.

Paul J. Burley, CCM, (Ret.)

A veteran of 40 years in the private club industry, associated with three clubs in the Washington, D.C. area, Mr. Burley was employed at the Congressional Country Club in Maryland, the University Club of Washington, D.C. and Woodlawn Country Club in Alexandria, VA. He has been affiliated with CMAA since 1947 and served eight years on the Board of National Capital Chapter of CMAA, acting as its president for two years. Burley has chaired CMAA workshops on two occasions and served on numerous national committees for the association. He was chairman of the 1976 National Conference held in Washington, D.C. He is a guest lecturer at the Northern Virginia Community College and guest speaker at the Washington Whirl-arounds as well as other hospitality oriented organizations.

G. Mead Grady, CCM

G. Mead Grady, CCM, is General Manager of The Commerce Club in Atlanta, Georgia. He attended Ball State University and has served as a guest lecturer on Food Service and Lodging Programs, Purdue University; lectured at Northwest Institute where he was designated a Fellow of the college; and lectured at Georgia State University. In addition, he was an instructor for CMAA General Manager Workshops and has authored numerous articles for *Club Management* magazine.

Mr. Grady has been a member of CMAA for over thirty years and has served on the Association's Board of Directors from 1974 to 1977. He has been an officer in the Ohio Valley and Georgia Chapters. He was elected to the CMAA Board of Directors in 1984 and was President in 1988.

Gerard F. Hurley, CAE

Mr. Hurley is Executive Vice President of the National Club Association, the Washington, D.C. trade association representing the tax, legal, legislative and policy interests of private clubs, including city, athletic, golf, country and tennis clubs throughout the country. He has been in association management for 22 years. He is Executive Director of the Conference of Private Organizations, national information exchange group representing private clubs, fraternal, and civic clubs. He is a member of the American Society of Association Executives and was certified by that organization in 1974. Mr. Hurley is a director of the Capitol Hill Club and the National Association Executives' Club, both in Washington, D.C.

He has a B.S. in Business Administration from the University of Maryland (1959). He has participated in numerous courses under the Institute for Organization Management of the Chamber of Commerce for the United States and has authored numerous articles for the club industry trade and consumer press. Mr. Hurley has frequently addressed CMAA chapters, national and regional golf associations and other business groups. He has lectured on club management and tax issues at Cornell and before other university classes on club or hotel management.

Michael L. Kasavana, Ph.D

Dr. Kasavana received his B.S., M.B.A. and Ph.D degrees from the University of Massachusetts. His bachelor's degree was in Hotel, Restaurant and Travel Administration; his master's degree carried an emphasis in Finance; and his doctoral studies were in Management Information Systems. Since receiving his Ph.D., Dr. Kasavana has taught at both the undergraduate and graduate levels at the University of Massachusetts and Michigan State University. In addition, he has been employed in numerous consulting roles, seminars, research directorships and faculty positions. During the past twelve years he has published several books and a host of journal articles on hospitality information systems.

Dr. Kasavana's works have pioneered many important industry/research fields. His book, *Hotel Information Systems,* (1978) was the first to address the area of hotel computerization; *Computer Systems for Foodservice Operations* (1984) was the first text to examine restaurant automation; and *Managing Computers in the Hospitality Industry* (1987) with John Cahill, provided a comprehensive overview of hospitality automation. He was also responsible for automating the concept of Menu Engineering.

H. Milton Keen

Mr. Keen is a graduate of Wagner College, Staten Island, New York, with a B.A. in Economics and Business Administration. He began his insurance career in Washington, D.C. in 1961 with Victor O. Schinnerer & Company, which was later acquired by Marsh & McLennan. He joined the Smithy Braedon Company in 1983. He has served as Underwriter, Account Executive, Consultant and Vice President.

He is a member of the Metropolitan Washington Association of Insurance Agents and of the Metropolitan Washington Board of Trade.

Dante M. Laudadio, Ph.D

Dr. Laudadio is Chairman, Hospitality Administration, Florida State University. In addition to his academic assignment, Laudadio is President of the Lassen Co., a management consulting firm specializing in the development of promotional plans and analyses, operational and cost control procedures. He has spoken to international and national groups, including CMAA, on such topics as menu development and merchandising, bar operations and controls, getting the most from employees, and how to increase check averages in food and beverage operations.

He holds a Ph.D (marketing) and an MBA (Hotel, Restaurant, and Institutional Management) from Michigan State University. He is a member of the Society of Wine Educators, and the American Marketing Association, as well as several state and national Hotel and Restaurant associations.

Gerald V. "Jerry" Marlatt, CCM (Ret.)

Gerald V. "Jerry" Marlatt was a club manager who devoted twenty-six years to the club management profession. He was, for six years, the Director of the Club Management Division of the National Golf Foundation. He has also given 32 years to the Club Managers Association of America, was a national director for four years, held all of the national offices and was the president in 1973. Jerry served as a member of CMI for five years and was twice its chairman. He has won the Fred Crawford Award, the Idea Fair, and in 1973 was the recipient of the CMAA Outstanding Leadership Award.

At the chapter level, Marlatt has served and been president of both the Oklahoma-Kansas and Greater Chicago chapters. He was the first distinguished speaker at the Conrad Hilton School of Hotel and Restaurant Management at Houston University. He has taught in CMAA workshops, PGA business schools and NGF seminars. He has lectured in GCSAA Club Management Program and for the USN Clubs Program. Marlatt is a member of the South Florida Seminole, Greater Chicago and Oklahoma-Kansas chapters. Marlatt is retired and living in Royal Palm Beach, Florida, where he works as a consultant to private clubs.

Patrick J. O'Meara, CPA

Patrick J. O'Meara is a Certified Public Accountant and a partner in the national accounting firm of Pannell Kerr Forster. Since 1958, he has personally worked on well over 200 club clients. Pat authored the chapter on clubs in the "Encyclopedia on Accounting Systems," published by Prentice-Hall. He has served as an advisor to the Budget and Finance Committee of the Club Managers Association of America and is an honorary member of the Club Managers Association of America, the Club Managers of the City of New York and the Metropolitan Club Managers Association. Pat served for 10 years as vice chairman of PKF's National Council which is the firm's policy-making board, and presently serves as PKF's Eastern Regional Managing Partner and National Director of Club Services.

Mr. O'Meara is a member of the American Institute of Certified Public Accountants, the New York State Society of Certified Public Accountants and the National Association of Accountants.

Robert Alan Palmer, J. D.

Robert Alan Palmer, J. D., is Associate Professor in the California State Polytechnic University's Center for Hospitality Management. Best known as the former legal counsel of the National Restaurant Association, he has also taught at Penn State University, and currently lectures and consults in the areas of personnel management, employment and wage-and-hour, alcohol-server liability and legal problems of hospitality management.

Mr. Palmer has spoken to such diverse groups as the American Society of Association Executives, the National Association of Convenience Stores, the International Racquet Sports Association and CMAA, among many others. He has guest lectured at major universities and has appeared on "Good Morning America" and PBS' "McNeil-Lehrer Report." His articles have appeared in *Cornell Hotel and Restaurant Administration Quarterly, Club Business, Restaurant Hospitality, Restaurants and Institutions, Fast Service/Family Restaurants, Restaurants USA,* and *Bar Business.*

A member of the Virginia State Bar Association and the American Bar Association, Mr. Palmer is listed in *Who's Who in American Law, 1987–1988.*

James E. Petzing, CCM

James E. Petzing, CCM, has been Secretary and General Manager of the Atlanta Athletic Club since 1970. After graduating from Cornell in 1955, he spent 15 years in the public sector of the food service industry before joining the Atlanta Athletic Club. Mr. Petzing has recently taught the club management course at Cornell University.

Mr. Petzing has had an active role in organizations that are allied to the club industry and those that foster responsible citizenship and community relations. He holds memberships in the Chaine des Rotisseurs, National Club Association, Atlanta Sommelier Guild, area Chambers of Commerce, the Georgia Athletic Hall of Fame, and Confrerie de Vigneron de St. Vincent Macon.

He has held all offices in the Georgia Chapter and was the 1986 President of the Club Managers Association of America.

Ronald E. Pickett, CCM, (Ret.)

Ronald E. Pickett, CCM, has now joined the ranks of retired club managers after being the General Manager of the Corpus Christi Country Club for 13 years and related service activities for a total of 33 years.

Mr. Pickett holds a B.A. degree in Hotel and Restaurant Management from Florida State University and is a retired Lt. Col. from the Air Force where he enjoyed club assignments at the two largest Air Force Clubs in Washington, D.C.—Andrews Air Force Base and Bolling Air Force Base. In addition to these important assignments, he was sent to the Air Force Military Personnel Center where he managed 450 Air Force Clubs—worldwide.

He has served the Texas Lone Star Chapter as President and held other positions at the state level and served on national committees.

Kevin F. Reilly, JD, CPA

Kevin Reilly is the Director of the National Tax Office of Pannell Kerr Forster, located in Washington, D.C. Pannell Kerr Forster is the international tax, accounting, and consulting firm whose expertise has served clubs for the past 75 years. Mr. Reilly is responsible for the Firm's tax publications and is principal Firm liaison with the Treasury Department and National Office, Internal Revenue Service. Prior to this position, Mr. Reilly was with the Office of Chief Counsel, Internal Revenue Service. He received his Juris Doctor from the Washington College of Law, American University and a Bachelor of Science in Accounting from Providence College.

Mr. Reilly is a member of the Virginia Bar and the American and Federal Bar Associations. He is also a CPA and a member of the Federal Tax Division of the AICPA. Mr. Reilly is a frequent contributor to *OUTLOOK* and is on the editorial advisory board of *Club Management*. He has written numerous articles for publication in professional journals and has participated in seminars on recent developments, including the Governmental Affairs Conference of the Club Managers Association of America.

Roger S. Ross, CCM

Mr. Ross joined CMAA in 1957. He has been a member of the Board of Directors of the New Jersey Chapter and served as secretary, vice-president and president of the Metropolitan chapter. He also serves as a National Director of the association.

He has managed clubs since 1955. These clubs include the Glen Ridge Country Club, the Morris City Golf Club, both in New Jersey, and is currently the advisory manager at the Piping Rock Club and General Manager of the Cornell Club in New York.

Ross graduated from Cornell University and has served as president of the New York City chapter of the New York Society of Hotelmen. He was also president of the Cornell Society of Hotelmen. He has been a guest lecturer at Cornell and the University of Massachusetts. Ross has also served as a director of the NYSC Association.

Margaret Shaw, Ph.D

Margaret Shaw, co-author of the chapter "Effective Marketing Communications," is currently a professor of hotel marketing and management in the Department of Hotel, Restaurant, and Travel Administration at the University of Massachusetts/Amherst. Dr. Shaw received her Ph.D. in hotel administration from the School of Hotel Administration at Cornell University. She also received her MBA from the Graduate School of Management at Cornell.

Dr. Shaw has held various positions in sales and marketing with the Sheraton and Hyatt Corporations. She has published several articles related to sales and marketing in hospitality journals. She is an active speaker at hospitality conventions and seminars.

Donald I. Smith

Donald Smith has over 24 years of industry experience and 11 years as a university professor. His broad industry perspective comes from his career as an entrepreneur, and former president and C.E.O. of Shakey's, Inc. where he directed a $3 million financial turnaround in two years. Smith was Director of the School of HRIM, College of Business, Michigan State University and is now the Westin Distinguished Professor at Washington State University. As Director of the School of HRIM, he received the 1983 outstanding MSU faculty award.

Professor Smith is an international lecturer for the National Restaurant Association, for universities and for business associations. He offers presentations concerning motivation of foodservices employees, service as a hospitality strategy, marketing, menu engineering and trends in the hospitality industry.

Brian G. Spaulding, CCM

Mr. Spaulding is General Manager of the Sky Club in New York City. He was also manager of the Stock Exchange Club; Manager of the York Club and General Manager of the Douglaston Club. He joined CMAA in 1976 and has been extremely active in the City of New York Chapter with positions ranging from Labor Relations Chairman to President.

Mr. Spaulding has been published in *Club Management* magazine. The focus has been on labor relations. He is a member of the Hotel Executives of New York and the Metropolitan Club Managers Association.

Norman J. Spitzig, Jr., CCM

Norman J. Spitzig, Jr., CCM, is Assistant Secretary and General Manager of the Fort Wayne Country Club in Fort Wayne, Indiana. He is a *magna cum laude* graduate of Boston College and recipient of a master's degree from the Ohio State University. Mr. Spitzig's previous club experience includes five years as General Manager of Losantiville Country Club in Cincinnati, Ohio, and two years as Assistant Manager at Scioto Country Club in Columbus, Ohio.

Mr. Spitzig is the author of *Perspectives on Club Management,* an anthology of articles for club officers, directors, managers and management student on a variety of topics pertinent to the private club industry. He currently lectures on club management at Indiana-Purdue University in Fort Wayne and at CMI's Business Management Institute.

Mr. Spitzig has served the Club Managers Association of America as an officer and education chairperson of its Ohio Valley Chapter, as a member of the Information, Publications and Magazine Committee, as a member and chairperson of the Textbook Committee, and as a contributing author to *Club Management Operations*. Mr. Spitzig also served as general editor of this fourth edition of *Club Management Operations*.

James W. Timmerman, CGCS

Mr. Timmerman is the golf course superintendent of the Orchard Lake Country Club in Orchard Lake, Michigan. He received a B.S. and M.S. in Soil Science from Michigan State University. Prior to going to Orchard Lake CC in 1970 he was employed as Eastern Agronomist for the United States Golf Association Green Section.

Mr. Timmerman has been a member of the Golf Course Superintendent's Association of America for 18 years. He was a national director for five years and served as President in 1984. In addition, he has been President of the Michigan and Border Cities Chapter of GCSAA and President of the Michigan Turfgrass Foundation. He currently is a member of the USGA Green Section Committee.

Charles R. "Chuck" Walter, CCM

Chuck Walter joined CMAA in 1966. He has been Secretary and President of the National Capital Chapter as well as an officer in the Paradise of the Pacific chapter, Southeast Asia Chapter and Southern California Chapter. He served as President of the Association in 1984.

He has served on numerous CMAA committees including chairman, Budget and Finance; trustee, Scholarship and Research; Certification, 1985–1987 Conference Committee; Governmental Affairs; Long-Range Planning; Student Development; Textbook; Public, Allied and International Relations; Executive Referral Service and Publications Committee.

He received a B.A. in Hotel and Restaurant Institutional Management from M.S.U. He has been assistant manager and manager at various clubs in the South Pacific, Europe and the United States for over 30 years. He was Chief, Air Force Club Systems, San Antonio, TX and attained the rank of full Colonel while on active duty as a regular officer in the U.S. Air Force. He is a member of NRA and was a winner of 2 gold medals for Best Menu Award. He is currently General Manager of the Jonathan Club in Los Angeles, CA.

Club Management Operations

Fourth Edition

1

The Private Club: Its Nature, Membership and Organizational Structure

Blue Mound Golf and Country Club, Wauwatosa, Wisconsin

Six Questions to ask

Private clubs offer superb food, well-served in elegant surroundings. They offer rolling golf courses that seem to go on forever. What are these clubs? Where do they come from? Who owns them? Who joins? Who runs them, and how? This book answers those questions.

The instinct to band together in compatible groups seems to be deep-seated in human nature and goes well beyond the goals of mutual protection and survival. Primitive societies recognized relationships based on status (determined by birth) which eventually gave way to relationships based on contract (the free agreement of individuals). As tribal communities settled down on defined land areas, territorial society arose, which further divided into religious and economic units. In the transition from nomadic hunting societies to more static agricultural societies, secret organizations with long, complicated rituals began to provide the substitute interest and excitement human nature apparently craves.

In medieval western Europe, the grouping together into voluntary associations moved from mutual aid and protection societies to religious confraternities, merchant and craft guilds, professional organizations, secret societies, and cults. People began to organize into groups completely independent of the state to further some common interest of their members.

Private social clubs have evolved now into voluntary associations not related to making a living. Nonsalaried, volunteer members constitute a majority of the participants—these are spare-time, participatory organizations.

The trend toward membership in a tightly knit club seems more pronounced in urban societies where kinship and neighborhood ties are weakest. The number of such clubs appears to be largest in America; we are truly a nation of joiners.

CLUBS IN THE UNITED STATES

The great private American social clubs that we know today—city clubs, country clubs, and others—do not (with few exceptions) date back much more than a hundred years. The Somerset Club in Boston dates from 1842; the San Francisco Commercial Club and Honolulu's Pacific Club were formed in 1851. The Pacific-Union Club in San Francisco dates from 1852; Delaware's Wilmington Club from 1859; The Olympic Club in San Francisco, the Union Leagues in Philadelphia and New York City, and the Rochester Club in Rochester, N.Y., were all organized during the Civil War.

The Country Club in Brookline, Mass., founded in 1882 with antecedents to 1860, is generally considered the oldest country club. The Myopia Hunt Club in South Hamilton, Mass., claims 1857 as its founding date.

A group of businessmen who habitually dined together at a downtown restaurant can no longer chip in a few hundred or a few thousand dollars for an option on some vacant land for a golf course and a clubhouse. Nor can they readily obtain a lease on an old brownstone mansion for an exclusive men's retreat. The origin of many present-day prestigious golf and city clubs no longer fits in the modern scenario.

The golf facilities of the last three decades (whether or not organized as private country clubs) appear to be, to a substantial degree, of the residential or resort development variety, established to increase nearby real estate marketability. They are clearly not the result of spontaneous community undertakings. Executive-type luncheon facilities organized as private clubs in conjunction with construction of new downtown office complexes have proliferated. Nonetheless, an analysis of the current membership of the National Club Association indicates that less than ten percent of its member clubs have been organized as recently as the 1970s and 1980s.

Today's private clubs can be broadly classified as social and/or recreational, but these categories are misleading. Clubs can be described as town or country clubs, although these terms simply hint at location, sometimes falsely; occasionally, the classifications suggest the nature of the club's primary facilities.

What is a private club today? For our purposes, E. B. White probably said it best: "It is easier for man to be loyal to his club than to his planet; the bylaws are shorter and he is personally acquainted with the members."

We all know what we mean by "private social club" at the far end of the spectrum—it's "private." Membership in such a club is generally focused on a certain group or common interest—university graduates, the press, women, military affiliation, certain ethnic or religious groups, members of particular professions or political parties. The public is excluded and membership is restricted to those people selected by participating members.

The "social" attributes of a private club seem largely dependent on its food and beverage amenities. Town clubs range from luncheon-only clubs that serve segments of the business community to fully integrated dining and athletic clubs, occasionally combined with living accommodations for members and transient guests. Country clubs tend to offer elaborate social amenities along with their outdoor recreational facilities; they cater to golf, tennis, swimming, horseback riding, boating, and other athletic interests. And yacht clubs take on the nature of town or country clubs as they take advantage of their particular marine locations and specialties.

As we move down the list of clubs from elegant clubs to more spartan ones, we see differences in the value and extent of physical facilities, stability of membership, permanency of management and staff, number of months of actual operation, and amount of membership fees and dues charged. The picture and dividing lines between what is and is not a club go from fuzzy to murky to blank.

What clubs, exactly, are we talking about? It's easier to define the ones we aren't. Gale's *Encyclopedia of Associations* counted more than 36,000 societies and fraternal and patriotic organizations in 1970—private social groups associated with national membership organizations. We aren't counting those. We also are not writing for managers of the neighborhood swimming or tennis club with snackbar facilities or less, or for groups of individuals that meet in a member's home. We are writing for groups whose members convene at a regular place, which they either rent, lease, or own. The accommodations themselves vary according to the purposes and services for which the club was organized. The members employ a manager to run their facilities and operations; they have a common bond or interest and a selection criterion for incoming members.

What Kinds of Clubs?

No comprehensive statistical surveys of such private clubs exist, but the Club Managers Association of America and the National Club Association recently estimated that about 13,000 organizations meet their definitional criteria as private social clubs. It is for managers of these groups that this book is written.

The National Golf Foundation now estimates that over 6,000 private country clubs exist, more than any other type of club. Activities of the typical golf and country clubs center around their golf courses, but the clubs usually provide members with outdoor swim and tennis facilities and, often, paddle tennis courts, saunas, and other athletic accommodations. Recent statistics indicate that in 1988 the average golf club had approximately 700 members and that average annual dues were in excess of $2000 per regular member.

The second most prevalent type of club is the city club, which serves the social needs of individuals working in the urban core. These clubs (probably no more than 2,000 of them) have varying types of facilities, including athletic facilities, overnight accommodations, and library or reading rooms. Their common goal is to provide a haven for social interaction or relaxation in the heart of the city.

The term city club covers a diverse group of organizations, with interests ranging from a desire to preserve the Union (Union Leagues) to sports (athletic clubs). Only a few hundred of these clubs qualify as old-line, social institutions. The typical city club in 1988 averaged nearly 2000 members, and the average dues per regular member was near $1000.

Other types of clubs popular today include yacht clubs, tennis clubs, hunt clubs, and beach clubs; in fact, the types of clubs are limited only by the common interest of individuals and their imagination.

Member-Owned Versus Proprietary

It is generally assumed that members own whatever financial assets exist in the club, but that isn't always true. Some clubs, or their assets, are owned by an individual or corporation.

Most clubs today, especially the old-line ones, are owned by their members and governed by a board of directors elected by the members. As in commercial corporations, member are considered shareholders; usually one member has one vote, although some clubs sell bonds to members who then have a favored voting position.

A proprietary club is one that is owned by an outside individual or corporation; the members have no equity interest in the club or effective control over its operation although they may have some influence. Such arrangements are popular with clubs built and operated by developers as an "amenities attraction" to a housing development. One variation on the proprietary club arrangement has the club's facilities owned by a corporation and leased to the membership, which then completely controls its own internal affairs.

Proprietary clubs are normally for-profit endeavors, and, therefore, pay corporate income taxes. Member-owned clubs have the option to be tax exempt. Qualifications for the exemption are discussed in the chapter on taxes and regulation.

Common Bond, Selected Members

The private club label is applied to many types of membership organizations, but there are two prerequisites of a private social, recreational, or athletic club in the context of this discussion. One is the common bond among members; the other, the membership selection process.

The term "private club" implies the existence of personal contact, commingling, and fellowship among members. It presupposes a common involvement among members in a given recreation or pursuit. Indeed, the Internal Revenue Service views this common bond and personal contact as criteria for a club to maintain an income tax exemption.

To be a "private" club, a club must not allow nonmember individuals to use club facilities merely by paying an admission fee; the club would then be a public accommodation. Individuals in the United States have a constitutional right of association guaranteed by the First Amendment. This right allows them to choose their companions and associates through membership in a private club. The selective membership process is basic to the American personality, but the psychological implications of exclusivity often dominate the issue. Groucho Marx probably stated it most succinctly: "I wouldn't join any club that would have me."

At issue here are not the pros and cons of a particular membership selection process, but, rather the need for the process as part of the definition of a private club.

Membership Maintenance and Promotion

A club must maintain its membership at an appropriate level. During recent years, several clubs have ceased to operate because of declining membership. Some clubs that once had waiting lists now find that, for the first time, they have fallen below the maximum level of membership dictated by their bylaws. Since membership increases mean more dollars and increased facility use, an active membership committee is imperative.

If a club is in financial difficulty and needs new members, the board of governors should not try to keep this fact from the present members. Some clubs are afraid to let their members know the true situation for fear that members may resign from the "sinking ship." But current members are the principal source of new members and as such should be kept informed and encouraged to enlist new members.

The membership committee should provide a professionally produced membership brochure complete with attractive photographs. After all, a club is competing for dollars that could be spent on a lavish vacation rather than a year-round membership.

One way to recruit new members is to encourage members of the board of governors and committee members to write personal letters to their friends in the club asking them to introduce new members. Club brochures are also helpful.

Finally, to assure continuing success of any club, young members are a must. Without them, a club is in danger of dying. For this reason, a club should take an occasional census to determine the average age of its members. If the average age is high, the club should make every effort to attract younger members. This is why some clubs provide members under 35 years of age with all the privileges of a regular member without requiring full dues. Young adults in their twenties are encouraged to join with even a greater dues reduction.

Membership Election

Clubs have varying requirements for membership, but generally a candidate must be proposed and seconded by two members of the club. Many times, neither sponsor can be a member of the board of governors. If membership is for a nonresident candidate, the proposer details the candidate's qualifications for admission. The candidate's name together with the names of the proposer and seconder appear on the club's bulletin board before the nomination is considered.

Election procedures should keep pace with the times, particularly procedures expediting candidate elections. A club may well lose prospective members because of complicated election procedures established in 100-year-old bylaws. For example, one club requires not only that a candidate for membership be proposed and seconded, but also that ten other members submit letters of recommendation on behalf of the candidate. If this particular club were experiencing membership problems some bylaw changes would be in order.

Membership Levels

Although maintaining a maximum level of membership, some clubs may want to increase this maximum if there is any financial difficulty. Some clubs oppose this approach based on the belief that adding members overtaxes the club's facilities and dilutes existing freedom and enjoyment. It has been found, however, that this is not necessarily a sound argument. Some members feel that they will not be able to play as many rounds of golf if membership were increased. But, in fact, the number of rounds per golfing member varies among even comparable clubs. The key is better organization of playing activity by effective club management. Similarly, increasing membership by 20 percent can readily be absorbed in the food and beverage departments of many country clubs. Enlarging locker and storage facilities, obtaining additional help, and similar expansion problems are not insurmountable. An increased membership also helps to finance major improvements and to spread the operational costs over a larger membership.

Clubs find the arbitrary resistance to membership expansion has broken down over the years with the movement toward special classifications such as social members, junior members, nonresident members, or tennis members. Expanded classifications increase capital resources and make use of otherwise underutilized facilities. In some clubs, these special memberships account for as many or more than the so-called "regular" members. Thus membership expansion is both feasible and financially advantageous.

Types of Memberships

Private clubs are not required to have more than one type of membership, but the desire for additional members who might otherwise be unwilling or unable to pay full membership dues and initiation fees has led some clubs to create a variety of "nonregular" membership categories. In a recent sampling of the bylaws of fifty clubs, all had a primary resident or regular membership; 91 percent had nonresident memberships; 93 percent had junior memberships; 91 percent, honorary memberships; 84 percent, social memberships; and 84 percent, senior memberships. The survey also identified some clubs with military, collegiate, widow, and other classes.

Many factors are considered in determining appropriate membership classes; age or location of business or residence are determinants in a city club; age, facilities to be used, residence, and other factors are considered in country clubs; age, location of residence or business, and number of years out of college are considered in university clubs.

The annual dues for each nonregular membership classification is generally established as a percentage of the regular dues, rounded to the nearest $10. The use of many different membership categories, with varying dues amounts, can cause administrative and accounting problems. Clubs should, therefore, limit their membership classifications to a reasonable number. Nonetheless, clubs should establish the membership classifications appropriate to the objectives and needs of the club and its members.

Following is a brief analysis of the major country and golf club membership categories, including examples of their respective bylaw provisions. Beach and yacht clubs, and those clubs with similar facilities, have the same membership classifications as country clubs. A discussion of the membership categories in city and university clubs completes the chapter.

Country Club Memberships

Regular Membership

All clubs have a "regular membership," which allows full access to all club facilities and, in the case of member-owned clubs, a vote in the election of club directors and the right to hold office. Regular members usually pay the highest dues and initiation fees of all member classes. In some country clubs, the dues established for a regular member covers the member and his family (children under 18 or 21, still living at home, unmarried) for the use of all facilities at the club. Other clubs charge an additional fee for golf privileges for the spouse or other family members. Or, a separate dues structure may be established for a "family membership" to cover the regular member's family.

Some clubs charge a "user fee" to all members, including regular ones, for the use of certain facilities, for instance, platform tennis added by many clubs in recent years. Many clubs include tennis and swimming pool privileges as part of the regular dues structure; others charge user fees for these facilities.

A regular membership in a golf club is generally a family membership in the name of the man of the house; however, clubs are increasingly making this category available to women, especially those related to members. The age requirement for regular membership varies, but averages from 30 to 35, reflecting a tendency to recruit members who have attained a certain business or professional status.

A member's family is usually granted access to all club facilities at no additional cost; the family often retains certain privileges if the male member dies. For instance, the wife may be automatically eligible to use the facilities at a reduced dues rate until she remarries. (See also the section of this chapter on Widow's Membership.)

Children of regular members, after reaching a certain age (usually 18 or 21), often must apply for junior membership status. They do not have to have their names placed on the normal membership waiting list. (See also the section in this chapter on Junior Membership.)

Sample Regular Membership Bylaws Provision: "Regular members shall have the right to vote at all meetings of the members of the club; to serve as directors; to hold office; to share in the assets of the club upon dissolution thereof; and subject to the rules and regulations as the board of directors may from time to time adopt or approve, to enjoy the use of the property and facilities of the club."

Organizations that set a maximum average age for a serving group can stimulate advancement for younger members by requiring newcomers to fit the "average."

Associate Membership

Associate members (or "weekday golf members") generally have all the rights and privileges of regular members except that they are not entitled to vote or hold office in the club. They may not be entitled to play golf on Saturdays, Sundays, or holidays and as a result their dues are usually less than those of regular members.

House Membership

House members are generally entitled to use the clubhouse and the food and beverage facilities of the club; normally they are not entitled to use the various sporting facilities without paying an additional charge. All members of a country club have the basic privileges of a house member; for example, a so-called "tennis member" probably pays dues that entitle him to all the privileges of a house member, and for the additional privilege of using the tennis facilities. A member who wishes to use only the swimming facilities pays the dues of a house member, plus an additional fee for the use of the pool. A member who wishes to use both the tennis and swimming facilities pays dues structured to cover the dues of a house member with tennis and pool privileges. This member may also be known as a "nongolfing" member.

Social Membership

Social membership is similar to a house membership and permits member access to the clubhouse only, usually for food and beverage and social privileges only. Clubs sometimes admit social members or house members when their facilities will not comfortably accommodate additional regular members. Many golf clubs use this mechanism as a way to expand their membership base; individuals join the club as social members until there is an opening in the regular membership.

Sample Social Membership Bylaws Provision: "A special membership, shall be available at the discretion of the Board of Directors. Such membership, which shall be nonvoting, shall entitle such members to the benefits of the clubhouse and social functions only. (Pool and tennis privileges shall be optional for additional dues fees.) The total number of social members shall not exceed 25 percent of the authorized regular membership."

Junior Membership

Some clubs have created junior memberships for persons between the ages of 21 and 30. This classification is also called "intermediate," "special," "under 30—golf," or "associate." Junior membership is ideally suited for children of regular members too old to use club facilities under their parent's membership; members' children usually do not have to get on the club's waiting list to join as junior members.

Junior members are entitled to use all club facilities, but they rarely have an equity interest in the club or a vote in its operation. Dues and initiation fees are lower than those of regular members, in keeping with the lesser incomes of persons under 30.

Sample Junior Membership Bylaws Provision: "A special membership, to be known as a Junior Membership, shall be available, at the discretion of the Board of Directors, to persons between the ages of 21 and 30. Juniors shall pay such annual dues (which shall not exceed one-half of the annual dues of regular members) as the Board shall from time to time fix; but no other fees shall be required of them, except that the Board may require an annual payment, to be applied to Regular Membership Fees."

Or, for a junior membership limited to sons and daughters of regular members; "Regular Members' sons and daughters who have reached the age of 21 but have not attained the age of 30, and who are unmarried and residing with their parents, shall be eligible as Junior Members. A Junior Member shall cease to be a Junior Member if the parent ceases to be a club member or when the Junior Member marries, leaves the household of his or her parents, or attains the age of 30. A person whose Junior Membership is to be terminated for any reason may apply for Regular Membership."

Senior or Life Membership

Recognizing the senior member's often limited ability to pay and his many years of support for the club, many clubs have created a senior membership category with a reduced dues structure. This type is usually based on some combination of age and years of club membership; for example, if a total of 90 gross points were required, a member 70 years of age, who had been a club member in good standing for 20 years, would qualify. Clubs must be especially careful, when creating this type of membership, that they do not set such a low gross total that a member can qualify on the basis of age alone.

The dues of a senior member are generally established at some reduced rate, for example, half the dues of a regular member. Senior membership can also be offered to members of other classifications, such as house members. Clubs must ensure that they do not become overloaded with senior members who pay little or no dues, because the dues load for the remaining regular members would increase.

Sample Senior Membership Bylaws Provision: "Senior members shall be those regular members who have enjoyed membership in the club for not fewer than 20 years and have attained the age of 70. A senior member shall have the rights, privileges, and duties of a regular member but shall have the obligation to pay one-half the dues of a regular member. Surviving spouses of senior members shall be eligible to become senior members if they were married to the deceased senior member during the entire period of the deceased's membership in the club."

Nonresident Membership

Country clubs may have nonresident members, whose status is determined by their legal residence and regular place of business. Nonresident members must usually live and work more than a specified number of miles (generally 50 to 75) from the club. Club members who move to new locations, and who thus have infrequent access to the club, sometimes do not wish to sever all their club ties. Nonresident memberships may be limited to former regular or social members.

The dues structure for a nonresident member is usually determined as a percentage of regular membership dues—generally less in a country club than in a city club.

Sample Nonresident Membership Bylaws Provision: "Nonresident membership shall be limited to persons who reside outside the County of XX. For the purpose of these bylaws, residence outside the County shall be determined by the actual place of abode irrespective of the legal domicile of the candidate for such membership. If a nonresident member who was formerly a regular member reestablishes residence in XX County, he or she automatically shall be reinstated to regular membership if a vacancy exists in the regular membership. If no such vacancy exists, the person shall have all the rights and privileges of a regular member, shall pay the dues of a regular member, and shall be entitled to fill the next available vacancy in the regular membership."

Widow's Membership

A widow of any member of the club, of any membership class, can usually become a "special member" in that same class on the death of her husband. The dues structure for a widow is usually somewhat less than the dues for the membership category in which she and her husband had belonged.

The membership of any woman member, in any class, normally expires at the end of her dues year if she marries or remarries. Her new husband can usually apply for membership at that time and, if approved, should be elected without delay. The husband is expected to pay an initiation fee, equal to the excess between the current initiation fee of the class he applied for and the initiation fee of the class membership his wife previously held.

Clergy Membership

Certain clubs grant clergy memberships to some clergymen in their communities. These members usually have all the rights and privileges of regular members, except they do not vote and they do not hold office. Clergy members generally pay no initiation fee and only nominal dues.

Honorary Members

Some clubs also elect honorary members to the club. These members generally have all the rights and privileges of regular members, except that they may not vote or hold office. Honorary members do not usually pay initiation fees, dues, or assessments.

City Club Membership

City clubs have fewer membership classifications than do country clubs, usually because their facilities are more limited. Some clubs have athletic facilities, and may or may not charge their members a user fee for them. Such facilities may include squash courts, swimming pools, saunas, gymnasium, or tennis courts. The demand on the facility may be such that a club institutes a user fee since some members benefit from the areas more than others. The membership classifications generally used by city clubs follow.

Regular Membership

Regular (or resident) members of a city club are those who are entitled to use all facilities and are over a stated age limit, generally 35 years of age. They are equity members, entitled to vote and hold office.

Junior Membership

Junior membership in a city club is usually based on an individual's age; generally anyone 35 years old or less qualifies. Junior members are usually entitled to all membership privileges and may even be entitled to vote on club affairs.

The junior membership category may include several classifications, determined by age—one classification for members between the ages of 26 and 30. This subdivision is used primarily for the dues structure; younger members pay lower dues.

Nonresident Membership

Nonresident members are those with no residence or place of business within a certain mileage radius of the club. The distance varies from club to club, depending on its location. Some clubs may set a 50-mile requirement; others establish a 100-mile boundary. Nonresident members are not entitled to vote or to hold office in the club. Dues are usually established as a percentage of regular membership dues.

Suburban Membership

Some city clubs have recently established a category of suburban membership. A suburban member is basically one who cannot meet the requirements of nonresident membership. His residence and place of business are not far enough away from the club for him to qualify for nonresidency status, although his residence and place of business are not far enough away that he cannot use the club as much as a resident member. Thus, some clubs have established a suburban membership category for those individuals who live and work outside the city limits. The dues of a suburban member are usually established somewhere between those of the nonresident and resident members.

Honorary Membership

Honorary membership is usually reserved for certain local or federal heads of government or other dignitaries. These members pay no initiation fees or dues and cannot vote or hold office in the club.

Senior Membership

Senior membership in a city club is usually restricted to those individuals 65 years of age or older who have been club members in good standing for a number of years, for example, 25 or 30 years' membership. The dues are usually reduced to half the dues charged a resident member.

Clergy Membership

City clubs elect certain clergy to a special membership classification. These clergy pay no initiation fee, but they may pay nominal dues. They are entitled to all of the privileges of resident members, except they may not vote or hold office.

Luncheon Club Membership

Luncheon clubs have basically the same membership classifications as city clubs. They are open for lunch only and offer no other amenities or accommodations. Their dues are generally less than those of other private clubs.

University Club Membership

University clubs generally have the same membership classifications as city clubs, but their junior memberships are based on time out of school, rather than age. For example, there may be one junior membership for individuals out of school for 3 years, and another for those out of school 6 years. Regular memberships are generally reserved for individuals out of school 10 years or more.

Military Club Membership

On most military installations two or more types of private membership clubs exist for military members, retirees, and civilians working on the installation. These are voluntary organizations, but membership is restricted by grade structure. There are two categories of active members (voting and nonvoting) and an honorary membership category for local and/or federal dignitaries.

Other Membership Classes

It is impossible to list all of the various membership classes that exist in private clubs today, because no two clubs are alike. Clubs near a military base may create a membership class specifically designed for a transient population; clubs in a state capital may establish an honorary membership class for key state legislators; clubs with extensive athletic facilities may have various membership classes, each relating to only one type facility.

Transfers

Clubs generally permit members to transfer from one membership category to another, if such openings exist under the club's bylaws. Members applying for transfers from one category to another may be given preference over a nonmember applying for membership. For example, if a golf club has a waiting list for golfing members, it may give preference to a house member who wishes to transfer to a regular membership. This policy, of course, encourages people to join clubs as house members while they are waiting to join as full members.

Club bylaws usually require that a member transferring from a lower dues structure to a higher one must pay the difference in initiation fee between the two classes. Of course, on attaining the higher dues category, the member must also pay the higher dues. Similarly, if a member transfers from a high dues category to a lower one, he receives a reduction in dues, although his initiation fee is not refunded.

Resignation and Discipline

Resignation

Generally, a member is not entitled to any rebate of any fees, dues or charges of any kind upon resignation, death, suspension or expulsion. Furthermore, the resignation of a member is usually accepted only if he has paid his dues and outstanding charges.

Suspension/Expulsion

The Board has the authority to prescribe rules for the use of the club by members and others and for their conduct in the clubhouse and on the club grounds. The Board of Governors generally has the right to suspend or expel any member of any class, at any meeting of the Board, for a violation of the club's bylaws or of the rules of the club or for conduct which, although it may not constitute such violation, in the opinion of the Board, is improper and prejudicial to the interests of the club.

The suspension/expulsion process usually requires an affirmative vote of at least two-thirds of the Board of Governors and the Board is usually the sole judge of what will be considered improper or prejudicial conduct. Usually a member may be suspended without prior notice, but before he or she can be expelled (except in the case of past due indebtedness) notice in writing, containing a specification of the charge or charges, is usually mailed to him or her (at his or her last known office address) that such action will be considered by the Board at a time and place mentioned in such notice. Many times the member in question is given an opportunity to be heard by the Board of Governors at the time it discusses such a serious matter. At such meeting, the bylaws of many clubs permit the member the right to his own witnesses and the right to cross examine other witnesses within such limits as may be determined by the Board.

To say that the Board should be very careful in its consideration to suspend or expel a member would be a gross understatement. To suspend or expel a member is indeed a most serious action and should not be taken lightly. Accordingly, the Board of Governors under such circumstances would probably be much better off requesting the member in question to resign. Should such request be disregarded, the Board may then proceed with its action to expel the member. Common sense would dictate that such matters be discussed with the club's attorney before any action is taken by the Board and that the facts and circumstances be documented very carefully in the event that they are needed in the future.

Discipline of Delinquent Members

Besides suspension or expulsion, there are certain other ways that a club can discipline its members. For example, when members do not pay their bills on a timely basis, many clubs "post" the name of such delinquent members. This is done in order to embarrass the members into paying their bills promptly. Here again, in order to avoid possible legal entanglements, the "posting" of members should be given very careful consideration. Perhaps, as a prerequisite of membership, the member should sign a document authorizing the posting of his name if he does not meet certain obligations. Even then, the accounting office should be quite certain that a particular individual has, in fact, not paid his bill prior to posting his name on the bulletin board. (Payments of house charges do sometimes get credited to the wrong account and it could be very embarrassing not only for the member but also for the club and officers of the club if a member's payment was recorded incorrectly and his name was posted without justification.) It may be wise to telephone the member a few days prior to posting to adivse him of the impending action, particularly if he has never been posted before and is not one of those few individuals who are constantly delinquent.

Furthermore, if a club intends to follow the procedure of posting delinquent accounts, it should bear in mind that *all* the members of the club are the owners thereof and certain individuals should not be exempt from the posting process. If an Officer of the club or a member of the Board of Governors is delinquent in the payment of his charges, his name should be posted in the same manner as the name of any other delinquent member.

As a further discipline to delinquent members, the Board of Governors may also have the authority to impose late payment penalties on those members who do not pay their bills on a timely basis. Some clubs charge a flat amount, regardless of the amount of the indebtedness. Other clubs may charge a percentage of the outstanding overdue balance. If a club uses the percentage method, it should verify the legal and other requirements of the "interest" charge with the club's attorney.

Other Disciplinary Action

Rather than outright expulsion or suspension from the club, the Board of Governors may also suspend a member's privilege to use a certain facility for a period of time. For example, suspending a member's golfing privileges for two weeks, yet permit him to use the other facilities.

Organizational Structure

Hundreds of members collectively direct their clubs; their wishes are interpreted by constantly changing boards of directors and their programs implemented by hundreds of thousands of employees. Every private club has its own established bylaws, house rules, and policies and many clubs have essentially the same printed rules and regulations but the clubs are totally different with respect to atmosphere, community standing, personality, and reputation. And these differences are attributable to the various clubs' employees.

Private club's personnel are as diverse as the members; the number of employees may range from 20 to 400, but the organization structure is basically the same:

1. Members;
2. Board of Governors;
3. Executive Committees;
4. Committees;
5. General Manager; and
6. Staff.

Successful club management depends largely on effective interaction up and down the chain of command. To be effective, participants must understand what their responsibilities are, how those responsibilities relate to the overall management of the club, and how they should be discharged. There are four major participants in a typical club's chain of command: the board of directors, the committees, the manager, and the staff.

Board of Directors

The essential function of the board of directors at a club is to govern. In its oversight capacity, the board determines club policy regarding all significant aspects of management, including establishing club policies for attaining membership and regulations for club use, setting and monitoring budgetary priorities, ensuring that club policies fulfill the needs of the members, and seeing that the club is being run efficiently and effectively.

One problem board members frequently face is particularly worth noting. Often committees, in seeking to achieve specific objectives for the club, have difficulty keeping within their established budgets—which are set by the board of directors. It is incumbent upon the board to ensure that the committees (as well as the other management elements) do not overspend while accomplishing their objectives. Ultimate fiscal responsibility for the club resides with the board members and requires continuous, careful monitoring.

The board's perspective is essentially a long-range one. It should look at the big picture: Where is the club going? What should it try to achieve? Is the club conforming to the principles established in its charter?

Although the board ideally remains apart from the day-to-day operational aspects of the club's management, it must not become aloof from the needs of the members, their problems, and their dissatisfactions. Indeed, the more "tuned" the board is to what the members are thinking, the more effective it can be in guiding the club successfully. At the same time, the board should not enter a day-to-day question of chocolate versus vanilla ice cream.

There will, of course, be occasions when the board will need to focus on specific operational aspects. Issues that affect the club's legal liabilities, for instance, or its fiscal integrity could require the direct attention and direction of the board.

If the effective functioning of the board of directors is essential to a well-run club, it follows that the board itself should be selected with care. Board service requires members to have the ability to lead and communicate effectively and to accept and delegate responsibility. Because the club is an integral element of the community at large, a member of the board should not only demonstrate a commitment to the club and a capacity for service to the entire membership, he should be responsive to those factors from the public domain—legal, social, and bureaucratic—that affect a private club.

Selecting a board member is primarily a matter of good judgment; the following profile, however, may be helpful. In general, the successful nominee will be:

1. Alert, knowledgeable, and mature;
2. Well regarded by others;
3. Open-minded, unbiased, unselfish, and reliable;
4. Able to work well with others, particularly the manager;
5. Sincere in desiring to serve the club;
6. Upstanding in personal habits and activities; and
7. Able to devote the time and energy required for board activities.

Although the responsibilities of the board of directors must cover a broad area, the critical factor in successful board leadership is HOW it governs. Essential to that success are:

1. Good communication, both within the board and down the chain of command;
2. Revitalization of membership;
3. Delineation of authority; and
4. Effective decision-making processes.

In a general sense, the board bases its policy decisions on the information it has about what is going on in the club. Thus, the quality of that information directly affects the quality of those decisions. Good communication among board members and with the committees, the manager, and—to some extent—the staff helps to ensure that the board members' decisions address the needs of the club in the best way possible.

The board can facilitate good communication in several ways. Internally, it can brief new members thoroughly—provide minutes of past meetings and reports and hold personal conferences—before they attend their first meeting. The new member can thus participate fully from the start. With the committees, the board can establish some type of liaison, either by appointing a representative of each committee to communicate with the board or by assigning board representatives of the committees who, in turn, report on the committee's activities and progress.

Revitalization of the board membership goes hand in hand with good communication. A static composition of the board can quickly undermine creative thinking, stunt communication with the club membership, and generally keep the club from prospering. A regular turnover on the board—or at least a staggered-term policy—enhances the vitality of the decision-making body and precludes the club membership from feeling that the club is not moving forward or that they are powerless to initiate change. Club members should be encouraged to serve on the board or on committees. They should be made to feel that *their* contribution is important.

It may be desirable to have an age-spread among group members, so that policy-oriented tasks can be generally assigned to older members and action-oriented jobs to younger ones. Above all, it is important to ensure that each task assignment makes clear the objectives, individual responsibilities, and budgetary constraints involved. This not only eliminates frustrating duplication of effort and confusion over lines of authority, it sets the stage for the most efficient use of manpower and the most effective results.

Delineation of authority is crucial to good club management. Most clubs have and attempt to follow an organizational chart, but the lines of responsibility can frequently blur as membership changes and new leaders set up relationships and communications links independent of those prescribed in the club's policy manual. One of the key concerns of the board, therefore, is to ensure that the agreed-upon chain of command and areas of responsibility be understood and maintained.

However wisely a board's composition is selected, the bottom line regarding its utility hinges on the effectiveness of its decision-making process. The following guidelines can help create a process that produces meaningful results for the club. In preparing for a business meeting, the chairman of the board (and of the committees as well) should:

1. Identify pertinent objectives to be discussed;
2. Prepare a concise agenda;
3. Ensure that the meeting room is properly equipped; and
4. Choose an accessible site and convenient time for the meeting.

During the meeting, the best results can be achieved if the chairman will take care to begin the meeting with items that members agree on before discussing decisive areas, although exceptions to this order are possible. Regardless, a careful chairman will be aware of the atmosphere being created in the meeting. Most meetings tend to engender more enthusiasm early, so it is wise to schedule items needing mental energy, creativity, and thought early on the agenda, and hold issues of great interest and concern to members for the later portion of the meeting.

In conducting the meeting, the chairman should make sure that all members present understand the issues to be discussed, why they are important, and what the goals are. Having succeeded thus far, however, many chairmen falter when it comes to actually keeping the meeting running smoothly. The successful chairman will:

1. Keep control of the discussion, and not allow others to dominate the discussion;
2. Talk only to the group;
3. Involve all members in the discussion;
4. Ensure that speakers are heard by all members;
5. Clarify all issues before moving on to a new subject;
6. Remain neutral, but positive;
7. Keep conflicts between individuals to a minimum, stress areas of agreement, and review progress made;
8. Close discussion when it becomes evident (a) that more facts are needed to proceed, (b) when discussion reveals that additional members not present are needed, (c) when members need

more time to consider the proposal, (d) when it appears that changing events may soon alter the basis of the decision, (e) when more time than is available is needed to cover the subject adequately, (f) if it appears that the issues can be settled better outside of the meeting;

9. Finally, wrap up the meeting effectively. Summarize the meeting's accomplishments, assignments, and decisions. Get a verbal commitment from each assignee (and be sure to follow up later).

Committees

Committees can be highly successful elements of a club's management. As a group, they can address a wide variety of issues; individually, they can encourage a sense of team spirit and commitment among club members, keep the club up to date in specific areas, help guide the club, and provide important opportunities for leadership.

Committees may vary in size according to the needs of the club. Generally, the larger the committee, the less participatory its members seem to be, although a larger committee can handle larger tasks. Smaller committees encourage interaction and contributions by individual members, but care should be exercised to ensure that the group is not so small that it cannot adequately address a project. Motivational experts believe that five members on a committee is optimal.

A committee chairman must not only guide the actual meetings; he should first bear in mind what it is that the committee is being asked to achieve, what is the best way of accomplishing it, and, in the final analysis, how its success can be evaluated.

The Manager

The relationship between a club's board of directors and its manager has more influence on the success, growth, and tone of that club than almost anything else. All other aspects—membership, pricing, controls, participation, facilities, communication, personnel, and so forth, are important as well, but the critical factor is how the manager and the board interact. This important relationship is sometimes negative or adversarial, largely because there is no established policy on the kind and type of club desired. The manager, therefore, should be given a sense of direction, a set of goals to pursue.

Boards should also be wary of false economies. It is not possible to "hire high but pay low." A good manager may be expensive, but it is a worthwhle investment in the future of the club.

The way a manager perceives his role and his relationship to the board is essential to the overall managerial process. The effective manager will deal with the board as a peer, providing advice as well as accepting it. This relationship will be satisfactory if both understand and agree to their roles and what they expect of each other.

Characteristics Common to Success

Some 100 successful association managers were recently asked to name the traits or talents they thought were most important in contributing to their success (and that of other successful association managers they knew) and the leading association officers of those managers were asked to name the outstanding qualities they thought made their managers successful.* The responses were comprehensive and revealing.

**The Why's of Association Success*, Samuel B. Shapiro, CAE 1977, American Society of Association Executives.

The responses were grouped under 11 major "trait" headings and ranked. Not surprisingly, there was high agreement between the managers and the officials; comments from both sources outline the specific bases of a board-manager relationship. The rankings follow:

Managers' Ranking	Officers' Ranking
1. Interpersonal relations	1. Interpersonal relations
2. Dedication-commitment	2. Dedication-commitment
3. Integrity	3. Organization-administrative ability
4. Organization-administrative ability	4. Intelligence
5. Creativity-vision	5. Knowledge of industry-profession
6. Intelligence	6. Integrity
7. Knowledge of industry-profession	7. Creativity-vision
8. Professionalism	8. Leadership
9. Communications abilities	9. Communications abilities
10. Leadership	10. Professionalism
11. Spouse	11. Spouse

As noted earlier, the board is authorized by the membership to set the course for the club—to set policy and establish goals. The manager, on the other hand, should be a participant in that planning, capable of and prepared to set in motion through programs and services the board's plans. Too, it is the manager's responsibility to ensure that the programs and activities of the club remain within the constraints of the budget. Above all, the club must be able to rely on a strong manager to provide a sense of continuity and ensure forward momentum during times of change.

Technically, the manager has the responsibility, under the aegis of and in conjunction with the policy formulated by the board of directors, to ensure efficient and profitable club operations. He must establish standards of personal administration, performance, and service to members and guests; determine room rates if guest rooms are involved; create appropriate publicity, oversee food selection and level of service; and plan dining room, bar, and banquet operations where applicable.

As if this were not already enough to keep a good manager busy, he is also expected to ensure that facilities are properly maintained, allocate authorized funds, authorize expenditures, help plan budgets, hire and fire personnel, field and remedy complaints, and delegate responsibilities down the chain of command.

The manager is essentially a team leader; he must keep the "team"—both staff and club members—informed of pertinent club information and cooperate with the committees and board in representing the views of the members.

It is a tall order for any manager. A well-considered, flexible, accepted management plan is, therefore, indispensible. It allows a program to be monitored and kept on course, and establishes a clear-cut direction for both the manager and the board. It also provides the manager with a mechanism for maintaining control by discouraging committees—or individuals—from taking unilateral actions that may alter a program's course. Even though the board retains overall control of policy, a good manager never loses control of operations. Instead, he will remain the junction through which a program begins, proceeds, and culminates.

As with all leaders, a manager must earn the trust and admiration of the club membership, the committees, and the board of directors. The manager who treats everyone with equal respect and warmth, who consistently "plays fair" regardless of with whom he is dealing, will be assured of that trust.

REVIEW QUESTIONS

1. List three types of clubs and the types of services they offer.
2. List five kinds of club membership, who is eligible for them, the privileges these members receive, and the relative dues structure of each membership type.
3. Who owns a club?
4. What are the elements of a club's management hierarchy?
5. Who does run the club? Describe the role of each participant.
6. What are some of the qualities of a successful club manager according to board members? According to the managers themselves?

Ans.

Clubs are < Social < Food - meals, Health - Facility (sports, golf, tennis; Recreational < boating, swimming, racket ball etc.

1. Country Club
City Club
Common interest of members < Type of activities or circumstance to gather yacht - tennis - hunt - beach

2. Regular
Associate
House
Social
JR - Sr
Non-resident
Widows
Clergy
Honorary

3. Member - Non profit individuals
or
Proprietary - profit corporation

4. Members
Board of Governors
Exc. Committees
Committees
Gen Manager
Staff

By Laws / house rules / policies
Differ by Type
Atmosphere
community standing
personality
reputation

Inter Action of Board - Manager

5. Board of Directors Long Range
Committees
Manager Day to Day operation
Staff

6. See Page 18

2

The Club Manager: Authorities and Responsibilities

Baltusrol Golf Club, Springfield, New Jersey

Managing a club is a highly specialized profession. The job often makes out-of-the-ordinary demands on a manager but provides a wide range of satisfaction as well. To understand what a modern club typically expects of a club manager, a brief historical overview of the changing role of a club manager is necessary.

THE CHANGING ROLE OF A CLUB MANAGER

The role of the club manager has changed considerably since the origin of the club. The first clubs in ancient Greece and the Roman Empire were political in nature, very exclusive and usually revolved around the communal baths. They provided relaxation, privacy and membership separation of the sexes. The employees were generally slaves and a favored slave was the manager. Much of the government's behind-the-scenes business was conducted at these baths.

Clubs during the turn of the 19th century were the exclusive preserves of the rich. Membership was the social "in thing." Clubs were used primarily in America to preserve this exclusivity. As most club members' homes were mansions requiring a full-service staff, the members equated club employees with their own maids, butlers and cooks. Although a few managers were treated as professionals and held the respect of their members, most were still treated as servants.

This servile attitude towards club managers in America was changed significantly by two events which occurred during the first half of this century.

One was the passing of the 16th Amendment to the U.S. Constitution in 1913, the legal foundation of and justification for federal income tax, and the other was the stock market crash of 1929. Prior to 1913, when a club facility ran into the red (and they did even back then!) certain affluent members would decide how much each would "ante-up" to sustain the club's operation for another year.

When the after-tax disposable income of these gentlemen was significantly curtailed, so was their willingness to accept a club's financial obligations personally. The system of sheltering the accumulation of wealth had changed drastically.

The 1929 stock market crash also significantly reduced the number of people able to afford the luxury of club membership. If clubs were to survive as a fundamental part of American life, professional managers able to provide for the social and athletic desires of their membership within the constraints of a limited amount of funds would be needed.

Today's club manager has a variety of management responsibilities covering the full spectrum of the industry. The club manager of the 1980s continues to encounter a wide diversity of problems, ranging from the current morass of wage and hour laws to the proper methods for maintaining athletic facilities. The spotlight is now on the experienced, well-trained professional club manager, a person rapidly becoming responsible for one of the most important facets of the hospitality industry. Clubs are at last acknowledging the fact that they are, in a very real sense, businesses and the club manager a true business person.

How does the aspiring club manager gain the professional skills necessary to enter and successfully remain in this most challenging and rewarding field? The most direct path, of course, is through formal study. However, until very recently, the profession of club management was largely overlooked as a specialized curriculum of study. Those wishing to acquire the specific knowledge needed to succeed as a professional club manager often enrolled in one of the hotel schools and, if they were lucky, learned the unique skills of their chosen profession under the tutelage of an older, more experienced manager through on-the-job training.

EXHIBIT 2.1

Sample Two-Year Club Management Course Curriculum

Year One—First Semester

Introduction to Club Management (Orientation in the history, growth and development of the club industry. Provides basic information in organization, personnel management, sales promotion, purchasing, production control, and includes the study of techniques and procedures of modern management.)

Hospitality Dining Room Service

Bar Management and Operations

Year One—Second Semester

Merchandising in the Hospitality Industry

Sanitation Safety in Food and Lodging

Seminar in Product Knowledge

Personnel Management

Year Two—First Semester

Club Management Practicum (On-the-job training in a local club facility with emphasis on front-of-the-house operations.)

Catering and Banquet Management

Club Management Certification (A seminar designed to acquaint students with the various local clubs. Managers from these clubs present information in seminar fashion related to management and operations of their properties.)

Year Two—Second Semester

Restaurant Purchasing/Cost Control

Club Management Practicum (On-the-job training with emphasis on back-of-the-house operations.)

Law for the Hospitality Industry

Club and Resort Management (A study of military and private club management which will encompass resort operations and management in the areas of lodging and food service.)

Food and Beverage Management

Today things are changing. Not only is the number of schools offering degrees in the hospitality industry growing, but many of these same schools are customizing programs specifically for those who wish to become club managers.

Exhibit 2.1 on this page details the curriculum of a typical two-year club management course curricula.

The number of higher educational institutions offering formal, specific training in club management is, however, far from adequate to accommodate all those wishing to enter the field. The continuing education programs offered by the Club Manager's Association of America (CMAA) are an excellent way to obtain or augment the specific training needed to succeed in club management in the 1980s. Ample educational opportunities are available through CMAA for club managers lacking in either the experience or formal education to become fully knowledgeable in the application of the sound business principles needed for the successful management of clubs.

National and regional workshops sponsored by CMAA are also excellent opportunities for managers to increase their management skills in areas specific to the club field. Courses are taught by highly trained professionals and offered in areas ranging from "Menu Engineering" to "Professional Money Management Techniques" to "Personnel Development." Furthermore, the educational content of all such workshops is re-evaluated regularly to assure the continued dissemination of current, meaningful information.

Other CMAA educational tools include *Club Management* magazine and the various "Information and Research" publications. *Club Management* is the monthly periodical endorsed by CMAA because of its continuing professional content and the "Information and Research" publications include several reference packets on items ranging from menu promotion ideas to the use of computers in clubs. A much more detailed description of the various educational services offered by CMAA can be obtained by contacting the association directly at the address listed in the front of this book.

A significant event in the evolution of the club management field as a highly specialized area of expertise occurred in 1965 with the establishment by CMAA of the "Certified Club Manager" (CCM) designation. Specific and rigorous educational and experience requirements must be met before a manager is able to attain this designation. This hallmark of professional knowledge and competence is not easy to achieve, as indicated by the fact that only 24% of current CMAA members are "CCM's." Statistical survey after survey indicate that "CCM's" are in great demand by quality clubs throughout the country and that their salary and compensation packages are proportionally greater than "non-CCM's." The Club Manager's Association of America is currently working on developing educational and experience criteria for an even more advanced professional designation, the "Master Club Manager" ("MCM"). Clearly the day is fast approaching when CCM's and MCM's will be fully recognized in the club industry as the professional equivalent of the CPA to accounting or the CLU to insurance.

Three other professional organizations merit mention for the quality educational programs they have continued to make available to both the aspiring and active club manager.

The National Restaurant Association (NRA) offers a wide range of educational seminars and workshops covering its sphere of interest. Typical courses include "Labor Costs and Management", "Banquets and Buffets" and "Computers and Food Service". Information on these particular courses, as well as the additional professional services offered by the NRA, can be obtained by contacting the national headquarters at 1200 Seventeenth Street, N.W., Washington, D.C. 20036, (202) 331–5900.

The American Management Association (AMA) is an excellent source of miscellaneous information in the area of management. AMA offers thousands of courses and seminars each year in general management categories including purchasing, research and development, human resources, general management, information systems technologies, finance and accounting.

The AMA's courses range from basic sources of information to the latest technical developments applicable to upper echelon management. A complete description of courses that are currently available can be obtained by contacting the American Management Association, 135 West 50th Street, New York, New York 10020, (212) 586–8100.

The National Club Association (NCA), the national industry association representing the common business interests of social, recreational and athletic clubs, offers a wide range of educational tools specialized for the club industry. Typical topics of NCA publications and seminars include financial controls, the intricacies of tax for private clubs, the law regarding selective membership policies, and wage and hour regulations for club employees. In the continuing attempt to fulfill its avowed purpose "to support a positive and economic climate for private clubs and their members", NCA will increase both its seminar programs and educational publications over the next several years.

Information on NCA seminars and educational programs can be obtained by writing or calling NCA Headquarters, 1625 Eye Street, NW, Suite 609, Washington, D.C. 20006, (202) 466–8424.

AUTHORITIES AND RESPONSIBILITIES

The duties of a club manager are, in large part, a function of the particular club in question. Some clubs prefer to employ a "general manager" while others choose to hire a "club manager" and/or a "clubhouse manager". The tradition, financial status and degree of board involvement in the day-to-day operations all contribute to which type of management style is best suited for the club in question.

A manager is considered a "general manager" if the basic flow of authority is from the club board to the manager to the rest of the employees—and that means *all* employees.

Although the title "general manager" was given to some men and women more than 50 years ago, only in recent years has it come into widespread use. The "general manager" concept is now believed to be the natural trend in clubs, according to most leaders in the industry. More and more general managers will be required to fill the leadership void that is growing in private clubs. Members themselves are becoming less willing to devote the time and energy needed to meet the growing demands of managing a club, as traditionally has been required of board and committee members. Members of the future will want to divest themselves of even more club responsibilities.

CMAA has endorsed the following language as suitable for explaining the ideal relationship between the general manager and the club board of directors, as well as his typical duties and authorities:

- The elected club officials (officers/directors/governors/trustees) formulate policy and provide guidance for the general manager but do not involve themselves directly in the management of personnel or operations. The general manager is completely responsible for all phases of management and accountable to the "governing authorities" for performance of the entire management team and for all operating results.
- The relationship between the "governing authorities" and the general manager must be carefully defined. Both relationships are identical to those in any business corporation. The first is similar to the relationship between the board of directors and the company president or chief operating officer. Club committees should work with the general manager the same as subcommittees of a corporation board of directors work with the president or chief operating officer.
- The general manager reports directly to the club's chief elected official or his authorized representative. He also works in tandem with the full body of governing authorities.
- The general manager serves in the capacity of chief operating officer of the entire club and implements the policy established by the governing authorities.
- The general manager develops operational policies and is responsible for creation and implementation of standard operating procedures for all areas of the club.
- The general manager prepares the annual budget and, after board approval, manages and controls the operations to attain the desired results.
- The general manager supervises all department heads, including the clubhouse manager, food and beverage manager, all professionals, golf course superintendent and controller/auditor.
- The general manager coordinates all management functions of the club.

The benefits to those clubs that choose to operate under the general manager concept are several:

1. Dollar savings (e.g., better interdepartmental utilization of equipment, proper management of human resources, central control of major expenditures.
2. A clear definition of everyone's exact areas of authority and responsibility.
3. Standardization of employee policies (e.g., salary scales, fringe benefits, holiday pay, overtime policies, meals, life and health insurance, etc.).
4. Better interdepartmental information and cooperation (e.g., more informative contributions to the monthly club bulletin, the successful implementation of major sporting events, etc.).
5. Organization of the club in a more efficient manner.
6. One more "line of supervision" when a department head is away. Board members of any organization are, or should be, policymakers, not operational supervisors.
7. Stability and objectivity. While committee chairmen at a club change on a regular basis, a long-term general manager is often able to provide a more neutral analysis of the many problems associated with each department, those between departments, the solutions that have proven workable and those that have not.

The duties and responsibilities of a "club manager" or "clubhouse manager" also depend on the organizational structure of the club in question. The fundamental distinction between a "manager" or "clubhouse manager" and a "general manager" is that not all employees report directly to the first two. In country clubs, for example, the golf, grounds, tennis and pool professionals (or any combination thereof) report directly to the appropriate committee chairman when a "club manager" or "clubhouse manager" format is utilized. Sometimes, clubs specify that certain athletic professionals report directly to the manager (e.g., pool manager) while others do not (e.g., golf professional) thereby forming a sort of hybrid between the "manager" and "general manager" concept. The uncertainty accompanying this sort of management concept often creates more problems than it solves.

A "club manager" or "clubhouse manager" typically performs the duties listed below:

1. The club manager is responsible for heading the line functions of the operation, such as the food and beverage, housekeeping, and engineering departments. He may also assist in the management of club recreational areas.
2. The club manager cooperates with the governing body of the club (and, if applicable, the general manager). He advises and furthers the goals of the club as specified in its organizational structure.
3. The club manager establishes policies and operating procedures for the clubhouse.
4. The club manager hires personnel in the clubhouse and reviews the hiring selections of various department heads.
5. The club manager writes directives covering policies, rules and regulations and approves those directives written by department heads.
6. The club manager has authority over interdepartmental disputes and implements policies concerning employee/employer relations.

7. The club manager carries out all established procedures which will result in the financial condition desired by the club's governing body (and, if applicable, the general manager).
8. As head of all departments within the clubhouse, the club manager is consulted in those decisions which influence a change in established policy. He also suggests changes and may direct the implementation of any such change.
9. Although the club manager delegates his authority to various department heads, he is still ultimately responsible for all operations within the clubhouse and may make any changes within his authority that he deems necessary for the successful operation of the clubhouse.

CLUB EXPECTATIONS

Not only have the authorities and responsibilities of a club manager expanded and become defined over the years, but the specific duties have as well. Needs vary, not only from club to club within a certain category, such as country clubs, but from category of club to category. These duties differ according to the type of club, but whether the orientation is primarily social, professional, political, or athletic, the club will have a basic set of expectations of its manager.

To begin with, a club requires a manager who genuinely likes people—someone who enjoys serving others and who derives real satisfaction from the close personal contact with a variety of people and professions. After all, the club is its people—its members and its staff. Because the club manager (unlike the manager of a hotel) must deal primarily with the same people over an extended period of time, the club needs to know that its manager is someone who will be available to the members and who will foster a cooperative, enjoyable club atmosphere.

The individual characteristics of a manager will vary widely from person to person. However, certain key qualities and abilities are common among those who excel:

1. Effectiveness in interpersonal relations
2. Dedication—commitment to the welfare of the club
3. Integrity
4. A strong sense of organization and ability to administer
5. Creativity and vision
6. Intelligence
7. Professionalism
8. Ability to communicate well
9. Strong leadership capability
10. Industry experience

The ability to communicate well with others, whether within the management chain of command or directly with the club membership, is a most important quality indeed. Specifically, the manager should be able to make the people he serves feel important as individuals and should ensure that the staff complements those efforts. Greeting members by name whenever possible is an excellent method to develop personal rapport. By being diplomatic, even under difficult or stressful circumstances, by really listening to what members have to say, by developing and maintaining a congenial atmosphere within the club, and by avoiding partisanship, a manager can successfully implement club policies and simultaneously promote a cohesive, progressive organization that remains attractive to the membership.

Accepting criticism is also part and parcel of managerial responsibilities. How well a manager accepts constructive criticism can greatly affect the general direction of the club. To accomplish the goals and maintain the progressive atmosphere desired at the club, a manager must often endure the unfavorable opinions of a vocal minority. In such instances, however, the successful leader will continue to press forward rather than opt for the false sense of security that comes when initiative is never exercised. Similarly, a manager should be prepared to receive less credit than is actually deserved; those who really matter are sure to be aware of a manager's contribution to a healthy club.

Levels of dedication necessarily vary among managers, but generally the more dedicated the manager, the more successful the club. True dedication involves more than a desire to "get ahead" in the business. It requires a firm commitment to the ideals and goals of the club and to satisfying the membership. The manager should always be motivated by a genuine desire to make the club work as well as possible and to constantly seek ways to raise its standard of operational excellence.

Managing a club is both complicated and demanding. It requires, therefore, a strong sense of organization and the ability to formulate and administer plans and programs to achieve specific objectives. The effective manager is usually one who has learned to establish priorities and then see them through to completion. This requires the continued implementation of management controls and the support of a cooperative staff. The manager is, after all, the leader of a team—the staff. Without that reliable, competent team, the manager has the proverbial "two strikes" against him before he even begins.

A good manager must also have a broad knowledge of current business methods, budgets and financial statements. Using these tools, the manager can continue to monitor potential problems that may affect the welfare of the club and then make an informed decision to prevent such problems from becoming unmanageable. It is essential, however, that the manager, as a consensus finder, work closely with both the board of directors and the club committees. Their support—or lack of it—can strongly influence the manager's effectiveness and success, particularly when strong, decisive action is called for.

Not only is a manager responsible for promoting a positive public image for the club within the community, but he must strive to foster an acceptable personal image as well. This requires a keen sensitivity to what the members want and expect of their manager. The extent to which members consider the manager a social peer will vary with each club, but in almost all cases the successful manager is someone who chooses to maintain a low profile within the club. The manager is, first and foremost, the professional who directs the club operations. In so doing, the successful club manager will promote understanding and acceptance of his managerial methods and, at the same time, retain the support and good will of the club membership.

MANAGER'S EXPECTATIONS

Just as a club has specific expectations of its manager, there are many things a manager can—and should—look for from a club if it is to attract and retain a competent professional. These expectations are equally valid for both general managers and managers.

1. *The authority to effect genuine, positive change by implementing the policy decisions of the board of directors.*

When a particular board of directors has accumulated sufficient information to arrive at a sound operating policy, it is then up to the manager, with the full support of the board, to implement that policy in the way he determines to be most effective.

In addition, the competent manager should be given the latitude to implement all such policy in the style unique to his or her personality, educational background and work experience. For it is the manager, in best knowing the abilities and needs of the staff under him, who also knows the most effective methods of getting his staff to do what needs to be done because they want to do it.

2. *A salary and benefits package commensurate with position, performance and industry competition.*

The manager who is a competent "professional", in the most basic sense of this word, justifiably expects to be treated as such by a board of directors. Essential to such treatment is a fair salary and benefits package, one that is commensurate not only with a manager's authority, responsibility and his actual performance of said duties, but one that is at least commensurate with "similar" positions at "similar" clubs and businesses.

It is entirely reasonable for a manager to expect his annual compensation package to keep pace with improved performance, expansion of responsibilities, salaries offered by the "competition" and/or inflationary pressures. The responsible board of directors is the one which provides a specified time for both an in-depth performance review of the perceived strengths and weaknesses of their manager and an accompanying salary review.

Many managers feel that it is preferable to have a contract, whether annual, biannual or renewable every three years, with the club. Some managers feel that such a contract serves as an instrument to remind the board of a regularly scheduled review of salary and fringe benefits. As binding agreements for both parties, contracts can be of substantial benefit if either the club or the manager decides to separate.

Not all clubs will agree to extend a managerial contract for a new employee. Some are willing to do so only after the new manager has demonstrated a satisfactory job performance. For those clubs willing to negotiate a contract, three years is usually the maximum span. Because most boards are composed of directors who serve on a rotating basis, there is a widespread reluctance on the part of any existing board to "tie the hands" of a succeeding board by entering into a lengthy contractual agreement with its club manager. Conversely, however, some boards may seek to negotiate an extended contract with their professional because of their strong belief in the importance of managerial continuity.

Assuming that the club and the manager have agreed to negotiate a contract, what should the manager expect to have it include? Basic to any contract, of course, are such things as salary, duration and cancellation provisions. It is in the area of fringe benefits that many managers are unsure as to how much they can reasonably expect. One relatively common fringe benefit worth negotiating is housing. Some clubs provide a residence on the club premises for the manager and his family. This arrangement is desirable not only from the manager's financial point of view but is also convenient for the club.

As another example, most clubs provide meals for employees while they are on duty. Occasionally, a club will also provide meals for the manager's family. Exhibit 2.2 provides a guideline for formulating a manager's contract and a list of the more common fringe benefits that are available to the aspiring club manager.

EXHIBIT 2.2

Sample Club Manager Employment Contract

(Wherever a masculine personal pronoun appears, please consider it nongender.)

Suggested Clauses for Use in Preparation

(This is not a pro forma *contract. No blanket contract could be formulated which would cover every detail of the business relationship between club and manager. Clauses here are guidelines for providing proper wording—for use in whole or in part as the situation dictates. Additional and/or alternate clauses are enclosed in slashes.)*

Opening Statement

This Employment Agreement is made this ______________ day of ______________________,

19 _____ between the ______________________ (hereinafter referred to as the Club) and

__________________ (hereinafter referred to as the Manager.)

/The Manager is, at the time of execution of this Agreement, employed as Manager of the Club and the parties are desirous of continuing such relationship for an indefinite period./
/All previous employment agreements are hereby superseded by this Agreement./

Employment

The Club does hereby employ the Manager, and the Manager does hereby agree to be employed by the Club. It is understood and agreed that the Manager will faithfully and diligently serve the Club to the best of his ability in this capacity.

Term

The term of this Agreement shall commence on __________________________, 19 ________, and continue indefinitely until terminated as provided for herein.

Termination

This Agreement may be terminated after one full year by either party upon written notice, delivered

at least _______ days prior to the effective date of any termination.

Duties

The Manager shall assume complete control of the management of all club operations/with the exception of (*list areas or activities for which* **not** *responsible*)/, and shall devote his time and capabilities exclusively to the welfare of the Club and its facilities within the framework of the general policy promulgated by the Club's governing body.

Responsibilities

The Manager shall be responsible to the Club's governing body for all actions concerning the Club's operation; and specifically to the presiding officer thereof in event of conflict of interest among the members thereof.

Enforcement of Rules

As part of his duties, the Manager shall use all reasonable efforts to ensure that club regulations are obeyed by members; and shall bring to the attention of the Club any violations, abuses of privilege, or matter of unbecoming conduct on the part of members.

EXHIBIT 2.2
Continued

Board Meetings

The Manager shall attend all meetings of the Board of Directors, for the purpose of learning and advising on factors influencing policy decisions.

Arbitration

In case any disagreement or difference shall arise between the Club and the Manager hereto regarding their respective rights, duties, powers, and obligations under the terms hereof, or arising out of the interpretation of the bylaws, rules, and policies of the Club, such disagreement shall be settled by arbitration in accordance with the rules then obtaining of the American Arbitration Association.

Club Privileges

The Manager and family, shall have the privilege of using the facilities of the Club, subject to the proper performance of his duties and the convenience of the Club.

Salary

The Manager shall initially receive a salary of $ ______________ per annum, payable in equal/ semi-monthly installments. Future salaries shall be at such rates as are agreed upon between the Club and the Manager; and shall be paid at such intervals as may be mutually agreed upon, from time to time, between the parties.

Bonus

In addition to the fixed compensation stated above, the Club will pay the Manager a bonus, annually, in lump sum, in an amount ranging between $ __________ and $ ____________, as a reflection of the Club's degree of satisfaction with the Manager's performance.

Retirement/Pension

In addition to salary, the Club agrees to contribute, at the rate of $ ______________ per annum for so long as this Agreement shall continue in effect.

Group Insurance

The Manager shall be entitled to inclusion in all insurance and hospitalization plans available to employees of the Club as a group.

Quarters

The club shall furnish suitable living quarters for the manager and family /which they shall occupy as a condition of his employment and for the convenience of his employer./

Extended Illness

Should the Manager be unable to perform his duties because of illness or other incapacity, he shall be retained at full pay and allowances until his return to duty / for one month / plus one week for each full year of employment / whichever occurs first. At the expiration of this period this agreement shall be deemed terminated unless, at the discretion of the Club, it may be continued.

EXHIBIT 2.2
Continued

Inurement

This Agreement shall be binding upon and inure to the benefit of the Club, its successors and assign, but shall not be assignable by the Manager.

IN WITNESS WHEREOF; the parties have executed this Agreement on the ______________ day of ________________, 19 _____

ATTEST: (Club) ______________

__________________ By: ______________

Title: ______________

WITNESS:

__________________ (Manager) ______________

Manager's salaries vary both regionally and according to the size and type of clubs. They may also be affected by the social or business status of the individual club and its unique financial position. Before a prospective manager determines in his own mind what salary level will be acceptable, these factors should be taken into consideration. Generally, a club manager's base salary will fall into the $50,000 to $100,000 per year range, depending on the above considerations and the manager's education and previous experience. Over and above salary, a manager is sometimes given a nominal cash bonus at the end of the year out of a member-sponsored "Christmas fund" or if the club has had an especially profitable year.

The manager should always exercise caution in negotiating a contract. Pushing for an excessive salary or exorbitant fringe benefits might very well create an initial spirit of ill-will with the board, whereas keeping the overall welfare of the employing club in mind could, in the long run, be the manager's best approach to lasting success.

3. *The opportunity and challenge to advance to greater responsibility within the club.*

The position of "club manager" is, in one way at least, a rather unique one. The majority of club managers begin their duties at a new club as the "general manager" or "manager"—that is, as the most responsible and best compensated of all club employees. According to most recent CMAA surveys, fewer than 20 percent of all CMAA member managers previously were employed at the same club they now manage as an assistant manager or department head.

Because of this rather startling statistic—startling when compared to the standard in-house promotion policies of major businesses—it is no wonder that many club managers develop the feeling over a period of time that they simply have no room to advance professionally in their present positions and consequently feel compelled to move on to "bigger and better" things within a few years.

In certain cases, of course, young, upwardly mobile managers of smaller clubs—clubs particularly limited in the salary they are willing to pay or in the responsibility and authority they are able to provide—will always actively seek and welcome the opportunity for professional advancement. However, most boards of directors can retain the services of these talented managers seeking the opportunity and challenge for professional growth *within* the framework of their own club.

One way, of course, for clubs to accomplish this would be to genuinely promote their manager to a bona fide "general manager" status, complete with the increased authorities and responsibilities concomitant with such a promotion. Another less radical method would be to allow a competent manager to gradually take over certain duties formally requiring explicit board approval (e.g., increasing the dollar amount a manager is authorized to spend on the club's behalf before he is required to directly consult with the appropriate member of the board).

Whatever approach is taken, it is clear that the competent manager can reasonably expect a club to provide continuing opportunities for new challenges and professional growth.

4. *Sufficient time and opportunity for leisure and community activities.*

Every responsible manager needs both the time and opportunity for meaningful leisure and community activities. He needs sufficient time and opportunity to be able to dissipate the accumulated stresses and worries of the work day in that activity uniquely geared to his physical and psychological needs.

The successful manager is one who is able to consistently adapt his working hours to both maximize his visibility and effectiveness at the club and still allow adequate time for the pleasurable pursuit of leisure and community interests. The club, in turn, expresses its confidence in the manager and its knowledge of the ill-effects of stress by allowing him or her to develop such a schedule (consistent, of course, with the underlying objective of maintaining a top quality club operation). The results of such an enlightened arrangement will prove advantageous to all concerned: an energetic, enthusiastically productive manager and a first-class, member-satisfied club.

5. *The opportunity for professional interaction with colleagues in club management.*

The professional club manager also needs the continued opportunity for meaningful interaction with both managers and officers of other quality clubs both on a local and national level. Active participation in CMAA provides the perfect opportunity for such interaction. Local and regional meetings often provide the manager with the chance for topical educational programs and relaxing social gatherings; national conventions give the manager the chance to keep abreast of the deluge of new laws and regulations applicable to the club industry.

The benefits to both club and manager of such interpersonal interaction are obvious. The club retains the services of a poised, cosmopolitan manager thoroughly schooled in the problems (and alternative solutions!) facing the club industry today; the manager develops the personal self-esteem and professional confidence that, in turn, can only bolster his performance at the club. Clubs which put a limit on the amount of professional interaction they allow their managers are in effect putting that same limit on the long-range quality of their managers' performance.

Landing the job as manager, as with all positions, is just the beginning. Most managers will approach their new opportunity charged with enthusiasm and full of ideas for improvement. Often, there is also the temptation to "put one's own mark" on the job and to establish a reputation as quickly as possible. Such aspirations are commendable, but they should be tempered with caution.

Having passed the first hurdle—being hired—the new manager should take some time to "get a feel" for the club—what the membership is like and what the club has been accustomed to. One of the best ways to become quickly acclimated is to establish an "open-door" policy with the staff. By being accessible to his employees, a manager can gain the invaluable support of those who are thoroughly familiar with the club and its operation. Such a policy can also help ease any possible frictions that may attend a managerial transition.

A manager should not enter a new job in a "blaze of glory," changing everything he sees. He first must show both the membership and the club personnel that the board of governors has made the right selection. Managers should first observe to see how the club normally operates. Many procedures currently in effect may prove better than those the new manager initially wishes to suggest. Changes should then be implemented gradually to improve the basic operation.

The manager should not expect employees to tell him to manage the club—they are only too willing to do just that. The first reaction to any suggested change on the part of the staff may be, "We've always done it this way". Techniques for motivating and training these employees are discussed in the chapter on personnel practices.

Successful operation of a club is strictly the result of coordinated organizational teamwork. No single person can accomplish it alone. The smart manager, then, is the one who, in selecting a staff, can select qualified personnel to successfully manage the various departments. They, too, should be able to work well with the others and display leadership qualities.

Many good managers attempt to visit every department of the club sometime during their work day. In very large clubs, this may prove difficult, if not impossible. Nonetheless, the desired cooperation and loyalty is more prevalent wherever a manager maintains close contact with the staff.

Perhaps the most significant thing a club manager can expect from his job is a strong sense of gratification. There are many personal rewards associated with the job, not the least of which is dealing with the variety of stimulating and frequently influential people who comprise the membership and the interesting people of all vocations who form the staff. Above all, it is important to remember that a manager—especially a new one—should be a coach, not a critic. It's the manager who develops and maintains a spirit of camaraderie and enthusiasm among the staff within the entire club community who will reap the rewards of success.

REVIEW QUESTIONS

1. What distinguishes a general manager's authority as opposed to a club manager's authority?
2. Name at least five qualities and abilities of a successful club manager.
3. What should the manager expect from a club?
4. Name significant clauses in a club manager's contract.

3

Personnel Management

Kansas City Club, Kansas City, Missouri

INTRODUCTION

One of the many roles that a good club manager must assume is that of a personnel manager. Personnel practices and the establishment of sound personnel policies are the foundation of a well managed and efficient club operation. While this chapter is dedicated to describing some of the fundamental principles of personnel management, the enthusiasm, work habits, dedication and personality of club employees are frequently a direct reflection of the same traits found in the manager. Sound personnel practices are the result of study, common sense, an appreciation of human dignity, and the desire to put them into motion.

Essentially, personnel management is concerned with recruiting, selecting, developing, maintaining, and obtaining maximum results from the people we hire to carry out the operations of our club. Scores of textbooks have been published on this subject and countless more have been written on the sub-functions of personnel management. This chapter is not intended, nor could it ever attempt, to include the myriad of theories associated with this major area of study. It simply portrays some of the key elements that can be useful in putting together a healthy personnel program. Included below are sections on organization, recruiting and interviewing, orientation, training, evaluation, compensation, communication, leadership and the legal aspects of personnel management. Hopefully, after evaluating its contents, the club manager will be able to compare the suggestions included with his or her club's present practices, and make improvements if needed.

Before getting into the nine main sections stated above, it is important to point out the importance that management and first line supervisors have in making them work. An open climate is necessary so that trust can be built between the employee and management. Throughout every function of personnel development it is the supervisor's responsibility to provide the climate for individuals to have a feeling of self-worth. This can be facilitated by allowing the employees, where possible, to participate in problem solving and goal setting. By creating situations for learning to cope naturally, work will be viewed as meaningful rather than fatiguing. Employees will work harder and have a greater sense of loyalty to the club if they perceive that they have some voice or influence in the areas of planning their jobs, carrying out the responsibilities entrusted to them, and measuring the results of their efforts. Although personnel management is only one of the important disciplines of a club manager, it could very well be the most important. We have all experienced the results of turnover and absenteeism in our operations, and we have all learned to appreciate the enthusiasm and dedication of the loyal and well-trained employee. As professional club managers it behooves us to constantly upgrade our knowledge in the personnel area. By becoming well-informed masters of the subject and by sincerely and humanly applying its principles, many of our repetitive employee problems will become history.

ORGANIZATION

If we were hired as the manager of a new club, and were told to go into the job market and recruit a staff, it is obvious that a plan of action would have to be developed. Based on the type of facility, major activities, and the number of members that are expected to participate in the club, a number of positions would be established. Initially, it would be logical to determine how many department heads are needed then estimate the types and numbers of employees that will be required in each function. The method of recording this plan on paper would be to draw an organization chart. Exhibit 3.1 depicts an organization chart for a typical city club. Obviously, country clubs, yacht clubs, military clubs, athletic clubs, etc., would have different types of major functions and the organization chart would reflect the various needs of each.

Since most managers usually do not have the challenge or opportunity to open a new club, we will focus on existing organizations. Basically, however, the same principles apply. Because of technology, turnover, changes in activities or a number of other reasons, most clubs are dynamic organizations. As such, the organization chart should be reviewed and updated annually or more frequently if a significant change in the operation takes place. Anytime there is a change in management, the new manager should review and revise the organization chart to coincide with his or her style of management. Naturally, any changes made should be coordinated with key supervisory personnel and any board of committee members responsible for staffing actions.

Earlier, Exhibit 3.1 was referenced as the organization chart for a typical city club. Although the key departments and type of positions are included in this chart, the numbers of each category of employee are not included. Many managers have found it helpful to develop a chart which includes each position in the club and then annotate the chart with the employee's names. Certainly, there are clubs where the larger numbers of employees would preclude displaying a chart this size, but in such facilities, departmental charts can be displayed in conspicuous places in employee's work areas. The utility of this concept is threefold: (1) the employee knows his or her fellow workers and any changes taking place among the personnel; (2) employees can readily see where they fit in the organization as well as who they work for and for whom their supervisors work; and (3) they can see the lines of progression up the organization ladder. The latter can be a valuable tool to supplement a club's upward mobility plans.

Whether or not the manager decides to use the graphic organization display, each club should maintain a position listing. Exhibit 3.2 is a sample form that should be updated by the personnel clerk every time there is an accession or termination of employment. Position listings become a ready reference in the planning and budgeting processes and an excellent tool in controlling labor costs. (More on controlling labor costs in Chapter 5.)

RECRUITING AND INTERVIEWING

Knowing the number and types of employees is important in the planning and budgeting processes, but a club operation functions successfully only when staffed with capable employees. The first step in selecting good employees is recruitment. This section considers recruiting techniques and the critical role of the interview in making quality selections.

Even in a well-established club there is a need to develop and cultivate sources for new employees. Due to the nature of the hospitality industry, most of us are in constant search for new talent. It is a fortunate manager who has the labor pool resource to fill those unexpected vacancies which seem to plague many of us. We all know that the lack of qualified people impedes growth, incurs extra training and payroll expenses, and can be a real irritant to our patrons who, in fact, may decide not to return to the club as frequently as they should.

The scope of sources from which to recruit is large, and the creative manager is probably aware of many more than will be discussed here. However, the first step in recruiting should be to analyze the local labor market. Once this is done, select the source which seems best for the type of employee being sought.

EXHIBIT 3.1
A Typical City Club Organization Chart

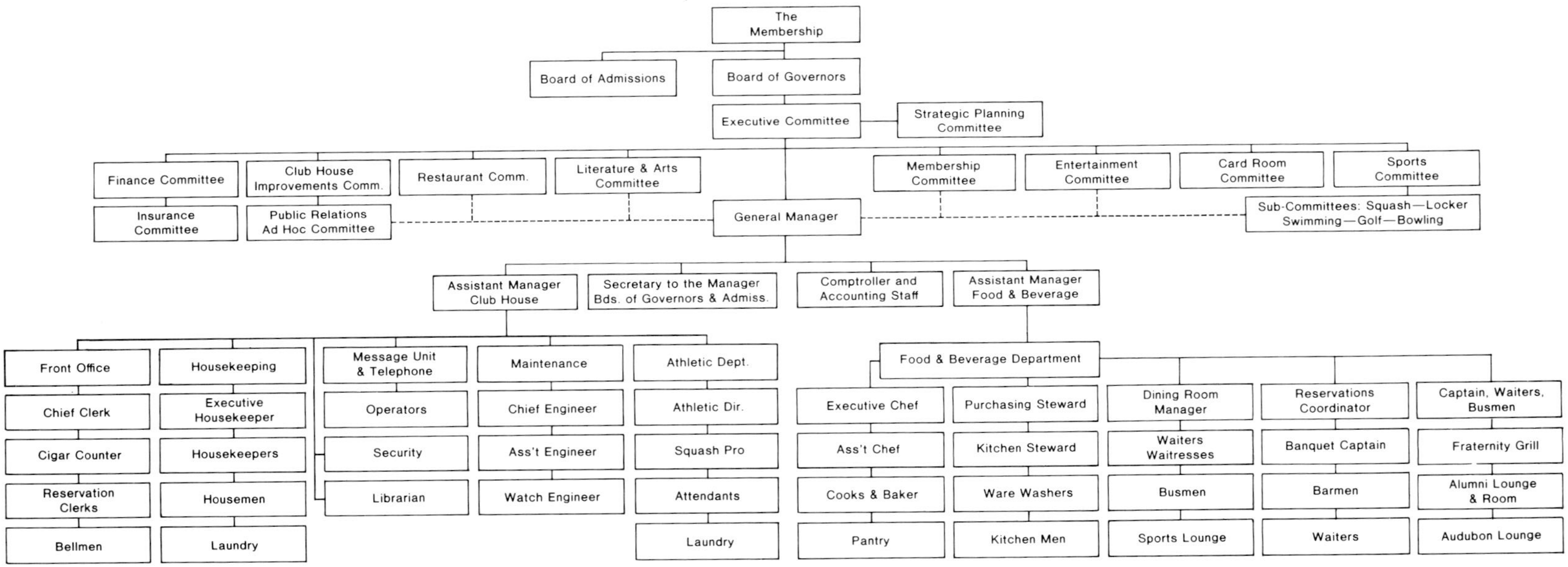

NOTES: 1. General Manager attends all committee meetings except Board of Admissions; prepares manager's reports for executive committee, in addition to the agenda for all committees and, in most instances, takes minutes of the meetings for distribution to committee members.

2. Assistant Managers have their own responsibilities; each is capable of substituting in the absence of others as well as to act with complete authority in the absence of the general manager.

EXHIBIT 3.2
Sample Position Authorization Listing Form

POSITION AUTHORIZATION LISTING		PAGE OF PAGES
1. DEPARTMENT	2. SECTION	3. PART
4. ☐ BASIC LISTING ☐ CHANGE (*Specify change number*)		
5. AUTHORITY	A. DATE OF BOARD REVIEW	
6. AUTHENTICATING OFFICIAL	7. SIGNATURE	8. DATE AUTHENTICATED

NO. OF POSI-TIONS 8.	POSITION NUMBER 10.	DESCRIPTIVE POSITION TITLE 11.	POSN CATE-GORY 12.	SPECIAL INFORMATION 13.	INVESTI-GATIVE RQMTS 14.	SCTY CLNC 15.	MEDICAL RQMTS 16.	ACTION/REMARKS 17.

Advertising in newspapers is probably the best method for reaching the most people at a reasonable cost. In using classified or display ads, care should be exercised to make the words appealing. The emphasis should be on the club's pleasant physical surroundings, pay or fringe benefits, and promotion opportunities.

Trade publications, such as *Club Management Magazine,* offer an excellent service when searching for managers, assistant managers, chef, greens superintendents, sports professionals, and other higher skilled personnel. The fee is low and the coverage is wide. Also included in these publications are "positions wanted" advertisements which are placed by qualified people seeking employment. Occasionally these ads may be of use.

Another viable alternative for skilled personnel is the commercial employment agency. We frequently shy away from this source because of the agency fee, which can range from a fraction of the monthly pay to more than a full month's wages. While the fee may seem steep, some club managers have found that those who have made the effort to use reputable employment agencies are earnest, serious job seekers.

Similar to the commercial agencies are the public employment services which can be found at city, state, and national levels. All types of people are usually on file with these agencies and, depending on the skill levels required and the amount of bureaucratic tape you are willing to submit to, they can be of service. Some states and the federal government have stay-in-school as well as head-start type programs which either supplement or pay the entire wage of the employee for designated periods of time. For the lower skilled positions, people with certain types of handicaps have proven to be excellent and loyal employees.

The old pros are now turning to colleges and universities to recruit assistant managers, chefs, and young sports professionals. A large number of schools are now offering excellent programs in hospitality, recreation and the culinary arts. Organizations, such as CMAA student chapters, are filled with highly motivated and very talented professionals of the future, who are also available during their student years for all types of work.

Some of the less frequently used but available methods include advertisements and visits to local high schools, notices to community and civic organizations, and booths at trade shows. Clubs located in the vicinity of military installations have an excellent source of skilled and unskilled part-time workers.

Before leaving this discussion on recruiting, it must be pointed out that we have at our disposal excellent sources of employees. Recruiting from within should be high on the priority list for replacing vacated positions. The employees themselves can be instrumental in recruiting new help, although the problem of nepotism should be carefully avoided. Finally, previously rejected job applications should be filed by the type of position sought and used to contact possible candidates. On many occasions more applicants apply than there are positions available, and a well-documented application can be very helpful in the future.

Successful recruiting hopefully results in a number of quality job applicants. All persons seeking employment should be required to fill out an application. Although applications vary from club to club, there are certain state and federal equal employment rulings which limit the type of pre-employment inquiries. Many states either prohibit or curtail any questions concerning race, color, religion, national origin, age, marital status, handicaps, or arrests. Other areas which are similarly prohibited except where required by the characteristics of the job include questions about a spouse, child-care arrangements, type of military discharge, membership in organizations, pregnancy, or whether an applicant owns or rents a home. Questions which are permitted include meeting minimum work age, proof of citizenship or ability to provide an alien registration number (after hire), recent convictions (seven years or less) with respect to fitness to perform the job, health or handicap problems specifically related to the job, and family relations for the purpose of avoiding nepotism.

Although prior work experience and education are permitted on the application, there are few managers who would make an employee selection without a thorough personal interview. The interview actually has several purposes. First, as an extension of the recruiting process, part of the interview should be devoted to a sales pitch for the club. The sales aspect, however, has to be realistic and portray not only the positive side of employment, but also include the frustrations and problems inherent in the position. If this is done properly by the interviewing supervisor, the new employee will have more informed expectations, which will cut down on the turnover that disillusionment sometimes creates.

But the principal reason for the job interview is to select the applicant who is best qualified and best suited for the job. Interviews can be highly structured and follow a specific, detailed checklist; they can be unstructured and allow the applicant to control the direction and content of the interview; or they can be a combination of both. Except for key management and professional positions, the interview should be conducted by the department head or responsible supervisor where the vacancy exists. This allows the first-line supervisor to become directly involved in selecting the person who will assist him or her in carrying out the assigned responsibilities of the section or department.

An informal guideline which can be used for an employment interview includes putting the applicant at ease before starting, following a simple outline, maintaining good communications by listening, staying clear of leading questions that require yes or no answers, and avoiding the human tendency to stereotype people. If the supervisor can concentrate on listening, avoid unnecessary interruptions, and keep the interview on relevant topics, the likelihood is good that applicants will reveal their feelings about the job, people, and most importantly their own abilities and personalities. At no time should the interviewer argue with job candidates or reveal negative reactions to anything discussed by prospective employees.

At the conclusion of the interview, and prior to talking to another applicant, the supervisor should annotate his or her impression. Even though there is an unknown quantity that some refer to as intuition, the results of the interview should be quantified as much as possible. This will significantly aid in the final selection, and when retained can be valuable if needed to defend the reason for the selection. Depending on the type of position being filled, the following are suggested areas for evaluation. The relative importance of each area should be weighed for the type of job being considered.

Quest #2

1. Educational background of the applicant
2. Prior work experience and level of accomplishment
3. Neatness, cleanliness, and overall appearance
4. Mannerisms, poise, and self-confidence
5. Ability to get along with people as expressed by involvement with groups
6. Logic and thought process
7. Personality
8. Ambition and resourcefulness (enthusiasm)

ORIENTATION

As soon as the selection is made and the employee reports to the club for the first day of work, the orientation process begins. All employees from the lowest paid to the general manager have various amounts of responsibility in providing information to new employees, and especially in making them feel welcome in the organization. Supervisors, however, have the major role and should be held accountable for a proper orientation to the job and the club environment. To minimize the normal anxiety employees bring with them to a new environment, supervisors must be sensitive, show empathy, and refrain from being haphazard in this induction process. Through the use of various tools and techniques each new employee needs to become familiar with co-workers, club facilities and their functions, employee benefits, where he or she fits in the organization, the management chain of supervision, job tasks, safety programs, training required, and very importantly the club's rules and policies. In this section we will discuss two important tools that most clubs should use in orienting the new club employee.

Since the main purpose of orientation is to help the organization and employee become acquainted with each other, and because first impressions are so important in developing a good mental outlook, nothing should be left to chance. When the supervisor begins the orientation process, there should be a structured check-list for his or her use. Exhibit 3.3 is a simplified example of a form that can be tailored to meet the needs of any club. Other than for actual on-the-job training, the supervisor should not delegate any of the orientation process. One problem that should be avoided where possible is overwhelming the new person with too much information, too quickly. If the orientation is too comprehensive or too complex, some important information can be missed, making the effort ineffective.

During the initial orientation, an extremely important segment is the explanation of club rules and policies. The good club manager will have a copy of employee rules made into a printed handbook. After the handbook is presented to the employee and its contents explained, it is wise to obtain a signed document from the employee to this effect. The purpose of the signature is to protect the club from future claims by the employee that the rules were never explained. Hopefully, this situation would not arise; however, there have been arbitration cases which could have been precluded by such a measure. While not all inclusive, some of the areas that should be covered are listed below. A section on each of the listed topics should be developed in the handbook.

1. Table of contents
2. Introduction by club manager
3. Purpose of the club
4. Work week and pay period definitions
5. Holiday observation and holiday pay
6. Vacation and leave policy
7. Sick leave and personal leave
8. Work schedule and timekeeping procedures
9. Hospitalization
10. Insurance
11. Retirement plan
12. Other benefits
13. Employee parking

EXHIBIT 3.3
Sample Supervisor's Orientation Check List

Supervisor's Orientation Check-List **Date** ______
Employee Name ______ **Department** ______
Position ______ **Supervisor** ______

Date / Time Completed

1. Prior to employee's arrival:
   a. review previous experience and training ______
   b. obtain job description ______
   c. prepare work area (uniforms, tools, supplies, etc.) ______
2. Welcome employee
   a. find location for informal briefing ______
   b. put employee at ease (coffee, soda) ______
   c. discuss background and interests ______
   d. show interest in housing, transportation, finances ______
3. Explain club's organization
   a. outline the organization ______
   b. explain department ______
   c. outline key supervisors and managers ______
   d. identify employee's position in the structure ______
4. Show layout and introduce to co-workers
   a. tour club and work area ______
   b. point out washrooms, lockers, break area, bulletin board, etc. ______
   c. introduce to co-workers ______
   d. explain each co-worker's position ______
5. Explain rules and regulations
   a. present and explain employee handbook ______
   b. discuss all club policies in handbook ______
   c. obtain signed form that employee has received handbook ______
6. Inform of job and assign training
   a. explain work standards ______
   b. assign workplace ______
   c. assign trainer and training program ______
   d. issue work tools, uniforms, etc. ______
   e. stress safety and security ______
7. Follow-up
   a. check that all front office paperwork is completed ______
   b. encourage communication after initial briefing ______
   c. check frequently on progress ______

14. Policies on drinking and drugs
15. Receiving telephone calls / using telephones
16. Unsafe practices / safety program
17. Reporting injuries / sickness
18. Employee meals
19. Use of facilities as a guest
20. Theft
21. Smoking
22. Possession of personal items / package passes
23. Tardiness
24. Use of radios and TVs
25. Fire protection responsibilities

TRAINING

The interviewing process helped us pick the best qualified and best suited individual to meet our needs. In some cases this person could be put into the job, and with only minor orientation, left alone to handle the task. For the most part, however, the employee will have to be entered into or put through a more formalized training program. This can range from a one-hour ware-washing class to a six-month job rotation type apprenticeship for a newly hired assistant manager. In general, some type of structured training program must be established for the majority of those we hire, and it will usually involve both skill level as well as human relations training.

The first step in setting up a program for the new employee is to review the job description and outline the major and minor tasks required of the incumbent. Where there are large numbers of employees in the same position (such as waiters/waitresses) and the position experiences relatively consistent turnover, it will be cost effective to print a training brochure. If one is not in use in your club, ask managers of other clubs for assistance. Training is one area that can be shared by managers everywhere. It is little short of amazing, the information that can be obtained by attending CMAA meetings, both in the formal education sessions and particularly the informal social events.

Once the job is broken down into its elements, the next step is to match the employee's previous training and experience with the tasks that have to be mastered. An outline should then be prepared, a trainer assigned, and a schedule established. Obviously, the most critical element in this formula is the staff member selected to do the training. This individual must be motivated, sincere, and have the ability to dedicate time to the trainee. Possession of a good sense of humor is an invaluable trait in looking for a trainer who will maintain composure and have the patience to do the job well. Training does not have to be routine or boring. Certainly a guideline is necessay to keep the training program on the track, but the more diversified, interesting, and challenging the program is, the more satisfaction and self-fulfillment will be experienced by both the supervisor and trainee.

In lieu of a formal training brochure for every category of employee, it is relatively easy to develop checklists for the routine tasks that have to be accomplished in a club. Similar to standardized recipes in the kitchen, printed checklists for dining room set-up, preventive maintenance, cleaning schedules, office procedures, etc. are excellent training tools. Experienced employees, working with first-level supervisors, can be asked to write down the procedures for each duty they perform. Management can then format the procedures, index them, and establish suspensed time tables for the accomplishment. As an initial training device, they are an excellent guide for the new employee to become familiar with the duties of his or her job.

Periodic training sessions are used by many managers and in a variety of ways. They can range from guest speakers on subjects such as safety, fire protection, the club's insurance program, and any number of informative topics, to classes on "dram shop" theory, salesmanship, data automation, etc. Supervisors should also be expected to give continuing refresher training, especially in high visibility areas such as the dining room and banquet department. A common technique used with waiters and waitresses is to hold a five-to-ten-minute session each day prior to opening the dining room. During the session one menu item is explained from preparation to service, a wine tasted and discussed with respect to pronunciation and the type of meals it complements, and a service tip reviewed. In large clubs where employee turnover can be expected, this type of training review is very helpful in maintaining professional standards.

Since employees are constantly in front of very discerning patrons (our members), human relations training is essential. Supervisors should constantly watch for breaches in courtesy both with members as well as in interpersonal relationships with fellow workers. The proper courtesy extended to the patron begins with a welcoming smile and has to continue throughout the member's visit to the club. An excellent technique which can be learned, is to recognize the member by name. This takes practice, name association systems, and concentration, but is a professional touch that goes a long way in making a member feel important. Everyone likes recognition, especially members in their club.

In summary, training is a continuous process. Supervisors have the responsibility to assess the training needs of their employees, understand their learning abilities, review their progress, and appraise and correct as necessary. Training brochures and checklists can help employees learn and practice routines they are expected to follow, but the key to a successful training program is the empathy and involvement of the supervisor. We can insist on high standards as long as discipline is fair and the example we show is not contrary to what we demand.

EVALUATION

Evaluation is a continual process that takes place in some form or another most of the time. People frequently evaluate each other consciously or unconsciously. So too, we evaluate employees' performance and/or potential when hiring, promoting, transferring, disciplining, training and rewarding. While informal appraisals tend to take place continuously, this section is concerned with the formal evaluation which is normally scheduled at regular intervals such as quarterly, semiannually, or annually.

There are a number of benefits which can be derived from using an evaluation system. As mentioned above, the strengths and weaknesses of the employee become a matter of permanent record to be used when considering promotions and pay raises. It also serves as a defensible document if the reverse is true. In completing appraisals, supervisors are made more aware of the differences between their people, hopefully making them better supervisors. The weak areas observed can also be transfigured into training needs and form the basis for accelerated or refresher training programs. Properly motivated employees in reviewing their appraisals will take pride in the positive accomplishments and exercise self-pride to improve areas which are legitimately rated below superior. The club manager can use employee evaluations to get a feel for the suprevisors' abilities to manage and fairly appraise the workers. It is doubtful that every department has all top-notch workers, and through personal observation a manager should be able to determine which supervisors are fair and credible in their ratings.

One of the most important activities a manager or supervisor performs in the evaluation process is developing job standards for and with subordinates. Good standards help structure clear expectations of what has to be done and how it will be accomplished. This clarity makes managing performance problems much easier, as well as developing and building on employee strengths. Usually performance standards are related to quality, quantity, timeliness, and/or work behavior. To be effective they should contain the following elements:

1. Be observable—can be tracked or viewed by the supervisor.
2. Be achievable—reasonable to accomplish and neither too lenient nor too severe.
3. Be clearly stated—understandable to the employee and supervisor and specifically indicate the expected level of performance.
4. Be differentiating—distinguish levels of performance.
5. Be consistent—represent a consistent level of performance for all employees within the same job classification.

Note that we stated they should be developed for and with the employee. Many managers have realized that employees who are allowed to participate in determining both their work goals and the standards upon which they will be evaluated, are more committed in their performance.

An objective and quantifiable evaluation is better understood and more defensible than a highly subjective rating system. Similarly, when a supervisor uses data on actual performance, the rating becomes more valid. In essence, the most valid evaluation occurs when the employee's actual performance is compared to the standards of performance which were derived from the job description (or a careful job analysis). In sitting down with the employee to establish the work standards, it is best to have a copy of the job description on hand. A careful review of this document will allow both the supervisor and the employee to mutually agree upon the key elements of the job. Each element can then be assigned the minimum standards for the job to be considered successful. A couple of examples might help clarify this point. Let's take the job description of a secretary (since most of us have direct association) and look at just two of the key elements of the position—typing and filing. Standards for the typing element could consist of spelling accuracy, typing accuracy and speed and accuracy format. We could then assign numbers or percentages against these to establish the expected norm of performance. Remember, make the standard attainable but not so strict that it cannot be exceeded. In the second case (filing), we may want the standards to include: filing of documents must be completed within two work days and must be filed in such a manner as to be found within five minutes of request. If the elements of the job are carefully defined and the standards fairly set, neither the supervisor nor the employee will have a difficult time during the evaluation interview.

The ability of an employee to meet or exceed the job standard is important, but only part of the equation for successful job performance. Equally important is the manner in which the job was performed. Certain work behavior can be observed and linked to the job standards. Exhibit 3.4 is an illustration of a work behavior rating form which can be used in conjunction with the job standards appraisal (Exhibit 3.5). The two, when used in combination, form an excellent basis for a meaningful and thorough evaluation.

EXHIBIT 3.4

Sample Performance Plan Form

I. Performance Plan			**Evaluation**		
In the area below, use the employee's job description to outline the major work elements of the job. Check the block as to the criticality of the element in the employee's total job performance. Then in consultation with the employee, determine the standard(s) for each job element. At the completion of the rating period, evaluate each element as to the degree the standard(s) was/were met.					
ELEMENT 1					
STANDARD(S) 1					
ELEMENT 2					
STANDARD(S) 2					
etc.					

EXHIBIT 3.5

Sample Employee Performance Evaluation Form

III. Appraisal Factors—Manner of Performance

Instructions

(1) Appraisal factors listed below represent work behaviors that can be observed in the context of the employee's current position as reflected in the Performance Plan in Part 1. Based on your observations of the employee's performance, rate EVERY appraisal factor. (2) Use the following scale in making the ratings. Mark "X" through the scale number in the appropriate box next to each appraisal factor.

Low Range
1. Very Poor
2. Far below Fully Successful
3. Below Fully Successful

Central Range
4. Slightly below Fully Successful
5. Fully Successful
6. Slightly above Fully Successful

High Range
7. Above Fully Successful
8. Far above Fully Successful
9. Outstanding

1. WORK EFFORT Exerts effort and shows initiative in starting, carrying out and completing tasks; spends time effectively performing work.	1	2	3	4	5	6	7	8	9
2. ADAPTABILITY TO WORK Picks up new ideas and procedures quickly; is easy to instruct; can adapt to the demands of new situations, understands and carries out oral or written instructions.	1	2	3	4	5	6	7	8	9
3. PROBLEM SOLVING Devises effective solutions to problems; or identifies effective methods and procedures for accomplishing objectives.	1	2	3	4	5	6	7	8	9
4. WORKING RELATIONSHIPS Sensitive to the behavior of fellow workers, supervisors and subordinates; maintains effective working relationships with others.	1	2	3	4	5	6	7	8	9
5. COMMUNICATION Communicates clearly and effectively, whether orally or in writing.	1	2	3	4	5	6	7	8	9
6. WORK PRODUCTIVITY Productive during work time, completes his/her work projects, duties, and tasks in a timely manner.	1	2	3	4	5	6	7	8	9
7. SELF-SUFFICIENCY Works independently with little need for additional supervision or help; follows through well; accomplishes all tasks required to complete a job on his/her own.	1	2	3	4	5	6	7	8	9
8. SKILL IN WORK Performs job-associated tasks well, whether they require physical, technical, professional, supervisory or managerial skills; is considered very skillful on the job.	1	2	3	4	5	6	7	8	9
9. WORK MANAGEMENT Effectively plans and organizes work; properly follows or implements management procedures, directives, regulations or technical orders; ability to direct or evaluate others or substitute for absent supervisor.	1	2	3	4	5	6	7	8	9

Probably the most important part of the rating is the actual conference between the employee and the supervisor. Even though most employees like to know how they are doing, many supervisors and some managers fail to realize the fact that they have a right to know. This happens because many raters dislike being in the position of having to defend their evaluations. This can be overcome by teaching a few key points and by stressing that evaluation interviews are among the few opportunities we have to motivate employees and significantly improve their performance. Because the appraisal can have such a positive impact on employee behavior, a good interview can be a powerful tool to improve performance.

By following four important steps, supervisors and managers can insure that the evaluation interview is conducted effectively. These steps include:

1. *Creating a positive climate* by insuring privacy, preventing interruptions, and removing any physical barriers that can result in psychological barriers. It is best to face the employee without a desk or table between you and hold it in a neutral area away from the office or employee's work area.
2. *Preparing a written agenda* to include the issues you are planning to raise and the outcome expected. Try to use the agenda, but if it is not used in its entirety, it will greatly assist in organizing your thoughts.
3. *Giving and receiving feedback*—Start with a discussion of the employee's strengths to establish a positive environment for discussion. Where possible, allow the employee to take the lead, especially when discussing problem areas. Employees who are given the lead will frequently identify the below standard areas of performance and even identify the causes and offer possible solutions.
4. *Establishing a performance improvement plan* that outlines the changes in behavior or activities and establishes a realistic date for the plan to be completed.

COMPENSATION

The reward for work performance is in the form of pay and benefits. The three primary components of compensation are base pay, indirect pay (tangible value), and employee perquisites. Base pay can be earned on an hourly basis or in salary increments. Indirect compensation, normally referred to as fringe benefits, includes such items as sick leave, vacation pay, military reserve pay, retirement, and bonuses. The third category of compensation consists of benefits such as free meals and use of the club vehicle, and morale programs such as enhancing the decor of the break room or recognizing an employee of the month.

When employees view their pay and benefits as being fair, they tend to refrain from being dissatisfied. Depending upon the types of perquisites they enjoy, they will usually disdain a modest wage increase if offered by another employer. On the other hand, they will consider themselves in a temporary situation and actively make themselves available on the job market when they think they are undercompensated. With this in mind, a club should establish compensation objectives that will attract quality people, reward and retain competent employees, provide a source of motivation, and still protect the club's membership's interests while remaining competitive with other hospitality employers in the area.

The first step in determining the pay scale for a particular job is to perform a job evaluation with regard to its value or worth to the club. Factors such as amount of responsibility, number of employees supervised, skills required, physical effort, and working conditions are considered in the job evaluation. Obviously, the positions which are rated the highest in worth to the club will be compensated the most. But the actual amounts to be paid should be based on a survey of wages and salaries. The competitive wage rate of the local area is the most important factor in determining the basic wage level for non-supervisory employees, while industry-wide comparisons should be used in structuring the salary levels of key supervisory and management personnel. The most difficult part of using survey figures, however, is equating the supplemental benefits of other clubs, restaurants, and hotels with those of our own club. All factors must be carefully analyzed when determining a fair and proper compensation package.

After completing the job evaluation and wage survey, a number of questions and decisions need to be considered before determining the actual pay scale for each position. Probably the most critical is that of the club's pay philosophy and whether or not it wishes or is able to pay amounts above, equal to, or below the local competition or national industry scales. If pay grades are to be established, a determination has to be made as to which jobs correspond to a particular grade, the degree of merit promotion increases within a pay grade, and very importantly the actual dollar amounts to be assigned to each grade. An issue which cannot be overlooked is the size of the pay differential between supervisors and subordinates as well as exempt and non-exempt employees. We want to avoid any perceptions of inequity. Inadequate differences, especially between exempt and non-exempt employees, can produce serious morale problems. Because of inflation and cost-of-living increases, consideration must also be given to periodic wage adjustments. A simple means of satisfying this requirement is to provide an annual pay increase according to the change in the consumer price index. This is a national average, however, and a club might find that an annual wage survey of the local labor market would more adequately satisfy its needs.

More and more clubs are realizing that employee benefit plans are vital to recruiting and retaining quality managers and employees. Costs of supplementary benefits can be a significant part of total labor costs and are increasing considerably faster than wage rates. Since employee benefits are part of the total compensation plan, benefit surveys should be made simultaneously with wage surveys if we want the total wage data to be meaningful. The obvious advantages of a good benefits program should include a reduction in employee turnover, increased morale, greater productivity, and a hedge against unionization.

There are numerous types of supplemental benefits available to a manager. Depending on the configuration of the club's work force, different benefits will have more value than others. For example, if the club has a large number of young employees (high school and college students), a good retirement program would not be of any importance. A liberal leave policy or a strong employee meal program would be viewed in a more positive light. On the other hand, if the majority of employees have families, there might be a lot of interest in group medical policies, life insurance plans, retirement, and other family security-oriented benefits. When establishing the types of benefits to be offered, the main factors that should be considered include age and seniority, marital status, sex, number of dependents, and the income level of the employees. It should be pointed out that fringe benefits are successful when they meet employee needs. Unfortunately, many club employees are on the lower end of the socio-economic structure. Since many of their needs are basic (food, shelter, etc.), benefits which they consider important include sick pay, unemployment compensation, workmen's compensation, life insurance, and medical plans. Until their shelter and safety needs are met, vacation plans and retirement cannot be used to compensate for a higher pay scale.

Before benefit plans are put into effect, detailed instructions and rules of administration should be developed. For example, if sick leave is to be paid, criteria should be set as to the length of employment before eligibility is obtained, when sick pay will begin, and whether or not a medical statement will be required as proof of illness. In the absence of detailed guidelines, policy will have to be established when problems occur. Also, without established rules, the club will not be able to budget the cost of the benefits, and inequitable treatment of employees could result.

There are intangible benefits of employment that do not have a monetary value, but can work well to stimulate retention and high morale. The attitude of management can have a great effect on the work force. Managers who show a legitimate concern for the well being of their employees will praise in public and admonish in private. Positive reinforcement and employee recognition infuse more loyalty than could be bought with wage increases or increased vacation time. An "employee of the month" program, when fairly administered, will encourage more competition among the staff. An easy and effective program to instill pride in the regular work force is to publicly and randomly recognize one or a few employees each month in the club bulletin that is mailed to the membership. This could be put into a column entitled "meet your friendly staff" with a picture of each and a paragraph to include length of employment, position, family, hobbies, and a short quote from the staff member on why he or she enjoys working at the club. Finally, managers who care will also insure that working conditions are safe, rest or break areas are sufficient, lockers are available, and rest rooms for the employees are properly maintained.

COMMUNICATIONS

Much has been written and spoken about the art of successful communications. It is difficult to attend an education seminar or pick up a management textbook without some type of information on this subject; and neither will we omit it in this chapter, primarily because of the tremendous importance the ability to properly communicate has in our life. The foundation of a good club operation has to be a sound communication system. Individuals giving instructions, reporting progress, sharing information and solving problems have to communicate effectively if problems are to be avoided. Information that isn't passed on, is incorrect, or is simply misunderstood is the usual reason behind a breakdown in service or a dissatisfied member.

Communication may be written, verbal, or physical. What we say and mean and exactly how it is interpreted may vary because of the perception filter each person possesses. The placement of an adjective, the inflection of the voice, or the raising of an eyebrow can create an interpretation much different from that intended. Some of the factors which influence how we perceive a particular event include previous experience, sentimental attachment, self-concepts, and our state of mind at a given point in time.

Before discussing some methods to help in the communications process, we will take a look at a few of the barriers to good organizational communications. Fortunately most of these barriers are created by the manager or key supervisors and can be corrected with an effective training program and the realization that they exist. The word "fortunately" was used because, starting with ourselves, these are the people with whom we have the most frequent contact and influence.

As has been mentioned throughout this chapter, our attitude is a major element in how we are perceived by the work force. It can be said that you only have to look at the enthusiasm, interest, and courtesy of the staff to be able to see a reflection of the manager. The cliche that actions speak louder than words is so evident with regard to the way an employee reacts to his or her boss. No matter what we way, if we are too brusque, talk down, or do not have the time to listen to our employees, we will not earn their respect. In other words, lip service will normally beget lip service.

A fact that is universally practiced by almost every loyal employee in our business is to tell the boss what he or she wants to hear. Employees who desire to be on the good side of their supervisor will seek out what they think is wanted and stress those traits that appeal to the boss. This is frequently seen when the manager makes a casual remark, but it is taken as a top priority by the supervisor who is genuinely trying to make a good impression. In the upward flow of communications, an opposite but related circumstance often occurs. Information considered valuable by the lower echelon employee is blocked from reaching the manager by the supervisor or assistant manager (even secretary) who in good faith thinks he is doing the organization a service, when in fact it can be a disservice to all. If, on the other hand, an "open door" policy is used to counteract a problem of this nature, and the manager makes a decision or provides an answer to an employee without consulting with the supervisor, there will be a communications gap in both directions from the supervisor's perspective.

Most of the barriers to effective communications are not as complex as the ones mentioned above. Recognizing some of the basic problem areas and making a sincere commitment to improve our methods will definitely help in overcoming them. One area we all need to concentrate on is our ability to listen to what the employee has to say. Too often the employee is stifled, and an excellent source of new ideas and solutions to club problems is overlooked. Often, too, a supervisor or manager can be guilty of being quick to blame upper management or the board for a policy and fail to listen to the real problem being expressed by the employee. Employees have a need to be heard and understood—they do not want to be shunted aside by a statement that is unrelated to their immediate environment. Also, a grave mistake in judgment is made by the manager or supervisor who thinks that everything he says is self-evident or self-explanatory.

Improving the art of communications begins with an awareness of the results of poor communications. Encouraging an openness between all levels of management and subordinates starts at the outset and continues throughout the process. There has to be thoughtful consideration for people's need to be informed of anything that might have an effect on their livelihood as well as their personal interests. Communications can be enhanced through the use of training packages, operating instructions, and certainly through the use of a well-placed bulletin board. Using various channels to get the information out will help, since repetition reinforces the learning curve. The selection of the type of words used is also very important. They should clearly communicate the message we want conveyed, and be geared to the people we are trying to reach. A simple rule is to keep words, whether written or spoken, accurate and specific. Once the message is conveyed, ask for feedback by encouraging questions and answers. As difficult as it may seem, a question should never be considered stupid. Above all, listen attentively. Since employees have more direct contact with the members than most supervisors, they usually have more knowledge of the members' reactions to club activities. One method of gathering information on what is really happening in the club is to encourage the use of an employee suggestion or comment box. It might be interesting to see what the employees have to say when the bottlenecks in the supervisory chain are bypassed.

A sometimes overlooked but extremely important communications tool is the weekly staff meeting. All key personnel should be required to attend and encouraged to actively participate. It is best to schedule the staff meeting at the same time each week, preferably on a Wednesday or Thursday. In this way ten or eleven days of club events can be discussed and the important weekend functions will receive double attention. The staff meeting is the perfect forum for reviewing past performances, introducing and explaining new policies and/or programs, and soliciting feedback from the responsible supervisors. Used properly, this hour spent each week sharing information will probably eliminate numerous hours of confusion and avoid the potential problems which result from misinformed or uninformed department heads.

A final comment on the communication process concerns getting feedback from those employees who are about to leave the employ of the club. The exit interview is used to get an appraisal of all the factors concerning the employee's decision to terminate his or her job. Questions related to the real reasons for leaving and what the club could have done to prevent it need to be asked. If the employee is willing to be specific about any problem areas affecting morale, this information may be of future value. An attempt should definitely be made to learn the employee's feelings about the club, both favorable and unfavorable. Information obtained from the exit interview should be analyzed for its validity, acted upon if possible, and filed for future reference. After a number of interviews have been performed, comparisons can be made to determine if the main problem areas are isolated or there are patterns in the organization which require attention.

LEADERSHIP

No chapter on personnel management could be complete without a discussion of leadership. Just as the preceding section pointed out the need for managers to understand the barriers to effective communications, managers must be aware of the factors that motivate employees before they can be effective leaders. Although some managers are blessed with a natural instinct for leading, most of us have to work hard to influence our employees to willingly accomplish what we ask and demand of them. The goals of this section are to outline some of the contemporary theories of need satisfaction and motivation, and to highlight a few of the styles of leadership that will help us to establish our own management style.

In order to understand why motivation works, we have to understand people. Many students of management credit Abraham Maslow and his theory on the hierarchy of needs as the leader of motivational study. Maslow determined that there are five basic needs in all people. Each one, from the lowest to the highest, has to be satisfied with sufficient frequency before an individual will be motivated to fulfill the needs at the next level. The hierarchy begins with the need to satisfy the physiological drives for food, water, sleep, muscular activity, etc. Once the basic needs are met, a person will seek the second level—security and safety. Commonly referred to as the need for shelter, an individual on this level is searching for housing, clothing, warmth and methods of defense. These needs also lead to desires for job security and fair treatment. The next step in the hierarchy is the need to belong and relate to other people. Human beings desire the company of others and to love and be loved. This can be fulfilled at work, with friends, and/or in family life. The final two needs are considered to be of a higher order and begin with the need for self-esteem and the esteem of others. This includes the desire for recognition, attention, appreciation, prestige, and status. If all four levels are satisfied, then an individual will strive for self-actualization. This drive, to become everything that one is capable of becoming, is only realized by very few people. In fact, it is theorized that most people remain on the first three levels (lower order) and only a minority of individuals actually satisfy their esteem needs.

Frederick Herzberg used the Maslow theory on need fulfillment to develop a more refined theory on what motivates and satisfies people. Known as the "motivation-hygiene" theory, Herzberg classified all job factors into two groups. Although they do not completely correspond with the Maslow hierarchy, many of Maslow's lower order needs align with Herzberg's hygiene factors, and the upper order needs tend to be linked with the motivators. Herzberg's hygiene factors consist of elements such as pay, supervision, interpersonal relationships, company policies, and working conditions. According to his theory, these factors will not motivate anyone to do a job better, but they will increase worker dissatisfaction if absent. On the other hand, factors such as the work itself, responsibility, advancement, achievement and recognition for achievement are motivators that create a need for personal growth. An absence of these motivational factors will not create dissatisfaction, but when they are present and viewed in a positive way by the employee, they will increase satisfaction and motivate individuals toward better effort and performance.

Herzberg's theory is useful in attempting to understand why workers tend to react the way they do, but it must be tempered with common sense. We can apply the theory in general, but we also know that people are individualistic, and while an increase in pay might not motivate a wealthy person, the reward of a salary hike will usually spur on-the-job performance of a more needy employee. What is apparent in both Maslow's and Herzberg's theories is that people have basic needs that must be met for them to be satisfied with their job. The needs for esteem, self-worth and recognition appear to be high on the list of factors that will motivate a person to perform well. By understanding the needs of people, managers are better able to establish policies and programs to maximize the performance of their workers.

A leader is a person who can influence the behavior of another in the direction of his or her own goals. Every manager strives to be a good leader, but not all succeed. If we take a look at the four typical forms of leadership and can apply the best factors of each in our daily managership, there is a good possibility that our effectiveness can increase. The first style of leadership that we will define is authoritarian leadership. Synonymous with autocratic, this type of leader emits a high degree of direction and allows the subordinates little or no control in any decision-making function. Contrary to the authoritarian is the laissez-faire style in which the leader gives little task direction and allows the individual or group complete freedom in decision making, with no regulation of the subordinates' performance. Bureaucratic leadership is characterized by a leader who relies on rules and regulations. It is closely aligned with the autocratic style because it is heavily structured and adheres to formal procedures. The fourth type is democratic leadership. This implies that the leader allows the group a high degree of participation in all decisions affecting the organization. This type of leader is very supportive of group interaction and committees to solve problems.

Each of the styles cited above is neither all good nor all bad. Given particular situations and circumstances, the style of leadership will usually require some change to be effective. The most effective style of leadership that a manager can employ will also depend on certain factors such as the degree of power in the position that the manager occupies, the type of task and length of time in which the task must be completed, and the amount of trust and affiliation subordinates have for their manager.

Many competent managers have a specific style of leadership that works for them, while many others believe in the situational approach. Listed below are some of the characteristics and behaviors of successful managers. With an open mind it would be well for us to consider how we relate to these factors and, if possible, modify our style for our own self-improvement. Some characteristics of an effective leader include:

1. Having technical competency with the ability to develop and teach better methods.
2. Being able to solve problems better than those supervised.
3. Being able to get along well with people.
4. Making decisions readily without a fear of reprisal.
5. Wanting and enjoying the role of a leader.
6. Having a strong desire for accomplishment and influence over others.

Some attitudes and behaviors that effective leaders have toward their subordinates include:

1. Having confidence in and conveying this confidence to subordinates.
2. Being friendly and approachable.
3. Carefully avoiding ego-threatening behavior.
4. Permitting subordinates to have some latitude in the solution of work problems.
5. Knowing that different leadership styles are required for different situations.
6. Encouraging subordinates to participate in short-range and long-range goal setting as well as establishing performance standards.
7. Appraising subordinates objectively and promoting and compensating on the basis of total performance.
8. Recognizing good work.
9. Using mistakes as an educational opportunity in lieu of punishment.

LEGAL ASPECTS OF PERSONNEL MANAGEMENT

The law now pervades nearly all aspects of personnel management in clubs and other hospitality operations. The purpose of this final section is to summarize the basic concepts of employment law for club managers and to provide necessary guidance for those managers in avoiding potential legal problems. Considering the great variation in state laws, this chapter is obviously not a substitute for specific legal advice on individual management problems.

Wage-and-Hour Law

The basic law in this area is the federal Fair Labor Standards Act, supplemented by regulations of the U.S. Department of Labor and by state wage-and-hour legislation. The FLSA covers minimum wage, overtime, meal and lodging credits, payment by salary, paycheck deductions and child labor. Most employers (except very small ones) are covered by the FLSA and frequently by state laws as well. If provisions of federal and state wage-and-hour laws conflict, the employer must usually observe the provision more advantageous to the employee. That is why, for example, states with minimum wages higher than the current federal minimum of $3.35 per hour may compel payment of higher wages by employers in those states.

Enforcement

Enforcement of the FLSA is the responsibility of the U.S. Department of Labor's Wage-and-Hour Division. Investigations are usually the result of an employee complaint, and the law protects such employees from retaliatory firing.

Penalties usually involve paying to employees or former employees back wages owed them as a result of FLSA violations. This liability generally covers the two-year period prior to the investigation, although this period may be extended in cases of "willful" violations. The Labor Department may take employers to federal district court to compel compliance with the FLSA, but most disputes with employers are settled before this happens, and several employer appeals levels exist within the Labor Department.

Requirements of Federal and State Wage-and-Hour Laws

The basic requirements of these laws are

- payment to employees of at least a minimum wage
- payment for all hours worked by employees
- payment of one-and-one-half times the employee's regular rate of pay for hours in excess of 40 in one week

These laws do not require an employer to pay for sick days, vacation days, holidays or any time when the employee does not work or is not under the supervision of an employer. Work time does include, however, extra hours which the employee may work, on or off the time clock, and whether or not the extra time is specifically authorized by the employer. The responsibility is therefore on employers to monitor employee hours and to specifically require employees not to report early or work late if the employer is unwilling to pay for that time.

Break time need not be paid for if the break lasts at least 30 minutes and no work is required during the break. Therefore, breaks shorter than 30 minutes or those during which employees perform work are counted as work time and must be paid for. There is no federal law requiring an employer to provide breaks, though some state laws do require breaks, especially for minors. Time spent in employer-required training sessions, meetings, etc., is also compensable work time.

Overtime compensation is required whenever an employee works more than 40 hours per week for one employer, even if that employee works two or more different jobs for that employer. If pay rates are different among those jobs, overtime will be calculated on the basis of a weighted average determined by the relative hours worked at each rate. Working beyond eight hours in one day does not create an overtime pay obligation, except under the law of California and a small number of other states and under some federal laws applicable to federal contractors. Likewise, there is no premium pay requirement for working Sundays, holidays, late nights or any particular shift though, of course, employers may agree to such special pay arrangements.

Deductions

Employers who provide meals or lodging to employees may deduct from employee pay the reasonable cost of meals or fair rental value of lodging, even if such deductions bring the employee below the minimum wage. However, the employer is responsible for substantiating these figures. Under federal regulations, the "reasonable cost" of a meal is limited to cost of food plus cost of preparation, but some states supersede this standard by limiting meal deductions to a particular dollar-and-cents amount.

Deductions for other purposes—uniform purchase or maintenance, shortages, check errors, credit card mistakes, breakage, walkouts, etc.—may not bring an employee below minimum wage or (in the case of tipped employees) take any portion of employee tips. In addition, some states require written authorization from an employee before any deduction in any amount may be taken.

Exempt Employees

Executive, administrative and professional employees are exempt from the minimum wage and overtime provisions of the Fair Labor Standards Act, but the Labor Department establishes criteria for which employees qualify as "exempt." In the executive area, these are generally employees who earn at least $250 per week, have management as their primary (most important) duty, and supervise the work of two or more other employees. Employees earning as little as $155 per week may qualify as exempt if they meet these management and supervisory tests in addition to other tests concerning their duties and responsibilities.

Those who qualify under the "exempt" tests may be paid on a salary basis, irrespective of the number of hours they work per week. Employees who do not fit the qualifications described above should be paid on an hourly basis to avoid possible wage-and-hour difficulties.

Child Labor

Federal child labor laws cover those employees 14 through 17 years of age. Employees in this age group may not, for example, operate "hazardous" equipment such as slicers, grinders, or various power-driven machines. In addition, 14- and 15-year-olds are generally barred from cooking and working in freezers or walk-in coolers, and may work no more than 3 hours per day and 18 hours per week during the school year, and only between 7 A.M. and 7 P.M. During summers, these employees may work up to 8 hours per day and 40 per week, and until 9 P.M.

Sixteen- and 17-year-olds have no time or hour restrictions (except under some state laws) and may cook, for example, or park automobiles or drive lighter vehicles (under 6000 lbs.) on private property but not on public streets. Since child labor violations carry a possible penalty of up to $1000 each, employers should obtain employment or age certificates from younger employees whose exact age may be doubtful. Employers should also pay attention to their state child labor laws, which may be more restrictive than federal standards. In the event of a federal-state conflict in this area, whichever provision is more protective of the employee generally applies.

Service Charge vs. Tips

Employees working under a service charge system must make the same minimum wage as any other employee. Of course, this may be paid from the service charge amounts collected. The federal 40 percent tip credit, which allows employers of tipped employees to pay less than the minimum, does not apply to service charge work.

Unless resticted by state law, service charge amounts may be distributed in whatever ways the employer considers appropriate. From a tax standpoint, however, it is expected that employers will pay such amounts through the payroll process, taking appropriate deductions for Social Security and federal and state income taxes. For this reason, employees who are compensated primarily from service charges (as opposed to tips) are not required to report these amounts (since they are already "reported" in the payroll process) and their employers are not subject to the federal tip reporting requirements applicable to most restaurant employers.

Recordkeeping

Employers are required under the Fair Labor Standards Act to keep the following information:

- full name of employee
- home address, including zip code
- date of birth, if under 19
- sex and occupation
- time of day and day of week on which employee's work week begins
- regular rate of pay in any work week in which overtime premium is due, and basis of wage payment (hour, day, week, etc.)
- daily and weekly hours of work
- total daily or weekly straight time earnings
- total overtime compensation for the work week, where applicable
- total additions to or deductions from wages paid each pay period
- total wages paid each pay period
- date of payment and the pay period covered by payment

Occupational Safety and Health

The Labor Department's Occupational Safety and Health Administration (OSHA) enforces the Occupational Safety and Health Act of 1970, which governs workplace safety. Department regulations set specific standards for various pieces of equipment or types of possible hazards, but employers are also obligated by a "general duty" clause to furnish a workplace free of recognized hazards likely to cause death or serious injury to employees, whether or not specific standards apply to these hazards.

Employees or unions have the right to file complaints if they believe unsafe or unhealthful conditions exist in their workplaces, and employees may not be fired or discriminated against for doing so. If OSHA inspectors find violations, a citation will be issued and penalties assessed. Serious violations may draw fines of up to $1000 per violation, and willful or repeated violations, up to $10,000. Optional fines may be charged for non-serious violations. Employers must generally keep records of work-related injuries and illnesses and must post these records.

In many states, safety and health laws are administered by state agencies rather than by OSHA. States may take over this function by showing that their programs are at least as effective as the federal one. Some standards, therefore, may be more strict and may differ from federal regulations.

The Immigration Reform and Control Act

This new immigration law, passed in 1986, penalizes employers who "knowingly" hire unauthorized alien workers. It is enforced by the U.S. Immigration and Naturalization Service, which now requires all new employees hired to complete a Form I-9. This form requires the employee to attest that he/she is legally entitled to work in the United States, by virtue of either U.S. citizenship or legal admission and authorization to work. The employee is also required to show documents establishing his/her identity and employment eligibility to the employer, who is required to verify on the form that these documents were shown and appeared genuine.

The required documents fall into three categories:

- single documents that establish both identity and employment eligibility, such as a U.S. Passport, Certificate of U.S. Citizenship or Certificate of Naturalization, Alien Registration Receipt Card (the so-called "green card") and others
- documents that establish identity, such as a driver's license, voter registration card, school ID with picture, U.S. military ID, etc.
- documents that establish employment eligibility, such as a Social Security card, birth certificate or various INS authorization forms

New employees must show either one document covering both identity and employment eligibility or separate documents for each purpose. The I-9 form is retained for at least three years (or until one year after employment terminates, whichever is longer) and must be presented to INS or Department of Labor officers upon request.

Fines for first violations of the law range from $250 to $2000; for second violations, from $2000 to $5000; for subsequent violations, from $3000 to $10,000; all of these amounts per unauthorized employee. Fines for failure to complete, retain or present the Form I-9 range from $100 to $1000 per form.

Anti-Discrimination Laws

The 1964 Civil Rights Act prohibits most employers from discriminating in employment on the basis of race, color, religion, sex or national origin. Although tax-exempt private membership clubs are specifically exempt from this portion of the Act, they are generally covered by similar legislation passed at the state level. In addition, other federal anti-discrimination laws, such as the Age Discrimination in Employment Act, do apply to private clubs. Club employers should, therefore, have some familiarity with these laws.

Applicant Questions and Qualifications

Obviously, no questions should be asked about an applicant's race, sex, religion, age or national origin. Furthermore, all questions (verbal or written) should be job-related; the assumption under anti-discrimination laws is that all information gathered by an employer will be used in determining which individuals will be hired.

Questions about marital status, parental status, plans for pregnancy, etc. should be avoided as having possible sex discrimination implications. Questions about economic status, such as home or car ownership, should be avoided as possibly impacting on certain minority groups. Questions about age should be avoided although, if liquor service or child labor is a primary concern, a question such as "Are you at least 18 years of age?" is permissible. Questions about arrest records are discouraged, though questions about past convictions are permissible and, in the case of some jobs involving possible harmful contact with members or customers, probably advisable. Questions about work availability for particular shifts, days, etc. are preferable to the questions about religion or child-care responsibilities sometimes asked to ascertain this type of information.

Any written or verbal tests used, or any physical or educational requirements placed on applicants, must be justifiable as job-related. The same or similar standards should be applied to all applicants. Employment advertising should be reviewed for discriminatory wording, such as "man wanted" or "girl Friday" or "young person." If information about sex, age, marital status, etc., is necessary for insurance or payroll purposes, this can be obtained on separate post-application forms which the employee would fill out only after he/she had been hired.

Sexual Harassment

Sexual harassment is a form of prohibited sex discrimination, and may consist not only of unwanted verbal or physical advances tied to job considerations, but also of pervasive acts, comments, etc. that create a threatening or hostile work environment for an employee.

Harassment situations generally fall into one of three categories:

- supervisor-subordinate. Possibly the most dangerous from a legal standpoint, since recent court decisions indicate that highly placed employees may be considered to be acting as agents of the employer when committing harassment, thereby reducing or eliminating the obligation of the harassment victim to complain to higher-ups. It should also be noted that harassment cases not only involve male employees harassing females, but reverse situations and same-sex harassment as well.
- co-workers of equal rank. Harassment victims in this situation generally must first complain to the employer and allow the employer to remedy the situation. Employers should be careful to provide channels for complaint, to investigate each such charge, and to appropriately discipline violations of the employer's sex harassment policy.
- harassment by club members or their guests. Though obviously a difficult situation for club management, an employer is legally obligated to take steps if harassment of employees by members or customers becomes a pervasive problem. Explanations of potential liability emanating from the club's board of directors might be a tactful and appropriate way to restrain offending members.

Pregnancy

Pregnant employees should be allowed to continue working as long as they are physically capable of performing their jobs. Any doubts about that capability should be resolved by medical professionals. Appearance alone is not grounds for dismissal, though certainly, normal grooming and dress standards may be applied in most cases.

For purposes of medical benefits, leave and reinstatement rights, pregnant employees should be treated similarly to those with other temporary physical disabilities, so that whatever provisions are made for those employees would apply equally to pregnant employees. California and a number of other states, however, have legislated special leave and reinstatement rights for pregnant employees, and employers should expect that other states will do likewise in coming years.

Religion

Employers are required to accommodate employee religious observances as long as such accommodation does not involve undue hardship to the employer. Hardship is usually defined in terms of amount of time-off required and its relationship to employer needs. If an employee's religion requires her to refrain from all Saturday work, for example, and the employer's busiest day of the week is Saturday, then accommodating this observance would normally be considered an undue hardship. But occasional days off, or time off required at slow business times, would not be deemed a hardship for the employer.

Age

Federal age discrimination law now protects those 40 years of age or older, since Congress has modified the prior law, which protected only those 40–70. Some state laws cover a larger portion of the population (18 and older in New York, for example) and a few states prohibit age discrimination in general regardless of age, though minimum ages for serving liquor would constitute a "business necessity" exception to the anti-discrimination law.

As with laws covering race or sex discrimination, age discrimination laws are meant to attack stereotypes about the capabilities of various groups. Thus, applicants over the age of 40 are to receive equal consideration with those younger, but older employees may still be held to work standards applicable to other employees and may be dismissed for work-related reasons. This is also true of any other employee, regardless of race, sex or other factors.

Documentation

Effective paperwork is the key to justifying performance-related disciplinary actions or dismissals. Though there are limits on the amount of documentation that an employer can create and compile, some guidelines are useful for the club manager:

- Use written job descriptions wherever possible. They not only inform the employee of what you expect, but they also show consistent standards and expectations are applied to all holders of the job.
- Conduct periodic written performance evaluations of all employees, and again be sure that standards are consistently applied.
- Notify current employees of job openings or promotional opportunities before recruiting from the outside.
- Be certain that employees know and understand workplace rules, and be sure that those rules are enforced consistently. Rules which are not enforced, or those to which exceptions are frequently made, should be modified or dropped.
- Look out for any rule which may have a "disparate impact" on persons of a particular race, sex, religion, national origin or age and either eliminate it or be sure that it can be justified as necessary to the operation of the club.
- Follow disciplinary procedures as outlined in your employee manual or other communications with employees.

In the discharge process:

- Be certain that poor or declining performance is documented.
- Counsel the employee, giving specific steps necessary for performance improvement. Memos or other documentation confirming or summarizing such discussions should be dated and signed.
- Make clear to the employee, in direct language, that failure to follow these steps within a stated time period will result in discharge. Do not surprise the employee with an unexpected firing.

Complaint Procedures

Anti-discrimination laws are enforced by the federal Equal Employment Opportunity Commission (EEOC) and by similar state agencies. Individuals who feel that they have been discriminated against file charges, which are usually handled first by the state agency, with EEOC assuming jurisdiction only after a state determination or after the lapse of certain time periods.

These agencies will review the charges, determine if a charge has merit, attempt to conciliate (settle) the dispute with the employer and, in some cases, hold hearings or even sue the employer on behalf of the employee. If the state or federal agencies do not file suit, the individual may do so after the agencies have completed processing the charge. Employees may not be fired in retaliation for filing a charge.

The complaining party, if successful, is entitled to compensation for his/her discrimination-related losses. This can take the form of reinstatement to the same or a better job with the employer, payment or reimbursement of attorney fees or, most commonly, back pay. Since the legal process can take some time, however, the complaining employee is expected to "mitigate" damages; that is, to continue working or to take other available employment while the charge is being processed. A back pay award is, therefore, reduced by the amount of wages earned, or which reasonably could have been earned, during the time the complaint is pending.

Settlement efforts by EEOC and state agencies are geared toward obtaining some amount of money, and possibly reinstatement, for the complaining party, and most cases are settled in this manner at the agency level, without going to court.

Handicaps and AIDS

Virtually every state has some law barring discrimination against physically handicapped employees or applicants. These laws generally require employers to give equal consideration to qualified applicants regardless of handicap if reasonable accommodation can be made for the handicap.

As with the similar requirement for accommodating employee religious observances under federal and state laws, most courts draw the line between major and minor expense. Reconfiguring an entire workplace and moving walls, for example, would not be required, but inexpensive construction of a wheelchair ramp or small-scale removal of architectural barriers might be considered a reasonable accommodation to make for a handicapped employee. State statutes usually cover not only those who are actually handicapped, but also those "perceived" to be handicapped.

These state handicap laws were passed out of a desire to expand employment opportunities for wheelchair-bound individuals or those with treatable medical conditions, such as cancer or epilepsy, that would not necessarily interfere with job performance.

In recent years, with the discovery and spread of Acquired Immune Deficiency Syndrome (AIDS), these handicap discrimination laws have become an important legal tool for employees or applicants with AIDS or related conditions.

As is now widely known, AIDS is a viral condition which attacks and undermines a person's immunity against disease, leaving the AIDS victim vulnerable to various illnesses, all currently fatal.

Certain groups—homosexual and bisexual men with multiple sex partners, intravenous drug users and their sex partners, hemophiliacs and others receiving blood transfusions—account for nearly all reported AIDS cases seen in the United States.

The federal Centers for Disease Control (CDC) declares that the AIDS virus is spread by sexual contact or by injection with contaminated blood and to children born to infected mothers, and that the kind of nonsexual person-to-person contact that occurs among workers and customers does not pose a risk for AIDS transmission.

Specifically regarding foodservice workers, CDC says, "all epidemiological and laboratory evidence indicates that bloodborne and sexually transmitted infections are not transmitted during the preparation or serving of food or beverages, and no instances of AIDS transmission have been documented in this setting. Foodservice workers known to be infected with AIDS should not be restricted from work unless they have another infection or illness for which such restrictions would be warranted."

This statement indicates that those with certain physical manifestations of AIDS, such as open sores or lesions, could legitimately be prohibited from working with food or beverages. And certainly those employees with AIDS may have a strong incentive to voluntarily leave their jobs if a disability or insurance plan will continue to cover their sizable medical expenses. But the CDC and most medical commentators reject any policy of automatically excluding persons with AIDS from foodservice employment.

The discussion of AIDS also encompasses:

- those with positive blood tests indicating exposure to the AIDS virus. This is not synonymous with having AIDS, say medical experts, who contend that not all of those so exposed will develop the disease.
- those with AIDS-Related Complex (ARC), an illness with some symptoms of AIDS but which is not AIDS itself. Here, too, medical researchers believe that not all those with ARC will develop AIDS.

Though persons exposed to the virus may have the capability of transmitting the disease to others, the methods of transmission still rule out workplace contagion. The CDC advises that "routine screening of foodservice workers for AIDS is not recommended as a method to prevent disease transmission. . . ."

This array of medical evidence has important legal aspects for employees with AIDS, ARC or positive blood tests who are fighting dismissal actions. State laws barring discrimination against the handicapped and those perceived to be handicapped are their main legal weapon and the weight of medical evidence is on the employees' side.

Most state civil rights agencies have declared that AIDS and its related illnesses constitute a handicap under their state law's definition. As a handicapped individual, the employee or applicant could not be dismissed or rejected because of the handicap if reasonable accommodation could be made. The medical evidence indicates that little or no special accommodation would be necessary in most cases, since these employees would not have to be isolated from others or required to use separate facilities. Their job rights would be protected until the time, if and when it arrives, when the employee could no longer perform the job in question.

A few states have moved to ban AIDS testing for employment and insurance purposes. Employers are generally advised not to institute testing programs even where they are not specifically prohibited, since any action based on test results could be considered handicap discrimination.

With other handicaps, possible future inability to perform the job or potential cost to an employee health plan due to a greater likelihood of illness are not sufficient legal justifications for refusing to employ. It is likely that courts would apply the same reasoning to employees with AIDS or, particularly, to those having nothing more than positive blood tests.

Drug Testing

Drug use, in the minds of many, is the country's fastest-growing employee relations problem. Over 20 million people are regular marijuana users, according to government estimates, and another 4 million indulge in cocaine.

Many argue that drug use is a private matter and that employers should not be able to prohibit off-hours use, at least as long as job performance remains unaffected. But drug enforcement officials and others knowledgeable about drugs and their effects urge employers to insist on drug-free employees. Under current law in most jurisdictions, employers have considerable freedom to do just that.

However, several states have already passed laws limiting employment-related drug testing, and more may be expected to follow. The key requirements of this new legal trend appear to be:

- Testing individual employees only when the employer has a reasonable belief, based on physical or behavioral signs or changes in job performance, that the employee may have a drug problem. Random testing is clearly disfavored under these new laws.
- Verifying the reputation and reliability of any laboratory used for test processing. Urinalysis, for example, has a high rate of false positive results if samples are improperly or carelessly handled. As more operators enter the testing business, such errors are likely to increase.
- Providing follow-up testing for individuals with positive urinalysis results. Even properly performed tests have a one- to five-percent error rate and cannot distinguish habitual from occasional use. A positive test may also reflect the use of legitimate prescription or over-the-counter drugs rather than illegal substances. New state laws are requiring follow-up testing, usually with the gas chromatography/mass spectrometry (GC/MS) method, a more specific way to determine drug use. Employment decisions in these states may not be based solely on the results of urinalysis or any other single test.

In addition to these guidelines, employers in any jurisdiction are well-advised to:

- Devise and clearly state the employer's anti-drug policy, including what circumstances will lead to dismissal for drug use. If the policy includes workplace drug searches, make clear to employees that personal belongings, lockers, lounge areas, etc. will be subject to inspection. This reduces employee expectations of privacy, which may be a key factor in legal challenges.
- Avoid singling out particular employee groups for testing. Do not, for example, require hourly employees to be tested but exempt management personnel from the requirement.
- Consider the establishment of an employee assistance program to help employees who want to end their drug use. Many employers find an assistance program less expensive than replacing experienced employees.

Polygraph

The polygraph, or "lie detector," records an individual's physiological responses to various questions. The purpose of the polygraph is to detect dishonesty, though there is much controversy over its effectiveness at this. Critics charge that the accuracy of the polygraph is heavily dependent on the skill of the polygraph operator and that many operators are untrained and lack the necessary knowledge to interpret test findings. The result is that some test-takers are unfairly labeled as dishonest.

Congress passed a bill in 1988 which limited polygraph testing. Under the new law, private employers may not use lie detector tests to randomly test employees or to screen job applicants. Employers may use polygraph tests in criminal investigations when there is a "reasonable suspicion" that the worker was involved in a crime at work. But the employer may not require the employee to take the test, nor may the employer make a decision to discipline or discharge solely on the basis of test results.

Standards to test procedures also have been established under the bill. The test must last at least 90 minutes, and the employee must receive a copy of the questions to be asked. The worker must also receive written notice of the date, time and place of the test and of the basis for employer suspicion.

REVIEW QUESTIONS

1. What is the purpose of an organization chart?
2. On what criteria should the job applicant be evaluated during a job interview?
3. What steps should the supervisor take during an employee's orientation?
4. What elements should effective performance standards contain?
5. What are some barriers to effective communication?
6. What are some attitudes and behaviors that effective leaders have toward their subordinates?
7. What are some key components of the Fair Labor Standards Act?
8. What information must employers keep on each employee?
9. How has the Immigration Reform Control Act changed hiring practices?
10. What do the Centers for Disease Control say about AIDS and foodservice workers?

4

Cost Controls: Food and Beverage

Paradise Valley Country Club, Paradise Valley, Arizona

Many authors have written about cost control systems and many professional managers have lived or died within this one important area. Controls only keep honest people honest; they do not make the dishonest man honest. Mainly, controls help managers identify problem areas so that they can be corrected.

Even the most experienced professional manager can get caught in a trap. He arrives at a new operation and reviews the procedures and the controls in place. Normally, he strengthens them, and then enforces his own program. He learns the facts, makes the required adjustments, and establishes a good, solid operation. The trap in the hospitality management industry is that, as the months and years pass, managerial surveillance, follow-through, and attention to controls often dwindle. One way to avoid this trap is for a manager to place regular quarterly inspection reminders in a new office calendar when he gets it.

The control mechanism is just as important as all the other attributes of a good professional club manager—personality, dedication, knowledge of good food, table service, etc. Without controls, managers are hard pressed to produce the bottom-line net profits required.

Unlike the commercial restaurant business, food in the club industry is often subsidized by membership fees. If the operation is subsidized, the managers must determine and aim for the specific target setup within the annual budget and then develop a program to meet that target.

Unfortunately, many club managers have no idea what their food costs are. They fail to recognize that the high cost of sales may well result from bad purchasing, poor issuing and receiving procedures, poor pricing, lack of control of guest checks and cash, or pilferage. The costs of sales including all operating expenses of a food department must be covered by sales income in order to achieve the predetermined target.

Frequently good bar profits in financial statements cause managers to relax and not really give bars the attention they deserve. Properly analyzed and checked, a good bar profit may really be a poor profit—when compared to what should be derived based on the price structure set and the recipes used. Again, attention to detail and review of procedures can ensure both the profit and fair treatment of the membership, based on their requests. Individuals new to the industry should recognize that bars are easy to steal from; traditionally they are the area where employee dishonesty is of primary concern.

This chapter discusses food controls managers develop controls through menu planning and pricing, establishing requirements, receiving, storing; issuing, preparation portioning; accounting for sales, including guest controls; and making inventories and scatter sheets. The chapter also details many of the bar control systems available to the manager.

FOOD DEPARTMENT

Menu Planning

The chef develops menus in many operations; the manager is interested in pricing but only after the menus are set. This practice can be a serious mistake. The menu truly reflects the club—both the food service and the manager's personal philosophy of that service. Menus must be aimed at total customer satisfaction. The menu also provides an opportunity to inject a "personality" into the food operation and the entire club.

Most members come from an affluent society and have varied geographic backgrounds. A well-developed menu should have at least one dish from each major region represented by the club members. Seasonal dishes might also be in order. Most members want quality and fine products on a year-round basis. Therefore, managers must know their sources for products (such as strawberries) that are not always available locally.

In developing a menu, managers should also consider the occupations of their members. Are they doctors? Attorneys? Are they weight or cholesterol conscious? There should always be at least one low-calorie meal available.

Menus should also be honest. If it says "Colorado brook trout," buy and serve Colorado brook trout year-round. If Maine lobster is listed, purchase Maine lobster, even when the price goes up drastically. Truth in advertising is of ultimate importance in private clubs.

Menus should have quality covers so that inserts can be changed as required to keep up with seasonal trends, member demands and product availability. The cost of changing menu inserts is significantly less than changing complete menus.

Refer to the many books available on menu planning, layout and development.

Menu Pricing

In developing prices, remember the budget and the direction indicated by the club's board of directors for the bottom-line percentage. An item's cost and its popularity also dictate its actual sales price. Managers should not go "across-the-board" with a specific food cost and price an entire menu. Consider the items with great popularity (as evidenced by their sales) and, perhaps, price those closest to the basic percentage goal. Price other items above and below the goal, depending on their cost factors.

Before computing the selling price of any item, first determine the cost of all the ingredients in the item. After developing a menu, prepare each item from scratch with the chef; note every ingredient used to ensure that all cost factors are considered. The cost of all items must appear somewhere!

Develop menu cost cards, as shown in Exhibit 4.1. Be sure to show the correct portion price, especially for meat. Use the *cooked* portion weight to properly account for trim, waste, and shrinkage. For instance, prime rib spec 109 RIB may cost $3.00 per pound before it is cooked and the cap removed. When cutting away excess fat, and removing the bones, also consider the shrinkage while it cooked. Indeed, the cost of the cooked product may well be $5.00 per pound, a considerable difference. So the real cost on the menu card for a one-pound serving should be the $5.00. Carry this process through on all items going into costs—for vegetables, meats, salads, and so on.

Post changes in costs to the club on the menu cards as the changes occur. Then the cards will show when the prices on a specific item should be raised or lowered or at least addressed. The cards thus help managers maintain the desired cost percentage.

Sometimes, however, it might be wiser to allow the change in the desired cost percentage rather than change the price of the item. Obviously, managers don't want to raise a menu price to the point where sales of that item decrease unless it is demanded. Tracking price-sales changes is easier on a scatter sheet. This record, discussed later in this chapter, shows sales activity (an item's popularity) on each specific item on a daily basis.

After setting a menu price, it is time to establish requirements.

EXHIBIT 4.1
Menu Card

CHATEAUBRIAND

ITEM:

Portion Size: 16 oz	HISTORY
Total Raw Cost: $29.70	Date: 7/16/88 Cost: $10.40 SP: $33.84
Selling Price: $38.00	Date: 10/15/88 Cost: $11.00 SP: $35.79
Cost Prior to Trimming: $5.94/lb	Date: 11/5/88 Cost: $11.68 SP: $38.00
Cost after Trimming: $7.68/lb	Date: Cost: SP:
Portion Cost: $7.68/lb	Date: Cost: SP:
Food Cost: $11.68/31%	Date: Cost: SP:
Date: 11/5/88	Date: Cost: SP:

Accompanying Ingredients

ITEM:	COST:
Bordelaise Sauce—4 oz.	.24
Half Tomato—2 each	.22
Baked Potatoes w/sour cream	.45
Broccoli w/polonaise sauce	.75
Carrots	.25
Salad w/bleu cheese	1.24
Bread and butter	.30
Beverage	.35
Garnish	.20
Total	$4.00

EXHIBIT 4.2
Standards for Ordering and Receiving Fresh Vegetables

Item	Grade	Specifications	Unit of Purchase	Approximate Net Weight
Lettuce, Iceberg	U.S. Grade 1	Compact heads. Firm. Leaves, pale green color. Free from red rib and decay. Product from Western United States whenever available.	Box 24 heads	35 lbs.
Romaine	U.S. Grade 1	Semi-firm heads. Elongated leaves. Dark green color. Free from decay. Western states.	Crate 18 or 36 heads	
Mushrooms	U.S. Grade 1	White or off-white. No dark discolorations. Cap closed around stem.	Basket	3 lbs.
Celery, Pascal	U.S. Grade 1	Firm stalks. Pale to darker green in color. Crisp. Western.	Crate—3 dozen	50 lbs.
Cabbage, White	U.S. Grade 1	Heavy heads. Firm. Off-white to pale green color. Free from discoloration.	Bag	50 lbs.

Establishing Requirements

The first item in establishing requirements is specifications. Many clubs have purchasing specifications; but few clubs have them in writing. There are three good reasons to write them down:

1. The club's buyer may become ill or quit; the manager will have no idea what the buyer has been using for specifications.
2. The manager himself may forget the specifications and have to rely on guesswork.
3. The club must establish and maintain a forthright business relationship with purveyors.

Before buying the first commodity, the manager should sit down with the chef and purchasing agent and develop specifications. Consider the member and his demands and needs. Normally, members will want high quality; specifications should, therefore, be developed toward that goal. The best grade sold to meet the need is the key. If eye appeal is important, such as for tomatoes to be stuffed for salads, the right grade may well be the highest grade, but certainly such uniformity and expensive quality are unnecessary if the tomatoes are to be cooked in stews.

Many textbooks and references deal with establishing requirements. And suppliers near the club will work with a manager to develop specifications—because they want to do business with the club. A sample specification appears as Exhibit 4.2.

Specifications should not stay just with the purchasing agent and buyer. A copy of those specifications must always be available at the receiving area so that managers can be assured that purchases are delivered in the same condition as ordered. Copies should also be given to each of a club's regular purveyors.

Pre-cut meats will solve some of the problems of setting specifications. Of course, portion meats are more expensive per pound than primal cuts, but the waste of the trim and a club's own labor costs to cut the meat should also be considered. In addition, portion control beef provides absolute control within the storeroom and in issuing. Carcass cuts also require regularly scheduled cutting tests to assure the yield expected from a bulk product is verified.

Establish requirements by weight. Bushel, box, bag, or crate does not guarantee yield. Pound and weight do guarantee yield. Specify fruits and melons by pound and size. Fresh items probably produce more acceptable food for club members, but some items in the convenience and instant food lines are good and can reduce your labor costs substantially. These products are also easier to store.

To establish requirements, analyze past consumption in the club, specialty program events over and above normal day-to-day use, possible menu changes, and, of course, seasons of the year. A profit- and quality-conscious food buyer normally purchases enough meat for only a few days' operation. Meat is one of the more expensive items in the food cost family; if overpurchased or overstocked, much of the operation's cash is obligated—when it could be working in other ways (like drawing interest in the bank). Market speculation is a full-time job and should be avoided, unless the club's purchasing agent is a true specialist.

Some other disadvantages of purchasing in large quantities include restricted storage space and pilferage (which becomes more possible as control becomes more difficult). Also, large inventories increase handling costs. Meats and some other items shrink while stored. Beef, for example, can lose up to 30 percent of its weight if stored for long periods; potatoes will go from 100 to 90 pounds in about three weeks.

In establishing requirements, it is often wise to do cutting tests. Take, for example, three generally available frozen broccoli products, and prepare each in exactly the same manner. Repeatedly, the product with the lowest initial cost may provide the smallest yield. An item with a slightly higher initial price may give a larger final yield and, thus, be a better buy. The same is true with canned and frozen goods and most convenience-type food items.

A well-laid out purchase order is very important. A four-part order, with each copy a different color, is shown in Exhibit 4.3. Copy #1 is the vendor's copy (white); #2 is the receiving copy (yellow); #3 is for the accounting office (pink); and #4 is the file copy (green).

RECEIVING

The next food cost control point is the receiving station. One copy of the purchase order should always be here. Many operations allow one person to do the buying, receiving, and issuing. This practice is bad; it leaves great openings for errors and provides ideal opportunities for fraud or dishonesty.

If the club's size does not allow for different people in each area, then, at minimum, a manager should assign someone from the accounting department to the storeroom and issue and receive only at specific times.

EXHIBIT 4.3
A Four-Part Purchase Order (Vendor's Copy)

Big Deal Restaurant Corp.
Building 5F
36 N. Taylor Street
Anywhere, USA 00000

Date: May 18, 1989
Purchase Order #38951—B
(please include this number on all packages shipped)

For Good Controls Country Club
5221 Covington Road
Anywhere, USA 00000

Ship To:

Storeroom
Building 5F
36 N. Taylor Street
Anywhere, USA 00000

Please Supply Items Listed Below

Quantity Ordered	Received	Description	Unit Price		Total
160 pounds		Ribs of Beef (#109)	$2.75		$440.00
200 pounds		Steamship Round (with handle)	$1.85		$370.00
40 pounds		Top Round of Veal	$11.75		$470.00
		TOTAL:			$1,280.00

Instructions and Conditions
Acknowledge promptly if you are unable to ship complete order by date specified. Law warrants goods shipped produced in accordance with applicable provisions of labor standards act. Charge for packing or crating will be accepted unless previously agreed on.

BY Cody Pollock
Contracting Agent
VENDOR'S COPY

EXHIBIT 4.4
A Sample Bin Card

Date: April 23

Daily Quotation Sheet

Quantity Required	On Hand	Order	Item	Unit of Purchase	Today's Quotation		
					ABC Company	DEF Company	XYZ Company
3	4	—	Produce: Lettuce, Iceberg, U.S. #1, 2dz./crt 40-45 lb. net	Crt			
2	1	1	Lettuce, Bibb, 2 dz./ crt, 26 lb. net	Crt	26.00	26.40	27.00
1-1/2	1	1	Potatoes, U.S. #2 100 lb. sack	Sack	8.40	8.45	8.60
2	2	—	Potatoes, Baking, Idaho, U.S. #1, 100/ ctn 55 lb. net	Ctn			
1/4	1/8	—	Radishes, U.S. #1, crt—5 doz. bunches	Crt	3.25	3.20	3.35

Note: Items and purchase specifications may be preprinted on the form if desired.

For receiving, always have large scales available at the back door. Club personnel should check all items, correlating the receiving document from the company with the purchase order.

Verify the order. Is it what was ordered? Weigh it; count it; check all the items and determine that the product's quality equals the club's specifications. Then stamp and sign the invoices. The stamp should include a "received on" blank for the date. This stamp will show how long an item sits in a warehouse and the specific time the order was actually received. Then post these documents to the bin cards and forward the papers to the accounting office. A sample bin card appears in Exhibit 4.4.

EXHIBIT 4.5
A Sample Meat Tag

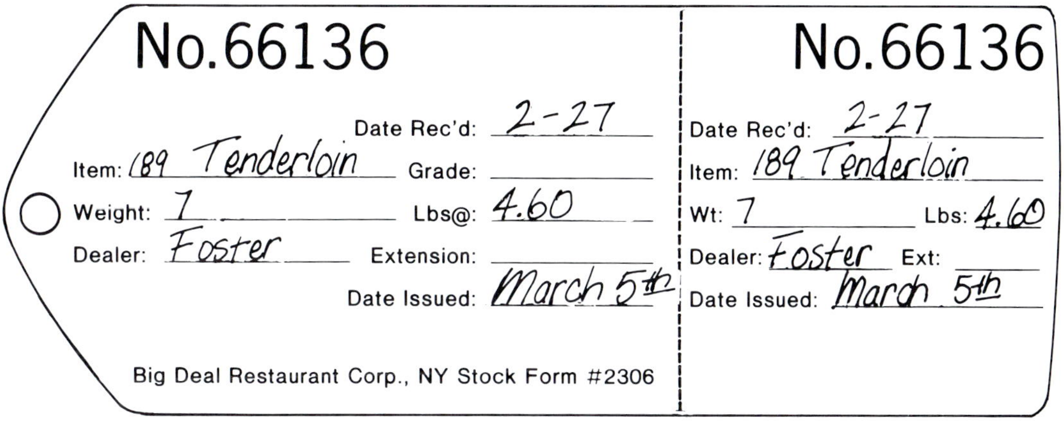

Some operations use a meat tag system to maintain a perpetual inventory and control. The tags, as shown in Exhibit 4.5, have numbers printed at the top and bottom, and indicate weight, size, and date of receipt. The top half is attached to the requisition when it is issued and forwarded with the requisition to accounting at the end of each day.

It is often wise to open some cases in the receiving area to assure that a full count of liquor, canned goods, and so on is in each case. Remove the ice packed around poultry occasionally to verify the product's actual weight. It is also wise to pull vegetables from the lug or case to verify that specifications, including the weight, are met. Such spotchecking is a sound business practice.

Storing and Issuing

Always keep the storeroom locked unless an attendant is on duty. Rotate the locks periodically whether or not theft is suspected. A storeroom, particularly one with high-value items, should be secure, clean, and neat. Draw an outline of the storeroom layout so the location of items can be easily identified. This diagram is especially important for freezers, because storeroom personnel and chefs should not spend long periods of time in cold areas. Staff tend to become frustrated and move food out of place and onto floors—which is unacceptable.

Directly issue daily and repetitive delivery items, perishables to be consumed within 72 hours, or staples in the amounts needed until the next delivery. Control direct issues from the storeroom, and consider them when computing daily food costs. Use requisitions to withdraw items from the storeroom or, at least, use bin cards to show issue dates. The two together, both the bin card and the requisition, form an excellent management tool. A sample requisition appears in exhibit 4.6.

Written requisitions can help managers calculate a daily food cost. The total cost of the requisition and of the direct issues provides a working daily food cost.

Managers should pull bin cards regularly to ensure that items are not sitting on the shelves and becoming "dead stock." Managers should develop special menus to use any such items so they do not go bad in the storeroom.

EXHIBIT 4.6
A Sample Requisition

Company:	Branch: Maryfield	# 298705
Big Deal Restaurant	Date: December 5, 1988	Section: 14-7

Item	Stock Number	Unit of Issue	Quantity Ordered	Quantity Issued	Unit Cost	Total Cost
Pastrami	3246	lbs.	20	20	1.88	37.60
Corned Beef	298	lbs.	35	35	2.35	82.35
Cherry Pepper	1749	Gal.	2	2	4.50	$9.00
Tuna Fish	E-14	Can	24	24	$7.79	$186.96
					Total	$ 315.91

Requested By	Date	Issued By
Requested By	Date	Posted By

Occasionally follow a delivery from its arrival, through the storage procedure, and into the operation to ensure that the commodity is actually received and processed *through* the club. Receiving storeroom personnel have worked with delivery truck drivers and issued receipts for items that never left the trucks. Such items can be sold elsewhere at a discounted price; the drivers and storeroom personnel pocket the proceeds.

After establishing that an item has actually been received and is in the storeroom, a manager should verify the amount issued into the operation. Occasionally a storeroom man and cook will work together to remove foodstuffs from the club. This area is also easy to spotcheck. Follow a product through the operation until it is served to a customer in the dining room.

Perpetual inventory is one of the best and most effective ways to control supplies, equipment, and other goods internally. A card, of convenient size for handling and filing (perhaps 5½ × 8½ inches), is adequate to maintain control of each item in inventory. The card should have a description of the item, columns for the date of receipt, the number received, cost of the present unit, date of issue, number of items issued, the unit price, and the extended value of the item. When the storekeeper or other individual responsible for the stored goods receives a requisition, the card serves as a record of the items disbursed.

The perpetual inventory system can be kept manually or on a computer. Post all items to the record as they are received and also systematically post items as they are issued. The remaining number shows the amount of goods left in storage. Simple calculations provide managers with a running total of the amount of goods purchased, the amount of goods consumed, and the value of the goods remaining.

Schedule a physical inventory regularly to prove or disprove the accuracy of the counts on each card.

Perpetual inventory thus provides two major advantages to management:

1. Control of goods and merchandise
2. Accounting and physical data necessary to manage efficiently

Preparing

The club's kitchen and food production effort has three basic requirements:

1. Produce quantities of food based on management forecasts
2. Determine and control the cost of the food produced
3. Set standard portion sizes

To accomplish these purposes, managers must forecast the number of meals to be sold, limit the requests for raw food to the quantity required, and prepare the food properly. Failure to accurately estimate how much to produce causes overproduction and leftovers. Occasionally, leftovers do appear; they should be used—not thrown away.

One of the keys in this area is the standardized recipe card, as shown in Exhibit 4.7. The card must list the exact quantities of raw food required for a particular number of servings and multiple copies of the cards must be kept in the kitchen. Enclose them in plastic so that food spills and grease do not soil them. Standardized recipe files not only simplify production planning and control; they also assure the customer the same product each time he orders it.

EXHIBIT 4.7
Sample Standard Recipe Cards

Shrimp Curry

Yield: 100 Portions — Each Portion: ¾ Cup

Ingredients	Weights	Measures	Method
Shrimp, frozen, raw, peeled, deveined	20 lb		1. Place shrimp in salted water; cover, return to boiling point. Reduce heat; simmer 5 minutes; drain. 2. Set aside for use in Step 9.
Water, boiling		3 gal	
Salt	5 oz	½ cup	
Onions, dry, chopped	3 lb	2 qt	3. Sauté onions and peppers in butter or margarine about 10 minutes or until tender.
Peppers, sweet, fresh, chopped	2 lb	1½ qt	
Butter or margarine, melted	8 oz	1 cup	
Flour, wheat, hard	1 lb 8 oz	1¼ qt	4. Add flour to butter; blend thoroughly. 5. Cook 30 minutes or until well browned, stirring frequently.
Butter or margarine	3 lb	1½ qt	

Ingredients	Weights	Measures	Method
Water, hot		3 gal	6. Gradually add water; cook until thick and smooth, stirring constantly. 7. Add sautéed vegetables.
Apples, fresh, cooking, chopped	4 lb	1 gal	8. Add apples, celery, and seasonings; simmer 20 minutes.
Celery, fresh, chopped	2 lb	1½ qt	
Curry powder	2 oz	6 tbsp	
Monosodium glutamate		¾ tbsp	
Ginger, ground		3 tbsp	
Pepper, cayenne		2 tsp	
Garlic, dehydrated		3 tbsp	
Horseradish, prepared		3 tbsp	
Salt	5 oz	½ cup	
Mushrooms, canned, drained, chopped	1 lb 8 oz	3 cups (3-8 oz cn)	9. Add shrimp, mushrooms, and juice; simmer 2 to 3 minutes, stirring constantly.
Juice, lemon		¾ cup	

EXHIBIT 4.7
Continued

Baked Chicken and Rice

Yield: 100 Portions (2 Pans) — Each Portion: 1¼ Cups

Pan Size: 18 by 24-inch Roasting Pan — Temperature: 350°F Oven

Ingredients	Weights	Measures	Method
Chicken, broiler-fryer, whole Water Salt Bay leaves Monosodium glutamate	45 lb 6 oz 	 9 gal 9 tbsp 9 leaves 9 tbsp	1. Wash chicken thoroughly inside and out under running water. 2. Place chicken in stock pot or steam-jacketed kettle; add water and seasonings and bring to a boil; reduce heat and simmer 2 hours, or until tender. 3. Remove chicken; strain and reserve stock for use in Step 8. 4. Remove meat from bones; cut into 1-inch pieces. Set aside for use in Step 10.

Ingredients	Weights	Measures	Method
Rice, parboiled Salt Water	6 lb 6 oz 	3 qt 9 tbsp 1½ gal	5. Add rice and salt to water; bring to a vigorous boil; reduce heat; cover and simmer 13 minutes or until the water is absorbed. 6. Keep covered for use in Step 10.
Butter or margarine, melted Flour, wheat, hard	8 oz 9 oz	1 cup 2 cups	7. Blend butter or margarine and flour together to make a cold roux; mix until smooth.
Chicken stock, hot		2 gal	8. Gradually add roux to stock, stirring constantly. 9. Heat to boiling point; boil 2 minutes; stir frequently to prevent sticking.
Peppers, sweet, fresh, chopped	1 lb 8 oz	1¼ qt	10. Combine chicken, rice, sauce, and peppers.
Salt Pepper, black	4 oz 	6 tbsp 2 tbsp	11. Add salt and pepper. 12. Place 3½ gal mixture in each pan.

EXHIBIT 4.7
Continued

French Fried Onion Rings
(Flour Method)

Yield: 100 Portions			Each Portion: ¾ Cup
Pan Size:			Temperature: 375°F Deep Fat
Ingredients	**Weights**	**Measures**	**Method**
Onions, dry, cut into slices ¼-inch thick	20 lb		1. Separate onion slices into rings.
Milk, nonfat, dry Water, warm	13 oz	2⅞ cups 3¾ qt	2. Reconstitute milk; pour over onions. Let soak 10 minutes. Drain well.
Flour, wheat, hard, sifted Salt Pepper, black	3 lb 6 oz	3 qt 9 tbsp 2 tsp	3. Dredge onion rings in seasoned flour. 4. Fry 3 to 4 minutes or until golden brown.

NOTE: 1. 22 lb dry onions A.P. will yield 20 lb sliced onions.
2. Other types of milk may be used in Step 2.

Remember, the chef won't be there every day. He may be on vacation or out sick, and a second cook will have to produce the product the chef normally prepares daily. If the recipe card is accurate and the chef uses it, the product will be the same, no matter who follows the recipe, and the customer won't notice any variation.

Items such as sauces are sometimes produced in large quantities. If so, the quantity should be divided and placed into smaller containers to meet daily requirements. Then the manager will always know how much is on hand and the pot won't "run dry." Inventory of smaller quantities is easier and normally the product is better also.

One of the advantages of producing food ahead of time and then holding it is the ease of inventory control already discussed. Other benefits also accrue—very little waste, good use of labor as food is prepared during slack periods, and mass production that permits qualified personnel to supervise more closely.

Some operations use convenience foods extensively because of their uniformity, quality and cost. Convenience foods also take up less kitchen space, reduce labor costs, and decrease total food inventories. However, many managers still prefer to develop their own food products with quality recipes and fine ingredients. They feel the product is better and more completely satisfies member demands. Some food items, particularly vegetables, should be prepared in small batches. Vegetables cooked in quantity often sit too long in steam units; they lose their color, texture, and nutritional value.

All food must go to customers. Failure to prevent unauthorized consumption by employees will drive food costs out of sight.

Portioning

Used effectively, portion control guarantees that the yields forecasted will, in fact, be achieved. Indeed, menus are priced on the assumption that portion size will be strictly controlled. Some ways to help maintain good portion control and uniformity are:

1. Making guides to cut cakes, pies, and other desserts
2. Allowing hot foods such as meats, cooked fruits, and custard pies to cool or gel before cutting them
3. Using ladles, spoons, and scoops of the exact size of the portion to be served

Ounce scales are a must in the kitchen. They must be convenient to the cooks and should be checked occasionally to assure their accuracy. Also, set up sample plates with portion sizes annotated; take pictures of the plates to ensure that correct portion sizes are served. These pictures also help servers know exactly how to lay out the plate so that the customer receives a consistent product.

Accounting for Sales

To account for the sale, the manager must compute the food cost. This process is not necessary on a daily basis, although many operations do such a daily accounting. Daily food costs, however, can be converted to weekly or monthly cost programs depending on the needs of a particular club. By using all of the control procedures outlined in this chapter, managers may find irregularities—that the kitchen is not meeting desired goals. Then it is beneficial to go back and compute the daily food cost.

Daily food cost is the total cost of all food and nonbar beverage items consumed, less the cost of employee meals and items transferred to other activities. Three systems are normally used to compute daily food cost. One is a requisition totaling method; the second is a daily kitchen inventory; and the third is information obtained from point of sale equipment.

In the requisition totaling methods, the manager totals all daily requisitions processed through the kitchen. This method does not really provide an accurate *daily* food cost, because the kitchen may requisition in bulk or may prepare items for general consumption later in the week or for a party on the following day.

The second method—daily kitchen inventory—is better to truly ascertain a daily food cost. However, this method is more labor intensive and, thus, more expensive. At the end of a day's business, and before the start of the next day, simply count or weigh all food items on hand in the kitchen. Managers can often estimate weights, but they shouldn't estimate until they have tested and practiced their abilities in this area. Estimate the weight first, and then actually weigh the item to see if the figure is "light" or "heavy." After a while, managers will come very close; then estimating is a good procedure. A sample of a kitchen inventory is displayed in exhibit 4.8.

EXHIBIT 4.8
A Sample Kitchen Inventory

Kitchen Inventory and Gross Income

Date: 12 Aug 88

Description	Begin Inv	Received	Avail	Ending Inv	Consumed	Unit Cost	Unit	Total Cost
FRESH FRUITS								
Apples	14	20	34	26	8	.26	EA	$2.08
Bananas	0	10	10	5	5	.30	LB	$1.50
Oranges	25	0	25	25	0	.30	LB	
FRESH VEG.								
Celery	5	10	15	13	2	.42	EA	.84
Lettuce	28	0	28	16	12	.27	EA	$3.24
Onions	0	10	10	6	4	.24	LB	.96
MEATS								
Chicken, Fryers	61	0	61	54	7	.72	LB	$5.04
Ground Beef	20	20	40	30	10	1.40	LB	$14.00
T-Bone Steaks	30	0	30	19	11	4.50	EA	$49.50
DAIRY PROD.								
Cheese, Amer.	2	10	12	11	1	.80	LB	$1.80
Cheese, Cottage	3	5	8	8	0	1.20	LB	
Milk, Fresh	41	20	61	30	31	.15	1/2 PT	$4.65
Milk, Fresh	0	10	10	6	4	.97	1/2 GA	$3.65
CANNED FRUITS								
Apples, Spiced	1	2	3	1	2	3.17	#10	$6.34
Apple Sauce	0	1	1	0	1	2.37	#10	$2.37
Pineapple Chunks	2	0	2	2	0	3.46	#10	
Pineapple, Sliced	1	0	1	1	0	2.66	#10	
MISCELLANEOUS								
Coffee	3	5	8	4	4	2.30	LB	$9.20
Flour	2	10	12	9	3	.14	LB	.42
Sugar, Granulated	1	5	6	3	3	.31	LB	.93
Sugar, Powdered	0	2	2	0	2	.56	LB	$1.12
Tea	1	0	1	1/2	1/2	4.40	LB	$2.20

Total Sales $302.25 (100%)

Total Cost of Sales $109.84 (36.4%)

Gross Income From Sales $192.41 (63.6%)

Total Sales Month to Date $3615.75 (100%)

Total Cost of Sales Month to Date $1358.08 (37.6%)

Gross Income Month to Date $2257.67 (62.4)

Inventory Taken By John Doe Verified By Richard Roe

The description column of the inventory form identifies the items to be counted. In the beginning inventory column, the figures represent the amount of the item on hand at the beginning of the workday. Figures in this column should be the same as the figures in the ending inventory column for the preceding day. The received column shows quantities (1) issued to the kitchen, (2) shown on cost of sales account on requisitions, (3) transferred to the kitchen cost of sales account on transfer between activity forms, and (4) charged directly to the kitchen cost of sales account for the day. Add the figures in the beginning inventory column to the figures in the received column; enter the total in the available column. The figures in the ending inventory column represent the amount on hand at the end of the day's business.

Figures in the consumed column represent the difference between the available column and the ending inventory column. The unit cost and unit columns represent cost of the item to the club, by unit. For example, on line 1, a pound of apples cost $0.26. Multiply this figure by the number of pounds consumed (which is eight in the example) to arrive at the total cost for the day—$2.08. Enter this figure in the total cost column. Extend all of the costs of items in this same fashion for the day.

Compute the figure on the total sales line by adding all the figures in the total cost column. Then subtract the cost of employees' meals and transfers out of the kitchen cost of sales account. Gross income from sales is the difference between the total sales and total cost of sales. Compute month-to-date figures in the same way, beginning with the first day of the current accounting period.

Compute the cost of sales percentage by dividing the figures on the total sales line by the figure on the total cost of sales line. For example, in Exhibit 4.8, divide $302.25 into $109.84. To find the gross income from sales figure in the Exhibit, divide $302.25 into $192.41. To check the accuracy of the percentage figures, add them together. They should equal 100 percent.

Many crosschecks are available to verify the accuracy of an inventory. For a guest check verification, take the kitchen copies of the guest checks, total the number of items sold, say T-bone steaks, and crosscheck this amount with the inventory. If the guest checks show 11 steaks sold and the kitchen inventory shows 11 consumed, the inventory was correct. Another crosscheck is the scatter sheet. The cashier normally maintains this form by posting it from guest checks. Thus, the scatter sheet is always totaled and easily available, on a daily basis, to confirm inventory figures.

It is often helpful to put a chart in the kitchen to display daily cumulative food costs for the month. Wherever possible, kitchen personnel should not be responsible for the daily inventory. Get another employee, either from the accounting department or an assistant manager to actually do the physical inventory.

Inventory and Scatter Sheet Controls

Exhibit 4.9 shows a sample scatter sheet. It is invaluable for determining the accuracy of inventories, controlling food cost, and forecasting the need to change selling prices or food portion size. If an item is not selling well, it could be because of portion size or selling price. Adjustments to both of these areas can be checked on the scatter sheet to see what effect changes have on sales of the item.

EXHIBIT 4.9

A Sample Scatter Sheet

Scatter Sheet — Date 12 Aug '88

Sales Price	Menu Item	Times Sold	Total	Sales Value
	25% Cost			
$4.25	Hamburger	卌 卌 卌 卌 卌 I	26	$110.10
2.00	Cheese Sandwich	卌 I	6	$12.00
3.50	Egg Salad Sandwich	卌 卌	10	$35.00
.75	Gelatin Salad	卌	5	$3.75
	30% Cost			
1.25	Pie, Cherry & Apple	卌 卌 III	13	$16.25
.95	Ice Cream	卌 卌 卌	15	$14.25
4.50	Cheeseburger	卌 卌 卌 卌 卌 卌	30	$135.00
4.95	Ham Sandwich	卌 卌 卌	15	$74.25
1.50	Waldorf Salad	卌 卌 II	12	$18.00
7.95	Baked Ham Dinner	卌 卌 卌 卌 卌	25	$198.75
6.00	Fried Chicken Dinner	卌 卌 卌 卌	20	$120.00
	35% Cost			
4.95	Pork Sandwich, Hot	卌 卌	10	$49.50
5.95	Beef Sandwich, Hot	卌 卌 卌 卌	20	$119.00
7.95	Shrimp Salad	卌 卌 卌 卌 卌 卌	30	$238.50
8.50	Turkey Dinner	卌 卌 卌 卌 卌	25	$212.50
8.50	Pork Chop Dinner	卌	5	$42.50
1.50	Ice Cream Sundae	卌 卌 卌 卌 卌	25	$37.50
	40% Cost			
6.50	Lobster Cocktail	卌 卌 卌 卌	20	$130.00
4.95	Club Sandwich	卌 卌 卌 卌 卌 卌 卌	35	$173.25
10.95	Pork Tender, Dinner	卌 卌 II	12	$131.40
12.95	Filet Mignon, Dinner	卌 卌 卌 卌 卌	25	$323.75
1.50	French Pastry	卌 卌 卌	15	$22.50
	45% Cost			
6.50	Oyster Cocktail	卌 卌 卌 卌	20	$130.00
5.50	Fruit Salad, Plate	卌 卌 III	23	$126.50
12.95	Rib Steak, Dinner	卌 卌	10	$129.50
12.95	Rainbow Trout, Dinner	卌 卌 卌 卌 卌 卌 I	31	$401.45
13.50	Prime Rib, Dinner	卌 II	7	$94.50
.75	Coffee	卌 卌 卌 卌 卌 卌 卌 卌 卌 I	46	$34.50
.75	Milk	卌 卌 卌 卌 卌 卌 卌	35	$26.25
	50% Cost			
2.50	Asparagus Tip Salad	卌 卌 卌 卌 卌 卌	30	$75.00
6.95	Prime Rib Sandwich	卌 卌 卌 IIII	19	$132.05
13.95	T-Bone Steak, 16 oz	卌 卌 卌 卌 卌 卌 卌	35	$488.05
13.75	New York Cut Steak, 12 oz	卌 卌 卌 II	17	$233.75
2.50	Strawberry Shortcake	卌 卌 卌 卌 卌 卌 卌	35	$87.50
	55% Cost			
6.50	Chef's Salad Bowl	卌 卌 卌 卌 卌	25	$162.50
10.95	Calf's Liver Dinner	卌 卌 卌 卌 卌 I	26	$284.70
18.95	Lobster Tails	卌 II	7	$132.65
				$4757.26

EXHIBIT 4.10
A Scatter Sheet Recap

Items	25% Cost	30% Cost	35% Cost	40% Cost	45% Cost	50% Cost	55% Cost	Totals
Cost % to Sales	0.1%	3.6%	5.1%	6.5%	8.9%	9.6%	6.6%	40.4%
% of Food Cost	0.2%	8.9%	12.7%	15.2%	21.0%	26.0%	16.0%	100%

The scatter sheet is also valuable for developing menu food cost on a daily basis. In the sample scatter sheet in the exhibit, note that items are grouped by food cost percentages. The first group (25 percent cost) includes four items—hamburgers, cheese sandwiches, egg salad sandwiches, and gelatin salads. The cost of each item is approximately 25 percent of its selling price. The number of times each item is sold is tallied in the times sold column of the scatter sheet. The total number of items sold is multiplied by the sales price to determine the entry for the sales value column. Therefore, the total of 26 hamburgers sold at $4.25 gives a sales value of $110.50. After entering all sales values on the scatter sheet, total the sales value column as shown in exhibit 4.9. To find the food cost for each percentage category, multiply the sales value by the cost percentage for that category.

For example, in Exhibit 4.9 again, the total sales value for the four items in the 25 percent cost group is $161.25. Multiply this figure by the 25 percent cost for the group; the food cost is $40.31. To find the percentage of total sales for each percentage cost category, divide the total cost of each percentage category by the total sales value of all categories. For example, the $40.31 cost of sales computed earlier for the 25 percent cost category is divided by $4,757.25. The total sales value is 0.1 percent. Thus, of the $4,757.25 for food sales, only $40.31 (0.1 percent) was spent on the cost of sales for the 25 percent cost items. Enter this figure (0.1 percent) in the cost percent total sales line on the scatter sheet recap as shown in Exhibit 4.10. Total the figures on the scatter sheet recap; the menu food cost is about 40.4 percent.

Compute the percentage of total food cost for each category in one of two ways. First, divide the percentage of each cost category by the total food cost percentage. For example, in Exhibit 4.9, divide the 0.1 percent entry by 40.4 percent; the result is approximately 0.2 percent. Or, divide the food cost for each category by the total cost of food. For example, the cost of sales for the 50 percent cost category is $508.27. The cost of sales for all food sold is $1,922.36. $508.27 divided by $1,922.36 is about 26 percent. Enter these percentage figures in the appropriate columns of the percent of food cost line on the scatter sheet recap. Compute and enter the percentage of each cost category; add them. The total should equal 100 percent.

Check the scatter sheet against the inventory; there may be variances. Some of the most common things to look for are incorrect unit cost entries, transposed numbers, extension errors, or figures entered on the wrong line. If the food cost seems too high and inventory errors are not the problem, check these areas: errors in computing selling price, poor portion control; waste; pilferage; failure to use leftovers properly; employee consumption of high-cost food items; poor cooking methods; or cashier embezzlement or mishandling.

Turn for a moment to guest check controls. Prenumbered guest checks are a must. Guest checks can be printed in any number of copies, depending on the needs of an individual club. At a minimum, there should always be three copies. The cashier, manager, or dining room supervisor controls and issues checks after they are received and their numbers are recorded. Checks can be issued to waiters and waitresses by number on a hand receipt or on another format. Exhibit 4.11 shows a possible control format for guest checks.

At the end of each shift, someone should reconcile both used and unused guest checks with the hand receipts. The unused checks are reissued on subsequent shifts. One wise procedure is to take all kitchen copies of guest checks and file them numerically; compare them daily with the order copies to ensure that all food orders from the kitchen are paid for. This procedure prevents waiters from bringing in their own guest checks, getting food from the kitchen, and collecting funds from the customer. Fortunately, many clubs do not allow cash transfers; all transactions are charged to the member's account. Therefore, the waiter's advantage of being able to get food from the kitchen to the customer is negated because no cash changes hands. Of course, the waiter can still get high-cost food items out of the kitchen for his own consumption or that of his friends, without having to pay for it—*if* you do not correlate the guest checks at the end of the day.

No cash exchange takes place in many of our private clubs. Either credit cards or chits are used as negotiable instruments. (A chit system is used in clubs where the customer comes in and writes his name on a chit. The waiter or cashier enters the amount of the charge and the customer either initials or signs the chit.) The club member's number is always placed on the chit. Account numbers are of ultimate importance when using a chit system, as is a signature verification procedure. One of the biggest fears of any manager is losing the chits. Therefore, many clubs attempt to use prenumbered chits and maintain a log, just as they do with guest checks.

Scatter sheets and inventories, when combined with effective guest check controls, well-trained employees, and managerial interest, can provide pinpoint control of food items. The inventory tells what was consumed; the guest check or scatter sheet shows what was paid for, and the cash register receipts should equal the food sales value as computed on the scatter sheet. If these figures do not agree, managers should be able to determine what items were lost by comparing the scatter sheet to the inventory. Then they look for the cause of the loss. Managers who control portions, price food correctly, take careful inventories, study the scatter sheets, tightly control guest checks, and investigate problems immediately will be able to control food cost and, of course, the budget's bottom line.

Most clubs do not have a food checker in addition to the cashier. The checker is normally located at the entrance to the dining area from the kitchen. If a club has a checker, compare the figures from the checker to those of the cashier. They should be the same. The additional labor cost of the checker can be offset by the control provided. The food checker can also supervise quality and portion control on plates as they leave the kitchen to be served. Each manager must weigh benefits derived against the cost in determining whether or not the club needs a checker.

EXHIBIT 4.11
A Control Format for Guest Checks

Date: Today

On Hand No. 00001 Thru 00100 No. of Books on Hand 2

Wait No	Beginning No	Ending No	Sign Out	Beginning No	Ending No	Sign In	No Used	No Acct
Mary	00001	00010	Mary	00009	00010	Cashier	8	8
SUSIE	00011	00020	Susie	00015	00020	Cashier	6	5

Checks Missing 00014

Checks Void None

Checked Against Kitchen Copy Head Cashier Checked By Restaurant Manager

Verified By Club Manager

BEVERAGE DEPARTMENT

Purchasing, Receiving, Storing, and Issuing

Purchasing for the bar follows the same basic principles as purchasing food, but a couple of warnings are in order. First, *beware of bargains*. Most bar customers order by brand name. Even though managers may be able to get a "good deal" on an unknown brand of the same basic quality, customers will normally not be happy with it. Within the club industry, quality bars are a must. Occasionally, a club's board of directors may decide to use a lower quality item for bar "well" liquor. (Pour brands, or "well" items, are those poured when a customer does not order by specific brand names.) Lower quality well items may improve bar cost if prices remain virtually stable. They should, however, be nationally known brands to build confidence in both the manager and his operation.

A second problem in bar purchasing is the *temptation to overbuy special bargains*. Compare the amount of money actually saved versus the interest the money could earn in the bank over the same time period. Also analyze the extra manhours required to take and extend larger inventories.

Consider purchasing cordials of the same brand in split cases. Normally split cases are cheaper than the case price. Cordials are one item frequently overstocked. So purchase limited quantities, establish low bar stocks, and make adjustments as necessary.

Managers should use the same principles in receiving liquor as they do for food. Storing and issuing are also the same as within the food department. One item to consider in storing is corked bottles. Always store them on their sides so the corks stay wet. Establish bin cards for every item in the storeroom. Exhibit 4.12 is a copy of a bin card. A bin card is also a good reordering tool. If a reorder point is established, and the manager knows the time it takes for delivery, each time the card reaches that level, the manager knows to order again.

Weigh cases of liquor and list the correct weights at the receiving point. Compare the list to a case delivered sealed to determine if breakage or pilferage has occurred. Requisition liquor as you do food and post the requisition to the bin cards. Give the keys to the liquor storeroom to only one person. If he leaves, change all the locks. The person who runs the liquor storeroom should never have access to either the requisition book or a blank requisition.

Establishing Cost of Sales and Price Objectives

Every club is different and no set rules apply to everyone. However, some general guidelines exist for establishing proper cost of sales objectives and prices. Again, the manager should consider the budget approved by the board of directors and a club's members when establishing prices.

Consider the bar operation as one entity when establishing cost of sales objectives. All drinks do not have to have the same gross profit. A good example of this is beer, which has a higher cost of sales and, therefore, a lower gross profit than liquor. It is generally better to increase bar prices than to ever decrease service and quality.

In establishing prices, try to limit the number of different prices. When establishing prices be sure to consider all of the ingredients that go into a drink. Develop menu or recipe cards for all drinks; include the cost of mix, fruit, sugar, cream, eggs, and even ice. Where possible, establish one price for bar pour items and highballs, one price for all call brands, one price for soft drinks, one price for all domestic beers, one price for imported beers, and one additional price for all

EXHIBIT 4.12
A Sample Bin Card

Date	Reference	In	Out	Cost	Balance	Date	Reference	In	Out	Cost	Balance	Date	Reference	In	Out	Cost	Balance

Hiram Walker—½ Gallon—Canadian Club

EXHIBIT 4.13

A Sample Beverage Recipe/Cost Card

C.C. & Coke

	Date:				Date:				Date:			
	Reg	RPD	Party	CON	Reg	RPD	Party	CON	Reg	RPD	Party	CON
Sale Price	1.10	.75	1.10	1.00								
Cost Price	.22	.22	.22	.22								
Percentage	20%	29%	20%	22%								

Ingredients | Bottle Data

	Size	Cost	Amt.	Cost	Cost	Cost	Size	Cost	Amt.	Cost	Cost	Cost
Canadian Club	59oz. 32oz.	MAR. 01, '79	at 103 5.97				7/3oz	.163	.17			
Coke	Gal.	2.44	.019				3oz.	.06	.06			
Water (Ice)	NC	NC	NC				4oz.	—	—			
Total												

Preparation & Procedure:

Pour ingredients into ice-filled glass; do not over stir or will result in a flat drink.

doubles and certain expensive drinks. When a manager establishes standard recipes and ensures that they are used, the customer is guaranteed the same drink at the swimming pool as he receives in the bar or main dining room. Consistency is very important in drinks.

If a manager hears customers say they would prefer to go "see Joe" because Joe makes a better daiquiri, he better find out what Joe is doing different from the other bartenders. Bartenders may indeed come up with better recipes—but Joe could be adding extra liquor and costing the club money. A sample recipe/cost card appears as Exhibit 4.13.

Dispensing Systems

There are many methods of dispensing alcoholic beverages; this section discusses only four. The first of these is the free-pour system—the bartender pours from the bottle into the measuring jigger. There is another definition of free pour and that is to pour directly from the bottle into the glass, but for the purpose of this chapter we will depict it as bottle to shot glass to glass. This system is the most frequently used within private clubs and it has some definite advantages and disadvantages. Free-pour is the cheapest to install and the simplest to use; it's faster than some of the other systems and easier to inventory. In addition, when bartenders are well trained, members will normally feel they are receiving a better and clearer drink. Unfortunately, the free-pour system is difficult to monitor and control, thus leaving the dishonest bartender with many opportunities and ways to cheat the club.

Training bartenders is important in this system, particularly to guarantee that they follow the club's recipes.

The second system is the measured prepour system—the bartender pours directly from a bottle equipped with a pouring head that measures the desired amount. The bottle heads are fairly inexpensive and the system offers slightly better control than free-pour. The heads require less bartender training and members feel they are receiving a fair drink. Shot sizes are uniform, and overpouring is almost eliminated. But there are disadvantages. The customer can be shortpoured without his realizing it, and many of the heads available are bulky, hard to store, and hard to clean. Measured prepour usually offers slower service than the free-pour system and provides only slightly better control.

The third system available is the automatic meter system—the amount of liquor poured registers on meters. This type of system, properly used and maintained, accurately accounts for all liquor dispensed. It produces a standard shot, reduces the time required for inventories (because the amount served is recorded on a meter), and is a more difficult system to cheat. The meter's strong points are its speed and consistency in making drinks, aid in inventory control and cost cutting, and pilferage prevention. However, this system is very expensive to purchase, hard to maintain, and causes dissatisfaction among some customers. Due to the high cost the number of brands carried in the dispenser is normally limited. Thus, a bar has to combine the use of the meter with the free-pour system—which can negate the use of the control. Meters malfunction occasionally and, thus, reduce service. If this system is used, it is wise to vault the bottles and meters away from the bars so the bartenders do not come in contact with them.

Unless a bar has tremendous volume, speed is really unnecessary. A good example of a bar that could use this system is a theater bar that has to serve many customers who come out for intermission and who shortly have to return to their seats. In general, meters discourage pilferage, but any system is capable of being thwarted, especially if it's resented by the individuals who use it. In private clubs, many customers actually do look on these devices as offensive—a sign that the bartender, their friend, is considered suspect by the manager. This attitude is hardly conducive to warmth and hospitality within the club.

The fourth system is the fully automated system, the drink price is rung on a cash register connected to a computer. The computer then dispenses and accounts for measured amounts of liquor, or, in some cases, even mixes the entire drink. This system has several advantages. Highly qualified bartenders are not necessary, thus payroll is less. The system provides increased control of sales and decreased cost of inventory. It is hard to cheat; the drinks are always uniform; the pricing errors are eliminated. However, the system is expensive to purchase and maintain. It is very complicated and, unless a bar has a very large volume, it is not really beneficial. Automation creates an unpersonalized feeling in the membership.

The best dispensing system is the one the manager can operate cheaply while achieving full control and maintaining a satisfied membership. The choice is up to the manager.

Draft beer dispensing systems are also available. The basic system is the regular head; the bartender pulls the lever, dispenses the beer into a glass, and serves it to the customer. Some of this system's advantages are its speed and the personal contact it provides with the member. It is also the cheapest and the easiest to use. It has one major disadvantage; it is very difficult to inventory—to determine the amounts left in quarter, half, three-quarter, and full kegs. Depending on the size glass used and the amount of head at the top of the draft, managers should know how many glasses to get from a keg. Wise managers occasionally will tap a keg and then watch the rings on the cash register for the life of that keg. Managers thus can verify that the numbers of glasses rung matches the number actually dispensed.

A second draft beer system uses meter control. Two types are currently on the market. For the first, the bartender presses a button and dispenses the exact amount of beer set on the computer. The machine counts each glass or each drop. The advantage to this is its inventory control. Disadvantages are probably greater, because often those drops will not be the exact amount required to fill the glass. Depending on the pressure, temperature, and the amount of beer in a keg, the glass fill can vary and make a poor glass of beer. The second meter system dispenses ounces and accounts for the flow through the system. This system still gives the presonal contact with the member; it is fast; and it controls inventory. Its disadvantages are its cost and its possible malfunctions, which, again, negate its quality control.

Inventory and Cost Controls

Each bar station should have its own locked storage cabinet. Establish par stock levels. They should be only as large as needed to reduce inventory time. Set par stocks by using a basic figure for each item served on one of the bar's busiest days. Then add a 25 percent safety factor. Stock bars daily against the par stock. One good system is to issue full bottles only for bottles returned. Take the empties to the storeroom and destroy them after issuing a bottle against each empty one. This process keeps exact par stocks at the bars.

In connection with this, prepare separate requisitions for each bar. If a bar runs short during operation, it is probably better to restock it from another bar. Always use a transfer between activities (TBA) form (Exhibit 4.14), rather than issuing directly from the storeroom. Issue keys to the liquor cabinet where the par stock is stored to bartenders as part of their banks. Keys are the bartender's responsibility while he is on duty. He must return them with his cash and/or charge slips at the end of his shift. Issue keys for the draft beer box or draft beer taps at the same time.

The best way to inventory, especially for inexperienced managers, is to use scales. Establish tare weights for all bottles in advance. (Take empty bottles and weigh them to establish their weight.) Someone independent of the bar operation should make the inventory and, if possible, someone independent of the inventory should extend the figures at least once a week.

EXHIBIT 4.14
A Sample Transfer Between Activities Form

Branch	Transfers Between Sections	Transfer Number

Stock Number	Description	Unit	Quantity	Unit Price	Amount

Date	Issuing Section	Signature
Date	Receiving Section	Signature
Date	Authorized by	Signature

FMB	ID	Branch			Date				
1	2	3	4	5	6	7	8	9	10

CD	CON		Document					GLAC			Sect		Invoice						DR Amount									CR Amount								
1	11	12	13	14	15	16	17	19	20	21	23	24	35	36	37	38	39	40	63	64	65	66	67	68	69	70	71	72	73	74	75	76	77	78	79	80

CD	CON		Document					GLAC			Sect		Invoice						DR Amount									CR Amount								
1	11	12	13	14	15	16	17	19	20	21	23	24	35	36	37	38	39	40	63	64	65	66	67	68	69	70	71	72	73	74	75	76	77	78	79	80

Exhibit 4.15 is a bar inventory. The first item is the description column listing the item. The second column is the number of bottles and ounces the bartender had at the beginning of the shift. These figures are obtained from the previous day's inventory and are normally recorded by the person extending the inventory. The receipt column indicates the amount of each item issued to the bar since the last inventory. Amounts in this instance are transcribed from the requisitions or possibly from the TBA's. Managers may even want to attach the requisitions and TBA's to the inventory to support the entries. The available column simply totals the main inventory and the receiving column and tells what is available at the beginning of the shift. The ending column records the amounts left at the end of the shift as weighed by the inventory taker.

Then comes the consumption column, which indicates how much was consumed at the end of sales. Find this figure by subtracting the end balance from the total of the beginning and receipt column. The cost column is the unit price per shot and should be preprinted. The retail cost column indicates the cost of one shot sold and should also be preprinted.

The total cost column is found by multiplying the unit sales price by the consumption column. Extend all the prices by multiplying the retail cost column by the consumption column. Total the entire column; it indicates how much money the bartender should have turned in from sales. Cross reference this total with his cash register tape and his cash turned in. Add up the total amount cost column; it indicates the cost of sales on that bar for that shift. Compute it daily to see if the bar is meeting its gross profit objective.

After extending and totaling the inventory, note the actual receipts from the cashier on a bar recap sheet, as shown in Exhibit 4.16. Enter the actual receipts figure in the total register sales block. If the amount is greater than the inventory accountability total, the bar is said to be "over." If it is less, the bar is said to be "short." Explain any differences larger than five percent in the remarks section.

Compute the cost of goods sold by dividing the total cost of sales by the actual sales. If the cost of sales continually exceeds the standard, investigate the bar operation to determine the reason.

Some private clubs can use point of sale equipment in their bars without offending the membership. This allows for an easy daily inventory and stock reorder to be accomplished. Such equipment, however, is inappropriate for use in many private clubs. Managers are thus forced to rely on the previously described manual control systems.

There are many reasons for overages and shortages: failure to follow standard recipes; ineffective security of stocks; incorrect computation on inventory form (or inaccurate weighing and counting of bottles); failure to follow standard price lists; failure to account for empty bottles; bartenders bringing in their own bottles and pocketing the sales receipts; under ringing of sales, with subsequent theft of receipts; bar employees drinking the beverages; careless handling of stocks, resulting in spillage, breakage, or evaporation; failure to ensure that each bartender has a separate stock and separate cash register; over- or under-pouring, as a result of inaccurate measurement; and watering of liquor.

This last item can be checked easily with a hydrometer; keep one in the operation. Occasionally take a bottle that looks a little off color or a little lighter than it normally would. Pour some of the liquor into a glass and check it with the hydrometer. The instrument will reveal the alcohol content of the liquid and, quite possibly, that the bottle contents have been diluted. Watering, of course, should be checked in gin and vodka bottles occasionally as a matter of course, since water won't change the color of those.

EXHIBIT 4.15
A Sample Bar Inventory

BAR INVENTORY AND GROSS PROFIT

Date ____________

Bar Number				On Hand Start Shift		Rcvd	Available		On Hand End Shift		Con-sumed	Unit Sale	Total Amt Sales	Unit Cost	Total Amt
DESCRIPTION		EM BTL	WT	BTL	OZ	BTL	BTL	OZ	BTL	OZ	OZ	OZ	XXXXXXXXX		XXXXXXXXX
Cutty-Sark	LT	3	23	1	16	2	3	16	—	6	106	$ 2.25	$ 238.50	$ .42	$ 44.52
Long John	LT	13	23	13	22	12	25	22	12	12	426	2.25	958.50	.41	174.66
Old Charter	LT	11	18	21	6	—	21	6	10	6	352	2.25	731.25	.33	116.16
Old Taylor	LT	0	18	2	4	—	2	4	2	4	—	2.25	—	.26	—
I. W. Harper	LT	1	18	—	30	1	1	30	1	2	28	2.25	63.00	.42	11.76
Canadian Club	LT	2	18	2	2	—	2	2	—	26	40	2.25	90.00	.32	12.80
Gen J. W. Dent	LT	5	19	5	14	12	17	14	12	14	160	2.25	360.08	.20	32.00
Old Grandad	LT	0	19	2	4	—	2	4	2	4	—	2.25	—	.51	—
Rum	LT	2	23	3	21	—	3	21	1	14	57	2.00	114.03	.26	14.82
Vodka	LT	3	18	11	12	—	11	12	8	18	90	2.00	180.00	.21	18.90
Beer Kegs				20	—	20	40	—	20	—	20	35.00	700.03	21.20	420.08
Cold Drinks				200	—	100	300	—	100	—	200	.20	40.00	.35	70.00
Mix				100	—	10	110	—	60	—	50	—	—	1.00	50.00
TOTAL ACCOUNTABILITY													$3,475.25	XXXX	$915.62
TOTAL SALES PER CASH REGISTER													$3,470.25	XXXX	XXXXXXX
DIFFERENCE (Explain in Remarks)													(5.00)	XXXX	XXXXXXX

REMARKS
*Spillage

SALES PER CASH REGISTER	$3,475.25	100%	
COST OF GOODS SOLD	$ 915.62	26.35%	INVENTORY BY (Signature)
GROSS PROFIT	$2,559.63	73.65%	VERIFIED BY (Signature)

EXHIBIT 4.16
An Inventory Recap

Bar: TR-1 TR-2 PUB TR SVC (LOUNGE — circled) WR CB WINE

Date: Nov. 12, 88

Day: Fri Foster

	Inv Acc	1/2 Price Sales	Adjusted Inv Acc	Total Register Sales	Over/Short + or (−)	Cost	Cost%
	1040		16.40				
Liquor	79.80	N/A	79.80	84.15	+4.35	13.23	17%
Beer	18.25	N/A	18.25	15.75	(2.50)	7.43	41%
Draft	N/A						
Food	N/A						
Wine	10.40	N/A	10.40	10.40	∅	7.54	73%
Misc	N/A	N/A	∅	2.35	2.35		
Total	108.45	N/A	108.45	112.65	4.20	28.20	26%

Bartender: Foster Inv by: RCK Computed by: ______

Bar Manager: RCK Officer Manager: ______ CAO: ______

Overages in excess of 10% must be explained.

Shortages in excess of 5% must be explained. Gross Profit ______

Good managers take inventories themselves periodically, often just after regular personnel have done the counts to confirm the results. This practice is beneficial, both to the club and to the manager.

One other way to ease the inventory procedure is to purchase cordials from those companies that preprint inventories on the sides of the bottles. These items simplify the inventory because the bottles do not have to be weighed, and the element of guesswork involved in "eyeballing" the quantity is also eliminated.

Another good control method, but one that should only be used in high-volume bars, is to have a bar cashier, separate from the bartender. Thus, sales making and cash handling functions are separated. In this system, bartenders and waiters present checks and cash to the cashier for payment. This system is expensive because of the labor cost of the additional employee, and it can be beaten by employee collusion.

One inventory system, often used in Europe, is to issue all liquor to bars at retail value. The bartender is thus responsible for assuring the club of the retail price of the stock. A daily inventory is taken, at retail, of what the bartender has on hand. Deduct that amount from the amount he started with to determine what was consumed, at retail cost. This figure should balance with the cash register reading for that day. Whether a manager follows the inventory control sheet at retail value or at cost value, inventory is still the key.

Clubs that permit the use of shot glasses should use those that have a serving line. The manager should also keep a measuring cup handy to verify that the bartenders don't replace the measured shot glass with a slightly smaller one. That bartender would thus get one shot out of every four or five for himself. Some clubs, of course, do not permit the use of control devices such as shot glasses.

Another skimming system bartenders often use is to replace bar glasses with new ones of a smaller size. This method is particularly effective for draft beer. If the manager normally figures the number of glasses based on a 12-ounce glass, and the bartender replaces the glasses with 10-ounce ones, that bartender nets two ounces for himself out of every glass he serves. Out of five glasses, he gets a full one. In a high-volume operation, that bartender makes a great deal of money, especially if there's no bar cashier.

No two bartenders should work out of one register; all accountability is lost. Also, a bartender should not work out of an open cash drawer, for, if he does, he has easy access to the money, without ever ringing sales. Further, tip jars should never be placed near the register. Place registers where they are visible and lighted so customers can see what the bartender rings.

In reality most bars should be slightly "over" since soft drinks are seldom part of the inventory. As a matter of general policy, all shortages and any overages in excess of 5 percent should be explained and investigated.

Spotcheck a bartender occasionally. Walk in, transfer him over to another bar, close his bar down, and do an inventory versus register reading in the middle of his shift. Dishonest bartenders will often take money, put it in the register, and plan to remove it later or at the end of their shifts. This inventory tactic will also catch the bartender who brings in his own bottles. If the bartender leaves without taking anything with him, the manager may count the inventory and discover a couple of bottles that don't belong to the club. That manager unwittingly had another unbudgeted partner.

One frequent problem is the bartender who shorts some customers and then overpours others to earn higher tips. This person is very difficult to catch and even harder to control. Shot glasses, as mentioned earlier, should have a serving line on them and the bartender should pour to the line—not to the top of the glass to eliminate shortpouring some customers.

One last problem is soft drinks. Very few cola sales are rung on bar cash registers—the drinks are served every day. If the bartender has a tip jar near the register, the chances of soft drink sales being rung are slim. This area is really difficult to control. Only by being aware of what's happening can a manager hope to limit the problems.

Many club managers are very reluctant to institute across-the-board price increases because of member resistance. Thus, managers have tried to achieve their bar cost objectives by cutting the size of the drink or cutting the quality. Neither of these methods is really acceptable; sooner or later, the members are alienated. One good formula is to increase prices slightly, and accompany the raise with an increase in the size of the drinks. Everyone is happy, and the bar nets the percentage needed.

One last remark on bar control: the bar has the highest profit margin in a club's operation. Its importance cannot be overemphasized. Don't ignore it just because it's producing what seems to be reasonable profits. Establish recipe cards, know the percentages that should be running based on the daily inventories, and then ensure that those are obtained.

WINE

Wine is normally the largest dollar inventory item of all bar items and therefore deserves a few special remarks. If you personally are not totally knowledgeable about wines, and if you do not have a highly skilled wine steward or sommelier, then it may be wise to consider having a small panel of two to three members who are knowledgeable about wines to sit in on tastings when considering the purchase of house and table wines as well as those wines that you will place on your wine list with the intent to move them out quickly.

The second category of wines, those to be laid down and aged for use anywhere from six months to fifteen years or more, must be purchased with great care. Normally, you will be dealing with foreign wines, predominantly Bordeaux and burgundies, some ports, as well as late harvest California wines or Tröcken Beerenauslese German wines, to mention just a few of the possibilities. In purchasing these wines, quality advice is once again vitally important, as they will become a long-term asset for the club.

Receiving wines is the same for either of the two categories of wine. Always make sure that the bottles are checked to insure there is no breakage.

In the storing of wines, again we have a deviation from other alcoholic spirits in that wines should be held at proper temperatures. Ideal storage for category one, short-term wines is a wine display area or holding area with separate temperatures for white and red wines. The temperature at which white wines normally should be held is 44° while red wines normally should be held at 56°. Storage for category two wines is crucial for allowing them to develop and grow over the years, and storage temperatures become more important. If, in fact, you are unable to properly store wines in category two, it is probably best not to attempt to hold wines of that nature, as your risk of losing the wines (and dollars) becomes very great. When storing long-term or short-term wines in either category, one should consider insuring that the bottles are on their sides to allow the corks to remain moist.

Following this, we get into the issuing of wines. Issuing wines, once again, is the same as it is for issuing spirits, with absolute controls and inventory maintenance of the wines once they go into use. Don't issue a wine from a temperature-controlled cellar unless you also have a temperature-controlled wine facility within your dining or bar area to maintain the same temperature, particularly those expensive wines that you've held over the years.

Next is the topic of sales and the pricing of wines. There are many theories on the pricing of wines in restaurants and in private clubs. One is to set a percentage of markup on all wines, thus, a wine that costs you $1 that you have set a markup of 75 percent on would sell for $1.75, or a bottle that cost you $10 would sell for $17.50. Many private clubs, however, are more inclined toward another system of pricing, which is to put a markup of a certain number of dollars that you wish to produce as profit on that wine. This system allows you to have a steady income and a steady profit on any bottle of wine that is consumed. Some profit can be made with more expensive wines, but certainly nothing to compare with a percentage markup. For long-term wines being held for a year or more, you might consider using two add-ons before applying your profit formula to determine the selling price of the wine. Each year, the wine prices in your cellar should change based on what you are making on any investments your club has. For instance, if your club has certificates of deposit and is making 10 percent on that investment, the wine should be increased in value by that 10 percent. If your club is borrowing money for a specific purpose or a capital program, you should consider putting the percentage of interest of the money you are borrowing against the wine, plus your investment return for the annual increase in the price of the bottle. Then, at such time as you are ready to sell the wine, you would put your formula to the price on that wine. If the wine was laid down for 10 years, it would have continued to improve or increase in value, which gets you a return on the money you laid down and invested in the wine. At the same time, it will allow you to sell your wine at far lower prices than commercial restaurant establishments and hotels in your area and show your members a tremendous value.

Obviously, inventory controls are vitally important when you are dealing with high-cost wines and assets of this nature. If wines are properly stored and stocked, by using the procedures as we discussed for hard liquor, you should have no problems.

Wines are a tremendous asset in the private club industry. There is a definite appeal for any club to have a fabulous cellar, it creates a great deal of pride within the membership. But, a wine program should be developed very slowly and very carefully due to the amount of money invested, and care must be taken to develop proper storage to insure there are no losses.

THE MENU AND FOOD SERVICE

Nothing succeeds like service. That's the good news. The bad news is nothing can fail like service as a survey conducted several years ago demonstrated. Asked why they did not return to a certain restaurant, 80 percent of respondents cited "service." This was four times other reasons: menus, prices, atmosphere, parking, entertainment, food quality.

Clearly, a do-or-die challenge confronts the club manager: achieve and maintain member-satisfying service. The manager must be prepared to come to grips with this challenge.

The menu reflects the wishes of the patrons; it is the basic influence on all club operations. The menu greatly determines preparation and service costs. In clubs, the menu represents all systems of food service. The pool snackbar furnishes hamburgers, hotdogs, other sandwiches, beverages, and desserts. The club may offer a continental breakfast of coffee and sweet rolls for the golfer, or a more substantial list of foods ordered either a la carte (food separately priced) or table d'hôte (food combined in groups and offered at a set price). The luncheon menu may be offered in a rathskeller and include only specialty sandwiches, potato chips, and beverages.

A fast-food service room may have a variety of titles; it will offer a limited group of entrees, salads, desserts, and beverages. In the main dining room, a more sophisticated menu will offer customers and guests, who can afford the time and price, a sociable get-together. The dinner menu is usually limited to appetizers, 6 to 12 entrees such as steaks, chops, seafoods, roast beef, and one or two less expensive entrees; selected vegetable; beverages; and desserts. Of course, the special-function or party menu for specific functions is extremely limited in scope so that the club can quickly serve quality food to a large number of people in the shorter time.

Some clubs may have only one type of service for lunch and another for dinner. Larger clubs may have three types of service going at the same time for lunch—the rathskeller with specialty sandwiches, a cafeteria line for hot entrees, and the dining room with more sophisticated service. The type of service definitely affects the cost of labor—and the combined food and labor costs cannot exceed a definite percentage of the gross or the percentage established in the club budget.

Dining room service is comparatively expensive. If a club can substitute a fast-type or self-help service and still please the customer, that may be all that is needed. For example, the club might offer a continental breakfast of Danish pastry and coffee. The member does not have to wait for the waitress—who will "catch it" if he then misses his tee-off time. Most golfers will more than pay for the free coffee and Danish when they finish their rounds and order more nourishment.

One club with a large luncheon clientele has a "Hofbrau," which prepares a fine but limited menu of sandwiches to the customer's order. Members receive their sandwich plates and pay the cashier. Then the guests proceed to a separate table to serve themselves with beverages, potato chips, potato salad, olives, hot peppers, and other condiments. The total cost is included in the price of the sandwich. This system needs only two or three employees, who are responsible for total food preparation, service, and cleanup. In addition, the same club has a lounge that serves a limited number of hot entrees, cafeteria style. The customer selects the rest of his meal and serves himself. Again, the cafeteria employees are responsible for complete food preparation, service, and cleanup.

With little attention to the rathskeller sandwich operation and the fast cafeteria service, the food manager can thus devote extra attention to the main dining room or special parties. The lunch menu of the dining room may repeat the items served in the rathskeller and lounge and offer additional main dishes for diet customers and those desiring the usual beef, veal or fresh seafood.

The dinner menu is usually more lavish and sophisticated; it is served in fine style to impress the member, his family and guests. The menu is typically more formal and includes an array of appetizers, salads, entrees and desserts.

The menu may be priced a la carte, table d'hôte, or both. Many clubs find it advantageous to plan a family night, with an extremely limited menu of one or two entrees. It may also include a free glass of champagne or other wine. The entire meal can be bargain priced. This family dinner has become very popular. The advantage to the club is easier preparation for the kitchen and faster service by the waitress. Both decrease the labor cost.

The buffet menu is usually low on labor cost but the guest can take as much as he desires. To keep some semblance of portion control, expensive items such as beef or pork roast should be sliced and served by an assistant chef. The portion served is governed by the quantity of food already on the plate; the larger the quantity, the smaller the serving. Place desserts at a separate table.

The buffet is excellent for many members who desire to select their own time of service. It is also a labor saver, but the buffet can waste food. Therefore, it must be monitored to ensure that replenishment is sufficient—but not overdone.

Physical Facilities

Physical facilities of the dining room and kitchen, the distance the waiter or waitress must walk to pick up an order, and the steps the cook must take to prepare a dish are prime considerations in labor cost. Setup stations placed conveniently in the dining room will shorten steps for table setups by offering the server easy access to the sugar, rolls, butter, cream, coffee, tea, condiments, napkins, and flatware. Curtain the station to fit the decor if desired. The distance from the dining room to the kitchen can be a killer for waitstaff. Any innovation to alleviate this difficulty will pay off.

Kitchen facilities must be balanced with the menu to ensure quick service. It is impractical to highlight fried fish, fried shrimp, fried oysters, fried chicken, the french-fried potatoes on the menu simultaneously if the kitchen has only one deep fat fryer. The kitchen is literally a madhouse during any meal's peak operating hours. Most present-day kitchens were built at the same time as the rest of the club. It is quite expensive to add kitchen space, to remodel the kitchen, or even to replace equipment. Therefore, a change in the kitchen is usually not a primary item in the club's budget.

Inspect the kitchen, and see if the equipment can support the menu. Always consider your kitchen equipment and design layout when developing your menu so as not to overload any one station as well as to confirm that all menu items can be produced in your existing kitchen. Study the work methods; it may lead to better equipment utilization and less movement by the cook. It may be possible to improve worker efficiency and morale just by regrouping some equipment. Perhaps an old fryer can be replaced with an automatic one so the cook will not have to continually watch the frying time to ensure maximum quality. An automatic fryer lifts the finished basket at the timed setting; food quality is consistent. A microwave oven may also save time by quickly preparing items that are ordered infrequently or by heating portion-controlled items that can be handled by less experienced kitchen personnel.

Time spent in analysis pays off. Reasonable changes can be planned and made saleable to the board. Depreciate capital expenditures over a period of years.

REVIEW QUESTIONS

1. What do food and beverage controls help the manager do?
2. In what areas of club operations can the manager set up controls?
3. Give examples and explanations of the "paper trail" necessary to maintain portion and cost controls.
4. Discuss bar inventory controls.
5. Discuss the significance of the menu in a club's foodservice operation.

5
Cost Controls: Labor

Grosse Point Yacht Club, Grosse Pointe Shores, Michigan

The efficient operation of any club today requires forecasting labor needs in order to meet the standards of quality and service demanded by club members. Labor planning is the effective way to control service costs.

Labor cost is relative; it is most useful when shown as a dollar percentage of the total sales of the club operation. Labor cost control is the analysis of the workload and the planning of staffing—employee's working hours and work procedures. Then managers have a relatively quick perspective on the efficiency of their labor force.

The manager must stay on top of the operation. His is not totally a "desk" job. He must ensure that his supervisors are knowledgeable and that they meet the standards and efficiency the operation demands.

In most private clubs today, the cost of labor substantially exceeds food costs. The payroll spiral continues with inflation. The requirement for more skilled labor at clubs has increased and so has the demand for shorter hours and more benefits, including retirement, hospitalization, and paid vacations. Add to these the "hidden" costs of accidents and injuries, employee turnover, and the expense of training. There is no set formula for setting staffing patterns in clubs. The pattern will differ for each club because many factors affect labor costs. Probably the most important of these is the philosophy of the club's board of directors.

All clubs' boards of directors insist that the quality of food and service must impress members and guests. Each club interprets the term "standard" in its own way. Clubs with affluent members may meet high standards by hiring personnel above and beyond the number really required to serve the number of customers present. On the other hand, members at some clubs accept inconveniences in order to minimize operational costs. Most clubs lie between the extremes and try to fit a planned or even a fixed budget into their operations. To do so, they use labor controls.

UNION VERSUS NON-UNION

A surprising number of club managers find unionized employees administratively and operationally simpler to manage than non-union ones principally because of defined wages and benefits and established disciplinary procedures. Though union clubs may be simpler to manage, a poorly worded union contract can create managerial headaches. The liabilities of such a contract can outweigh its benefits, whereas a properly worded contract can benefit and protect management as well as employees. Such mutually arranged advantages can be achieved despite the often stated opinion that "unions and the process of contract negotiations foster a continuing erosion of managements rights and authorities." In fact, management of some non-union clubs voluntarily relinquish rights and authorities through careless compromise and unthinking accommodations to employees.

Every club manager inherits assets and liabilities. Assets include club facilities, reputation, membership and staff; liabilities include club facilities, reputation, membership and staff. This chapter deals with how to make the club staff an asset.

To strengthen and utilize the asset, you must manage employees skillfully. In a unionized club you must familiarize yourself with the union contract and any prevailing benefits not covered in it. In a non-union club you must learn personnel procedures and policy. Generally, less written material is available in non-union clubs except for those which have written employee manuals. Unionized clubs maintain records on negotiations, grievances and arbitration hearing, all valuable information for the club manager.

UNION CLUB OPERATIONS

Quest I

A. The Collective Bargaining Agreement

The Collective Bargaining Agreement is for a fixed period of time. Many clubs negotiate contracts for three years. While it is not unusual for a contract to run less than three years, it is uncommon for a contract to exceed three years.

The agreement generally includes the following clauses:

1. Scope of Agreement—states who is covered under contract;
2. Union Recognition—the employer recognizes the union as sole bargaining agent for employees listed under the Scope of Agreement;
3. Union Membership—employees must maintain membership in union to work in club. This is unlawful in states which have Right-To-Work laws;
4. Dues Checkoff—authorizes club to deduct union dues from employee paychecks and submit to union. Employees must sign deduction authorization form;
5. Grievance Procedures—lists justifiable discharges for cause, such as intoxication and insubordination. Also outlines procedure if union challenges suspension or termination of union member;
6. Hours of work, overtime, meal periods—lists hours of work per classification and outlines when overtime is payable. Also establishes meal periods;
7. Holidays, vacation—lists number of holidays per year. Generally lists major holidays such as Christmas, July 4, etc. Also states vacation benefit based on years of service: (e.g., two weeks after one year, three weeks after eight years, four weeks after 15 years);
8. Wage increases—lists increases in wage rate by classification and effective date(s) of such increases. Many club contracts attach a schedule at the end of the contract defining wage rate by job description;

EXAMPLE

Weekly Pay Rate

TITLE	HRS	1/1/89	1/1/90	1/1/91
Busboy	40	250.000	270.000	290.00

9. Benefits—outlines medical benefits including hospital and surgical coverage. Lists pension benefits and employer contribution rate(s);
10. Bereavement Pay, Sick Days—lists sick day benefit and perhaps bonus—for good attendance. Bereavement pay is separate from sick day benefit for the death of a member of the immediate family;
11. Seniority Principle—outlines procedure for layoffs and promotions. It should include the sentence: "The seniority principle will be followed when practical;"
12. Management Clause—this critically essential clause re-enforces management's right to operate the club limited only by what is clearly stated in the contract. Below is an acceptable Management Rights Clause:

"The Union recognizes that, except as expressly limited by the terms of this Agreement, The Employer has and retains every right to manage its business, including but not limited to the right to plan, direct and control operations, to hire, promote, transfer and lay off employees due to lack of work or for other lawful reasons; to maintain discipline and efficiency; and to assign work and to combine one or more jobs."

Collective Bargaining Agreements include a wide range of miscellaneous clauses defining such issues as cost of living increases, meal allowances and personal days. Yet many union contract "benefits" are customarily offered in non-union clubs or required by law.

Disability requirements and overtime provisions are legal obligations to all employers. A true benefit is one that exceeds legal obligations or is unlikely to be granted in a non-union club. With these considerations in mind, remember the cardinal rule of collective bargaining: Everything is negotiable.

B. Negotiations: Who Should Negotiate a Club Contract?

The club manager entering a room to negotiate a union contract has been likened to a boxer stepping into the ring after a long layoff. The manager may not have negotiated a contract in several years. During these same years his "negotiating opponent"—the union representative—may have dealt with scores of contracts.

To offset the experience advantage of the opponent, the manager, together with appropriate legal counsel, must strengthen and sharpen bargaining skills before entering the negotiations arena. Furthermore, the manager must assemble and analyze all pertinent facts and information that can affect the "opponent's" strategies and tactics.

Such a regimen demands that the club manager be success oriented, dedicated and determined. Understandably, many clubs elect to spend a sizeable amount in legal fees to spare managers this rigorous challenge. Nevertheless, experience confirms that the high-caliber professional club manager is often well qualified to meaningfully participate in the negotiation of a contract that achieves an optimum measure of efficiency, effectiveness and economy. Attuned to the club operation's specifics and nuances, the manager who negotiates well can foster and strengthen contract terms to achieve maximum club operations success.

C. "A Contract is a Contract"

Once the contact is ratified both parties are obliged to live up to the terms and conditions for the contract period. The club manager should study the contract and operate his business accordingly. Most contractual disputes center on disciplinary decisions rather than wage and benefits. Contracts are usually very clear concerning salary structure and benefits and rarely will the club and employees disagree on these issues.

To avoid the grievance procedure the manager should be patient in his dealings with employees. Firing an employee without contractual study can result in being forced to re-hire the employee with back pay and penalty.

Never "shoot from the hip." Before taking any action against an employee or instituting a work rule change you must:

1. Be *knowledgeable* of any contractual objections which might be raised by union representatives;

2. Be *prepared* to state management's interpretation concerning the objections;
3. Be *determined*.

Never implement a directive unless you are determined to follow through on your objective. Rescinding a management directive after union resistance may increase the union's perceived "status" while at the same time undermine management's control over club operations.

NON-UNION CLUB OPERATIONS

Most non-union clubs have developed their personnel policies and procedures over many years. Unfortunately, such policies are often established on a "need basis." Issues such as jury duty, pay and sick leave pay require a defined policy. When these types of issues arise, their resolution signals the foundation of an "unwritten policy" which will be followed in similar situations. It is imperative that the club manager during the decision-making process evaluate his options with the understanding that his decision will affect *all* employees. Policy decisions should never be made on an individual basis.

Although a club manager may leave his present position, his personnel decisions remain intact and continue to guide the new club manager in his role as "personnel director."

Personnel policy, whether verbally enforced or written, is equally binding. It is beneficial in a non-union club to prepare a policy manual for proper administration. Such written documentation will be of great assistance to both the club manager and club employees.

The wording of a club personnel policy manual is extremely important. The manual should be constructed in such a way that managerial rights are not limited.

Some club managers believe that a written personnel policy manual limits their authority and, therefore, opt not to prepare such a manual. Nothing could be further from the truth. Past practices are the foundation of your club policy. Any grievance before a local, state or Federal body will weigh heavily the past practices of management in evaluating disputes between the club and its employees. Remember: Be Knowledgeable! Be prepared! Be Determined!

A Personnel Policy Manual which is concise, flexible, and has legal counsel approval is of mutual benefit to management and club employees.

When preparing a policy manual give serious consideration to employee input. Meeting with employees and gaining insight into their concerns can only enhance your club image and foster employee support. Managers who independently tackle this task and implement a personnel policy are subject to employee resistance which can undermine your image and employee productivity. Although such a manual may be reasonable and in conformance with legal requirements it may not produce the desired results.

Certainly a club policy manual which is clearly understood and supported by management and employees can only improve overall club operations. Once such a manual has been prepared, it should be distributed to all employees.

Regardless of whether your club has a personnel policy manual or not, the club manager must realize that, in most cases, "an employer may no longer hire and fire at will." Most states have passed laws curtailing an employer's ability to terminate employees "without just cause."

Employers have a responsibility to honor commitments made to employees. More and more terminated employees are seeking legal advice and filing suit for wrongful discharge. In many cases the personnel policy manual is cited for violations. As with union clubs, the club manager must follow a standard of behavior which is consistent with past practice and in conformity with the law.

Discrimination laws also play an important part in management's operational policy. The club manager is required by law not to discriminate against any employee based on union membership, race, age, sex, national origin, color or creed. Club managers must be mindful of potential discrimination suits filed by discharged employees based on one or more of the above points. You must be consistent in your treatment of your employees. The well-known union slogan "equal pay for equal work" applies to union and non-union club operations. This is not to say that employees with tenure should not be paid a higher rate of pay, but rather that such difference should be reasonable. The time may come when you may be required to justify such difference in a court action.

UNION VERSUS NON-UNION: MOVING CLOSER TOGETHER

Question #2

Over the years the distinctions between union and non-union operations have narrowed and reduced in number. Government regulations and employee readiness to question management's decisions which adversely affect their employment rights have played a major role in moving the club labor force closer together. Many labor organizations have agreed to wage concessions and productivity improvements while non-union staff have gained in wages and benefits. All workers are aware that gains in wages and benefits can only be achieved through increased productivity and bottom-line performance.

All club managers should develop an overall approach to labor relations which is consistent with their abilities and personality. The club manager should strive towards establishing a working relationship which encourages employee support and is dependent upon those managerial traits which enhance recognition and acceptance.

In summary, a well-planned labor relations plan possesses the following qualities:

Question #3

1. It is clearly understood among employees and supervisors;
2. It utilizes the professional expertise of all members of the management team;
3. It has employee support;
4. It meets contractual obligations and is in conformance with State and Federal wage and hour laws; and
5. It includes the input of the club manager.

The club staff is potentially the club manager's number one asset. If not developed properly it can become his major liability. The manager who develops a labor relations plan which fosters employee support and respect will increase club efficiency, reduce manhours lost relating to grievances and simplify the decision-making process relating to personnel procedures.

PRODUCTIVITY

Productivity is the art of getting things done to the satisfaction of the board and the club members at the least possible cost and with the smallest number of employees. The success of any organization depends on the productivity of its people. Top-quality leadership hires qualified people to do a job, trains them, and instills the morale and motivation they need for the team. Management must understand and respect the psychological and material needs of the employees. Only then will the required atmosphere of teamwork prevail so that all staff members can strive to find the best way to do a job. If not, management will have costly personnel problems.

1. Identification of qualified personnel for each job requires taking the time and effort to interview candidates. A good position description will help the prospective employee understand his possible duties, responsibilities, place in the organization, whom he reports to, and whom he may supervise. The candidate and the interviewer can then communicate with a definite degree of understanding, and the employer can judge the knowledge, skills, and motivation of the applicant. The position description should be as simple as possible. (Sample position description for food and beverage director, catering manager, and waiter/waitress appear as Exhibits 5.1, 5.2 and 5.3.)

For the positions of supervisor on down, employees must understand that jobs require good physical stamina for standing, walking, and lifting.

2. Training unfortunately, is accomplished at many clubs through the "buddy" system. The new employee's knowledge is limited to that of his "buddy." A well-trained employee is an asset to the team only if he feels the club has taken the time and expense to train him. It is a work incentive that leads to good morale.

The best method of learning is on the job, but it should be backed up by, or fortified with, planned training. The employee should also be encouraged to take academic training in subjects helpful to his advancement. If he shows such motivation, the club should be willing to pay a minimum of 50 percent of his tuition, provided he attains a passing grade or better. Some clubs encourage students by paying 100 percent of the tuition if they get a grade equivalent of an A or a B.

Many community, technical, and senior colleges throughout the country offer associate or bachelor degrees in culinary or food service management. These colleges welcome qualified representatives of club management as guest lecturers or even as teachers of club management. With the use of a textbook, course outline, and club experience, the club representative may enjoy teaching and also bring the student practical information he needs to implement classroom training.

3. Job standards and the productivity expected of each worker should be established first. The number of customers the waitress can serve per hour, the total number of entrees or covers a cook can prepare per hour, the number of drinks the bartender can pour per hour, and the quantity of dishes the dishwasher can handle per hour are all determined over a period of time and combined with a preplanned volume of business. These figures will be the basis of the staffing table.

EXHIBIT 5.1

Sample Position Description: Food and Beverage Director

FOOD & BEVERAGE DIRECTOR

Job Summary: Directs the formal areas of the club. Supervises employees, orders supplies, helps plan menu, and maintains payroll and bookkeeping records.

Work Performed:

1. Is in charge of all formal dining areas of the club and may also be in charge of informal areas such as grills and cafeterias. Supervises club food and beverage service employees in accordance with operating policies which he may help to set up.
2. Responsible for maintaining records of personnel performance and bar and dining room costs.
3. Inspects food and beverage personnel as to their appearance.
4. Checks special function sheets against room set-up and personnel scheduling functions. Supervises the service of club, cocktail and dining areas.
5. May schedule periodic food and beverage service employee meetings to assure correct interpretation of club policies; covers proper procedures of food and beverage service in club areas.
6. Trains HEAD WAITERS, CAPTAINS, BARTENDERS and STAFF to handle the various types of food service.
7. Handles complaints of members and guests.
8. Executes the general responsibilities necessary to minimize the costs of operating the club.
9. Assists in the planning of menus with the MAITRE D'CLUB or EXECUTIVE CHEF for special parties.
10. May schedule employees for each dining room.
11. Establishes standards of performance such as the amount of linen to be used in dining areas, number of covers to be served per employee, setting of labor cost goals and brands and amounts of liquor served.

Relation to Other Jobs:

Promotion from: CAPTAIN, WAITER, DINING ROOM CASHIER

Promotion to: MAITRE D'CLUB, ASSISTANT MANAGER

Job Combination: The duties of this job may be combined with those of EXECUTIVE CHEF, MAITRE D'CLUB, CAPTAIN, HEAD WAITER, DINING ROOM CASHIER, FOOD AND BEVERAGE DIRECTOR, BANQUET MANAGER, ASSISTANT MANAGER.

Special Qualifications: The DINING ROOM MANAGER must be thoroughly familiar with the organizational procedures of the club. He must be knowledgeable in proper methods of food and beverage service; knowledge of food costs may be required. He must have knowledge of etiquette and social customs especially in regard to club banquet functions. He may be technically, as DINING ROOM MANAGER, an understudy of Food and Beverage Director where size of the club warrants such specialization.

EXHIBIT 5.2
Sample Position Description: Catering Manager

CATERING MANAGER

Job Summary: Operates in function of a sales manager in promoting and selling the club's dining facilities for private banquets, weddings, or convention activities. Having made the sale and agreed on date and details, manages all administrative and operational aspects of preparing and holding the event.

Work Performed:

1. In charge of all advertising and marketing for club dining and social event facilities.
2. Makes arrangement with guests, in person or by letter, for banquets, luncheons, conventions, weddings, dances and any other social event the club facilities are equipped to handle. Obtains pertinent information from guest including: number of persons expected, seating arrangements desired, decorations, music and entertainment, etc.
3. May show guest through facilities offering suggestions in effort to sell the merits of the club facilities for the occasion.
4. Decides on and quotes prices; draws up contract securing guest's signature.
5. May suggest menu or help guest plan menu in conjunction with EXECUTIVE CHEF.
6. Transmits necessary information to CHEF, HEAD WAITER, STEWARD and other employees concerned; arranges for printing of menu, procurement of decorations and entertainment, table set up, food service time schedule, and publicity, if desired.
7. Inspects finished arrangements and adds final touches at last moment; may be present to oversee the actual service and greeting guests.

(In city clubs this position is often the basic function of the club house manager. As the SOCIAL DIRECTOR in other type clubs this position might be more restrictive, including the responsibility of all the details of the event excluding food & beverage arrangements which may be handled by the FOOD AND BEVERAGE DIRECTOR.)

Relation to Other Jobs:

Promotion from: HEAD WAITER, PURCHASING AGENT, CHEF, SOCIAL DIRECTOR

Promotion to: CLUB HOUSE MANAGER

Job Combinations: HEAD WAITER, STEWARD, SOCIAL DIRECTOR, PURCHASING AGENT, EXECUTIVE CHEF, CLUB HOUSE MANAGER, FOOD AND BEVERAGE DIRECTOR

Special Qualifications: Some establishments require graduation from a hotel or restaurant training school. Many clubs employ a BANQUET or CATERING MANAGER who has had European training. Must have ability to sell the club's services and facilities; a practical knowledge of food costs, preparation, and pricing is important, knowledge of social customs and etiquette essential, and imagination and initiative are great assets.

EXHIBIT 5.3

Sample Position Description: Waiter/Waitress

WAITER—WAITRESS

Job Summary: Sets tables and serves meals to club guests according to well established rules of etiquette, and performs various incidental duties to furnish satisfactory service.

Work Performed:

1. Reports to HEAD WAITER and/or WAITER CAPTAIN to receive instructions about the menu, and to obtain checks for writing orders; familiarizes self with menu, paying particular attention to "specials."
2. May set tables assigned to him, spreading clean linen, and placing glasses, condiment holders, flowers, and silverware on table or inform BUS BOY or GIRL to perform this duty.
3. Receives guest and takes order: Assists HEAD WAITER seat guests by pulling chairs away from table; distributes menus and may fill glasses with ice water while guests decide upon order or instructs BUS BOY to perform this duty; writes order on check; answers questions about the food and menu, or makes suggestions about various dishes and wines.
4. Tells COOKS of order: assembles food on tray, procuring items from each station or from a central serving counter; carries tray to the FOOD CHECKER who prices items listed on check.
5. Serves meal: Places tray (when tray service is used) on a stand near the table being served; places dishes, by course, in front of each person, serving from the left of the patron; may replenish water and butter if needed, or requests BUS BOY or GIRL to perform this duty. An efficient WAITER places dishes in front of each guest in such a manner that the guest may start to eat immediately upon being served.
6. Removes soiled dishes or requests BUS BOY or GIRL to do so; procures and serves dessert; may place finger bowls in front of each guest.
7. Gives check to guests when they have finished eating, and either receives immediate payment (in which case it is taken to CASHIER), or permits members or guests to sign check (in which case the amount is subsequently charged to the member's account).

(This job makes numerous exacting demands upon the worker. A meal may consist of seven courses, and may be accompanied by various wines. The worker must know how to regulate his service so that each course will immediately follow the one preceding it, so that guests do not feel a lack of attention. To perform this job competently, the worker must know the types of wines that accompany a meal, how long it takes to complete any course on the menu, and must be able to intelligently plan for, and regulate the service of, numerous different meals when serving several groups simultaneously.) The following general guidelines are basic serving knowledge required of all WAITRESSES and WAITERS:

a. Be courteous, obliging, and attentive. Always greet patrons with a smile.
b. Inspect all dishes, glass, and silver for cleanliness before serving.
c. Place and remove dishes from the left. Never "stack" dishes in front of guest when removing them.
d. Place and remove beverages from the right.
e. Never place fingers or thumbs inside dish or glass.
f. Handle cups and silver by handles, handle glass at base.
g. Serve ladies first if gentlemen are seated at the same table.
h. Clean table well before serving dessert.

EXHIBIT 5.3
Continued.

Relation to Other Jobs:
Promotion from: HEAD BUS BOY, BUS BOY or GIRL, BELL CAPTAIN, BAR BOY
Promotion to: WAITER CAPTAIN, HEAD WAITER

Job Combination: The duties of this job may be included with those of HEAD WAITER, WAITER CAPTAIN, or may be combined with those of BUS BOY or GIRL, CAFETERIA MANAGER, CASHIER, COFFEE MAN, HEAD BUS BOY or GIRL.

Special Qualifications: Worker must be thoroughly familiar with American and foreign dishes, and all types of alcoholic beverages. Must know how to pronounce the names of foreign preparations and what beverages to serve with them. Must know proper methods of serving meals of all kinds.

*NOTE: More specialized service might include a WINE WAITER with extensive knowledge of wines, their usage and service.

Unfortunately, many variables preclude the exact determination of job standards. In industry, the use of time-motion studies and other methods of job analysis have produced the assembly line. The line is feasible when the end product is of one type, as in the automobile industry, or for institutional-type food operations such as those in hospitals, schools, and airline kitchens. Their standards can be measured fairly accurately. Clubs just have too many variables: thus, job standard setting is an art based on experience rather than a science. Each club's standards apply to that club only. Standards may not be comparable even for similar-sized clubs with equivalent memberships.

For instance, the number of waiters or waitresses required will depend on the following:

- Type of service, whether American, French, or Russian style (American service—food plated in the kitchen and served by the waiter; French service—food plated from the service cart near the guest in the dinner room; Russian service—food placed in servicing containers in the kitchen and taken to guest's table where portions are served from the serving dish onto the guest's plate;
- Menu;
- For special parties, whether there are salads, appetizers, and other items;
- The serving of wine or alcoholic drinks by the waitress or by the wine steward or cocktail waitress;
- The presence of the serving station;
- The distance traveled by the waitress to the preparation area;
- The bussing of tables;
- The variations in the number of customers from day to day, as compared to the philosophy of a club to be ready to serve the maximum number of prospective customers at all times.

Discussions with club managers have produced the following staffing standards for waitresses and waiters:

Standards for Waiters and Waitresses

Event	*Number of Customers to Be Served*
Lunch	15–20
(Sandwich grill)	20–25
Dinner	
American style	15–20
Russian or French	10–15
Special Functions	
Preset salad and appetizers	25–30
Full service	10–20

At some city clubs, the member prepares the dinner check at the table. All the waiter has to do is serve; therefore, this waiter can handle about 15 to 20 percent more covers. This system, it should be noted, often produces confusion because the kitchen crew is unable to read the member's order. To alleviate this problem, the waiter should always verify any item he or she is unsure of *before* leaving the table to turn in the order.

Dishwashers

The productivity of dishwashers depends on the following:

- Menu;
- Number of customers;
- Equipment (whether the flatware, dishes, pots, and pans are to be done by hand in a sink, or with the aid of a single- or double-tank dishwasher or a flight-type dishwasher. In larger clubs, the vegetable cleaner may also use the deep sink and be the pot washer. A warewasher would, on the average, be expected to take care of 120 to 150 covers.

Cooks

The productivity of a cook is probably the most difficult to measure. His efforts depend on the following:

- Menu;
- Quality, quantity, and layout of his equipment. His utmost effort is required during the preparation for the meal hours and special functions. Other than during meal hours, his job may be classified as "busywork." Managers usually figure about 100 covers per cook.

To meet the above standards, the employee must be experienced and well trained. In most instances, however, we deal with less qualified personnel. Thus, in the club industry, it is difficult to have reliable standards which will apply to all categories of employees.

Forecasting or planning statistics are defined as information gathered and analyzed so the club manager can predict his workload with some degree of success. Many club managers say that the number of luncheon or dinner guests varies a great deal from day to day and, thus, they cannot preplan with any degree of accuracy. Yet they insist that their food and labor costs are well within the percentage guidelines. These managers are using some method of forecasting, albeit one based on experience. Formal data collection, properly analyzed, will reinforce their experience.

As mentioned in the previous chapter, the cashier or another employee checks off on a scatter sheet the quantities of each entree sold daily. This list permits the chef to know the acceptability of each item on the menu and is the basis for future changes in the menu. In large clubs, the cash register is keyed to the food items, and the price is stamped on the checks. The manager receives an automatic readout each night. The cashier's scatter sheet or the readout also lists the cash sales and the number of covers or customers. The average dollar value per check is then easily determined. The list also provides a running inventory of major food items which can be listed on the daily report.

The bottom note on Exhibit 5.4 should also list the variables that might affect attendance—weather, a sports event near the club, or a special television program. The daily information (and the inclusion of staffing notations or difficulties encountered) serves as a food reference. It is also the basis for the monthly manager's financial report to the board (exhibit 5.5). Granted, the daily number of customers and dollar sales will vary, but sharp fluctuations can be noted immediately, the reasons determined, and corrective action taken.

A manager who waits for the monthly report may lose such detailed information; the monthly report does not reflect daily variations. That report is prepared so the board can see dollar trends; it is primarily used for budgeting. Daily items, such as dollar value, customers, labor costs in each category, productivity, and other variables, can be noted or graphed and used for future planning.

The scheduling of personnel systems used in industry, and in some clubs today, is the shift concept. In clubs, the first shift takes care of breakfast and lunch; the second takes care of dinner and afternoon or evening special occasions. The shift system is simple for accounting purposes; however, it does have the disadvantage of maximum work activity during the meal hours only. Idleness occurs at other times. Granted, busywork may be found for all employees, but highly skilled ones may resent doing work "beneath" their stations. (Busywork assignments may also violate a club's union contract.)

Under the shift concept, clubs are usually staffed almost entirely with full-time or solid core employees. At the opposite extreme is the club staffed with a minimum of full-time employees; it augments its staff with part-time workers. There are two types of employees—regular ones and those available on call. This staffing pattern gives the manager the greatest flexibility on labor costs. Part-time employees work during heavy periods to supplement the efforts of the regular staff, but also for other short periods. If conditions such as bad weather or cancellations occur, a few telephone calls will keep the temporary help from coming in. Most managers prefer a middle-of-the-road position between full-time and part-time staffing; the control over the number of employees who actually report for work at a given time gives these managers a feeling of security about the control they can exercise over their labor costs.

All managers willingly accept lost production from cooks as long as they are experienced, reliable, and conscientious. If managers must, they will employ permanent part-time, well-paid cooks to help carry an overload. Club members are willing to endure slower service when they know the food will always meet their expectations.

EXHIBIT 5.4
A Sample Daily Report

Day *Friday* Date *Sept. 1* Weather *Fair*

Grill		Main Dining Room	
People	274 *	People	117 *
Food	798.15 *	Food	787.25 *
Liquor	176.10	Liquor	686.60
Beer	59.15	Beer	36.05
Wine	26.05	Wine	36.75
Soda	33.35	Soda	4.90
Cigars	5.85	Cigars	
Cards		Cards	
Service Charge	165.00	Service Charge	232.84
Sales Tax	50.51	Sales Tax	71.38
Total for Day	1314.16	Total for Day	1855.77
Total for Month	1314.16	Total for Month	1855.77

Pool		Tee Snack Bar	
Food	4.75	Food	15.60 *
Soda		Soda	15.20
Beer		Beer	15.40
Service Charge	.73	Service Charge	6.95
Sales Tax	.22	Sales Tax	2.16
Total for Day	5.70	Total for Day	55.31
Total for Month	5.70	Total for Month	55.31

	Day	Month
Total Sales	2700.65	2700.65
Total Service Charge	405.52	405.52
Total Sales Tax	124.27	124.77

* See cashiers summation

EXHIBIT 5.5
A Sample Monthly Food and Beverage Report

FOOD AND BEVERAGE INCOME AND EXPENSE
For the month of December, 1988
and the two months ended December 31, 1988 and 1987

	Month of December		Two months ended December 31,		Increase or (decrease)
	1988	1987	1988	1987	
Revenues:					
Food sales	$134,171	$145,844	$220,279	$232,901	($12,622)
Bar sales	42,897	40,209	69,510	63,817	5,693
	177,068	186,053	289,789	296,718	(6,929)
Expenses:					
Cost of food	52,171	53,308	94,072	97,469	(3,397)
Cost of liquor	10,914	9,390	17,497	15,666	1,831
Salaries and wages	73,182	72,914	132,058	129,746	2,312
Employee meals	3,514	3,292	6,700	6,302	398
Laundry	201	568	201	1,008	(807)
Maintenance	0	1,047	192	1,047	(855)
Supplies	2,335	2,682	6,434	7,059	(625)
Sundries	322	313	644	626	18
Total expenses	142,639	143,514	257,798	258,923	(1,125)
Net operating income (loss)	$34,429	$42,539	$31,991	$37,795	($5,804)
Food cost percentage	38.88%	36.55%	42.71%	41.85%	
Bar cost percentage	25.44%	23.35%	25.17%	24.55%	

For planning the staffing, the manager should review the statistics from the past and present records to augment his own expertise and draw up his employee schedules for each job category. Exhibit 5.6 is an example of the anticipated workload and the scheduling of cooks for a club's normal Wednesday. At this club, all full-time cooks work a minimum of 40 hours per week, and the part-time cook works three days to help out. If additional hours are required, the full-time cooks work and are paid overtime. The cooks' hours are rotated for the week because the club is open six days and closed on Mondays.

This scheduling principle applies to all categories of club personnel. Scheduling must consider the standards of productivity, the workload, and the serving hours. It does not matter whether full- or part-time employees are used. A sample of the weekly scheduling for the salad department and cooks appears in Exhibits 5.7 and 5.8.

EXHIBIT 5.6
Sample Staffing Table

Staffing Table—Cooks
Wednesdays

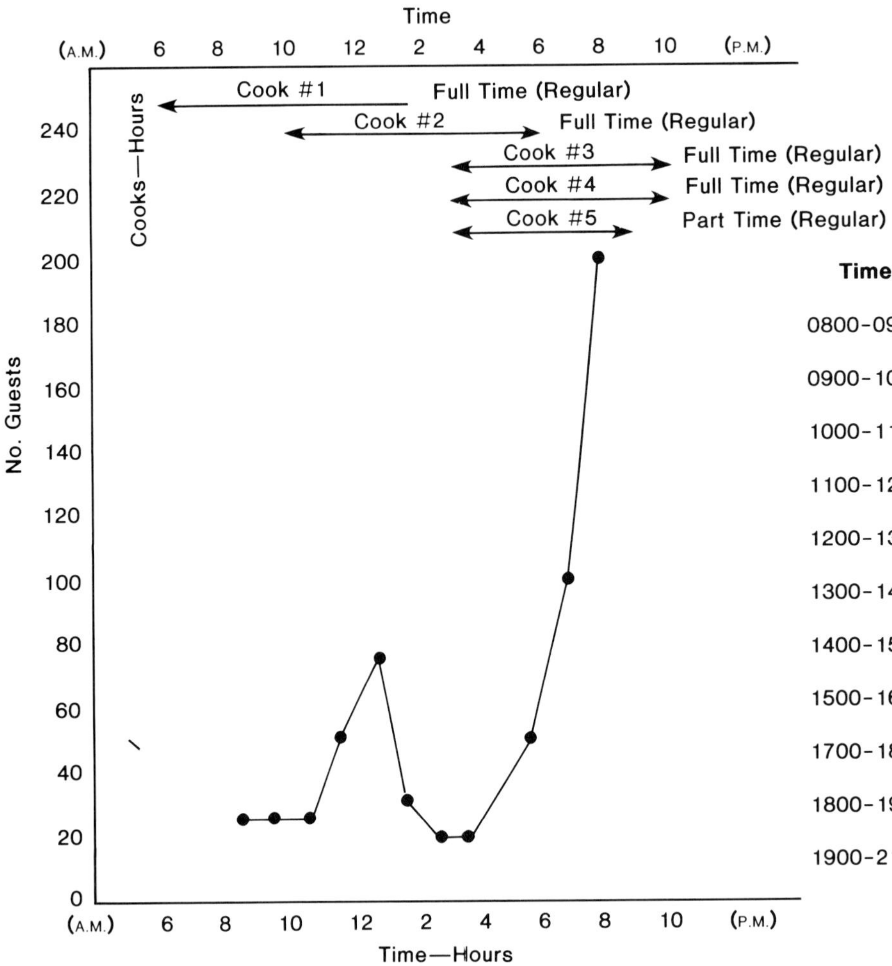

Time	No. of Guests
0800-0900	25
0900-1000	25
1000-1100	25
1100-1200	50
1200-1300	75
1300-1400	30
1400-1500	20
1500-1600	20
1700-1800	50
1800-1900	100
1900-2100	200

EXHIBIT 5.7

A Sample Salad Department Schedule

Department: *Kitchen*

Sub Section: *Salad Dept. Staff*

Dates From: *January 3, '79*

To: *Undefinite*

Employee	Sunday	Monday	Tuesday	Wednesday	Thursday	Friday	Saturday
John Thompson	Off	Off	8:00 5:30	8:00 5:30	8:00 5:30	8:00 5:30	8:00 5:30
Terry Brendt	Off	8:30 5:30	12:00 9:00	12:00 9:00	Off	8:30 5:30	8:30 5:30
Chuck Wendemann	Off	3:00 11:00	3:00 11:00	Off	3:00 11:00	3:00 11:00	3:00 11:00

Prepared by: *John Thompson*

Break Time: *10:00-10:15, 3:00-3:15*

Approved by: ____________

Meal Time: *2:00-2:50, 6:00-6:50*

Let's imagine that a group of workers has worked several weeks and still has not met the club's productivity requirements. The manager can take the following steps:

1. Break down the workload by floors or areas and instruct each employee thoroughly as to what his responsibilities are and how they should be accomplished.
2. Make certain he demonstrates the quickest and best way to do the job so that it will not have to be unlearned.
3. Leave the work area so that the employees are free to carry out the tasks.
4. Restrict himself to training, coaching, and supervising—offering suggestions only when asked or when judged necessary by observation.

EXHIBIT 5.8
A Sample Cook's Schedule

Department: Kitchen
Sub Section: Cooks
(See Reverse

Dates:
From: 14 Jan
(Day) (Month)

To: 20 Jan
(Day) (Month)

	14	15	16	17	18	19	20
Employee	Sunday	Monday	Tuesday	Wednesday	Thursday	Friday	Saturday
Waldo	Off	1400 2130	Off	900 1730	1000 1400	1300 2130	1300 2100
Taylor	Off	Off	900 1730	900 1730	1000 1400	900 1730	1300 2100
Tyler	Off	Off	900 1730	Off	Off	1300 2130	1300 2100
Walton	Off	Off	1400 2230	1600 2000	1400 2230	1500 2330	1500 2330
Rockey	900 1500	1300 2130	Off	Off	Off	1500 2330	1500 2330
Schadl	900 1500	Off	Off	Off	Off	1400 2200	1700 2000
Corpus	Off	Off	Off	Off	1500 2200	1500 2300	1500 2300
Echon	Off	Off	Off	Off	1500 2200	1500 2300	1500 2300

Prepared by: C.W. Approved by: ______ DPSO FORM 3A

Break Time ______ Meal Time ______

5. Encourage initiative and independence of decision when workers are sufficiently skilled.
6. Avoid needless rules, so that workers can be responsible for the means of accomplishment as well as the task itself.
7. Expand assignments as workers gain experience.

Many club employees, especially those in the more servile tasks, are transient or temporary, but it is still important to make the attempt to train them for the future. Nothing prevents a lower-rank worker from eventually acquiring a supervisory role.

In most clubs, department heads conduct training programs for both new and existing personnel. Job descriptions, orientations, and substantial supervision are a few of the essential tools.

Accounting for Productivity Time

The work schedule is the basis for salary payment. Unfortunately, employees find excuses for not being at work on time, and some supervisors are lax in reporting such absences. Therefore, managers must enforce strict rules to account for an employee's time.

Many clubs use timeclocks. Other clubs use a "sign in" sheet kept by the supervisor. Variations of both methods combat the numerous cheating methods possible. One club uses a timeclock and has the employee punch a card (Exhibit 5.9) at his regularly scheduled time. No compensation is provided for extra hours, other than those scheduled, unless the extra time has been authorized. The employee carries the clocked card to his supervisor, who initials it after considering a reasonable time lapse for the worker to appear at his duty station.

At other clubs, an officer worker collects the punched cards after about 15 minutes and gives them to the supervisor, who initials the cards. This ensures that workers arrive at their work stations. About 15 minutes before quitting time, the reverse procedure takes place. The supervisor initials the card and gives it to the employee, who then has enough time to change and clean up before he punches out. This method prevents a worker from clocking in or out for an absentee buddy.

The personnel officer collects the cards and makes his required notations for each worker in the daily personnel report.

The sign-in system is effective, provided the supervisor is conscientious. If he is not, his labor costs will probably exceed his planned costs for the work scheduled. Regardless of the method used to account for attendance, some clubs have a member of the personnel department, or the assistant manager, spotcheck employees' on-the-job attendance.

The employee will be paid only for appropriate hours on the job. If the hours vary from those scheduled, there must be a written document, from an authorized person, explaining the reason. If the employee does not report, or does not report on time, the supervisor forwards that information to the manager. For overtime, the request must be forwarded in writing (such as on the form in Exhibit 5.10) and authorized by the signature of the manager or the assistant manager. The employee must request authorization before working the overtime.

The new computerized time clocks give management a great deal more control and information on variances (as well as the reason(s) why).

EXHIBIT 5.9
A Sample Time Punch Card

Pay Period Ending

A Punch This Side: 1st to 7th / 16th to 23rd

Category

Name

Basic Workweek ____________

Schedule:

Supervisor:

	16	1-17	2-18	3-19	4-20	5-21	6-22	7-23	
Daily Totals									

Employees are paid as scheduled and approved by their Supervisor. Pay starts when an employee is scheduled to report for work, if they clock in at or prior to reporting time. Employees clocking in late will be paid for time worked.

OFFICERS' CLUB BOLLING AIR FORCE BASE

8—214309 SIMPLEX TIME RECORDER CO., GARNER, MASS., PRINTED IN U.S.A.

B Punch This Side: 8th to 15th / 24th to 31st

Hours Scheduled ____________

Name

Reg. hours worked		Including	
1st Shift	____________	Annual Leave	____________
2nd Shift	____________	Sick Leave	____________
3rd Shift	____________	Holiday	____________
O.T. Hrs.	____________	Taxable Tips	$ ____________
LWOP	____________	Change Tips	$ ____________
AWOL	____________	Other	$ ____________

	8-24	9-25	10-26	11-27	12-28	13-20	14-30	15-31	
Daily Totals									

Supervisors must approve and initial time cards daily.

Overtime must be approved in writing.

8—214309 SIMPLEX TIME RECORDER CO., GARDNER, MASS., PRINTED IN U.S.A.

EXHIBIT 5.10

A Sample Overtime Request Card

To be Completed by Supervisor

To	Thru	From

Classification (Include details requiring overtime	
	Pay Period
	RC/CC
	Request Number

SSAN and Name, or Number of Employees by Grade, and Office Symbol	Grade	Hours Re-quested	Date Overtime will be Worked	Estimated		Compensatory Time	
				Overtime/ Holiday Rate	Total Cost	Hours	Date
Total							

Date	Typed Name, Grade, and Title of Requester	Signature of Requester

Fund Certification	Approving Authority
Accounting Classification	☐ Approved ☐ Disapproved
☐ Funds are Available ☐ Funds are not Available	Signature

Date	Signature of Certifying Official	Typed Name, Grade, and Title

SUMMARY

This chapter only touches the surface of labor relations in the club industry. The club manager has an obligation to himself, his employees and his club to develop his managerial and club personnel skills. *Club Management Magazine* and *OUTLOOK* are excellent references for *current* legislation and pending changes in wage and hour laws. Many local and state agencies publish pamphlets covering a wide range of labor-related topics which are available free of charge. For example the New York State Department of Labor publishes contract settlements throughout the state detailing wage increases and benefits.

Many law firms host seminars on a wide range of topics, such as discrimination in the work place and liquor liability law. The accounting firm of Pannell Kerr Forster publishes a periodical newsletter outlining changes relating to the Fair Labor Standards Act and other annual issues such as "Trends in Clubs." The information needed is there for the asking. Be knowledgeable! Be prepared!

This chapter has also discussed methods to hire qualified personnel and to train them to become productive members of the club team. More material about employee training and standards appears in the chapter on personnel practices. A club's manager judges effectiveness by the quality of service to the member, and by the labor cost percentages in the daily report. The daily reports are compared; on some days, conditions will cause an 80 percent or even a 90 percent labor cost. Hopefully, these days are balanced by days of low labor costs and high dollar sales.

The monthly report is usually compared to preceding reports; unless the budgeted percentage of labor shows an upward trend, the manager and the board are unconcerned. The manager may find many things to correct. Also, he may find that despite the fact that he followed the rules, he was mistaken in believing he had a stable work force. What he thought was normal turnover for the industry really may be excessive for a club. Most of this loss will probably occur within a few weeks to a few months of hiring a new employee.

The cost of employee turnover is expensive and includes the following:

1. Loss of production after the present employee decides to leave, and during the period it takes to train a new one.
2. Advertising and time costs in recruiting and interviewing a replacement.
3. Increased breakage and spillage.
4. A possible increased accident rate.
5. Loss of efficiency among remaining employees.
6. Cost of pre-employment physical exam.

Most employees today want to be successful. They are willing to work in order to enjoy those things that go along with success. If the work incentives are provided to permit them to climb that ladder, they become interested and have the desire to achieve.

EXHIBIT 5.11
A Sample Evaluation Sheet

Name ____________________ Date ____________

Employer ____________________ Position ____________

Supervisor ____________________

Please Rate According to the Following:

	Superior	Good	Average	Below Average	Unsatis-factory
Attitude Toward Work					
Quantity of Work Accomplished					
Quality of Work					
Professional Growth on the Job					
Ability to Get Along with Others					
Growth in Self Confidence					
Willingness to Learn					
Ability to Communicate					
Tact, Poise, Courtesy					
Dependability					
Conformance to Rules and Regulations					
Potential for Leadership					

Please comment on strengths and/or weaknesses. Include other comments you would like to make.

____

____

____

Signature of Evaluator ____________ Date ____________

What are some of those incentives?

1. The most important incentive is recognition. Make the rewards dependent on accomplishments.
2. The employee must feel that he is part of the organization. The supervisor must see that the new employee is introduced to all of his co-workers, and explain to him his part and responsibilities in the organization.
3. He must be placed into a meaningful training program. For hands-on training, he must be placed with a proficient operator.
4. The employee must be briefed on the rules and regulations of the club so he can understand the requirements of management.
5. He must be briefed on the benefits such as pensions, hospitalization, sick leave, and incentive awards.
6. Maintain friendly relations; explain that there is an open door policy for discussions of difficulties through the supervisor.
7. Discuss the successful employee's possible career progression at the club.

To complete management's motivation efforts, the supervisor must meet periodically with each employee to discuss his weaknesses and strengths and how well he meets the standards of the club. Every employee wants to know where he stands and what he must do to improve himself. A written analysis of these meetings should be placed in the employee's personnel folder; a simple evaluation sheet appears as Exhibit 5.11.

Ultimately, the molding of people into a truly well-balanced motivated organization still depends on a quality manager.

REVIEW QUESTIONS

1. What are the elements of a collective bargaining agreement?
2. How have the distinctions between union and non-union operations been reduced?
3. Why should the club manager have a well-planned labor relations plan?
4. What can the club manager do to support employee productivity and satisfaction?

6

Interior and Exterior Housekeeping

Library of Union League Club, New York

Before a prospective member or a member's guest ever plays a round of golf or eats a meal at a club, he has already formed an opinion of the club, based on the general appearance and attractiveness of the building from the outside. In a country club, the walks and gardens also create part of this impression. In a city club, such a little matter as the shine of the brass or cleanliness of the windows may attract the visitor. The lobby also conveys an impression about the club being entered; there are no substitutes for clean air, freshly painted walls, unworn upholstery, and, above all, cleanliness.

Housekeeping affects the entire club and all its operations. The finest food, not served in an attractive setting on clean linen with shining silver, loses some of its appeal. Soiled carpets and stained walls behind tray stands detract almost as much from fine food as poor service. On the other hand, dining rooms with a warm, inviting atmosphere can only add to the pleasures of dining at any club.

A club with bedrooms, apartments, or cottages available for members or guests is reflected by those rooms to a degree that is second only to the club image conveyed by the membership itself. The rooms might be traditional, with colonial or period furnishings, or they might be ultramodern, but the important thing is that their decor reflect the image a club has of itself—and, of course, be inviting, attractive, well furnished, practical, and clean.

Most managers have backgrounds in the hospitality industry, frequently including knowledge of the food and beverage operation and sometimes of accounting. An extensive background in construction, decorating, or housekeeping is equally important. Just as it takes years to become a chef, so it requires extensive training or experience to become a builder, decorator, or housekeeper. The manager of a club does not have to be an expert in each of these fields, but he must have a working knowledge of how to get things done through others—whether they be club maids and porters or construction contractors.

The purpose of this chapter is to assist the club manager in dealing with the various levels of help that he will need. Like the private homeowner, the club manager is responsible for an entire range of work—from laundering linens to cleaning gutters, painting, and perhaps even building. The homeowner might choose to do some chores around his home and hire help to do others. Likewise, the club manager must decide who will do what in order to get the chores done—but on a larger scale; i.e., will he hire a laundry to supply clean table and bed linens or will he hire employees and develop an in-house laundry? How should he train maids to handle their functions efficiently? What about upkeep or preventive maintenance on club equipment? Should staff take care of it? When major renovation or building projects come up, what kind of contract is advisable? These and other pertinent questions are discussed here. The chapter ends with a glossary of technical terms to help club managers work with architects, engineers, and contractors.

Finally, although there are times when a manager may feel otherwise, club members are reasonable and do not expect him to be an architect or a decorator. Engineering knowledge or building experience is certainly a plus, but the manager should not be afraid to call on members for their skills in those fields. Most members are flattered and glad to share their expertise to help their club. There is a wealth of talent in the membership—the manager might as well use it!

EXTERIOR HOUSEKEEPING
CLUB HOUSEKEEPING

Responsibilities of the Housekeeper

A large club may have an executive housekeeper to supervise the activities of the housekeeping staff. At a small club, the manager may have to assume the role of housekeeper among many other responsibilities. Even if the manager is his own housekeeper, he should write a job description for the position. Preparing the job description and thinking about the responsibilities involved help in performing that function. The following is a sample job description:

HOUSEKEEPER

Function—To be responsible to the manager or assistant manager of the club for administering and coordinating the housekeeping staff in all areas of the club.

Responsibilities

1. Develop standards for the proper care of buildings, furnishings, and equipment. Prepare work schedules for employees, ensuring equal distribution of workload. Allow adequate time for work to be completed and provide flexibility so that unusually heavy activities in one area or another can be accommodated.
2. Prepare and implement training plans for instructing new employees in the housekeeping department.
3. Advise employees about their on-the-job performance. Discuss grievances, suggestions, and complaints. Recommend appropriate action.
4. On a regular basis, inspect the work of the housekeeping staff and check to see that desired standards are being maintained. Provide continuous instruction for all housekeeping employees. Demonstrate proper methods of cleaning different surfaces, as well as preferred procedures for waxing, sweeping, dusting, window washing, and care of bathroom facilities.
5. Be responsible for the inventory of cleaning supplies and equipment, as well as linens used. Order or requisition the necessary supplies and equipment and verify orders received.
6. Control and issue supplies and equipment to employees as required.
7. Coordinate work with club manager and other department heads in their areas of responsibility.
8. Implement policies and procedures of the club. Make recommendations or suggest changes in policies or procedures when deemed necessary.
9. Perform other duties as assigned.

Training Housekeeping Employees

The average club member is probably rather affluent and owns a home that is attractive and well kept. His standard of living is high. On the other hand the standard of living of most employees on the average club housekeeping staff is not so high. Housekeeping involves a low level of skill, low pay, and what many consider to be a lack of prestige; the combination can create problems for the club manager. With the proper strategy, the problems can be solved.

It is of primary importance for the manager to let housekeeping employees know that he cares about them as human beings, that he doesn't speak to them only when the windows aren't clean or the brass isn't polished. For the person whose job, day after day, is to vacuum the same bit of carpet, it is nice to hear the manager say that the carpet always looks clean and that the employee's dependability is appreciated. Just as anyone likes to be praised for a job well done, so does the housekeeping staff.

One of the most important steps toward assuring that the club's standards of cleanliness are met is to develop a routine for all cleaning activities. Each employee should have a schedule of the routine tasks he is expected to perform. Standards for these routine tasks should be developed so that the services rendered by a maid and her substitute are exactly the same.

There is more turnover in the average housekeeping staff than in almost any other department. Therefore, a program must be developed for training new employees in their jobs and in the standards expected at the club.

It would be nice for a club to be so well staffed that it would have a supervisor to oversee the training of housekeeping employees. But most clubs do not, so the manager must develop a strategy or plan that will work, given the limited staff available. The "buddy system" sometimes works very well. Under this method, an experienced employee is assigned to work with a newcomer and to teach him the job. Ideally, the experienced worker takes pride in his or her own ability and helps instill the same attitude in the trainee. The experienced worker should be able to express himself well and should be very patient, as trainees must learn why or how certain methods are used. If possible, the trainer should develop and use a checklist of areas to be taught. Obviously, best results are obtained if the teacher and the trainee understand each other—that is, if they use the same vocabulary for the chores being discussed and can communicate comfortably with each other.

New maids should first be taught the standard procedures for cleaning club guest rooms. (Cleaning procedures are discussed below.) Efforts should be made to see that maids develop good work habits, are neat in appearance, follow daily work schedules, develop good health habits, adhere to house rules, respect property, and have safe working habits.

Maids and porters are more cooperative and efficient if the manager takes the time to talk over pertinent matters with them and to advise them of such things as decorating plans, improvements, or additions that are being undertaken. The employees will frequently offer suggestions and opinions that can be very practical from an operating point of view.

An outstanding club housekeeping operation requires planning and work. One aspect of planning that the club manager must tend to is setting up a standard procedure for cleaning guest rooms. In a large club with many rooms, maids report to the housekeeper who assigns them rooms to clean that day. In a smaller club with fewer rooms, maids may know in advance which rooms they clean. In any event, the maids must first check the status of the rooms to which they are assigned; that is, whether the rooms are occupied or vacant; whether guests are scheduled to check out or check in. The work of the maids should not disturb the guests. If there are checkouts or if it has been requested that certain rooms be made up early, maids should start their work in those rooms. They should never knock when a "Do Not Disturb" sign is displayed, nor should they knock or try to enter a room that is double locked. If, by a predetermined time—usually early afternoon—the room is still inaccessible, the maid should ask the housekeeping department or the front desk to check the room by phone.

Before entering any room, the maid should have gathered her supplies—toilet tissue, facial tissues, ashtays, matches, menus, stationery, drawer liners, bath and bed linens, soaps and other giveaways. If the guest rooms are all on one floor, it is usually convenient to carry these supplies on a cart. Carts should never be taken into guest rooms; they are normally left at the door of the room being cleaned.

Before entering a guest room, the maid should knock and say "Housekeeping." If the room is occupied, she asks if the guest wants service then or later.

If the room is ready for cleaning, the maid usually begins by opening the windows to freshen the air. Next, she usually makes the beds so that the room looks neat in case a guest enters. Beds can be made various ways, so a standard procedure should be decided upon and followed unless, for example, a regular guest asks for his bed to be made up a certain way. It might be a good idea to have a poster in the linen room showing how beds are to be made. In any case, in a well-run club the linen is changed daily.

The bathroom is usually cleaned next. The room and fixtures can be cleaned in this order: tub, shower curtain, walls, basin and vanity counter, toilet, and floor. Glasses used in the guest room are sent to the main kitchen for washing and sterilizing. Throw-away plastic glasses are being used more and more as they require less handling and transporting.

The next cleaning step is to dust the bedroom with a cloth dampened with an all-purpose cleaner (for plastic furniture) or with furniture polish (for wood furniture). Finally, the room is vacuumed. The maid then checks to see that all guest room and bathroom supplies are replaced as needed.

Guest Room Inspection: Guest rooms should be inspected regularly by the club's housekeeper or manager. It seems simple enough to walk in and look around to see if everything looks neat and clean, but it might be helpful to have in mind an inspection checklist. Here are some suggestions for bathroom inspection.

1. When inspecting a bathroom, first see if the floor is clean; then check the walls and ceiling to see that they are clean and free of cracks or broken or loose tiles.
2. Check all chrome fixtures including the faucets and shower head, to see that they are polished. Look for leaks or drips.
3. Check all soap recesses.
4. Inspect the toilet bowl, tub, shower, and washbasins to see if they are clean and if all drains are working. Occasionally check the water pressure by turning on the faucets and flushing the toilet. See that the toilet seat is clean on top and bottom.
5. Open the bath cabinet and see that it is clean, that the shelves are not broken, and that the door works.
6. Check soap, paper, and towel supplies.

The following steps are helpful for bedroom inspection:

1. Check the carpeting for spots; ascertain that it has been properly vacuumed. In particular, check under the beds, radiators, and furniture, since these areas are more difficult to clean.
2. Check windows, windowsills, and draperies to see that they are clean.
3. Inspect the furniture for spots and, in particular, examine any upholstered furniture for stains.
4. Be sure that the beds have been changed and made properly.

5. Pictures and wall decorations should be clean and level, and lamps and shades dusted and in working order.
6. Open the closet and check it for cleanliness, making sure that the shelves and clothes poles are dusted, that there are sufficient hangers, a laundry bag, and extra blankets if they should be there.
7. Open bureau drawers to see if they have been washed. Make sure that the desk or night table is supplied with guest stationery, and that the telephone is cleaned and the phone book is in place.
8. Check to make sure that television sets, air conditioners, and heating units function properly.
9. After checking all of the individual items, step back and imagine that you are a member or a guest coming into that room. Is it inviting? Does it reflect a true image of the club? If not, why not?

During room-to-room inspections, written notes should be made of conditions that need to be corrected. The notes are then passed on to the housekeeping and maintenance personnel.

Employee Rooms

Rooms available at a club for employee occupancy are a great asset and should be cared for and treated as such. The cost of maintaining the rooms is relatively low, and their value in lowering payroll costs is high. If some club employees are required to live on the club grounds, the rooms provided for them are usually considered nontaxable income other than for social security and FUTA purposes.

Country clubs are frequently located in suburban areas where there are few single rooms available for rent at prices employees can afford. Room and board substantially increases an employee's income, at relatively little cost to the club. To encourage live-in employees, it could be pointed out to them what they would have to pay for meals and a room if they live away from club property, and it might be emphasized that those expenses would have to be paid with "after-tax" dollars.

A regular program should be developed for refurbishing employee rooms, just as for member-occupied rooms. If there are quite a few employee rooms, a maid should be assigned to clean the baths and halls. There should be an area where live-in employees can relax and prepare a snack if they so desire. Such attention to the needs of the live-in help doesn't cost much and pays large dividends. A community "TV" room with a small refrigerator and hot plate should suffice.

LAUNDRY AND LINEN SUPPLY

One of the largest expenses of a club is for laundry. Clean linens whether club-owned or rented, are needed for the dining room operation, guest and employee bedrooms, swimming pool or beach, and locker rooms.

A member dining at his club expects to see fine linen that is kept clean and attractive. Table linens should not be wrinkled and should not have tears, holes, spots, or stains.

In recent years, clubs have leaned more toward using in-house laundry operations rather than services from rental companies.

A few strategies can improve a club's service from an outside laundry service and, at the same time, lower costs so that an in-house operation may not really be necessary to meet club needs.

In selecting a laundry service for a club, it should not be assumed that just because there are several competing services in the area, their prices are the same. A study of several clubs in a major metropolitan area, receiving services from five different laundries, showed that prices varied as much as 60 percent. Even more surprising is the fact that one company serving several clubs had price variations of up to 20 percent for the same item. There may be justifiable reasons for these variations, such as the distance traveled to the club or the volume of business that the club does with the laundry. However, a club that continues to use a laundry service should check prices with other area clubs using different companies and also with clubs using the same one. If the prices charged neighboring clubs are lower, the manager will want to find out why.

Laundry received from a linen supply service should be counted on receipt; it is equally important to count it when it is sent to the laundry. Some laundry services charge for linen lost during the year and bill for its cost. Even if a laundry bill does not show that specific charge, it is built into the cost of laundering each item. Therefore, a club should always count laundry being delivered or picked up. Not counting it can prove to be very costly.

One factor affecting the decision to have an in-house laundry or not is the space required to house the operation. If the club has an unused area available, the only cost is for buying and installing the equipment itself. However, if the installation of a laundry requires the construction of a new room, the actual cost is substantially increased.

If a club enjoys good relations with another club nearby, the two might explore the possibilities of a joint laundry operation to see if costs for both clubs can be reduced.

In-House Laundries

If the club purchases good linen, basic quality is assured. If the club launders its own linen, the quality of the laundry work can be controlled. An in-house laundry reduces exposure to theft and other losses. (Linens can still be stolen by people having access to them at the club, but the risk of pilferage while it is out of club control and off the premises is eliminated.)

Use of milder washing products in-house helps preserve the life of linen, and, together with less theft and loss, contributes to a lower laundry cost. The harsh detergents and strong bleaches used by commercial laundries greatly reduce the life of the linen. Also, a laundry service must employ drivers and buy trucks to pick up and deliver linens and these costs obviously have to be passed along to the club.

Many clubs that have switched to in-house laundries report that their laundry costs have gone down as much as 60 percent from when they used commercial laundries. Measurement of these savings depends a great deal upon the allocation of payroll when persons working in the club's laundry perform dual functions and have other duties. It also depends on what percentage of the equipment and installation costs is charged back to the operating costs each year.

If a club decides to have an in-house laundry, another decision must be made: whether or not to use no-iron linen or the very fine cotton linen that requires pressing. Permanent-press linen has improved greatly in the last few years, but many clubs consider the freshly ironed appearance of cotton damask to be more attractive. The initial outlay for mangles and presses is considerably greater, but the improved appearance of the linen may be worth it.

Many clubs started their in-house laundry operation with only a washer and dryer for washing the numerous towels used at their swimming pools. As they gained confidence in their ability to handle an in-house laundry, they then added dining room linen and, in some cases, bed linen. Some have gone a step further and added the mangles and presses that have enabled them to use fine linen and to do their own uniforms.

Before a club installs its own laundry, management must take several steps: the first is to analyze the cost of the equipment involved. Second, the club's linen needs should be analyzed to determine what quantities have been used during peak periods from the outside laundry. It is obvious that the club will need a large enough supply to carry through the period required to launder soiled linens. The supply should be large enough to get through the busiest 3-day weekend that the club has, particularly if laundry personnel do not work on weekends.

The machinery selected should be well built and easy to operate. Many washers are made with preprogrammed cards for various types of washing—e.g., towels used at the swimming pool just to dry already clean bodies do not require as much detergent nor as long a wash cycle as linen used in your kitchen. Intelligent, well-trained employees may do a fine job without preprogrammed cards. However, if the laundry employees lack skill and experience, it may be better for them to use a card system.

The selection of detergents is important. The detergent that is cheapest by the pound may end up costing more in the long run because it is more caustic and may actually destroy the laundry machinery. Vendors of different detergents frequently offer to program the amounts of detergent, bleach, and softener to be used. That can be very helpful, but it should be remembered that these people are salesmen first; and the amount of laundry product used by the club affects their commissions. Equipment manufacturers know a great deal about their own equipment. Therefore, when a club purchases equipment, part of the deal should be that the manufacturer instructs the club's employees in the operation of the machines and in the amount of different chemicals to be used.

When purchasing quality towels and linen, it is also a good idea to buy rags and wiping towels. Quantities of these should be available in every possible area that they can be used. Napkins used to wipe grease stains from floors or ranges can probably never be cleaned well enough to be placed on a guest table again. Soiled linen, particularly, if it is wet, should be laundered as soon as possible. Grease and moisture cause cotton fabrics to deteriorate. For no-iron linens, extremely high water temperatures should be avoided. Heat tends to set stains and cause the linens to lose their no-iron quality. Excessive amounts of bleach or soap also greatly reduce the number of washings that can be expected from either permanent-press or regular linen.

Linen Supplies

Towels embossed or imprinted with the name of the club will far more likely be taken as souvenirs by guests than will the harsh towels usually supplied by commercial laundries. The club might charge a nominal fee for bath towels at the pool or beach or might issue them without charge. In any case, costs will be greately reduced if the member signs for a towel and is charged for its loss if he fails to return it. Tennis players who drape towels about their necks after playing frequently forget to return them. It is always a good idea to count the towels that go to each department so that the cost of replacement can be properly allocated.

Linen purchases must be planned ahead. For many items that clubs use, the time between placing an order and its delivery can be several months. If club linen is crested and special-ordered, the delay may be even longer. A record should be kept of all linens that are laundered and from which area of the club they are received. This helps spot losses more easily and provides information that helps when ordering supplies. Periodically the manager should measure the amounts used in a given period to compare costs with then-current rental prices charged in the area. Only in this way can the manager determine the monetary savings from an in-house laundry.

REPAIR AND MAINTENANCE

Maintenance and repair expenditures, depending upon the facility, take approximately ten percent of all income, except dues, that a club receives. If the clubhouse and facilities are relatively new, the cost of repairs and maintenance may be less than ten percent, but if the building is 50 years old, it may require as much as 15 percent of the club's income. Thus, maintenance and repair constitute an important part of overall operation and a strategy should be developed to ensure the maximum return for each dollar spent.

Decisions in this area of operations involve questions like these: Can certain jobs be performed best by outside contractors or by club personnel? Is there sufficient work to justify employing a full-time carpenter or plumber or mason? To answer the second question, analyze the expenditures that the club has made in each category (carpentry, etc.) during the past five years. If plumbing expenses were $40,000 and three-quarters of that amount represented labor costs, it would seem that, unless a plumber could be hired for less than $30,000 a year, the club should continue with outside contractors. On the other hand, if the club could hire a person skilled enough in plumbing to do the required work in one-half of the week, the other half would be available for other assignments. If the time not spent on plumbing assignments can be utilized effectively, the labor portion of the plumbing bill is in effect cut in half. The same type analysis can be made for carpentry and painting work. It is quite possible that neither of these expenses on its own would allow for the employment of a full-time employee, but it is possible that their combined costs would exceed the cost of engaging a carpenter who also paints.

An outside contractor frequently must pay workers a higher hourly wage than the club manager pays, because the contractor does not employ the help on a year-round basis whereas the club manager does. The contractor must also cover overhead expenses and make a profit, all of which may result in the club's being charged double the hourly rate that would be paid directly to a craftsman working for the club.

There are many advantages to having certain skilled employees on your payroll. During the winter, a skilled painter can do the fine interior work. In the summer he can oversee the less-skilled exterior painting often done by college students on vacation. The question of hiring skilled in-house maintenance men cannot be answered in terms of dollars alone. If a club experiments by employing skilled personnel for a year or two, another important question comes up: have the standards of maintenance and repair of the club been raised by the program, or lowered? If the costs remain roughly the same and the standards are raised, the program should be considered a success. If the costs are not lowered, but the general level of maintenance appears to have dropped, the program should be considered a failure.

If one person on the staff is responsible for repairs and maintenance, it is a good idea to review his plans regularly and establish priorities. The manager should know what projects are being worked on each day and should take the time to inspect work in progress. Periodically he should walk through the club as if visiting a club he had never seen before, looking for shortcomings, for work that needs to be done—walls with paint flaking off, disconnected downspouts, and such. On such a tour, the manager should list all possible work that could be done to improve the club. Then he should analyze this list and establish the order of priority for the work to be done. The work should then be discussed with the maintenance foreman and a realistic program set up for its accompaniment.

PREVENTIVE MAINTENANCE

Preventive maintenance is work done, usually according to a schedule, to postpone major repairs or prevent breakdowns and costly expenditures. Following are a few examples of work that can be considered preventive maintenance: Cleaning leaves and debris from the gutters of the clubhouse is preventive maintenance as it may prevent conditions that could ultimately result in water damage to ceilings or walls of the building. Touching up or repainting a building when it begins to show wear may prevent its needing all the paint scraped or burned off prior to repainting. Timely painting can prevent having to replace wood that has rotted because of exposure. Cleaning a typewriter in the club office can prevent a costly breakdown. Regular carpet shampooing extends the life of a carpet. In the club's kitchen, cleaning the flues and filters regularly considerably extends the life of the exhaust motors.

Preventive maintenance services can, of course, be obtained from a service contractor or performed by a club-employee. Whichever, the goals are the same: extend the life of equipment and reduce cost.

If a service contract on a particular piece of machinery costs $500 per year and the cost of replacement or of maximum possible repair is less than $500, the maintenance contract appears to be a bad investment. That may not always be the case, however. An equipment breakdown has other costs—costs that could have been prevented by a maintenance contract. For example, if the club's dining room had to close for a day or so while workmen replaced the exhaust fans in the kitchen, there would be a loss of business. Therefore, a club manager must take a practical approach to a preventive maintenenace program. If breakdown and service interruptions of certain equipment create only minor problems, then an extensive preventive maintenance program for that equipment might be a waste of money.

The club manager should first set basic goals for the club's preventive maintenance program including the following:

1. Lowered total costs of repair and maintenance.
2. Extended productive life of the equipment and building.
3. Proper functioning of equipment and machinery.
4. Improved working conditions.
5. Increased employee production (because equipment is less subject to breakdowns).

Having established goals for the preventive maintenance program, the manager must, with the assistance of others, set up a plan whereby those goals can be reached. A refrigeration contractor can estimate how frequently the cooling tower should be drained and cleaned. An electrical contractor will advise on how often electrical motors, disconnect switches, relays, and other related items should be checked.

Each piece of equipment to be included in the plan should have its own record card. The card should show the name of the item, the manufacturer, the date of purchase, and the source of repair parts. It should then list the preventive maintenance procedures and tell how often they need to be performed. There should, of course, be a space for the person performing an inspection to indicate the date of the procedure and his name. There should also be a space on the card for listing other than routine work so that the history of that particular piece of equipment and the cost of its maintenance are available when needed. There should also be a determination made of when a piece of equipment has reached its useful economic life. The history of repair and maintenance costs can be compared with new purchase prices and expected maintenance costs to determine an optimum time for replacement.

A preventive maintenance program can be no better than the person who implements it. If a club owns a $20,000 piece of equipment that not one employee knows a thing about, the club should consider using an outside service contract for preventive maintenance. Very few in-house maintenance personnel have all the skills necessary to service the complicated machinery of today. Maintenance and repair work requires both specialized equipment and the specialized experience of repairmen trained to inspect and test that type of equipment.

Before going to an outside service contractor, the club manager should check the contractor's credentials: Is he properly licensed? What is his reputation with other clients for whom he has provided the service that he is proposing to sell? Is he willing to submit a list of other clients who have similar contracts? How long has he been in business? Is he fiscally responsible? And, finally, does the contractor have enough personnel and an adequate supply of parts for your equipment?

MORE ABOUT IN-HOUSE LABOR VERSUS CONTRACTED SERVICES

When the club manager is considering whether or not to use an outside service contractor for a particular job, he should answer two basic questions: (1) Who will do the job best? (2) Who will do the job at the least cost to the club? Outside service organizations will say that they can do the job better and do it for less, but in each case, the manager will have to make a judgment.

For instance, the ducts and flues to the club's oven ranges have to be cleaned regularly and the average club does not usually have the specialized equipment for this job. Thus, an outside service contractor is in order. Similarly, the regular servicing of fire extinguishers, standby generators, electronic billing machines, computers, and typewriters is probably best handled by outside service organizations.

However, preparing the club pool for summer operation is a different matter. Although pool service companies will acid wash the pool and check out the filtration system, their work may be quite costly. None of the jobs involved requires great skill, so the work may be better handled by club personnel—the decision is the manager's.

The same analysis must be made for all services. Does the club have the equipment and trained personnel to shampoo carpeting? If the club doesn't own a shampooer, how much would a good commercial machine cost? Is there an employee capable of operating the machine and free to do so when needed? How many years of service could be bought for the cost of the machine? How advantageous is it to have the equipment on the premises so that stains and spots can be removed rapidly after a carpet is soiled?

A professional floor-polishing service costs a known figure each month. If the housekeeping staff is so busy that an additional employee would have to be hired to polish the floors, then it is probably advisable to keep the outside service. On the other hand, if there is time available for a club employee to do the work without adding to the payroll, the manager should consider using club personnel. It may be that dropping certain outside services will save enough money for the club to pay a higher rate to employees who have the skills necessary to perform the services.

Service organizations claim that their personnel have the necessary technical knowledge and experience for the jobs they perform and that their employees are trained and well supervised. Those claims may be true, but it is still a good idea to ascertain who did the training and what his qualifications were. The question of supervision is even more suspect. Some contractors are present at the time of the signing, but never appear again unless there is a complaint. On the other hand, outside service contractors eliminate a club's having to train its own personnel and that type of training is seldom a one-time item, as labor turnover is unfortunately high in the club industry.

Janitorial Services: If the house staff is efficient and adequately supervised it may be able to perform most of the janitorial tasks that outside contractors provide—at substantially lower cost to the club. Most contractors spend between 60 and 65 cents of each dollar on labor and supervision, between three and five cents on supplies, and another three cents on equipment; the remaining 30 cents is split between overhead and profit. In-house janitorial work can eliminate the cost for supervision as well as the costs for profit and overhead that a service contractor requires. Service contractors must also maintain a fleet of trucks to transport workers and their equipment, and this factor is included in their overhead.

The club manager must decide whether to use contractors for some of the routine housekeeping tasks that could possibly be done by the club's crew. The outside service assumes some of the manager's responsibilities and worries—the question is, at what cost to the club?

Contracting for Housekeeping Needs: Before entering into a contract for outside service for a particular function, certain steps should be taken. First, write a set of specifications for the desired service. The specifications should cover such matters as how frequently the service is to be performed and include a fairly detailed description of the work needed. With specifications in hand, the manager should then discuss the job with the contractors from whom he wants quotations, to be sure that the prospective contractors understand the extent and quality of the work expected. The number of contractors asked to bid should be limited; that is, if 25 firms in the area offer a night cleaning service, do some investigating and select a few firms to submit a quotation. Reliable firms welcome this approach and will provide references and list other companies that have used their services. If possible the manager should arrange to visit a customer where the services are provided and the conditions are similar to those at his own club. He also needs to ascertain what provisions a company makes to provide the service if the regular serviceman is ill. The organization contracted with must have sufficient personnel to cover such an emergency. With this type of service, price is important—but the quality of the work performed must measure up to the standards of the club. Legal advice in this area is highly desirable.

CONSTRUCTION CONTRACTS

During the course of their careers, most club managers are involved many times with construction contracts. These may range from contracts for the construction of a completely new facility to small contracts for repair and renovation work.

A contract serves several purposes. In essence, it defines the parties to the contract; the nature and scope of the work to be done; the contracted price for the work; the method of payment; and conditions such as time of performance and acceptance procedures. More important than the wording of even the most carefully phrased and defined contract is the good faith and integrity of both parties to the contract. For that reason, any club manager taking bids for a contract must thoroughly investigate the past performance records of those bidding on it.

Types of Contracts

Although there are many types of contracts, five basic types are most generally used: (1) lump sum, (2) cost plus, (3) guaranteed maximum or upset price, (4) negotiated, and (5) informal. Following is a brief explanation of each of the five types.

Lump-Sum Contract: Under a lump-sum contract, the club agrees to pay a definite, stated amount after completion of construction work. The amount is determined either by competitive bidding or by negotiation with selected bidders. This type of contract is sometimes called a risk contract, for the obvious reason that the contractor exposes himself to the risk of being unable to complete the work for the lump sum to which he agreed. Because of this risk, particularly on renovation jobs where it is difficult to foresee all the problems that might come up, contractors tend to submit high bids to protect themselves against unanticipated expenses. Another risk involved is that, after the contract is signed, the contractor might do the job as cheaply as possible in order to maximize his profits; consequently the quality of the work may suffer. It is argued that, if specifications are clearly and precisely drawn, no risk is involved. However, it is extremely difficult to foresee and specify every detail in any construction project.

The principal advantage of a lump-sum contract is that the cost is known before the contract is signed. If the contract and specifications are well written, there will not be too many unanticipated additional costs. It is usually easier to obtain competitive bids for a lump-sum contract, so the club has the advantage of obtaining the lowest possible cost for the project.

Cost-Plus Contract: Under a cost-plus contract, the contractor agrees to perform the work for his actual cost of construction plus an additional fee. The additional fee might be either a percentage or a lump sum agreed on in advance. A cost-plus contract has some advantages and disadvantages. The contractor is protected against price rises and unanticipated problems during construction. The quality of work should be the best possible because there is no profit motive for the contractor to cheapen his work or to use inferior materials. The contractor is also protected from price rises. In bidding on a lump-sum contract, the contractor may anticipate price rises and, in order to protect himself, raise his bid. Then if there are no price increases, the club ends up paying more than it should. With a cost-plus percentage contract, the club has full control of any desired changes, and changes are made at cost. Changes made under a lump-sum contract are frequently passed on at a much higher figure than normal with a substantially increased profit margin.

A cost-plus contract has several disadvantages. One is that the final cost of the building is unknown until the project is completed. Another is that the contractor gains by every increase in the cost of the building.

If there is complete faith between the club and the contractor and if the contractor is comletely competent, this type of contract may be ideal. (However, a cost-plus contract might also be sought after by unqualified contractors, because they are not taking on any risk.) Other disadvantages are that costs submitted by the builder must be checked out by the architect's staff or the manager to verify that they are legitimate. Also, under this type of contract, questions that arise during construction are placed before the club or his representative. Unless the club manager is experienced, he may not really be competent to make those decisions.

Cost-plus percentage contracts are best used when the conditions to be met during the contract are unknown and when a fixed-price contract would be unfair to either the club or the contractor (that is, the builder might underbid and lose a great deal or he might overbid and the club would spend more than is justified).

Guaranteed-Maximum-Price Contract: The guaranteed-maximum contract is essentially cost plus with an upper limit. The obvious advantage is that the final figure will not exceed a predetermined amount. Also, there is incentive for both the contractor and the club to keep costs down—the savings are usually split between club and contractor. On the other hand, if the contractor sets a maximum price that is too high, on this type of contract any "savings" are really artificial.

Negotiated Contract: Negotiated contracts are not competitive. They are based on faith between club and contractor. They are not desirable and should be entered into only when time is severely limited and plans are incomplete. Such contracts may be negotiated for a lump sum, a unit price, cost plus, or cost plus fixed fee. These arrangements usually offer no advantages to the owner and very few to the contractor. The disadvantages are many: negotiated contracts require a great deal of knowledge to administer and are extremely risky for the club. There is a similar risk of loss to the contractor, as plans are usually incomplete when the contract is made. The club is subject to many extras. This type of contract holds many potential problems for everyone; as a result it often ends up in court, where nobody really wins.

Informal Contracts: Informal contracts may be verbal and closed with no more than a handshake. This type of contract is used more frequently than the other types to obtain services such as removal of debris or patching of a road. Before entering into any informal agreement, both parties must clearly understand and agree to the scope of the work and the means of compensation. Otherwise, a lawsuit may ensue. In the case of debris removal, for example, it is to the owner's advantage to obtain a lump-sum contract so that his total cost is known. The contractor might prefer a unit-cost agreement whereby he would receive a fixed amount for each truckload of debris removed from the club's grounds to the city dump. For patching a road, on the other hand, the owner would prefer to be charged for the actual material used, plus equipment, labor, and profit. Why? Because if a paving contractor is to patch the club's entrance road for a set cost, he might, in order to maximize profits, consider his job complete when the owner thinks it is still inadequate. Problems frequently result from such an arrangement, even if all parties entered into the agreement in good faith.

Some General Rules

As stated at the beginning of this discussion on contracts, the most important aspect of entering into any contract is the good faith and integrity of the parties involved. Other general rules to follow, no matter what form the contract may take, are the following:

- Do not sign a contract until you have obtained legal advice.
- Do not sign a contract unless completely satisfied with the wording and meaning.
- Obtain approval from the Board of Governors.
- Be sure that there is no question about the scope of the work and the specifications for the job.
- Do not hesitate to ask questions about any provisions.
- Never take anything for granted.
- Protect the club's money.
- Do not let the contractor receive more than he is entitled to at any time.
- Make payments only in accordance with the schedule agreed on.
- Make final payment only after all work has been approved.

The glossary at the end of this chapter contains an explanation of the technical terms used in contracting work.

SELECTION OF CONTRACTORS

Selection of a general contractor to construct a major new facility that costs hundreds of thousands of dollars is sometimes easier than choosing the contractor to do a small job involving only a few thousand dollars. Before most clubs undertake major building projects, the plans are studied by committees, engineers, architects, and board members, many of whom are experts with a great deal of knowledge about the contracting firms in the area and who thus are able to select qualified contractors to submit bids.

Small alterations or minor jobs may be entirely different. The resident experts of the club may leave the choice of contractors up to the manager. If the manager knows something about the work involved and knows the contractors in the area, the task is relatively simple. On the other hand, if he is new in the area and does not know the local contractors, he needs help locating capable, honest firms. A good place to start is with the membership list. If any architects or engineers belong to the club, they would be happy to recommend contractors. Or, perhaps a member with a business or plant in the area has had experience with local contractors.

Having obtained a list of contractors, the manager should then obtain as much information as possible about them, including references. Any contractor who has completed 100 jobs will be able to come up with a few satisfied customers; therefore, the manager should attempt to find customers for whom the contractor has worked other than those he names. Were customers satisfied with the quality of the work? Were there extra charges? Was the work completed on time?

It is not necessary to know how to mix concrete and lay bricks in order to hire a mason, nor is it necessary to be able to thread pipe in order to engage a plumbing contractor. What is necessary is the ability to locate reputable contractors who take pride in their work and are honest in their dealings with others.

After selecting a contractor and signing a contract with him, but before he starts work, make sure that he provides a certificate of insurance showing that he carries adequate comprehensive general liability insurance in addition to workmen's compensation and employer's liability coverage. (See the chapter in this text dealing with insurance.)

Even if the club has been doing business with a particular group of contractors for years, you must request certificates of insurance from them each year. Contractors have been known to do poorly in business and lose their insurance. No manager wants to face a loss that the contractor caused and for which he was insured.

REVIEW QUESTIONS

1. What are the advantages and disadvantages to in-house laundry facilities at clubs? Commercial service providers?
2. What other types of work at clubs might be performed better by outside contractors? Why?
3. When is it more cost effective for a club to provide its own services, rather than hiring outside personnel? Use concrete examples, such as painting (interior or exterior), plumbing, floor care.
4. Describe the supervision necessary for the club to provide over outside service agencies (such as laundries or floor contractors).
5. Under what circumstances should the club purchase service contracts on machinery or equipment?
6. Discuss contracts generally as they apply to clubs. What preparations must a manager make before entering a contract? With whom should he contract? What terms should be in the contract?
7. Describe the various types of contracts available, advantages and disadvantages of each, and for what circumstances each particular type is suited in the club.

GLOSSARY

The club manager is not expected to be an expert in all fields and was not hired for his knowledge of architecture and construction, but in the course of club employment, he will come in contact with architects and builders and will better be able to look after the club's interests if he has a working knowledge of the terms they employ.

The following is a glossary of terms to help club managers deal with these professionals, architects, and engineers. It does not contain all the technical terms that might come up, but it does list frequently used terms that managers will encounter. Very elementary and widely understood terms have not been included. There is no point in describing a floor or a roof, but the difference between a gable roof, a hip roof, and a mansard roof is explained; similarly, what constitutes a parquet floor is included.

Abstract of bids. See *Bid abstract.*

Accepted bid. The bid accepted by the owner as the basis of an agreement for construction or other work.

Accepted engineering practices. Practices in accordance with standard procedures recognized by architects, engineers, and other authorities.

Addendum (Addenda). Written instruction(s) that modify contract documents by adding, deleting, or clarifying specifications.

Advance payment. Money paid to a contractor in anticipation of performance under a contract.

Alternate bid. Amounts to be added or subtracted from the base bid for changes in construction or for the use of alternate materials.

Appendage. A structure attached to the outer wall of a building.

Application for payment. The contractor's request for payment of completed portions of the work.

Approval. An architect's or engineer's written approval of materials or constructon methods, or approval of a contractor's request or claim.

Approved equal or equivalent. Equipment or material accepted by the architect or engineer as being equal to that specified in the contract.

As-built drawings. Revised drawings that indicate changes made during construction.

Bank run gravel. Stones that are more than one-quarter inch and less than six inches in size used as aggregate in mixing concrete.

Basic agreement. A written agreement between contractor and owner listing provisions and standard contractual clauses that will be part of future contracts.

Basic services. The architect's or engineer's basic services consist of five phases: schematic design, design development, construction documents, bidding procedures, and construction contract administration.

Batt. A thickness of insulation sheathed in paper or metal foil for installation between framing members.

Batten. A narrow strip of building material used to cover butting joints or panels or boards.

Beneficial occupancy. The date when the facility can be effectively occupied for the purpose intended.

Bid. See *Proposal.*

Bid abstract. A summary of the bids received, listing all bidders and showing their prices for the project under consideration.

Bidding documents. Documents, upon which bidders base their bids, consisting of instructions to bidders, plans, construction documents, and addenda.

Bill of materials. A complete listing of all materials required for construction of a given project.

Bonus and penalty clause. A provision that provides for payment of a bonus to a contractor for completion of work before a given date or for a penalty charge payable by the contractor for failure to complete the work by the same date.

Budget, construction. The sum established by an owner for the purpose of constructing a project.

Budget, project. The sum established for all costs including land, financial costs, compensation for all professional services, contingencies, other project-related costs, and the construction budget.

Building line. The line beyond which a structure may not extend except for uncovered entrance platform or steps.

Building permit. The document issued by the governmental authority having jurisdiction for the construction of a project.

Cant. To set at an angle from horizontal or vertical; to slope, tilt, or bank.

Cantilever. A structural projection supported only at one end.

Ceiling price. The maximum price under a contract that the owner will pay a contractor.

Certificate of occupancy. The document from the appropriate government agency certifying that the building complies with applicable statutes and regulations and further stating that it may be occupied for its designed purpose.

Change order. A written order authorizing a change or an adjustment approved after the execution of the original contract, which is signed by the owner's representative.

Codes. Governmental regulations or requirements relating to construction and occupancy.

Completion bond. A document provided by the contractor for the owner guaranteeing that the work will be completed.

Construction documents. Working drawings and specifications, including all addenda.

Contingency. The sum of money set aside for unforeseeable events that might increase construction costs.

Contract bond. The guarantee provided to the owner by the contractors assuring that the contract will be completed and that all legal debts incurred by the contractor during construction will be paid.

Contract documents. The agreement between the owner and contractor, consisting of the drawings and all specifications and addenda that have been issued prior to execution of the contract.

Contractor's affidavit. The certified statement by the contractor, issued for the protection of the owner, relating to the contractor's payment of debts, claims, and release of liens.

Cost-plus-fee agreement. Under this type of agreement the contractor is reimbursed for his direct and indirect costs and is paid an additional fee for his service. The fee may be a specified amount or a percentage of costs.

Cross section. A drawing revealing the inner elements of something shown from a slice perpendicular to the axis of that thing.

Culvert. A pipe for water drainage under a road or embankment.

Damages. Sums that can be recovered from the contractor if it can be proved that he is responsible for delays that constitute a breach of contract.

Datum. A point of reference from which to measure elevation.

Detail. A portion of a drawing enlarged to show in greater detail the composition of all construction elements.

Direct lighting. A lighting system in which fixtures distribute all or nearly all of the light downward.

Distribution Box. The main feed line in a circuit to which branch circuits are connected.

Downtime. The time a machine or piece of equipment is not working, due to repairs.

Drip Mold. Molding that prevents rainwater from running down the face of a wall.

Dry batch weight. The weight of the cement, sand, and aggregate before the addition of water in making a batch of concrete.

Dry construction. Construction without plaster or mortar, using prefabricated building sections.

Due care. A legal term requiring exercise of reasonable care, skill, and judgment in performance of services consistent with a normally acceptable level of such services provided in the same geographical area and during the same period of time.

Eaves. The part of a slanted roof that projects over the side wall of a building.

Elevation. (1) In surveying: The distance above sea level or a datum plane. (2) The vertical view of a building or part of a building as it may be viewed from the front, rear, or sides.

Extra work. Additional construction items not included in the original contract and for which there may be additional cost.

Facia. A flat board usually used in combination with moldings and frequently located at the outer face of the cornice.

Factor of safety. The number, used by a structural designer, indicating the margin between the stress allowed in his calculations and the stress at which the structure will fail. A factor of safety of four would mean that failure would occur when stress was four times greater than that set as the maximum by the designer.

False ceiling. A ceiling built lower than the floor from which it is suspended, providing space for the installation of ducts, cables, and pipes.

Fiberboard. A building board of wood or fiber compressed and bonded into a sheet.

Field order. Orders written for minor changes in work that do not involve adjustments to the contract as originally written. Field orders are usually written by the architect during the period of construction.

Final acceptance. The owner's physical acceptance of the project from the contractor, acknowledging the project is complete and in accordance with the contract specifications. May include signing a document.

Final payment. Confirms final acceptance and is usually made only upon certification by the architect or engineer.

Fire block. Bridging built into floors and walls to reduce the risk of fire spreading.

Fire partition. A wall built to prevent or restrict the spread of fire.

Fire-rated doors. Doors designed to resist the spread of fire. They are rated by standard tests and labeled for identification.

Foundation. The substructure below the frame of a building. It includes footings, as well as the soil or rock upon which the building rests.

Frost line. The maximum depth to which ground in a particular area may be expected to freeze.

Gable roof. A double-pitched roof that terminates at one or both ends in a gable.

General contractor. The prime or main contractor.

Grade (*Gradient*). The change of elevation along a particular route, surface, channel, or pipe.

Grantee. The person or corporation to whom property or property rights are granted by legal documents.

Grantor. The person who transfers property or property rights by legal document.

Gross area. The total of all enclosed floor areas of a building, measured from the outside surface of the exterior walls.

Guaranteed maximum cost. The amount agreed to in writing for the maximum cost of performing specific work, including labor and materials as well as overhead and profit.

Hardwall. Gypsum base coat plaster.

Hip roof. A roof formed by the inclined planes of all four sides of a building. The line formed by two adjacent sloping sides of a roof is called a hip.

Hollow block. A concrete masonry unit that is 25 percent hollow.

Hollow core door. A flush door with plywood face glued to a skeleton framework.

Implied indemnification. (See *Indemnification.*) Implied by law rather than arising out of a specific contract.

Impregnation. Forcing preservatives into timbers to make them resistant to dry rot or insects.

Indemnification. A contractual obligation whereby one party agrees to secure another against loss or damage from specified liabilities.

Indirect lighting. A system for general illumination whereby light is directed at a ceiling or wall and reflected upon the area to be illuminated.

Insurance. The types of insurance that a manager, as representative of his club, is most likely to come in contact with in dealing with contractors and architects are the following: bodily injury, builder's risk, contractor's liability, employer's liability, owner's liability, property damage, public liability, and workmen's compensation. (See the chapter in this text dealing with insurance.)

Interior finish. The material used to cover interior floors, walls, and ceilings.

Invited bidders. Those contractors from whom the architect and owner have chosen to receive bids.

Jamb. The exposed vertical members used to frame a doorway or window.

Joist. Vertical beams used to support floors or ceilings.

Junction box. A metal box within which sheathed cable coming from different directions are joined by insulated connectors.

Kalamein door. A fire-resistant door with a metal covering.

Laminate. A sheet of many layers of paper, fabric, or wood cemented together with a resin at high pressure to produce a durable material such as plywood.

Lease. A contract securing the tenure of real property for a specified period of time.

Licensed contractor. A person or an organization approved by a governmental agency to engage in construction contracting.

Lien, mechanics or material. A charge made against a project for the satisfaction of unpaid debts for work performed by the contractor or materials supplied for construction purposes.

Longitudinal section. A drawing resulting from a perpendicular slice along the length of a thing revealing the inner elements of that thing.

Lowest responsible bidder. The bidder who is considered by the owner or architect to be fully able to satisfactorily perform the work and who submits the lowest bona fide bid.

Mansard roof. A roof with two slopes or pitches on each side. The lower slope is steeper than the upper.

Membrane waterproofing. The waterproofing of masonry or concrete surfaces with built up layers of canvas, burlap, or felt and pitch. Plastic coating is also considered membrane waterproofing.

Mill work. Finished wooden materials that are built in plants and shipped to the job in finished form, e.g., doors, windows, frames, mantels, panel work, and stairways.

Modification. A change order or written amendment issued by the architect or engineer.

Module. A repetitive dimensional or functional unit used in planning, drawing, and constructing buildings.

Non-load-bearing partition or wall. A wall that merely separates space into rooms, but does not carry any of the load from the overhead structure.

On center. The distance from the center of one structural member to the center of another adjacent member.

Out of plumb. A vertical member that is not in alignment with a true vertical line is said to be out of plumb.

Parapet wall. The portion of a wall that serves as a guard at the edge of a roof and extends above the roof line.

Parquet floor. A floor of hard wood laid out in small rectangular patterns to form various designs.

Plenum chamber. A large area or chamber into which heated or cooled air is forced for slower distribution through ducts.

Power of attorney. A written instrument authorizing another to act as one's agent.

Precast. Certain concrete members such as beams, columns, tiles, parts of walls, etc., are cast and cured at a location other than on the job and then transported to the work site to be placed in position.

Prefabrication. Standard or modular parts of buildings constructed in a factory and then shipped to the job site where they are assembled.

Prime contractor. The principal contractor who has a direct contract for all work with the owner and who in turn is responsible for the work of all subcontractors in addition to his own.

Progress payment. Payment of an amount previously agreed to for the completion of certain amounts of work.

Property line. The line that defines the boundary of the building or property as indicated on the deed.

Proposal. An offer by a contractor to furnish all labor, materials, and equipment to perform the work specified in the contract within a particular period of time for a stated sum.

Purchase order. Written authorization for the purchase of materials or services.

Radiant heating. Coils or pipes containing either hot water or steam placed in the floor, walls, or ceiling to heat an area.

Reducer. A fitting such as an elbow or tee that is designed for joining pipes or tubes of different sizes.

Reinforced concrete. Concrete that contains steel reinforcing rods and is designed to provide much greater strength.

Retainage. The sum that is withheld from progress payments to the contractor. The retainage is paid within a specified period of time after completion of the project.

Right-of-way. The land that is secured and reserved for public use for such items as utilities, highways, and sidewalks.

Rough floor. The plywood or floorboards upon which the finished floor is laid.

Roughing-in. The preliminary work that is done in connection with the installation of pipes, plumbing, and electrical work. It usually includes all concealed work but not the actual lighting or plumbing fixtures.

Schematic. A drawing or chart showing the method of construction or operation without supplying accurate dimensions.

Sealed bid. The proposal submitted by the contractor to furnish all necessary services and materials called for in the contract. It is prepared for opening at a particular time, is sealed and placed with other sealed bids.

Secondary beam. A beam supported by other beams rather than by columns or walls.

Shop drawings. Drawings and other data that show how specific portions of the work will be fabricated or installed. They conform to contract drawings but are not part of them. Normally they are furnished by suppliers and manufacturers and are approved by the architect or engineer.

Shop work. The term refers to work performed in a shop or location other than on site.

Shoring. Props that are used for the temporary support of excavation and form work.

Spread footing. A rectangular prism of concrete larger in dimension than the column or wall it supports.

Staggered course. Courses of roof shingles laid with butts not in a horizontal line.

Standard provisions. Common to many jobs and used unless the project requires special provisions.

Stop-work order. An order issued by the owner or his representative to stop the project work. Stop-work orders may be issued because of unsatisfactory work, labor disputes, failure to meet contract specifications, etc.

Subcontract. The agreement between the prime contractor and other contractors to supply certain materials or labor as called for in the contract documents.

Subcontractor. The secondary contractor who supplies a portion of the prime contractor's work as called for under the contract.

Take-off. The list of materials and quantities needed that is obtained from the drawings and plans that are part of the contract.

Tamp. To ram the earth so as to compact it or to ram freshly poured concrete so as to increase its density.

Telltale. A device designed to indicate movement of formwork.

Time of completion. This can be the date established in the contract for completion or the number of work days specified for substantial completion of the project.

Two-coat work. A term applied to substances that are applied in two layers, usually a first coat followed by the second or finishing coat. It may be plaster, paint, or asphalt.

Unbalanced bid. A bid in which the contractor attempts to collect a greater portion of the money that he will receive than the amount of completed work justifies. This may be done so that the contractor will be able to finance the balance of the job using the owner's capital rather than his own.

Underwriters Laboratories label. The Underwriters Laboratories are financed by the different insurance companies throughout the country. When an electrical item complies with their standards of safety and construction, the UL label is attached to it.

Unit-price contract. Under this type of contract, the contractor is paid a specific amount for each unit of work completed.

Valley. The angle formed by the meeting of two inclined sides of a roof.

Vee gutter. A wall that has a facing of some material that is attached to the backing.

Wainscot. Usually that part of an interior wall beneath a chair rail which is covered by a different material than the wall itself. Most frequently wooden paneling that is less than four feet in height from the floor is considered wainscoting.

Wall-bearing construction. In this type of construction the floors and roofs are supported by the masonry walls rather than by the structural frame.

Water-cement ratio. The ratio of the amount of water to the amount of cement in a concrete or mortar mixture. The least amount of water that will satisfactorily mix with the cement provides the strongest concrete.

Wire gauge. A system for measuring the size of wire. The larger the number the thinner the wire.

Woodwork. Most usually refers to the finished woodwork in a building but in actuality is the total portion of the building that is constructed of wood.

Work order. A written order directing the contractor to undertake work without negotiations as to price. Work orders are extensions of the original contract.

Working drawing. A drawing that is sufficiently detailed to permit construction of the item shown without any additional information.

Workmanship. The quality of executed work.

Yardage. (1) An area in square yards. (2) A length in linear yards. (3) Volume of earth or other material measured in cubic yards.

Zoning. Rules established by governing authorities to restrict land use and size or character of buildings that may be constructed on that land.

Zoning permit. The permit which is issued by the governmental authority having jurisdiction over the land that is to be used and stating for what specific purpose it may be used.

7

Financing of Clubs

Tam O'Shanter Golf Club, Long Island, New York

FUNDING SOURCES

Clubs can derive their income from many sources, but members of member-owned clubs generally share the costs of operating club facilities. The philosophy as to how these costs are shared differs from club to club. In some clubs, membership dues are an all-inclusive charge for the right to use all club facilities. In others, basic membership dues are for the general areas of the club and members pay additional dues for using any special facilities. In practice, most clubs follow a path somewhere between these two extremes.

In any event, the funds to operate the facilities and provide for replacements and improvements must eventually come from club members. The following section summarizes and briefly describes the various sources of funds available to a club, accounting systems, budgeting, long-range planning, capital expenditures, and general fiscal management.

Fees and Dues

Depending on a club's bylaws, the board of governors establishes membership fees and dues, and changes them when deemed appropriate. Declining membership during the early 1970s forced boards of many clubs to reduce (or waive entirely) initiation fees normally paid by incoming members. The initiation fee amount is usually left to the discretion of the board of governors, but some clubs limit changes that the board can make in the membership dues structure or the imposition of an assessment. Such restrictions probably have some merit, although they sometimes tie the hands of the board. For example, the board knows the club's financial situation better than the membership as a whole and may decide to increase dues by $200 annually to keep the club financially sound. Unless the board of governors can appropriately market the necessary increase, the members, naturally, will have no desire to raise their own dues. In fact, there have been cases where the membership has voted against increasing dues to the club's detriment. Furthermore, members have denied capital improvements that would attract new members because the importance of such improvements was not clear to the membership. If the board of governors can be trusted with running the affairs of the club, it should be empowered to raise dues or impose assessments as they deem appropriate.

At the same time, the board cannot know membership desires without asking. Certain board members will swear that they know what the members want, when in reality they only know what some of their friends at the club want. Recently, more clubs have used membership questionnaires to determine exactly what kind of a club the members want, and their priorities. The board of governors uses the questionnaire results to develop an overall club philosophy from which the club can operate.

Philosophy of Membership Dues

There probably are very few club members who, at one time or another, have not asked themselves, "just what are we paying for when we pay dues?" If the question cannot be answered in a convincing manner, the club has no real reason to exist. Therefore, it is important that each club review the services it offers, assess the cost of doing business, and justify its dues structure.

There are as many theories about club finance as there are theories about businesses in general. The theory that probably best fits club operations is "the operating loss absorption theory."

Patronage is limited to members and their guests. Unlike a commercial enterprise, a club has large areas of unproductive space when viewed from a revenue standpoint. The limited market of members (and their guests) generates a relatively small income for the operating departments after they absorb direct costs. Unproductive space simply does not generate revenue.

The club thus cannot sustain itself as an operating entity, so it must be subsidized. This subsidy is provided by dues income. After deducting carrying charges on the club's property, there must be sufficient dues income to cover fixed charges and to absorb the operating loss. Additionally, there must be sufficient income to meet mortgage amortization requirements and to finance additions and improvements to the physical facilities. These items may be financed either from operations, by capital improvement assessments, or by initiation fees which would then be considered to be capital contributions rather than income.

Membership dues should not be used to subsidize waste. Before increasing dues, management should ascertain that operations are efficient. This is particularly important where there is keen competition for prospective members among similar nearby clubs.

Variances in Dues Structure

Club Types

Some businesses generally cost more to operate than others. City and country clubs are no exception. Membership size and the financial requirements for membership vary among the different kinds of clubs.

Among city clubs, a luncheon club generally has a smaller membership than an athletic club; a select social club has a smaller membership than a university club. A luncheon club probably costs less to operate than does a select social club, and a select social club costs less than an athletic or university club. Yet the dues rates of the athletic clubs and university clubs are generally lower than the others due to the greater number of members in these clubs to share overhead expenses. A select social club with 700 to 1,000 members, occupying and owning attractive, well-located city premises will generally be one of the most expensive city clubs, and the dues rates will reflect it.

Among country clubs, a general "rule of thumb" is that a golf club is more expensive to operate than a beach club or a yacht club. The yacht club, however, may present the greatest financial burden to a member if it includes the cost of purchasing and maintaining a yacht.

Membership Dues

Membership dues represent a per capita charge to members, as determined by management, usually on an annual basis. Dues vary by membership type and in proportion to the club privileges granted.

Life Membership Fees

Certain clubs permit members to purchase a "life membership," exempting them from paying dues to the club for the rest of their lives. Life memberships are rarely sold at a price commensurate with their real worth; they generally cost ten times the current annual dues amount.

Although the club receives additional cash immediately by selling life memberships, such transactions can drain a club's finances later since the club will not receive the appropriate amount of dues income from all of its members. Sound long-range financing for a club probably prohibits life memberships, although they may provide an attractive way to obtain short-range funds and, conceivably, could be appropriate in some instances.

Membership Certificates

A membership certificate is similar to a share of stock in a corporation. Membership certificates show evidence of a member's investment in the club and his right to share in the net proceeds of the club in the event of its dissolution. The purchase of a membership certificate is usually a prerequisite to membership in a club that issues them. A certificate is generally refundable to the member if he resigns and the certificate is then resold to an incoming member. Clubs with membership certificates may charge a transfer fee to the outgoing member for transferring his membership certificate to an incoming member.

Initiation Fees

An initiation fee is a nonrefundable fee paid by a new member on election to the club. Some clubs charge an initiation fee as well as issuing membership certificates. Other clubs charge only an initiation fee; in these instances, the bylaws of a member-owned club will probably stipulate that the net proceeds in the event of the club's dissolution are to be shared pro rata by the then regular members.

Membership Bonds

Some clubs require a member to purchase a membership bond as a prerequisite to membership. Such bonds may be non-interest-bearing or provide for nominal interest; all regular members must own one bond in the same face amount. (Clubs must remain well attuned to the possible tax implications of membership bonds.)

Some clubs will offer membership bonds to members, to be purchased voluntarily, rather than go to a bank to borrow funds. These bonds would generally carry more interest, although less than the club would have to pay a bank.

Operating Assessments

When membership dues for a specific period do not generate sufficient income to cover the operations of the club, some clubs impose an operating assessment to make up the deficit. An operating assessment generally indicates that the membership dues as established by club management were not sufficient to cover the operating expenses and, therefore, could suggest "poor management" to some members. Surprisingly, some clubs will plan to impose an operating assessment at the end of the year, rather than raise the annual membership dues, under the belief that this procedure puts the club in a better position when they are discussing annual dues with prospective members. An operating assessment can, however, cause membership dissension, particularly on the part of new members.

Capital Improvement Assessments

Many clubs prepare two budgets for the year: an operating budget to be covered by the annual membership dues and a capital budget to be covered by a capital improvement assessment on an annual or a monthly basis. A capital improvement assessment of $10 or $15 per month, for example, is generally not a financial burden to members but does generate $120 or $180 per member for the club each year. The monthly capital improvement assessment can fluctuate, based on the planned capital improvements of the club for any one year.

Voluntary Contributions

Voluntary contributions from the members can be a good source of additional revenue. For example, certain clubs have successfully raised funds for specific purposes by asking the members to voluntarily contribute $2 or $5 per month for programs such as reducing outstanding mortgage indebtedness. The nominal amount appears on the monthly house charge statement with the understanding that, if members do not wish to contribute, they may simply deduct that amount from their payment. Active participation in such a voluntary program has generated considerable revenue for a few large city clubs.

Food, Beverage, and Other Sales

Most clubs maintain a clubhouse with food and beverage service. Management must be flexible in setting menu prices that adequately cover the expenses of these facilities. Generally, there is a much higher "mark up" and corresponding higher gross profit margin on beverage sales than on food sales. Setting these prices is discussed at length in the chapter on food and beverage operations.

In addition to food and beverage sales, clubs sell other items, such as cigars, cigarettes, club ties, etc.

Minimum Charge

To encourage members to use the food and beverage facilities, some clubs specify a minimum dollar amount that a member must spend on food and/or beverages during a certain period of time. The member receives a bill if there is a difference between his/her actual expenditures and the minimum charge. Food and/or beverage minimum charges may be set on a monthly, quarterly, or annual basis.

There are advantages and disadvantages to imposing a minimum charge for food and/or beverages. A minimum charge will increase the use of the club facilities with a corresponding increase in net income while overhead charges remain the same. Also, it provides the club with additional income in those cases where members do not spend the specified minimum amount.

However, minimum charges may be extremely distasteful to the members, who might object to such regimentation, and may cause dissension to the point that a member might even resign. Further, restaurant and bar facilities may be strained at the end of the month when members suddenly realize they have not yet met minimums, and crowd the facilities.

Although computerization has substantially reduced the time required to account for minimum charges, some additional time is often required to field complaints from members who were on vacation, etc.

Some say that nonpatronizing members do not carry a fair share of club costs. This is not necessarily true. Dues paid by a member who uses none of the club's facilities could, in effect, be subsidizing a member who frequently uses the facilities.

There is no substitute for good food, drink, service, and surroundings to ensure patronization of a club's restaurant operation. A minimum charge conceivably could dampen management's incentive to provide the necessary ingredients for voluntary membership participation.

Food and Beverage Service Charges

Most clubs impose a percentage service charge on food and beverage sales that is a gratuity for service employees. Gratuities are disbursed through the payroll and taxed accordingly when the club controls them.

Some clubs keep the service charges and reflect them as "other income" in the financial statements. The club that keeps the service charges necessarily pays higher salaries to food service employees. Clubs keeping the service charges may be subject to local sales taxes on these charges.

Some clubs no longer assess a monthly food and beverage minimum and now have a fixed "service charge." They also eliminated the percentage service charge formerly imposed on each member's individual food and beverage bill. This change rewards those members using the club the most since all the members pay the same "service charge." For instance, a member who did not use the club pays a $25 service charge; another member spending $500 one month would also pay the $25 service charge, rather than $75 if a 15 percent service charge had been used.

Surcharges

A surcharge is simply an additional charge on the member's bill. Some clubs have a fixed administrative charge added to each member's monthly statement, which is then kept as regular operating revenue.

If a club retains the service charge mentioned in the preceding section, the term "surcharge" rather than "service charge" should be used, thereby eliminating any possible misunderstanding that this charge is a gratuity.

User Fees

Clubs may charge a fee for the use of certain facilities. For instance, a country club may have an additional daily or annual charge for using the tennis courts, platform tennis courts, or swimming pool. Such fees are based on the amount of revenue necessary to cover the expenses of a particular facility divided by the number of members using that facility.

Guest Fees

Many clubs charge a guest fee to members when they have guests use a facility. For example, a lunch club or a city club may charge a guest fee for nonmembers using dining facilities and a country club will typically charge a guest fee for nonmembers using athletic facilities.

Other Fees

Other fees can be imposed on the members for certain privileges, such as golf club cleaning and storage by the golf pro, instructor charges for lessons, golf car rentals, greens fees for guests, or check cashing fees.

Room Rentals

Some clubs have sleeping accommodations for their members and, accordingly, charge rentals for such rooms.

Private Dining Room Rentals

Some clubs have private dining room accommodations. This feature is particularly common in city and luncheon clubs that have private dining rooms to accommodate private luncheons for members and their guests. A predetermined charge for using private dining rooms is added on to the cost of food and beverage service to the member.

Space Rentals

Large city clubs may generate revenue from renting space to commercial enterprises such as travel agencies, theater ticket agencies, gift shops, or clothing stores.

Other Rentals

Most clubs with sporting facilities provide lockers to their members and charge an annual rental for their use. The amount of the rental charge depends on the size of the locker. Beach clubs charge for bathhouse or cabana rentals on an annual basis.

Late Payment Penalties

To improve cash flow, some clubs charge a late payment penalty to members who do not pay their bills on time. Some clubs charge a percentage of the outstanding amount, which is akin to charging interest on the unpaid balance. In other cases, however, the late payment charge is for a fixed amount, regardless of the amount of the indebtedness. If a late payment fee is considered, consult with the club's attorney for compliance with various legal requirements.

Employees' Christmas Fund

Many clubs have an employees' Christmas fund created by voluntary contributions from the membership. The club asks for Christmas fund contributions by mail one or two months prior to Christmas. The members who wish to participate, either write checks to the club or have the club charge their house accounts for a specified amount.

The Christmas fund contributions are earmarked for distribution to the employees. Many clubs have devised formulas for determining how much each employee should receive based on years of service, salary, and amount in the fund. Some clubs base their distribution solely on merit as determined by management. Regardless of the method used to disburse Christmas contributions, the Internal Revenue Service (IRS) has ruled that such funds are considered additional employee wages and the club must withhold appropriate taxes.

Unrelated Business Income

Any income derived from sources other than members, such as earned interest or "outside" parties, is considered unrelated business income and is subject to Federal income tax on the net income from such sources. Furthermore, clubs exempt from income taxes under section 501(c)(7) of the Internal Revenue Code could lose their tax-exempt status if their outside business from sales or fees to nonmembers exceeds 15 percent of the club's gross revenue, including dues. A club could lose its tax exempt status if its total nonmember income, including passive income such as rents or interest, exceeds 35 percent of its gross revenue. The Internal Revenue Service also imposes certain recordkeeping requirements, which are discussed in another chapter of this book.

ACCOUNTING (BASIC SYSTEM)

The Club Managers Association of America (CMAA) has published the "Uniform System of Accounts for Clubs" as a guide for establishing a basic accounting system. The objectives of this uniform system are to allocate operating income to separate operating departments and to charge such departments with the direct costs and expenses attributable to the production of the operating income. For example, food sales are credited to the food department, the cost of food sold and any other direct expenses of producing the food sales, such as salaries and wages, payroll taxes and employee benefits, linen, china, glassware, and silver, are charged against the food department. All unallocated expenses are grouped into various overhead departments. Unallocated income (such as membership dues) appears separately on the statement of income and expenses and is not allocated to operating departments.

Operating Departments Income Allocation

Allocating income to a club's operating departments is simple since the revenue can be readily identified with the appropriate operating departments.

Club officers who are businessmen sometimes allocate dues and all overhead costs to the various operating departments in an effort to determine if there are any "losing" operations. This method fails because allocating membership dues is arbitrary and, for the most part, depends on the prejudices of the person making the allocations. A golfer might say that the golf department should get the major portion of the dues allocation. But a tennis player might say that if there were no tennis courts the club would not have as many members hence the tennis department should receive a substantial portion of the dues allocation. Those individuals frequenting the dining room and lounge might say that practically all of the membership dues should be allocated to the food and beverage department, since that is the most popular of all the facilities.

Costs and Expenses Allocation

Costs of Sales

Costs of sales are readily identified with appropriate operating departments. The term "costs" refers mainly to the cost of food and beverages sold. It also refers to the cost of cigars, cigarettes, or any other items that the club holds for sale such as club ties, gifts, and golf shop inventory, if the club rather than the golf pro, operates the golf shop. Inventories must be taken periodically. The counting and inventory valuation is usually simple. After items are counted, they are valued on the basis of the last invoice price, since stock is moved on a first-in, first-out basis. The inventory turnover in the food and beverage department is usually quick enough so that the last invoice price, if consistently applied, may be used.

When there is work in process in the kitchen during inventory, a physical count is not usually required. Here, an estimated value is generally used.

The cost of food sold and the cost of beverages sold are considered to be two key operating ratios. Accordingly, to determine these ratios, most clubs count the food and beverage inventories at the end of each month. Any large variances in these cost ratios must be investigated immediately because an increase in either the food cost ratio or the beverage cost ratio will be questioned by anyone reading the financial statements (see chapter 5).

Expenses

As mentioned previously, CMAA's uniform system does not provide for the allocation of certain overhead expenses to income-producing departments. For example, administrative and general expenses are reflected in the administrative and general (overhead) department and are not redistributed to income-producing departments. All club expenses must be allocated to a particular income-producing department or to an overhead department.

Computing the direct charges to the various operating departments is easy. For example, menus are charged to the food department; fertilizer is charged to the golf course maintenance department. Problems arise when a club purchases supplies for various operating departments from the same vendor and receives one statement for all the supplies purchased. The club's bookkeeper then determines the proper charges for each department. For instance, a club purchases towels and linens from the same vendor. The food and beverage department, the swimming pool department, and the rooms department all use these supplies. Although the club receives only one bill, the amount must be allocated to appropriate departments. Also, the electric bill should be allocated on some reasonable percentage basis to the various departments.

The major expense of any club is payroll. Payroll allocations are based on identifiable department positions. If an employee works in different departments (a man working as a busboy during lunch and as a houseman-porter during the late afternoon), an adjustment should be made so that the proper department is charged an appropriate amount. Payroll taxes and related expenses are usually divided among the various departments based on each department's payroll. The percentage of allocation may be determined each month.

Books of Account

All accounting transactions appear in one or more of the following books of original entry: sales journal; cash receipts journal; voucher register (purchase journal); cash disbursements journal; payroll journal; membership journal; general journal; and monthly journal.

Sales Journal

A summary of all the day's sales appears in the sales journal. Membership dues are not generally included in the sales journal, but rather are posted in the membership journal described later. The sales journal debits consist of accounts receivable, and the credits are the various sales—such as food, beverage, cigars, and cigarettes, or guest fees. Certain clubs post minor cash sales as debits in the sales journal with the credits going to the appropriate revenue account. Exhibit 7.1 shows a sample sales journal.

EXHIBIT 7.1
Sales Journal

Debits			Credits										
Date	Accounts Receivable	Cash Sales	Food Sales		Beverage Sales		Room Rentals	Tobacco Candy, etc. Sales	Telephone Charges	Service Charges	Sales Tax	Other*	
			Regular	Banquet	Regular	Banquet						Account	Amount

*This Journal should be expanded to meet the needs of the Club. For example, in a country club, there would be separate columns for such items as greens fees, golf car rentals, tennis fees, swimming pool fees, due to golf pro, due to tennis pro, etc.

Cash Receipts Journal

All cash received by the club is recorded in a cash receipts journal, as shown in Exhibit 7.2. The term "cash receipts" applies not only to actual cash, but also to any checks received in payment of accounts. The debit column of the cash receipts book refers to cash, and the credit columns refer to the accounts receivable.

In smaller clubs, the cash receipts are posted on a separate line for each separate payment. In larger clubs, a daily summary of the total cash received appears in the journal. Posting cash receipts in summary form requires maintaining some detailed records that show the cash receipts by individual, such as batching all the statement stubs returned with the payments. The summary of these receipts should always be signed by the individual responsible for compiling the form and verifying it.

EXHIBIT 7.2
Cash Receipts Journal

Date	Name	Debit	Credits				
		Cash Receipts	Accounts Receivable House Charges	Accounts Receivable Dues	Cash Sales	Other	
						Account	Amount

Note: Some Clubs will not separate members' house charges and dues. Under such circumstances, only one accounts receivable column would be required.

EXHIBIT 7.3
Voucher Register

Date	Vendor	Voucher	Paid		Credit	Debits							
					Accounts Payable	Inventory		Operating Departments*		Balance Sheet A/Cs		Other Expenses	
			Date	Check No:		Food	Beverages	Account	Amount	Account	Amount	Account	Amount

*A separate column is usually provided for each operating department, such as food, beverage department, various sports departments, etc. In addition, separate columns are also used for the unallocated expense departments, such as clubhouse expenses, administrative and general expenses, etc.

Voucher Register (Purchase Journal)

A voucher register is a journal recording all the club's bills. The credit column in the voucher register is the accounts payable column and the debits consist of the departmental allocations of the bill. An example of the voucher register (also called purchase or accounts payable journal) appears in Exhibit 7.3.

Invoices are recorded in the voucher register upon receipt to maintain accurate monthly financial statements. This way, if committee chairmen and club officers borrow the invoices (for review and approval, for use at meetings, or for preparing reports and budgets) and do not return them, subsequent preparation of accurate financial records is not jeopardized.

EXHIBIT 7.4
Cash Disbursements Journal

Date	Payee	Check No.	Credits		Debits		
			Cash Amount	Cash Discounts	Accounts Payable	Other	
						Account	Amount

If a vendor sends more than one invoice during the month, most clubs tend to wait until the end of the month before recording the purchases. At that time, the club reconciles the open invoices to the vendor's final monthly statement and posts the consolidated vendor statement in the voucher register. The voucher register serves two purposes: it records purchases and distributes the amount to the proper balance sheet or expense accounts.

Cash Disbursements Journal

If a club uses a voucher register system, the cash disbursements journal (Exhibit 7.4) records, in numerical order, all the checks that the club has issued. The credit column for the cash disbursements book refers to cash; the debit column refers to accounts payable.

Clubs that pay their bills promptly may find it advantageous to use a combination voucher register/cash disbursements journal. Under this method, the club lists all check payments as they occur during the month, and allocates the expenses to the various departments. At the end of the month, the bookkeeper records in the accounts payable credit column all the accounts payable in the open accounts payable file, and also allocates these expenses to the appropriate departments.

The following month, when the prior month's accounts payable items are paid, the club records the checks. The offsetting debit is listed in the accounts payable debit column rather than being allocated to the various operating departments in the cash disbursements/voucher register journal. For this system to function properly, a club must pay its bills promptly. Bookkeeping becomes confusing under this method if a club has bills that are two, three, or four months old.

Payroll Journal

Most clubs have a computerized payroll system (either in-house or service bureau) to maintain their payrolls. Smaller clubs use a pegboard system wherein the checks, the earnings cards, and the payroll sheets are prepared at one writing. The payroll journal is a summary of the payroll sheets and is the source for posting to the general ledger. Usually the summary of the payroll is broken down by departments so that the proper department is charged with the appropriate salaries and wages for the particular pay period. The credit for employees' meals can also be posted from the payroll journal since it is usually a number of meals times a set cost.

Membership Journal

The membership journal records membership changes on a cumulative basis. This journal serves as the book of original entry for recording dues billings to members, dues billings to new members, and credits for deceased, resigned, or dropped members. Member transfers from one category to another also appear in the membership journal, together with any change in the billing rate resulting from such transfers. New members' billings for initiation fees and membership certificates are also recorded in the membership journal, eliminating the need to record all such items in the general journal. Exhibit 7.5 is a sample membership journal.

General Journal

The general journal records various journal entry adjustments at the end of each month. It is used when recording such entries in other journals is inappropriate. The general journal usually consists of two columns (a debit column and a credit column) on the right-hand side of the book, with enough space to record the journal entries explanations on the left-hand side. One type of entry in the general journal might be a club-authorized write-off of a portion of the member's accounts receivable when a charge is in dispute.

Monthly Journal

The monthly journal consists of a "name/description" column and 24 "amount" columns (a debit and credit for each month) as shown in Exhibit 7.6. This journal records entries that recur each month and eliminates rewriting repetitious journal entries in the general journal. In addition, it reminds the bookkeeper of certain entries that must be made at the end of the month. The actual journal entry is written only for the first month of the year and, in subsequent months, only the amounts have to be recorded.

EXHIBIT 7.5
Membership Journal

	Total	Regular	Junior	Nonresident	Dues	Initiation Fees
Balance, January 1, 19XX	273	210	30	33		
Meeting of January 10, 19XX						
John Doe, Elected	1	1	—	—	$1,800	$2,500
James Thomas, transfer to nonresident	—	[1]	—	1	[900]	—
William Smith, resigned	[1]	—	—	[1]	—	—
Robert C. Brown, transfer to regular	—	1	[1]	—	900	1,000
Balance, January 31, 19XX	273	211	29	33	$1,800	$3,500

Note: There would be a separate column for each membership category.

EXHIBIT 7.6
Monthly Journal

Account Name	January Debit	January Credit	February Debit	February Credit
Fixed Charges—Real Estate Taxes	X		X	
Prepaid Expenses—Real Estate Taxes		X		X
To Record Monthly Proportion of Real Estate Taxes				
Fixed Charges—Insurance	X		X	
Prepaid Expenses—Insurance		X		X
To Record Insurance Expense for Month				
Unearned Income—Membership Dues	X		X	
Membership Dues Earned		X		X
To Record Dues Earned for Month				

This journal is set up in 24 columns with a debit and credit column for each month of the year.

General Ledger

At the end of each month, all the books of original entry are totaled and cross-totaled, summarized, and posted to the general ledger. The general ledger serves as the source of the club's financial statements.

Club operations are highly departmentalized, and the general ledger should be set up in columnar form by balance sheet and operating department categories ("railroad"-type ledger) rather than maintaining a separate ledger page for each individual account ("T account ledger"). Using the railroad-type ledger, all income and expenses affecting a particular department are posted in separate columns on ledger sheets prepared for that department. The railroad-type ledger provides for efficient and timely preparation of monthly financial statements because the profit or loss for each operating department is recorded in the ledger prior to financial statements preparation. For example, one immediately sees the profit or loss of a particular department for any particular month just by turning to that page in the general ledger.

The Accounting System

The basic accounting system in any club revolves around processing and recording sales and cash receipts, membership dues and fees, accounts payable and cash disbursements, and payroll. Also involved are inventories (including purchasing, receiving, storing, and issuing procedures), and daily and monthly financial reporting procedures.

Processing and Recording of Sales and Cash Receipts

Processing and recording of sales should start with the control of the sales chits. The sales chits should be serially numbered when they are printed to allow for numerical control. Preferably, each income-producing department (restaurant, bar, rooms, or cigars) should have a different colored sales chit. The chits for each department should be prenumbered with a different series of numbers to facilitate their handling and control. Unissued chits should be placed in a secure location under the control and responsibility of someone in the accounting office. This same person should maintain a control sheet showing the quantity of supplies on hand, by serial number, and the quantities of supplies issued to departments, also by serial number.

The various departments should receive chits in serial number sequence and in small enough quantities for efficient control. In very small operations, the accounting office may issue the chits directly to each waiter or bartender each day and maintain a detailed record. In larger operations, each day's sales chits may be issued to the department heads, who in turn should keep records of the chit numbers issued to the individual service employees.

In a proper system, missing sales chits can be traced to the individual service employee responsible for them. After all the daily chits are accounted for, the sales chits for each department are totaled and posted in the sales journal. This posting may be done in conjunction with the preparation of a "daily report" to management—a report indicating the total sales for each day. A sample daily report appears in Exhibit 7.7. The sales chits should then be sorted by member order and posted to the accounts receivable records. This sorting and posting can be done by hand or by automated data processing equipment.

EXHIBIT 7.7
Daily Report

				Date:	____
				Day:	____
				Weather:	____
	No. of Covers Served	Day		Month to Date	
		This Year	Last Year	This Year	Last Year
Food Sales					
Breakfast		$	$	$	$
Lunch					
Dinner					
Total					
Beverage sales					
Service charges					
Sales tax					
Tobacco, candy, etc. sales					
Room rentals					
Golf cart rentals					
Greens fees					
Tennis fees					
Swimming pool fees					
Telephone					
Other (identify)					
Total		$	$	$	$

Note: This is a "Flash Report" for management purposes only. If service charges and sales tax are computed at a later time, they may be omitted from this report.

Manual Processing of Accounts Receivable

For those clubs still using a manual system to record members' accounts receivable charges, the "envelope" system is most common. This system provides an individual envelope, as shown in Exhibit 7.8, for each member, on which the accounting office indicates the total daily charges for each member. Under this system, the work flow in the accounting office, after the sales chits have been processed (numerically controlled, added, prices test-verified, etc.), is as follows:

1. Sort the sales chits into membership number order.
2. Run an adding machine tape of individual members' total charges and staple the tape to the corresponding group of charge tickets. (Separate totals have to be maintained in clubs with "minimum charges.")
3. Post the total in the appropriate space on the member's envelope and insert the sales chits in it. (Separate memo postings have to be made for minimum charge purposes.)

EXHIBIT 7.8

Accounts Receivable Manual "Envelope" System

Member's Name: ______________________

House Charges for Month of: ______________________

			Fwd.			Fwd.		
1			11			21		
2			12			22		
3			13			23		
4			14			24		
5			15			25		
6			16			26		
7			17			27		
8			18			28		
9			19			29		
10			20			30		
Total			Total			31		

Total Charges		
Balance Arrears		
Amount Due		

Note: If club has minimum spending requirements for food and beverages, separate columns must be maintained segregating food and beverage charges from other charges.

4. Run an adding machine tape of the amounts posted to members' envelopes for the day and match the total to the daily charges as posted to the sales journal.
5. At the end of the month, the envelope totals are recorded on members' accounts receivable ledgers (usually card forms) and statements.
6. When the grand total of the outstanding balances has been reconciled to the control account in the general ledger, the statements are mailed to the members. Clubs that do not maintain duplicate sales chits generally send the member his sales chits only after he has paid his bill.

Posting Machine Processing

Another way to record members' accounts receivable is the bookkeeping/posting machine. The work flow, up to the point of posting to members' accounts, is basically the same as the work flow described for the manual system. Under this system, however, either the total daily charges or the individual charges each day are posted to the members' accounts receivable statement which is then duplicated and attached to the members' ledger card. At the end of each month, the statement is detached and mailed to the member; the ledger card is retained as the club's accounts receivable record.

EDP and Accounts Receivable

Many functions of a club's accounting department can be computerized. The most common computer application is billing for members' dues and house charges. Since a club's membership is fairly stable and all sales are usually charged to members' accounts, the billing of accounts receivable is particularly well suited to computerization. A second major application is the payroll. Other areas, such as accounts payable, cash disbursements, general ledger, and financial statement preparation, can also be computerized. (The appropriate use of computers in clubs is discussed in detail in a later chapter in this book.)

Generally, electronic data processing (EDP) is used in the club industry in one of two ways: either by using an outside service bureau or by using an in-house computer. Either way, the work flow, up to the point of posting the members' accounts, is basically the same as under the manual system. With the use of EDP equipment, it is important that batch controls be maintained over the data being processed.

Cash Receipts

After the accounts receivable have been properly controlled and billed, it is easy to record payments in the cash receipts book and the accounts receivable detail records. The most important point here is that the outstanding accounts receivable should be reconciled to the control account in the general ledger at the end of each month and any differences should be investigated before mailing statements to the members.

Dues and Fees Billing

Control over membership dues is maintained by using a membership journal (Exhibit 7.5) that provides a strict accounting of all membership changes by membership category. Billing data assembled (usually on statements) should be carefully checked against the membership journal to ensure that a dues statement has been prepared for every member and that the bill is for the correct amount.

EXHIBIT 7.9
Receiving Stamp

Date Received	
Quality O.K.	
Quantity O.K.	
Price O.K.	
Extension and Footing O.K.	
O.K. for Payment	

The accounting department has control over membership dues but must depend on information made available to it by the club secretary. For the accounting department to adequately control dues revenue, all membership changes must be authorized in the membership committee or the board of governors meetings and written in the minutes of these meetings. From these authorizations, entries are then made in the membership journal.

Processing Accounts Payable/Cash Disbursements

The chapter on food and beverage operations contains information on buying and accounting for food purchases on a daily and monthly basis. Information includes calculating stock requirements, purchase specifications, vendor relations, monthly inventories, and cost accounting. Clubs generally do not use formal written purchase orders but rather telephone purchase orders to vendors who are chosen from favorable competitive quotations. To ensure that vendors quote on the same merchandise, the club writes and distributes specifications to various vendors for goods the club intends to buy.

The vendors usually submit invoices upon delivery of the goods or services. The club should stamp and sign these invoices to indicate certain approvals. A sample of such a receiving stamp is shown in Exhibit 7.9.

The following procedures should be followed to process purchases properly. All invoices should be properly stamped and initialed (as evidence that the merchandise has been received) before being sent to the accounting department. The invoice should indicate to what account the purchase should be charged. This account designation should be subject to subsequent scrutiny by the accounting office. The accounting department should also compare the invoice with the purchase order and/or the competitive bid received. The mathematical accuracy of the invoice should be checked. All invoices containing discount terms should be separated so that prompt payment can be made to take advantage of such discounts. Invoices should be entered in the voucher register immediately. If many invoices are received from the same vendor during a month, the invoices may be filed alphabetically by vendor name. At the end of the month, such invoices should be checked against the vendor's monthly statement to verify the balance. After verification, the statement should be entered in the voucher register using only one line per vendor. When all the invoices have been entered for a particular month, all columns in the voucher register should be added and cross-added to verify that the total of the debit columns equals the total of the credit columns. All columns in the voucher register should then be summarized by account name or account number so they may be posted in the general ledger according to their account classifications.

Cash Disbursements

After an invoice is recorded in the voucher register, a check is written and clipped to the invoice for the manager's review and approval. After the manager initials the invoice as evidence of his approval, an officer may give final approval for payment. The officer usually signs the check as a cosignatory with the manager or another officer. The checks should be entered in the cash disbursements book when they are written.

Manager's Checking Account

In many private clubs, every check drawn on the regular checking account requires the signature of at least one officer. None of the employees is an officer of the club. Accordingly, it is sometimes difficult to obtain the necessary signatures for quick payment of debts. Some officers may scrutinize the supporting documents less carefully than others when signing checks. Some clubs have solved this problem by opening a "manager's checking account," maintained on a so-called "imprest basis" (similar to a petty cash fund) and for which the manager is the authorized signatory. An amount sufficient to cover the operations of the club for one or two weeks is deposited into the manager's account and all receipts of the club continue to be deposited into the regular checking account. Periodically, the manager's account is reimbursed from the regular account for exactly the total amount of the checks the manager has drawn. At the time of reimbursement, the officer signing the reimbursement check must carefully scrutinize and cancel in some manner all of the vouchers the manager has paid during that period.

Payroll

Timekeeping

Processing and recording payroll should not be too difficult.

Probably the most difficult timekeeping area to control is the golf course maintenance department since the crew reports for work to the maintenance building, usually located apart from the clubhouse where other employees report for work. It is, therefore, generally the greens superintendent's duty to record the numbers of hours his crew works. The other hourly employees generally use a time clock to keep track of their hours. But if time clocks are not used, the department heads maintain a time book showing the hours that subordinates work daily. For control purposes, overtime hours should be approved in advance.

At the end of each pay period (usually weekly), the time cards or books are submitted to the accounting office where payroll data are assembled. Employees generally receive paychecks, usually distributed by department heads. For control purposes, the duty of distributing the payroll checks should be rotated among responsible employees from time to time.

Recording Payroll

Most clubs are completely departmentalized, and the payroll records should be arranged in departmental categories to simplify the distribution of payroll expense. Probably the simplest method of recording payroll is through the "one-write system." With this system, the payroll check, payroll sheet, and earnings card are prepared at the same sitting through the use of a check with a carbon stub, and a pegboard. Although some smaller clubs may still use one-write systems, most clubs generally have a computerized payroll system.

Gratuities

Many clubs have instituted nontipping policies and automatically add a set percentage of food and beverage sales chits as a gratuity. These gratuities are considered wages and should be added to the payroll and taxed accordingly if paid out to the service employees.

When tipping is permitted, the employee receiving the tip is required to report it to his employer for proper tax withholdings. To properly declare cash tips received, the employee fills out Form 4070 (Exhibit 7.10) and submits it to the accounting department.

EXHIBIT 7.10
Employee's Report on Tips

Form 4070 (Rev. March 1975) Department of the Treasury Internal Revenue Service	Employee's Report of Tips to Employer	Social Security Number
Employee's name and address		Tips received directly from customers . . . . $
Employer's name and address		Tips received on change receipts . . . . . . $
Month or shorter period in which tips were received from , 19 , to , 19		Total tips . . . . $
Signature		Date

Financial Reporting Procedures

The club's daily report and the monthly financial statements are the two most common financial reports. Besides these reports, the club bookeeper usually has to prepare special reports for various committees and, perhaps, special reports for the board of governors.

Daily Report

In any business, management requires financial information to manage the operations efficiently. A private club is no exception. The daily report is an important management tool. In addition to financial information, it contains information such as the day of the week, the weather and indicates any other unusual circumstances that may affect the day's activity. A simplified daily report is shown as Exhibit 7.7.

Daily reports keep management informed of the current business activity so that decisions can be made quickly. Also, when the daily reports are prepared over a long period of time, they can help management plan and staff activities for particular days.

Monthly Financial Statements

The bookkeeper prepares the monthly financial statements for the monthly meetings of the board of governors. Typically, the monthly financial statements consist of a comparative balance sheet and a comparative statement of income and expenses (monthly and year to date cumulative) and are supported by comparative departmental schedules. Many clubs also include statistical information besides actual operating results, and comparisons with budgeted income and expenses enabling them to pinpoint variances from the budget and allowing for corrective action.

A sample club balance sheet is shown in Exhibit 7.11. Regardless of club size or type, the balance sheet of one club will be fairly similar to the balance sheet of another. There can be wide differences, however, in the presentation of the statement of income and expenses. As an example, the statement of income and expenses of a lunch club (Exhibit 7.12), a city club (Exhibit 7.13), and a country club (Exhibit 7.14) are quite different because the lunch club does not have all the operating departments of a city club and a city club does not have all the sports departments of a country club.

As mentioned previously, many clubs include certain statistical information in the monthly financial statements. The major revenue contributor in clubs, with the possible exception of membership dues, is usually from food and beverage sales. Accordingly, the most important statistical information presented is in regard to the food and beverage departments. The key food and beverage operating ratios are the cost of food sold ratio, the cost of beverage sold ratio, and the ratio of combined food and beverage payroll to combined food and beverage sales.

The cost of food sold ratio is computed by dividing the cost of food sold by the food sales. This ratio will vary depending on the type of club and operation. The cost of beverages sold ratio is computed by dividing the cost of beverages sold by the beverage sales. The ratio of combined food and beverage payroll to the combined food and beverage sales is computed by dividing the combined payroll by the combined sales. This ratio fluctuates depending on the club's location and size and whether or not the club assesses members for employee service charges.

EXHIBIT 7.11
Sample Balance Sheet

Assets

	December 31 Current Year	December 31 Prior Year
Current Assets:		
Cash:		
In bank	$	$
On hand		
Accounts receivable:		
House		
Dues, fees and assessments		
Other		
Total		
Less: Allowance for doubtful accounts		
Inventories, at cost:		
Food		
Beverages		
Other		
Prepaid expenses		
Insurance		
Real estate taxes		
Other		
Total current assets		
Cash Restricted for Capital Improvements		
Fixed Assets:		
Land and improvements		
Buildings and improvements		
Furniture, fixtures and equipment		
Total		
Less: Accumulated depreciation		
Total Assets	$	$

Liabilities and Members' Equity

	December 31 Current Year	December 31 Prior Year
Current Liabilities:		
Accounts payable:		
Trade	$	$
Other		
Taxes payable and accrued:		
Payroll		
State sales		
Accrued expenses		
Salaries and wages		
Workmen's compensation insurance		
Interest		
Other		
Portion of long-term debt due within one year		
Special purpose funds		
Unearned income:		
Dues		
Special fees		
Scrip		
Rentals		
Total current Liabilities		
Long-Term Debt:		
Mortgage note payable		
Less: Portion due within one year		
Total Liabilities		
Capital Improvement Fund		
Members' Equity:		
Membership certificates:		
Issued and outstanding		
Retained earnings:		
Balance, beginning		
Net income for the year		
Balance, end		
Total Liabilities and Members Equity	$	$

EXHIBIT 7.12

Small Lunch Club

Statement of Income and Expense

	Schedule	This Year	Last Year
Income [Loss]			
Membership dues earned		$	$
Restaurant	B-1		
Beverages	B-2		
Cigar stand	B-3		
Other income	B-4		
Total income			
General and Unapportioned Expenses	B-5		
Income before Fixed Charges			
Fixed Charges:			
Rent			
Depreciation and amortization			
Total fixed charges			
Net Income [Loss]		$	$

Other useful food and beverage operating statistics are the number of food covers served, the average receipt per food cover, and the average food covers served per service employee.

For those clubs that have sleeping room accommodations for their members, information such as the number of rooms available for rental, occupancy rate, and the average daily rate is also useful to management. Finally, comparative membership statistics are appropriate in monthly financial statements as a valuable management tool.

UNRELATED BUSINESS INCOME

Unrelated business income tax raises a lot of questions. (1) What is unrelated business income? (2) What records must be kept concerning the use of club facilities? (3) How much unrelated business income can the club earn, and still remain "tax exempt"?

Before passage of the Tax Reform Act of 1969, the tax imposed on unrelated business taxable income of most tax-exempt organizations was not applicable to exempt social clubs. The Tax Reform Act extended this tax to social clubs, but under a new concept. A social club became subject to the tax on *all* income except "exempt function income," which was defined to include (1) dues, fees, and charges paid by members for services provided for members, their dependents, or guests;

EXHIBIT 7.13

City Club

Statement of Income and Expenses

	Schedule	This Year	Last Year
Membership Dues Income		$	$
Clubhouse Operating Income [Loss]:			
Rooms	B-1		
Food	B-2		
Beverages	B-3		
Cigars, cigarettes, etc.	B-4		
Squash courts	B-5		
Telephone	B-6		
Laundry, valet, and lockers	B-7		
Other income	B-8		
Total		$	$
Deduct: Undistributed Operating Expenses:			
Clubrooms expense	B-9	$	$
Administrative and general	B-10		
Heat, light and power	B-11		
Repairs and maintenance	B-12		
Clubhouse Operating Income [Loss]			
Income Available for Fixed Charges			
Fixed Charges	B-13		
Income before Provision for Depreciation and Unrelated Business Income Taxes			
Provision for Depreciation			
Income before Provision for Unrelated Business Income Taxes			
Provision for Unrelated Business Income Taxes			
Net Income		$	$

EXHIBIT 7.14
Country Club

Statement of Income and Expenses

	Schedule	This Year	Last Year
Membership dues		$	$
Golf and Other Sports:			
Golf course maintenance	B-1		
Golf tournament and caddy expense	B-2		
Golf carts	B-3		
Total golf expenses			
Less: Greens fees and cart rentals			
Net golf expense			
Swimming pool	B-4		
Tennis courts	B-5		
Net Cost of Sports Activities			
Dues—Available for Clubhouse Operation and Fixed Charges			
Clubhouse Operating Income [Loss]:			
Food	B-6		
Beverages	B-7		
Cigar stand	B-8		
Locker rooms	B-9		
Other income	B-10		
Total			
Deduct undistributed operating expenses:			
Clubhouse	B-11		
Entertainment	B-12		
Administrative and general	B-13		
Heat, light and power	B-14		
Repairs and maintenance—clubhouse	B-15		
Total			
Net Cost of Clubhouse Operation			
Dues Available for Fixed Charges			
Rent, Taxes and Insurance	B-16		
Income before Provision for Depreciation and Amortization			
Provision for Depreciation and Amortization	B-16		
Income before Provision for Unrelated Business Income Taxes			
Provision for Unrelated Business Income Taxes			
Net Income [Loss]		$	$

(2) investment income "set aside" for charity; and (3) gain on the sale of property used by the club for exempt purposes if proceeds are used to replace the property sold within a period beginning one year before, to three years after, the sale. The law allows a deduction against the unrelated business income for expenses "directly connected" with the income. In addition, the law allows each club a $1,000 statutory deduction. This law became effective for taxable years *beginning* after December 31, 1969. Even though a club is subject to an income tax on nonmember income, it is still subject to the nonmember income guideline percentage and excessive nonmember use of its facilities will cause a club to lose its tax exempt status. Furthermore, the law provides that a taxable club will not be able to offset membership losses against the net income from outside business. For example, a taxable club may suffer an overall loss of $50,000 for the year, consisting of an $80,000 loss on regular membership business and a $30,000 net profit on outside business. This club would be subject to an income tax, at regular corporate rates, on the $30,000 net profit from outside business. The $80,000 loss attributable to the members may be used only to offset future or past membership profits in a taxable year.

Guidelines for distinguishing unrelated business income from tax exempt income are presented in the chapter on taxes, as well as a discussion of various sources of and uses for such funds. Clubs need to be especially careful not to jeopardize their tax exempt status and should probably seek professional advice where appropriate.

BUDGET PREPARATION

An effective method for controlling costs and improving efficiency is budgeting. All clubs can use budgeting advantageously, regardless of their size.

Budgeting is not complex. In our daily routine each of us calculates what to buy, when to buy it, and compares the costs of two similar items. Budgeting for a business merely extends this process. A club budget helps avoid the pitfalls of operating without a plan. Good organization is essential to successful budgeting. It is not practicable to attempt to control expenditures if authority and responsibility for incurring them has not been well defined.

Often budgeting seems unsuitable for a small club's requirements. Although convinced of budgeting merits, the club believes that a budget is too involved or too time consuming. Actually, budget procedures are fundamentally the same for small or large clubs, and they are simpler to apply in the small club.

Some believe that budgeting is a guessing game of writing down figures which are compared later with actual figures to determine how accurate the "guess" was. A budget is much more than that; it is a plan of operation.

A properly constructed budget provides many rewards.

- It provides definite objectives for future operations.
- It helps formulate and clarify management policies for the future.
- It is a convenient yardstick for measuring operational efficiency.
- It fixes responsibility for achievement on specific individuals or departments.

Finally, employees try to attain budget objectives. There is no better way to coordinate financial sales, and operating results than through budgetary control.

The Procedure

Income and expense estimates are made by carefully weighing past performance, current business trends, projected prices and taxes, increased labor costs, and other pertinent data to determine their effects on operating results. Once determined, these factors lay the foundation for the operating plan.

How does the manager estimate a budget? First, he produces an operating plan covering all operating departments. This must be an adequate financial plan including fundamental information such as:

1. Monthly revenue estimates for each operating department together with reasons for deviations from past experience;
2. Planned cost and expense ratios to sales, representing management's preestablished standards.
3. The expected profit or loss realization from each operating department and a summary report indicating the projected income or loss from all operating departments.

Budget figures are not "guesstimates," but a complete detailed projection of planned results. Club management prepares, submits, and recommends this part of the budget as the first step of the overall program.

The next step is to estimate the unapportioned expenses (that is, house expenses, heat, light and power, greens and grounds, and general and administrative costs). The manager estimates expenses based on past experience and current expense policy as indicated by committee appropriations.

In preparing the budget, management should not assume that the prior year's expenses are justified and merely increase those expenses by a certain percentage to allow for inflation. Each department must be reviewed to determine whether or not expenditures in the prior year were cost justified. That is, were the benefits commensurate with the cost? Benefits here do not necessarily mean dollars. They can mean additional services that the club member expects and to which he is entitled.

The difference between the estimated net income from all operating departments and the projected total unapportioned expenses equals the estimated operating loss. The club's fixed charges (that is, rent, real estate taxes, interest, insurance, and depreciation) are added to the estimated operating loss to arrive at the total projected cost of operations.

While preparing the budget, the club ideally should be able to project the required membership dues for the coming year and establish the dues figure based on the budget. More often, however, the membership dues figure has already been set and the projected total membership dues is calculated by multiplying the total estimated number of members in each membership category by the dues amount for each established category.

A somewhat more detailed procedure is followed if the budget is used to determine what the membership dues *should be.* If the requirements for the amortization of indebtedness plus the estimated cost of capital improvements and additions exceeds the depreciation charge and any other revenue sources besides operating income (such as initiation fees or capital improvement assessments), this excess requirement is added to the total operational cost to calculate the dues requirement. The dues requirement should then be distributed over the membership according to membership classification and the number in each class. For example, if a resident member pays twice the dues of a nonresident member, and a junior member pays one-half the dues of a nonresident member, then each resident member will have a weight of four, each nonresident member will have a weight of two, and each junior member will have a weight of one. The total dues requirement should then be divided by the total membership weight, and the resultant figure would be the junior dues rate. Twice this amount would be the nonresident dues rate and four times the amount would be the resident dues rate.

In addition to the operating budget, a capital budget should also be prepared. Management should recommend capital improvement projects required or contemplated for the future.

If improvements or new equipment costs can be justified in savings, the cost and savings are detailed in budget documents. If the cost can be justified in added gross profits through increased sales or revenue, these increases are illustrated, as well. If new equipment or improvements are desired solely because they improve services, this must also be discussed in the budget documents. In all cases, carefully prepared estimates of each project or item of equipment should be submitted to the budget committee.

Budget Committee Organization

The club manager, knowing the club's operations, can advise the board as to the proper composition of the budget committee. A budget, since it is a business and financial plan, should be handled by a small committee capable of cutting red tape and steering it through final board ratification.

As a permanent standing committee, it would ideally include the chairman of the executive or finance committee, the club treasurer, and the chairman of the house committee. The club accountant should assist the budget committee by assembling figures and preparing estimates. The club manager provides assistance as necessary.

The budget committee requests budget estimates from all officers or committees authorized to control and disburse club funds. The club manager provides a projected budget for operating departments, as well as for the unapportioned expense groupings. The club accountant prepares forecasts of all fixed charges such as insurance, taxes, interest and depreciation.

The membership committee chairman submits a proposed membership quota by classification to ascertain anticipated revenue from dues and initiation and transfer fees. If the club has a capital additions and improvements committee, its chairman also submits his budget.

A net earnings objective, which ties the operating budget to the capital budget, is essential in this planning process. Essentially, a net earnings objective is the summation of profit and depreciation expense that can be added to previous years' reserves, to provide the cash flow for planned capital expenditures. Unless a loan is contemplated, realistic budgeting must be in line with the above equation.

Budget Form

The budget has two parts: the operating budget and the capital budget. There is no set form for the operating budget, but it should follow the same format as the club's regular financial statements.

Execution

A budget defining each department's responsibility is the key to successful planning and execution. After carefully studying and revising the budget, the budget committee forwards the final budget with its approval to the board. The board of governors has the final authority to accept the budget as submitted or amended. Club management then has its operational map. The destination and the route to get there are laid out.

The budget is a plan, not a law. It instructs operating and administrative heads about the program to be executed and the financial results expected. The club manager's responsibilities are clearly defined, and his performance rating will be measured against them.

Control and Follow-Up

The committee and the board should periodically study budget reports that compare actual results to the budget figures so that all are aware of the current fiscal position of the club. Regular status reports spotlight problems that warrant special attention before they get out of hand. The budget should be revised, when appropriate, during the year.

Budgeting Advantages

The advantages of budgeting (including budgeting procedures) are:

1. It draws the increasingly diverse and complex operations of the modern club into overall club planning.
2. It defines the responsibility for the manager, officers and committee chairmen.
3. It is a means of effective and organized communication between the directing body and operating personnel, particularly between the club manager and the board.
4. It assumes an annual review of all club activities and operations, and opens the way to orderly, systematic changes.
5. It solves the recurring problem of educating incoming officers and directors, giving them an understanding of the scope of the club's operations.
6. It forces planning, particularly long-range planning, which is necessary for intelligent club management.
7. It offers some protection against unsound fiscal policies and decisions.
8. It provides a way of periodically measuring performance against objectives.

Of course, there can be many refinements beyond this fundamental system to tailor effective budgetary control for any club. The fundamental ingredient in any system is the manager—the one who should know most about club operations. The manager must play an important role in forecasting, planning, controlling, and improving operating results.

Communication

Budget preparation affords an excellent opportunity to inform the officers and board about repairs and maintenance requirements, and proposed capital expenditures. Board members sometimes are surprised when management points out that obsolete and inefficient kitchen equipment must be replaced at great expense or that some of the public rooms need refurbishing. The club manager, on the other hand, may feel that the board should have known that such expenditures would be necessary since the conditions were obvious or previously discussed. If the need for such expenditures is clearly presented in the budgets, a potential stumbling block to harmonious operations is removed.

A budget also provides a basis and opportunity for discussions regarding policies and plans of club operation. If analysis reveals a loss will result if meals are priced at amounts determined, by the house committee, the finance committee, and the board of governors, then there is a need to recognize this fact in advance, rather than criticize the manager's performance later.

Staff Requirements

Budgeting does not apply only to income and expenses in dollar amounts. Budgeting also applies to staffing and is a means of effective payroll control. Labor is the most costly component of club operations. In an average club, payroll and related expenses comprise approximately one-half of the total expenses. Consequently, it is imperative to meet desired service standards at a minimum of payroll cost. Management must provide efficiency and good service while maintaining minimum costs.

Generally, management controls payroll expense through efficient staff use, that is, by proper staffing and scheduling. Actual employee performance must be checked against work performance standards. Overtime hours should be approved in advance. Work schedules should be reviewed periodically and changed where appropriate. Perhaps a club should close for two or three weeks during a slow period so that all employees take their vacations at the same time, eliminating the need for temporary employees. Perhaps a country club should be open only five days per week instead of six, particularly if the sixth day is staffed with overtime help. Perhaps a city club should be closed certain nights of the week if statistics indicate inactivity.

The board of governors could consider many ways to maintain acceptable payroll costs. Of course, any such decision would have to be supported by appropriate facts and projections.

Briefly, effective payroll control procedures consist of the following:

1. An accurate determination of probable club activity during a given period.
2. Comparison of staff performance standards with actual staff activity.
3. Scheduling staff to cover the expected volume of activity without overtime hours. Overtime should be authorized by management in advance.
4. Payroll reports reviewed daily so that management can control this expense more effectively.
5. A weekly report relating payroll cost to dollar volume of sales.

Many refinements can be applied to this system of preplanning or budgeting staff and payroll requirements. Applying these essential principles to the payroll of any club will pay dividends many times over.

Cash-Flow Budget

In addition to the regular operating budget, a cash flow budget is useful. A cash-flow budget takes into account the anticipated cash receipts from operations, initiation fees, and capital assessments, plus anticipated expenditures both for operations and capital additions. Using the cash-flow budget, club management determines the periods in which there will be deficits (and possible borrowing requirements). At the same time, it indicates when excess cash is available for investment.

The cash-flow budget saves the embarrassment of suddenly discovering that the cash available is not sufficient to meet normal expenses such as payroll or real estate taxes.

Managing Cash

Many clubs bill their membership dues annually and, accordingly, receive a large amount of cash at the start of their dues billing year. As in any other business, it is prudent to invest any excess cash in order to obtain interest income. The club that maintains a high checking account balance does not have sound fiscal management. Proper fiscal management dictates that cash not be tied up unnecessarily in inventories or accounts receivable and that excess cash be invested appropriately.

Cash Advances

Sound fiscal management also dictates that clubs be prudent with cash advances to members. For example, some clubs allow members a cash advance of up to $100 any time they sign a cash advance voucher. This, of course, means that the club must keep a large amount of cash on hand to accommodate its members and must process the cash advance slips for the next month's billing. The member then pays for the cash advances with his house payment the following month. In effect, the member is using the club's cash for nearly two months. Despite this, if the board believes that cash advancing is a valuable service, then there should be a service charge. Not only is the club's cash tied up but also there is additional accounting work.

Caddy Fees

A similar cash advance problem exists in those country clubs that permit members to charge their caddy fees. When a club pays a caddy fee on behalf of a member, it is, in effect, advancing the caddy fee to the member. This can add up to a sizeable sum that is not available for investment. It may be more appropriate to sell scrip books with five or ten caddy slip charge tickets that caddies redeem. This way, the club would be paid in advance for caddy payments.

Check Cashing

Many clubs permit members to cash personal checks. This practice requires the club to maintain a large amount of cash for just that purpose. If there is a large check-cashing fund, the club should charge a check-cashing fee. However, careful consideration should be given to charging this fee since it could be considered a nuisance, and the service provided to the members could far exceed the loss in interest income.

Managing Accounts Receivable

Most clubs can certainly improve their cash flow through determined efforts to get the members' bills out and collected on a timely basis. If a club must borrow funds for operating purposes, it is unfair to members who pay their bills on time to also pay interest on debts caused by other members' late payments. Several clubs now impose late penalty charges on overdue accounts.

Discounts

A club should buy at discount prices whenever possible. If a vendor offers discounts on goods or services, a club should take advantage of the opportunity.

Price Adjustments and Minimum Charges

In commercial operations, management is free to adjust prices to maintain profits. Unfortunately, the club manager often has no such freedom to adjust prices. A manager may decide that food prices must be increased, but the chairman of the house committee and the board of governors may not approve the decision because of potential membership reaction. Gross profits can then decline to the point where the food and beverage operations may sustain an operational loss which is borne by the general membership in increased dues.

It is not necessarily true that members who frequent the dining rooms and bar support the club, whereas others who use them less do not. It could be argued that the member who pays the annual dues and does not use the club's facilities is, in effect, subsidizing the members who do. This is not necessarily true either if the club has a waiting list of potential members who would use the facilities.

Management Accounting

Accounting reports serve two primary purposes: to furnish financial data to people outside of the business, such as stockholders, lending institutions, and regulatory and taxing authorities; and to provide management with information for operating the business. Routine financial statements are, of course, needed for management decisions. More facts than are normally included in routine financial statements, however, are required for effective management control. This area of accounting dealing with operations control is termed "management accounting" as distinguished from historical or financial accounting.

One difference between financial accounting and management accounting is the type of information reported. Management accounting is concerned with whether the information is useful, rather than whether it conforms to generally accepted accounting principles. Some examples of management accounting information not included in financial reporting would include:

1. Average days' charge sales in accounts receivable, used to measure collection procedure effectiveness.
2. Inventory turnover during the month or year, to determine if there is adequate amount of inventory. A reduced inventory produces a corresponding cash increase which is then available for investment.
3. The number of food covers served during the period, to determine increased or declining usage, or the average receipt per food cover.
4. The number of service employees. When compared with the number of food covers, management can determine the ratio of meals to each service employee, and measure it to predetermine standards.
5. The number of kitchen employees, by category. When compared with the number of covers, the number of meals prepared by the kitchen workers or the number of dishes washed per dishwasher can be determined and measured against work performance standards.
6. Sales analysis. Data on food service or season of the year can be evaluated for patterns of market demand. Perhaps a dining area should be closed during proven slow periods. Perhaps the menu should be redesigned.
7. Gross profit per cover (contribution margin).

There are other helpful reports based on information not included in financial accounting. In most instances, the data needed to compile these reports can be garnered from the existing financial accounting information-gathering system. Furthermore there are industry-wide averages that serve as yardsticks for evaluating standards. These averages are useful, but they are just that—averages. They offer guidelines for evaluating club operations but no two organizations are alike.

LONG-RANGE PLANNING

Committee Selection

The first and most important step in long-range planning is selecting a long-range planning committee. Members appointed to this committee should represent a cross-section of the club's entire membership. Leaders in various club activities should be on the committee as well as young and old members. An engineer, architect, accountant, and other professionals are good choices as committee members. Most important, the club manager, who has the most intimate knowledge of the club operations, should sit on the committee. The committee should be large enough to handle the workload without being unwieldy. Moreover, because it is a hard-working committee, those appointed to it should have a committee track record indicating a willingness to work.

Capital Expenditures

Expenditures for capital replacements and improvements have far-reaching ramifications and may affect the success or failure of a club. Incurring indebtedness to finance capital expenditures commits future club revenue to repaying principal and interest on that indebtedness. Accordingly, during poor economic times, club management may be reluctant to embark on capital expenditure programs. Conversely, failure to engage in an appropriate capital expenditure program could result in membership dissatisfaction, a more costly operation for the club in the long run, and the general physical decline of the club.

Planning the capital budget can be more important than planning the annual operating budget. If there is an operation deficit for any particular year it is taken into account when planning the operating budget for the following year. Since the capital budget has great long-range effect on the club, capital expenditure programs should not be entered into on a hit-or-miss basis.

Project Evaluation

Any club is likely to have a number of potentially necessary projects. Efficient project analysis and execution will directly influence future club operations. In a business venture, factors such as competitive position, future earnings, and growth enter into the capital improvement evaluation. A club may not necessarily have to consider future earnings and growth, but it must consider competitive position because a dissatisfied member or a potential new member may go elsewhere. A club must maintain good facilities.

Purpose

The primary purpose of the long-range planning committee is to make some practical recommendations to guide the club's future. The committee's focus is the financial means and social needs of the club and its members, and how capital expenditures meet the stated goals. The expenditures must be given priority.

The major product of the committee is a detailed long-range budget and cash flow statement showing the probable effect on the club's operations resulting from recommended changes in facilities, activities and services. The plan details the capital improvement program along with its financing, whether it be membership bonds, capital assessments, loans from banks, or a combination of these. The plan must take into account interest rates, along with the rate of inflation. The committee studies the long-term aspects of the club and its community so that any current action cannot permanently injure the club's future. A club cannot afford to develop a project independently of a master plan. It cannot be run by crisis management. Permanent planning (with a resultant course of action for the governing body to follow) is needed. Although a club's facilities are currently adequate, major improvements and other developments costing considerable money may not be far down the road.

Considering such items challenges management to the utmost for they must be studied in light of present debts, future membership limits, dues and entrance fee structure, property ownership or disposition, economic projections, and any known or foreseen problems. The committee is responsible for preparing a long-range plan for improvements, which is then approved by the board of governors and ratified by the members. After the long-range plan is established, all major improvements to club property should be made only by approval of the long-range planning committee and the board of governors. If the board of governors and the long-range planning committee do not agree on the need for a proposed improvement, the matter should be referred to the membership for a final decision.

Financial Aspects of Planning

When there are numerous necessary projects some process must be used to set priorities. Setting priorities presupposes that someone evaluates proposed capital expenditure projects. Long-range planning committees help the board of governors set priorities for these projects. These committees ensure continued maintenance of the club's facilities to the membership's satisfaction. With this knowledge of club operations, the manager should be part of the committee discussions.

Effective long-range planning for an established club can be initiated by determining whether past operational patterns can be used to project future needs. The planning committee studies both financial and nonfinancial aspects of club operations dating back for ten years or more. Examples of useful financial materials follow:

1. Prior financial statements, including the balance sheets, income and expense statements, and statements of changes in financial position.
2. Prior budgets, including comparisons of budget figures with actual operating results.
3. Comparisons with national club statistics such as "Clubs in Town and Country," published annually by the accounting firm of Pannell Kerr Forster. Also, comparisons with the operating results of local clubs if possible.
4. Prior cash-flow projections and cash-flow requirements.
5. Detailed lists of prior capital improvements and the related costs.
6. Additional assessments, if any, for capital improvements or for operating deficits.
7. Dues structure analysis broken down by member classification and average revenue per member.
8. Long- and short-term debt analysis.

Nonfinancial Aspects

Examples of useful material for reviewing nonfinancial aspects of club operations follow:

1. Number of members by membership classification for the ten most recent years, including admissions and resignations.
2. Number of members, by age bracket each year.
3. Changes in age bracket, income level, or geographic location of members over a representative period of time.
4. Number of inactive members per year.
5. Basic services and activities provided by the club.
6. Club's policy on fees for golf, swimming, tennis, or related activities (in addition to dues).
7. Changes in dues, assessments, fees, and menu prices occuring each year.
8. Employee turnover, particularly that of key employees.
9. Changes in employee benefits provided by the club.
10. Changes in the number and type of club committees.
11. Changes in the club's waiting list in recent years.

In addition, the club must maintain data on nonmember income to safeguard its tax-exempt status, and not exceed IRS guidelines. The club's accounting records should also provide sufficient detail to support its position with respect to unrelated business income taxes.

If necessary records for the long-range planning committee are not readily available, a mechanism should be set up to assemble them.

Pertinent Questions

After data collection, members of the long-range planning committee should have the answers to pertinent questions, such as the following:

1. Is there a changing pattern in the total membership represented by various membership classifications and age groups?
2. Are there significant changes in the pattern of admissions and resignations?
3. How do the changes affect the club's future?
4. What can be done about negative changes?
5. How does the trend of the club's dues, assessments, fees, and menu prices compare with that of other clubs in the area and with the general economy?
6. Are the present dues, assessments, fees, and menu prices higher or lower than those of other clubs?
7. If they differ, are there corresponding differences in quality and services?
8. Does a review of past financial statements indicate that the club is being operated on a businesslike basis?
9. Can weaknesses be identified and eliminated?

Membership Survey

Although the long-range planning committee can learn much from the past, it should also gather current information. A survey of the present membership can be conducted to determine each member's age and occupation, length of membership, reasons for using some club facilities more often than others, which facilities or activities should be added and which might be eliminated and how the club ranks in reputation and social standing, and whether there are concurrent memberships in other clubs.

The long-range planning committee should know whether the club's facilities are sufficiently broad for the current membership and adequate for growth, whether the club is responding to changing needs, and whether any club being planned for the area might eventually affect the memberships of existing clubs. The committee also needs to know the club's standing in the local community and how to strengthen its public image. The club's current service standards may be too high, and if they are, membership might accept changes in them. Other survey questions might be also posed:

1. What can be done to increase member participation in club activities?
2. Will the general membership be willing to move to another community if an increase in assessed valuation and resultant higher real estate tax make such action advisable?
3. Will the membership accept a merger with another club?
4. Will the club benefit from increased participation by women in its activities?
5. Are the facilities and activities of clubs likely to change significantly in the next ten or 20 years? If so, what are some of those changes likely to be, and how can the club keep up with the changes?

Committee Recommendations

It is most important that the plan be flexible, so when it is reviewed periodically, changes can be made as required.

One way for the planning committee to make its recommendations is along these lines:

1. Make a statistical presentation showing the probable effect of all recommended changes on the operation of the club.
2. Make a list of any members' objections to proposed changes.
3. Weigh the importance of each change against the club's well being and against the relative importance of those objections.
4. Outline a strategy in advance for overcoming possible objections to change.
5. Be selective. Proposals of doubtful importance should not stand in the way of those that carry a more significant impact.

Whenever the planning committee tries to reconcile economic feasibility with member preferences, it is possible to recommend some changes that will be accepted. Implementing some important proposals to strengthen the club is better than trying to implement too many and winding up with membership rejection.

Financing Capital Expenditures

In reviewing proposed projects, a club can consider the following:

1. Finance the projects from operations.
2. Assess the membership.
3. Borrow the required funds.
4. Do nothing at all.

Financing projects from operations seems to be the most favorable alternative, but it presupposes that there is income available from operations to finance the projects. If a club has funds available from operations for capital expenditure projects, it is indeed fortunate, but this is not frequent.

Assessing the membership requires that the cost of the capital expenditure or replacement be offset by what is called a capital improvement assessment. Most clubs prepare an operating budget to determine membership dues. They could have, in addition, a capital improvement budget to determine capital improvement dues. Many clubs use this method although they are not referred to as capital improvement dues, but rather as capital improvement assessments. It is not uncommon for country clubs to charge a monthly capital improvement assessment of $10 or $15. These assessments are set aside in a capital improvement fund to finance the various projects approved by the board of governors. Assessments may also be used for repaying incurred debt for past capital improvements. One advantage of a monthly capital improvement assessment is that the club can adjust the assessment to meet the planned expenditures.

If money is borrowed from a lending institution, the amount borrowed plus interest, must be repaid from future operating revenue or from assessments. Some clubs borrow funds from their members for capital improvements by issuing noninterest or low interest bearing bonds. Sound financial management dictates that a sinking fund be established for redeeming such bonds. The sinking fund resources can come from operating revenue appropriations, initiation fees of future members, or membership assessments.

The club that does nothing about capital expenditures may have an already burdensome debt, or an overly assessed membership, or low operating capital. Doing nothing is regrettable when capital improvement projects are necessary since it can be more costly for the club in the long run and, more important, can result in membership dissatisfaction and facility decline.

The capital improvement assessment method thus is the best method for providing funds for capital expenditures when clubs do not generate sufficient funds from operations. A club must identify those capital expenditure projects to be funded and completed. Long-term and short-term priorities should be developed for projects that will maintain the club in good condition.

Accounting for Fixed Assets and Related Depreciation

The accounting for fixed assets and related depreciation in the club industry is quite varied. There are conflicting philosophies on the question of whether or not clubs should provide for depreciation of fixed assets. The philosophy supporting depreciation is based on the concept that depreciation is an element of the cost of doing business; that the cost of an asset should be depreciated over its useful life, and that operations should be charged with a pro-rata portion of prior years' expenditures for capital additions.

The opposing philosophy is based on the premise that a club should be operated on a year-to-year, "pay as you go" basis, leaving new members in a position no better or worse than when the club started. Under this philosophy, depreciation is eliminated as a charge against the operations of the club, and as new facilities are needed or desired, the active membership has the responsibility of financing the cost of such improvements by means of special assessments or borrowed funds, with the concomitant obligation to repay the amount borrowed. It is the view of the no-depreciation proponents that to assess the membership to raise funds for a new facility and then to provide for depreciation of the new asset would, in effect, have the present membership paying for the new facility twice if the dues structure was increased to cover the additional depreciation expense.

Because of these conflicting philosophies, one may find a wide range of policies related to the treatment of fixed assets and related depreciation in clubs (for example, the capitalization of all fixed assets purchased; the charging of all capital expenditures to expense as incurred; the charging of fixed assets purchased to special funds—i.e., capital improvement fund—and not capitalizing them). Since the purchase of fixed assets is afforded such a wide variety of treatment by membership clubs, it follows that the depreciation accounting methods are also diverse. Among the methods used are (1) depreciation in accordance with generally accepted accounting principles by providing for depreciation over the estimated useful lives of the various assets, (2) no depreciation at all, (3) providing for depreciation at a predetermined fixed amount, (4) providing for depreciation of only those assets acquired through general funds, and (5) not providing for depreciation of assets acquired through special funds.

It is generally an accepted accounting principle that fixed assets should be capitalized and depreciated over the period of their useful lives in a systematic and rational manner. In order to establish a simple depreciation schedule, assets are normally grouped together by year of purchase, type of asset, and estimated useful life; and depreciation is provided on the straight-line method.

Depreciation for Tax Purposes

For tax purposes, private clubs—whether or not exempt from income tax under Section 501(c)(7)—are required to compute depreciation under the rules prescribed in the Internal Revenue Code and its numerous amendments. The Internal Revenue Code stipulates prescribed times and methods in which to recover the cost of any asset that is used in a trade or business. If a club reports any unrelated business income (generally food, beverage, rooms, green fees, and investment income) the deduction allowable for depreciation against the unrelated business income has to be computed in accordance with the provisions of the tax law.

REVIEW QUESTIONS

1. Discuss the relative dues structure of clubs. What kinds of clubs have higher dues? Which membership types carry higher dues?
2. What additional charges can be imposed on members just joining the club?
3. What charges, besides dues, should members expect to pay? Why?

4. What is an "operating assessment"? Describe the advantages and disadvantages of a club's charging members for an operating assessment.
5. List the various books required for a basic accounting system, the entries made in each, and the reason for each book. What use is made of the material in the ledgers?
6. Who should participate as a member of a club's long-range planning committee? Why? How big should the committee be?
7. What does the long-range committee do? What should its annual report contain? How can the committee gather the material it needs?

8

Communications and Public Relations

Mayacoo Lakes Country Club, West Palm Beach, Florida

Any discussion about communications and public relations must include two basic tasks in which a club manager should be vitally concerned: internal and external communications.

In chapter 1, it was stated that every club has its own established by-laws, house rules and policies, whether written or unwritten, and that these guidelines are interpreted by a constantly changing board of directors. Thus, the first assignment you have in your job as club communicator is to determine the attitude of your club's board and members in communicating with the community and the membership. Does the policy under which you'll be working encourage outside-the-club publicity, or does it tend towards anonymity? Does your board encourage direct communication with your club's members in all matters, or does it prefer that some announcements come from one of your club's officers? How far does the board want you involved in both of these areas?

Some clubs prefer to protect the privacy of its members; other clubs welcome any type of objective publicity because they believe it promotes the community image of the club and helps to encourage new members. These policies, however may change with the election of each new board. Once you've determined answers to these questions, you are ready to plan your program.

BASIC FUNCTION OF COMMUNICATIONS

The basic function of communications for a manager is to keep the board, the membership, the staff, and the community informed. Do it in a concise and easy-to-understand way. Don't be wordy in your communiques and don't use words that may not be understood by the person or persons with whom you are communicating. Tell your dishwasher to "get the dishes clean", not to "strive harder to rid the dishware of impurities and extraneous matter". Don't use "street" language when talking with your club members or the board. If there is a question in your mind about whether or not you completely understand a discussion, repeat your intrepretation to those with whom you desire to communicate and ask, "Is that right?"

COMMUNICATING WITH STAFF

The time to begin communicating with your staff is the day the staff member is hired. If you are the manager of a small club, you will handle this assignment yourself; if your club is large, utilizing a number of department heads, it will be up to them. You should have written instructions or job descriptions that outline in detail the assignment or assignments of each employee. You may hire a person for the job of waiter, but if you expect that person to fill in at times in other jobs, it's wise to have that understanding the day he or she commences their employment. Your service personnel should know the day they begin that they will be expected to work several stations, possibly helping others with their duties or whatever else you may require. Your club's "Employee Handbook", as discussed in detail elsewhere in this book, should take into consideration such contingencies and be explicitly explained to a new employee as soon as possible.

For special functions make certain that all employees of the club are completely familiar with all planned procedures either verbally or through written communiques posted at advantageous spots around the club—kitchen, service elevator, dining room entrance, employees' rooms, etc.

In a small club you should strive to hold staff meetings at least once a week; in a larger club your department heads will undoubtedly handle these meetings, but you might sit in on them from time to time. If you manage a country club, you should strive to meet with your club's golf professional and golf course superintendent at least weekly in order to coordinate club activities. You wouldn't want the golf professional inadvertently away from the club or have the grounds superintendent unknowingly doing major course maintenance the day of a special club event.

COMMUNICATING WITH YOUR BOARD

When communicating with your board members, be tactful. Don't attempt to impress board members with your knowledge; they'll find out soon enough whether or not you know what you are capable of doing in the way you manage the club and handle yourself and your employees. Just as in any job, you have to earn respect. You have an advantage as a new manager, so use it. The board will be observant to see how you handle things under fire before they step in. Don't use first names; use "Mister" or "Misses." Such terms convey respect for the person you are addressing.

You should expect to sit in on all board meetings, with the possible exception of when the board may be discussing your salary or a promotion. If you've followed the "Manager's Employment Contract" form outlined in Chapter 2, this prerogative has been written into your contract with the club. During board meetings you can offer counsel based on your experience and training. It is during these meetings that through constructive advice and suggestion you earn the respect of your board members. You should work especially closely with your club president and the other club officers who make up the executive committee. You can improve your chances to be better listened to during board meetings if you can influence the chairman to ask for your opinions, rather than indiscriminately volunteering advice. Regular informal meetings and/or discussions with board members and officers can often produce valuable, advance "feedback" on new subjects or anticipated projects before they become a part of the formal board agenda.

COMMUNICATING WITH YOUR MEMBERS

Most of your communicating with members will be verbal or through letters, announcements and club bulletins, but also through actions. When communicating with members, keep in mind clarity and costs. You'll be working with the various committees and you may be editing the club bulletin or working with a "volunteer" editor.

The key to promotion and publicity is getting the message across. There are several methods of transmitting messages: verbal through telephone calls, announcements over the club's public address system, word of mouth, newsletters, notices, telegrams, etc. The best method is the printed word because it can be saved for reference. Repeat—if not twice, three times—because some people misplace things. Club members are busy people. They receive lots of mail. Much of it is junk. So, if you have an important message, see that they get the word through a letter, your club's publication, bulletin boards, table tents, etc. Greater emphasis is given to a single piece of promotion received in an envelope; so, if your message is of special importance, you may want to send just the single announcement rather than bunching a group of pieces together in one mailing. Color, although expensive, adds to the impact of a mailing piece and may be well worth the additional expense. Finally, promotional mailings often generate additional response when they are sent to *both* the office and the home.

GROUND RULES

Certain ground rules should be followed in creating communiques with your members.

Clear request: Accept requests for communications, letters, bulletin board notices or whatever only from your club president, club secretary, committee chairman, or those who have been specifically authorized by the board. If a request comes from someone else, it is your responsibility as manager to clear the request with the proper authority. Before publishing or posting a notice, be sure that the person making the request has proper authorization. Never fail to closely proofread *all* mailings from the club to the membership. There may be times when you will want to check with the president and board—the tennis or golf pro may want to use club stationery and postage to announce a sale of clothes or equipment, or to write a "letter to the editor" to the local newspaper. Again, remember, if in doubt, ask for authorization. *Your club letterhead should never be used for personal mail without proper authorization.*

Know the five Ws. In every announcement you should answer the five Ws: The XYZ Club (*WHO*) cordially invites you to the President's Ball (*WHAT*) to celebrate the inauguration of the new officers and directors (*WHY*) on Saturday, February 26, 1989 (*WHEN*) at the clubhouse (*WHERE*). Also, add the *HOW:* dress—formal, $25.00 per person, RSVP by February 22.

Before you mail your monthly newsletter or a dues notice, or before you give written instructions to your staff, ask yourself, "What's missing? Is my message clear?" Ask another person, your secretary or even a club member, to read the message and then in his or her own words tell you what message you are trying to convey. You'll soon determine if part of your message has been left out and if your writing is clear and understandable.

After your message has been checked for completeness and clarity and before it is duplicated for mailing or posting, have a third person proofread it, a person other than the one who wrote it. Most publication offices have a policy requiring that every item for publication must be proofread at least three times: once before the item is set in type, again after the item has been set, and a third time on page proofs before it is printed.

Items about social events should be sent to the home of each member because the wife is usually the social secretary of a family. In addition to your club's regular events such as the New Year's Eve party, spring dance, etc., all of which should be listed on your club's "Calendar of Events," you might use a publicity "blitz" to alert your members before each major event. Mail notices at least three weeks ahead of the scheduled date so your members and you will have plenty of time to make plans for the event. Follow up with a second and a third mailing if the event has special significance or if reservations are slow in coming in. Post notices on all club bulletin boards and on menus. Use table tents in the dining areas. If reservations are still slow, encourage members of the entertainment committee to organize a phone campaign or work up individual table reservations for themselves and their friends.

Tally the responses and reservations through self-addressed acceptance cards in the invitation, or request telephone reservations so you can record the names of those who will attend the function, and the number. Include the club's phone number in the announcement in order to make it convenient for the members to call. (Sure they know it, but a reminder can't hurt.)

Many stock promotional pieces such as announcements, invitations, club calendars and informational brochures can be purchased. The number, design, format and cost of these depends on your audience and the function. A mimeographed letter will not serve as a formal invitation to the inauguration of the club's officers. On the other hand, a formal invitation is not appropriate for a western party. Stock photos and cartoons, which can be used to illustrate your announcements, may be purchased in book forms from a variety of sources, such as your local stationery store.

Seek out and use a print shop that has someone who can work closely with you in creating announcements, and who will know the best type of paper stock and the most suitable type-face for the promotional piece you are creating. Your print shop should supply you with a style book displaying the various type-faces the printer has in stock, which may be used as a reference when working on the design and layout of your promotional piece. It can be referenced to when decisions are being made by phone.

Don't overlook the new generation of typsetting equipment which has made commercial work relatively inexpensive and an in-house printing set-up within the price range of most clubs. Duplicating equipment has been improved to the extent that many print in four or five colors. Artistic posters are available at a small cost and often today adorn the bulletin boards in the locker rooms as well as the front lobby of a club.

Because of the tremendous advances being made in word processing, consider this type of equipment in order to more economically and efficiently create and get out personalized letters, announcements and other mailing pieces. There are numerous word processors on the market that have built-in vocabularies that enable an operator to check and change the spelling of thousands of words, revise a letter by inserting or deleting whole paragraphs or just a word, and then process the letter at a rate of more than 100 pages an hour while the operator is free to do other chores.

Some clubs use closed circuit television in the lobbies to show waiting diners menus and a schedule of coming events. The television set in the locker room can be used to show an up-to-date weather picture including temperature, wind speed and direction, humidity indexes and forecasts for the day and week. This could be interspersed with automatic slide shows used to entertain and inform members.

When talking with your members, again—as you do with board members—use the last name and respected form of address. Train yourself to do this. Even if members suggest you call them by their first names, stick to the last name salutation. There could be an occasion when a slip-up in using a member's first name might not only be embarrassing, but in bad taste.

It is good communication to be present at major club functions. It will help you build a good rapport with your members because your appearance makes them feel more secure, and they will feel that the manager is interested in the club and the members' well-being. However, proper training of your staff and delegation of duties should preclude the need of your being present until the functions end.

EXTERNAL COMMUNICATIONS

Working with the media: As pointed out in the first part of this discussion, some clubs encourage objective publicity in the local or even the national media because they believe it promotes the club in a favorable light and also promotes membership. Other clubs are publicity-shy and have strict policies against divulging members' names or club activities. Regardless, both kinds of clubs promote themselves, and whatever the policy of your club, as manager you will have to be diplomatic in handling your club's public relations.

John Sherry, associate professor of law at Cornell School of Hotel Administration, made the following points in a workshop sponsored by the Club Managers Association of America:

> "Media and women's groups are trying to ascertain club membership policies, particularly with respect to the denial of membership privileges to classes of persons otherwise protected by federal and state civil rights laws.
>
> "Women's groups argue that denial of membership denies women executives the business contacts essential in furthering their professional careers.
>
> "*Although the media have a Constitutionally protected right to comment upon a club's right of privacy, media may not compel you as a club member to disclose your membership policies unless such disclosure is voluntary. Once voluntary disclosure is made, the Constitutional protection is waived, meaning the media are free to pursue the matter without threat of legal recourse by you or your club.*"

In short, don't open a Pandora's box. Stick to club activities and not policies when dealing with the media.

Club promotion can be as open as advertisements for special events or memberships, or it can be as discreet as word-of-mouth information passed along from member to member to non-member. However, few are the clubs that can rely simply on a word-of-mouth information system for informing old members and attracting new. In some clubs, managers are expected to send out news releases, newsletters, club calendars and other promotion pieces to the media. The pro may be expected to call in tournament results to the media and participate in clinics. The golf superintendent may be asked by the local paper to write a column on yard care.

If your club policy encourages objective publicity, first develop a friendly relationship with members of the media with whom you'll be working. Invite them to lunch or for a game of golf from time to time. Get to know the sports editor, the editor of the society column and the others to whom you'll be sending publicity items. Ask them what they are interested in specifically, what sort of information they are looking for and will accept. Determine the format they want you to use, not overlooking the formula of the "Five Ws". Whenever you have a special super function such as the club's big anniversary dinner-dance, invite the media people and their spouses as your guests. A little favor goes a long, long way, and they might show up with a reporter or cameraman!

Keep in mind that the likelihood of your club events being published depends to a great extent on the area in which your club is located, as well as the significance of the event. In large metropolitan areas there are many demands for time and space, so very few of your club's events will be reported. In smaller communities the club probably is the hub of the town's social activities, and the media will be anxious to cover your functions.

Types of news releases that TV, radio and newspapers are interested in, are the results of your club elections (because usually the people who are elected to office are well-known community leaders and news makers), and special events such as golf, tennis or other sports that attract players from outside the area, or events open to the public. Of secondary importance are the results of your members' golf, swimming and other athletic events.

If your club holds a major event, you'll want to set up a "press room" for the media where interviews can be held with the outstanding players. You'll also want to arrange for food and beverage facilities, or use of the clubhouse; but determine with the board ahead of the event whether or not your club will compliment these services or charge cash. The various associations such as the United States Golf Association, Professional Golfers Association, Ladies' Professional Golf Association, United States Tennis Association, and the National Golf Foundation can provide information on how to handle the press during tournaments.

Favorable publicity and promotion are possible with little or no budget, and without sending out news releases. If you've done your job of cultivating the media properly, not only will they be more receptive to the club news you send them, but, very likely, your club's name will creep into their talk or writing.

If club policy permits, invite influential people outside the media world to have lunch at your club. A delicious meal warms a person and personal knowledge about the club will encourage that person to think and speak favorably about your club in the future. Often it is to the advantage of the club to have civic groups such as the Rotary Club and Lions' Club use the facilities for their weekly and monthly meetings. Not only does it keep the food operations busy during possible slack luncheon periods, but it is good publicity; and the members of these clubs are excellent potential members of your club because they are community leaders and club oriented.

There are ways of getting your club promoted objectively on TV, radio and in the newspapers. Contact the producer of a TV cooking show and offer your club's chef for a cooking demonstration. Arrange an interview between your chef and the newspaper's food editor. Offer the expertise of your golf course superintendent to talk about proper lawn care. Feature writers for newspapers are looking for human interest stories, so they would appreciate knowing about charitable events, caddie programs and banquets, swims for the handicapped, visits by your pro to hospitals or clinics given at schools, or special programs such as managerial training for employees.

If you have employees who are talented in public speaking, you might consider writing to the program chairman of your community's civic groups, since they are often seeking speakers. Get board approval in advance, then write, giving the names of your available speakers and their subjects. The topics might include the greenbelt legislation, open land policies, and what the club contributes to the local economy in taxes and payroll.

All of this constructive promotion and publicity keeps the public informed, and when the public is informed it will be supportive of the clubs. Many times clubs have poor images because of a "closed door" policy, which leads to community antagonism. Far better for a club to keep the door partially ajar than to risk the ill feelings of the community and public criticism that could lead to rezoning around the club, higher property taxes, and possibly a forced move out of the area. Newspapers, radio and TV help create a club's image in the community. If the media become part of the club's extended family, they won't attack it in editorials or commentaries, but instead will adopt a kindly attitude when reporting about the club, which will create an image that is favorable.

There are special types of paid promotion a club may want to consider in its public relations program such as advertising public-invited charitable events or tournaments. Advertising of these events will include buying spot announcements on TV and radio and space in your local papers and your area business journal or magazine. The amount you spend will depend on the importance of the event and the amount of revenue you hope to generate from the event. Where you place your ads will depend on the audience you are trying to attract. If you are trying to attract as large a crowd as possible for a golf or tennis event, you'll want to advertise in the general media—newspapers, TV and radio. If your audience goal is to reach potential members, you'll want to analyze the circulation of the various media in your area and advertise in your city's magazine, the Chamber of Commerce magazine, or possibly the publication put out by your local city club if you manage a golf club, or a golf club if you manage a city club. Through publications of this type you'll reach a greater number of business leaders who can afford club memberships, and people who are the most interested in joining clubs.

DIRECTOR OF COMMUNICATIONS

A club manager's responsibilities are much like those of the director of a cruise ship. A manager wears many hats and he is responsible for many of the activities in a club—the food and beverage operations, the sports facilities and the entertainment events. A good public relations program should continually stimulate activities in all of the areas of the club. No detail should be left untouched. Integrate promotion for one event with publicity for another. An announcement on the locker room bulletin board should inform the club athletes about the up-coming dinner dance; the bulletin board in the lobby should list future sports events. Every opportunity should be used to call your members' attention to coming events in all areas of the club.

Few clubs have a static membership. It is constantly shifting and changing and with these changes come different interests. Thus, periodic surveys through a written questionnaire should be made to determine these changes. Membership studies are good morale boosters because they get your members involved and then indicate to the members that the club is interested in their likes and dislikes.

Membership studies can backfire, so be careful how the questions are worded. Phrase your questions in general terms, and don't get into costs. Don't make promises you can't keep. When the questionnaires have been tallied, communicate the results to your membership.

The results of your membership survey can be used in several ways. Your committees can use the results of the study to plan their progress so they appeal to the greatest number of members. Questions asking for biographical information should provide you with the names and ages of spouses and children, residential and business addresses, telephone numbers and special interests of the family members. This information is helpful if you send a birthday invitation to your members for a free lunch or dinner, and when planning special parties, or considering new and additional facilities. It's helpful if you want to know if a member's children are old enough to order alcoholic drinks; or if they are old enough to use the sports facilities; or who should get announcements of specialized instructional classes. It could be helpful when one of the members parks a car blocking the entrance or drive!

Membership participation in club functions is a delicate thing, and if it falls off there are a number of things a manager and the board can do to correct this. Using the membership study as a basis, committees can be appointed to better plan club events and pre-plan events on the agenda. Committee members, assisted by management, should provide the agenda and at the meetings ask some baited questions in order to start the members thinking. Implement plans for social functions for men, for women, for men and women, for families, for teenagers, and special membership groups like the under-forty group.

If you manage a downtown club, you may find your members totally absorbed in their suburban living, which could be disastrous. Consider their needs. Provide functions and services that will motivate them to come downtown. Add valet parking. Theatre nights. Football trips. Parties featuring a free cocktail hour. The race track. If you don't have enough parking space, make arrangements with a nearby garage or parking lot, so when members return from a club-sponsored trip and stop to pick up their cars, they'll probably pop in for nightcaps. Provide the means and your members will probably respond.

Once you have your members returning for club functions, or if your party attendance is good, keep them coming back. Get a camera. Possibly a Polaroid, or one of the new models that are self-focusing, self-setting with a built-in flash, and so simple to operate that they even advance the film to the next frame after the exposure is made. Take pictures at parties and tables filled with members. Snap a picture of the widow member who comes in only once a month or so. Play up your house residents, the birthday and anniversary party. The bride during her reception. Post the finished prints on your lobby bulletin board. Almost everyone wants his or her picture taken, and your members will soon start coming to the club more often just to see themselves on the picture display. Now capitalize. Publish the better pictures in your club bulletin, but don't publish the ones where you might have caught a member off guard (it could be embarrassing to the member and you). Have one of your office staff or one of the waiters or even a "volunteer" member take the pictures. Almost anyone can learn to operate the new cameras.

Through photographs you're making your club functions visible. Although pictures focus on the past, members reading your club bulletin are seeing the results today and will be interested in what's going to happen tomorrow.

Buy or rent a movie camera and projector or a video recorder and player. During the year take shots at your various functions. You can build an entire party around these historical films which should result in a sold-out house.

As you develop these programs, you'll find more and more members interested in what's going on at your club, members who will become active in club functions. You'll be flooded with suggestions of what to do and when to do it. Listen carefully. Adopt and implement the better ideas and shelve others for the future. Never discard ideas, but file them for future reference.

Welcome complaints as constructive criticism and accept them graciously. Listen attentively. Keep in mind that the member registering the complaint is just as interested in his or her club as the person who doesn't complain. If the complaint is about service or someone under your jurisdiction, a complaint that you would ordinarily handle, thank the person making the complaint and do something about it. If the complaint is about something that requires board action, ask the person to please put it in the form of a letter so you can take it up with the board. You'll find that when you take care of a legitimate complaint you'll have a better club member, and a person who will probably be one of your boosters and a better supporter of the club. Accept the fact that many complaints arise because the member is unfamiliar with all of the club's policies and procedures.

The range of public relations and promotion is far reaching. Many of your members are also members of other clubs. Many of the friends of your members are members of other clubs. As word gets around about the great club functions your club sponsors, more and more people will become interested in becoming members of your club. This indirect selling may even stimulate other clubs to increase their events.

NEW IDEAS

New ideas! Where do they come from? How do you find them?

There's an old saying that there's nothing new—only new applications of old ideas. This is true in any business, and especially true in the profession of club management.

However, nothing is so uninteresting as an old idea merely warmed over. So, be on a constant lookout for ideas to which you can add a new application. Few of us are eternally creative or original, so look for techniques used by other clubs or businesses that can be used at your club.

Stroll through a supermarket and note how the grocers merchandise their products. Can you use one of their display ideas for your Sunday buffet? Or to sell more desserts? Or wine? Or can you use their idea of a "loss leader" to attract more of your members?

Check the discount and department stores to learn how they feature their special items, or their sale items. Could you offer a "sale" price on a menu clip-on? Or possibly on one or two of your menu items? Or a special drink?

Study advertisements to learn how various companies promote their products. Could you "borrow" one of their headlines to use in a mailing piece to tell members that your dining room is "not just another restaurant, but something special for special people?"

Study the fliers you receive from airline and travel companies. Does one of them give you an idea for a different type of entertainment program, a different and unusual menu item? Or possibly an exotic dessert?

Is it possible to borrow an idea from the cigarette companies that use attractive young women to hand out free samples to passerbys.

Look to the radio and TV for ideas. Listen to the way announcers work in commercials between music and drama. Could you follow their format on your club's PA system?

Examine the ads in your special management magazine and other food service publications. Are there some unusual items advertised that you can add to your menu that will attract your members to dine at your club? That will set off your club's menu from the menu of your competitor down the street?

Examine church bulletins and trade association newsletters. Visit other club managers, the daily fee courses. Exchange your club publication with other clubs.

Attend your association's annual meetings and talk with your peers. Sign up for CMAA workshops where you'll find many ideas you can use.

Whenever you find an idea that offers even the slightest possibility, make a note or tear it out of a magazine or letter and put it in your "idea file." Every manager should have such a file where he keeps every idea he comes across for ready reference.

New ideas are like the air—they're everywhere just waiting for someone to recognize them and put them to use. No one will hand you an idea and tell you how to use it. But somewhere, someplace or from someone you'll find an idea that with a little innovation may fit your problem to a "T". Be brave enough to try ideas never used at your club before. Keep an open, inquisitive mind and you'll find ideas popping out at you from the most unexpected places.

Keep an open mind when talking with your members and your staff. Communications go both ways, from sender to receiver and back again. Solicit feedback from both members and staff.

Your club records should provide you with information as to how your members use the many facilities of your club. Your sales analysis should indicate what the majority of your members prefer in the way of entrees so you can work out menus with your chef that will appeal to the greatest number, and will feature the most preferred items. The golf staff should be able to tell you how many rounds of golf were played each month and each day of the month so you can determine why play is dropping off or increasing. Your records of the use of the swimming pool will indicate the most popular days and hours—and whether a party held at poolside was a success.

Reports from your athletic director should tell you about the use of the gym, the exercise room and classes, the running track, etc. Your records should include information about the tennis courts, food operations, bars and other function areas of the club so you can direct your concern to specific problems and intelligently discuss with the board the need for new equipment or enlarged facilities. Do you need new or additional exercise equipment? Is your kitchen too small to take care of the many additional diners your promotions have generated? Is your 20-year old pool without a wading pool inadequate for today's membership, or should the club simply wait for the children to grow up?

These are problems for the board to decide, but as manager you should bring these problems to the attention of the board and be prepared to make recommendations. Don't wait for your membership to seriously decline.

Communications is a never-ending job, but it is a job that's rewarding. Good communications will help provide the lubricant that will make for a more efficient, understanding, and outstanding staff. Good communications will provide one of the keys that build harmonious relations between the club manager and his board. Good communications will help build a better rapport between management and the club's members.

Good communications will help build a better understanding and acceptance of the club by the community.

Most important, good communications will help build a winner. And it's fun, exciting and exhilarating to build a winner.

REVIEW QUESTIONS

1. What are the five W's of good communication?
2. How will most of your communicating be conducted concerning your membership?
3. What types of written and oral communications should be provided to club personnel?
4. What methods could be used to focus attention and participation on special club events?
5. What type of information should be given to the media? What type should not be given?

9

Recreational Sports Programs

Cherry Hills Country Club, Denver, Colorado

People join private clubs for many reasons; among these is the desire to share social pleasures and enjoy recreational opportunities with friends. Specifically, recreational opportunities in the form of various sports activities often motivate people to become members of private clubs. Contemporary emphasis on physical fitness and health and body building, together with people's natural desire to participate and to compete, means that the active sportsperson may well play golf and tennis and swim in warm months, play platform tennis, iceskate, ski, or snowmobile during cold weather and, at any time of year, with friends who enjoy sports, he may bowl, play handball, squash, or racquetball.

America today is a society of "doers." Spectator sports of a few years ago may well be participatory sports now. Leisure time, better understanding of sports through school physical education programs, television, and actual practice (sometimes resulting from more travel to snow areas for skiing or to the sunbelt for golf in the winter) have promoted interest and generated the desire to participate in several sports within a given season.

Today's club must provide more than one participatory sports facility or activity to satisfy members' wishes and athletic needs. In fact, clubs should offer as many choices as are economically feasible; however, best use of land or available building space can limit these choices. Market and feasibility studies should be made and carefully analyzed before funds are committed for new facilities and caution should be exercised when planning club expansion to provide a new sports activity that may be of interest to only a small group of members. Any sports facility that is not enthusiastically supported will soon lose favor with the club's governing body which approves its operating budget. Then, again, a new sports activity may create new interest and thus increase membership.

Clubs with sports programs will need someone to oversee all sports departments—perhaps the club manager will serve, or it could be *an athletic director* responsible just for recreational management. After describing the duties of the club manager with regard to club sports, this chapter discusses management of specific sports activities.

If a club chooses to have a diversified sports and/or recreational program, serious consideration should be given to adding an athletic director to the staff. This trained professional can be of tremendous assistance to the club manager in scheduling and supervising the club's sports program. In selecting the athletic director, club managers should attempt to get a person who is "multi-talented." He or she should: have a sound knowledge of how to implement physical fitness programs, preferably be experienced in aquatics, and be skilled in the sports to be offered at the club, i.e., racquetball, squash, handball, badminton, volleyball and basketball. The athletic director can be charged with hiring full- and part-time assistants needed to carry out the programs.

DUTIES OF THE CLUB MANAGER IN RECREATIONAL MANAGEMENT

The role of the club manager in recreational management is typically one of coordination rather than of specific leadership. However, this can also depend upon the size and type of club the manager is managing. In small clubs, the manager may be required to more often market the recreational facilities on his own rather than have the tennis professional, golf professional or athletic director take that leadership role. In larger clubs where a staff of recreational professionals is present, the manager's role changes to that of coordination between the departments rather than devising, supervising and organizing specific athletic recreational endeavours.

Small Clubs

As so often happens in clubs with small membership or limited financial resources, the club manager himself must oversee the basic recreational areas other than golf. Here he becomes an operator rather than a manager. Areas he may oversee include the operation of the swimming pool, tennis courts, any summer programs for junior members, day camp, etc., and the recreational rooms which may include billiards, pool, bowling, dance instruction and beach and boating activity. Many small clubs will have one or more of each of these areas that the club manager must be knowledgeable of and have the time available to develop the programs properly. Few good management people are seldom expected, or required, to know all the rules and details of any recreational or sports activity. However, he/she should have a good working knowledge of that activity and preferably have participated in it from time to time. With the many "caps" that a club manager of a small club has to wear, it can sometimes be difficult to supervise and promote extra activities. With no specific professional and/or assistant manager to monitor the activities of these particular areas, it sometimes becomes important that the manager participate with the members in order to better understand their needs. The manager's participation, of course, can come under criticism, but the successful professional club manager can limit his activities while participating with members. He should never prohibit another member from participating because of lack of space, equipment, etc. One objective should be kept in mind by the manager at all times—the monitoring of that recreational activity to give him the management capability to plan for the future for those activities that the members need.

Assuming that the manager has a good reading of the pulse of the club for these extracurricular recreational activities, he should be able to staff these activities adequately. On many occasions small clubs' members so often feel that once an activity is established it can generally run itself. However, successful programs of any type must be monitored and supervised by a professional or the manager. For instance, the committees, board or the ownership must be given proper feedback on the cost of these recreational activities so that they can be handled to the best of the club's ability. Proper budgets should be established so that the club can keep up the facilities, the equipment and the supervision of said activity. Rules and regulations should be recommended by the committee and then be approved by the Board of Governors or ownership for posting in that activity's location. These rules and regulations can obviously help avoid problems that may develop between members and participants at a later date. It also establishes the time of operation and gives the manager the opportunity to see that proper housekeeping is given prior to and after opening hours.

Managers of small clubs can also be faced with the marketing and promotion of these recreational activities. Generally, this can be done through the manager's secretary or, preferably, assistant manager. The club's activities must constantly be resold to the members and they must be reminded of those activities that the club wishes to provide. Swimming lessons, bridge instructions, tennis tournaments must be publicized well in advance in order to expect good participation. Generally, the recreational activity of club managers in areas other than golf and tennis do not generate large amounts of revenue. However, they can become very necessary for the well being of non-athletic members to those members who, because of some physical disability, may not be able to participate in the more active sports. Proper development of these programs and the direction these programs take must be handled by the club manager. To some degree he is responsible for evaluating the membership's needs. For instance, are the spouses of many of the members active in bridge? Although very little financial revenue can be gained from bridge parties, the participation by the spouse can strengthen the position of the small club in the eyes of the community and its own members. In addition, it can create, if timed properly, additional revenues for luncheon and dinner. It can also heighten the activity of the member through participation in the afternoon or evening as mixed couples bridge events, etc. Other recreational activity such as lectures, ladies teas, demonstrations, tournaments in billiards, bowling, etc. can sometimes satisfy the needs of certain select groups of members who may not otherwise be served by golf, tennis, boating, etc. While the manager need not concentrate all of his efforts on these smaller activities, when regularly scheduled well in advance, the manager can plan the time to handle these activities properly and give those members a feeling of belonging to their own club.

Large Clubs

The role of the manager in recreational management in a large club changes considerably from one of operating to one of managing. In most cases, the manager has specific professionals that handle each named activity. The golf professional is generally a member of the Professional Golfers Association (PGA) and should be competent enough to run that program's activities. Through the PGA he/she receives much instruction on shop merchandising, personnel, marketing and, of course, the art of administering golf lessons and tournaments. The tennis professional is generally a member of the United States Lawn Tennis Association (USLTA) and also receives instruction and direction from his own professional association in the same general areas that the golf professional does.

Another professional that may work with the club manager is the athletic director. In many large clubs, his job would include the administering of programs of racquetball, squash, badminton, volleyball, basketball, exercise equipment, health and nutrition seminars and housekeeping of his own facility.

On many occasions the athletic director will also supervise the activities of the swimming pool and aquatic programs or a special aquatic manager may be hired for that purpose.

In the instance of a larger club, the club manager takes a separate route of managing. Here he is not so finely attuned to operating the specific programs that are offered, but more to the proper administering of these programs for the betterment of the membership. In most cases at a larger club, these recreational managers—golf, tennis, athletic, yachting, etc.—may answer directly to the manager. His job now takes on more responsibility in that he must manage these individual professionals. Specifically, he must see that they are administering their budgets properly, insure that complaints are directed to the proper committee, and insure that overlapping tournaments, programs and activities between departments do not conflict. This last area can be tremendously important when preparing the annual sports and recreational programs scheduled for the membership. A master calendar of events must be put together to insure that to the best of the club's ability, no two major programs or tournaments are scheduled at the same time. If not, then participation can be lowered, revenues can be significantly affected and dissatisfaction among the members can result.

In this specific case the manager must set deadlines for each recreational and sports department professional to submit a request for specific programs/tournaments. It is here that the manager takes a major role in leadership.

Additionally, during so many club sporting recreational events, food and beverage activity can also be planned. If these professionals agree, the entry fees to these programs and tournaments can include food and beverage. This automatically insures the club of food and beverage revenue that may not have otherwise been realized. It also promotes the image of the club as being a complete facility without the need for outside catering.

A final and most important area in the role of the club manager in recreational management is one of housekeeping and repair and maintenance. On so many occasions the manager is relied upon to provide these services although he may not be on the premises on a daily or hourly basis. Good housekeeping can also be beneficial in promoting the image of the club. Clean and tidy public areas give members a feeling of pride and enjoyment in the use of the club.

The active sports areas such as tennis and golf generally require large locker rooms. While the assignment of lockers may be completed by the sports professional, the manager may be charged with assigning lockers and conducting the general housekeeping in that locker room area. The basic knowledge of health and sanitation rules and close attention to day-to-day housekeeping can prevent many problems and enhance the club's prestige. Through budgeting of certain toiletry items and towels, adequate supplies can be provided for the convenience of the member and his guest. Uniformed housekeeping personnel who can be attentive to the member's needs can create a feeling of true relaxation for the member.

The manager must also pay close attention to the heavier needs of repair and maintenance by providing the continued quality upkeep of a facility that was originally intended for the membership. Proper annual budgeting for repair and maintenance can prevent the need for major renovation or restoration. It is here that generally the manager's input is paramount to the members' investment. Proper selections of replacement carpets, tiles, counter tops, tables and seating fabrics can all play an important part in the type of recreational sport facility being used. Obviously spike resistent carpet must be placed in the men's and ladies' locker room areas. Nonskid tiles must be present in both golf and nongolf locker rooms to prevent slipping in both the shower and the lavatory areas. Proper temperatures must be maintained in jacuzzis, whirlpools, saunas and steamroom operations. An efficient and knowledgeable maintenance staff is highly necessary here to assist the manager in insuring these proper temperatures are maintained. As future repair and maintenance can be directly related to these proper temperatures, the manager once again becomes involved because of overall revenue impact upon the club's entire budget. Some recreational facilities can be a tremendous drain on the energy budget each year. Close management monitoring of these areas can prevent serious financial problems.

The final area that the club manager can become involved in recreational management is the proper *forecasting* of recreational and sports activity. In close coordination with the Board of Directors or ownership of the club, the manager must have adequate feedback from each of the sport professionals and managers on activities in their area. Proper records must be maintained by each sports manager to monitor these activities over an annual basis for long-range planning.

While the general manager concept, as discussed in other chapters of this book, may not work in all clubs, it is at least necessary that the club manger have a good working relationship and understanding with the proper recreational/sports professional in order to achieve a maximum in services for members' pleasure. The lack of communication between the club manager and recreational/sports manager can only result in less professional programs for the members and uncomfortable atmosphere for the employees. The club manager must be looked upon in this particular case as a coordinator for all activities.

MANAGING THE GOLF PROGRAM

The private club's golf committee and greens and grounds committee establish policy, approve budgets, and review the standards of day-to-day golf operations. The club must employ properly trained and experienced professionals for all aspects of the complex assignment of managing the golf program.

To provide the services the membership desires, certain information must be gathered and analyzed. The data should include the following:

1. Number of golfing members in the club.
   a. Number of men, women, and juniors.
   b. Number of members playing more than fifteen rounds each golf season.
   c. Number of guest rounds per season.
2. Total number of rounds played annually and by the month.
3. Number of months the golf shop will be open. Whether the golf merchandise will be a concession of the golf professional or the golf shop will be operated as a club department.
4. Number of lessons given annually.

The answers to the foregoing questions provide information about members' use of the facility and thereby permit certain judgments to be made regarding departmental budget requirements. Additionally, the data greatly assist the club manager, golf course superintendent, and golf professional in forecasting their staff requirements and planning golf and social activities. The data also indicate member satisfaction.

A well-conceived and well-developed golf program, designed and presented for the enjoyment of club members, is the result of cooperative efforts of the golf course superintendent, the golf professional, and the club manager.

Golf Course Superintendent

Qualifications: Special qualifications of the superintendent vary depending on the club's size, its standards of excellence, and its terrain. However, every golf course superintendent should have a degree from one of the many recognized and accredited schools of agronomy. Receiving the degree is one important step in a customary sequence of events, described briefly as follows: the typical superintendent probably acquired his first work experience as a young person employed on a golf course during the summer. Then he would have entered an agronomy school and, after earning a degree, would have spent two or three years more as an assistant under the tutelage of a seasoned superintendent. Then he would be ready to become superintendent of his own course.

The superintendent must have management and organizational capabilities. He must be able to get work done through others; he must be able to delegate work among his staff. In so doing, he will seek the most qualified person for each assigned task. (The ability to make good assignments, of course, requires extensive experience in all the work required and performed by each member of the club's grounds department.)

Responsibilities for Land and Plants

The golf course superintendent is responsible for maintenance of all the club's land and plants. How much land do clubs have? A nine-hole golf course requires 60 to 100 acres, and an eighteen-hole course requires 120 to 160 acres, but many clubs have much more acreage than these minimum course requirements. The golf course superintendent is also responsible for the additional acreage required for tennis courts, a driving range, swimming pool, platform tennis courts, access roads, and parking lots. He might develop unused land into a sod nursery or tree nursery (an acceptable and economical method of providing for sod or tree replacement.) He might leave some unused land in its natural state, to serve as a bird refuge; or he could develop an arboretum in conjunction with a nature trail—perhaps boasting of all the trees native to the state and providing an excellent ecology program for any club.

The golf course superintendent takes care of the club's trees, shrubs, cacti, and flowers on the golf course and club grounds, and works to mold the natural elements of grass, trees, rock formations, hills, ravines, streams, lakes, or ponds into a beautiful golf course. These duties are important because the serenity and natural beauty of a golf course add immeasurably to the golfer's enjoyment of the game. Without the aesthetic value of a beautiful and well-groomed golf course, the game would be far less appealing.

The superintendent must understand the golfer's viewpoint about playing conditions of the golf course. There can be great differences of opinion on standards, and the wise grounds committee sets reasonable, long-range standards for its superintendent. For example, it is virtually impossible and impractical to make greens play fast one week and slow the next. Placement of the pin (the flag marking the hole on each golf green) should be challenging, but not impossible. An experienced superintendent will have his staff place the pin to challenge the golfer, but not to penalize him.

Maintaining the Golf Course: The superintendent makes his contribution to the club's golf program by keeping the course in the best possible playing condition at all times. The superintendent should consider the golf schedule carefully before undertaking any procedure that will inconvenience his golfing members. However, he must, occasionally, ask for cooperation and understanding when it is necessary to perform inconvenient procedures, such as aerifying greens, tees, and even fairways, to loosen compaction. Immediately after aerification, golf balls do not run true, and the appearance of the course is adversely affected—but the result is improved turf.

The golf course superintendent must constantly monitor the environment for changes that will affect his golf course. An infestation of insects attacking either the turf or trees can be properly dealt with if it is noticed and stopped before irreparable damage is done. (Golf course superintendents must be licensed to apply pesticides. See the chapter on taxes and regulations for details.) Likewise, extremely hot and dry conditions can reduce lush fairways and greens to stubble in a matter of hours if immediate corrective action is not taken. During the critical growing season and in seasons of extreme weather conditions, the golf course superintendent and his staff must pay constant attention to their golf course.

It is highly desirable to have a forester on the golf course superintendent's staff. A forester is trained to take care of both weak and healthy trees and other plants, know how to prune, guy weak limbs, and provide the nutrients and proper soil composition for the plants and trees under his care. (Biologists and nursery researchers are constantly developing hardy plants and trees that will adapt to extreme conditions.) Proper care by professional foresters increases the value of the club's trees and shrubs and adds to their beauty and long life.

Besides caring for grounds and plants, the superintendent's staff maintains all required mechanical equipment used in their daily work. Such equipment often costs more than $100,000. The Golf Course Superintendents Association of America (GCSAA) has prepared a list of suggested equipment for maintenance of nine- and eighteen-hole golf courses. National Golf Foundation Information Sheet GC-3 also lists the various pieces of equipment.

It is extremely important that rigid preventive maintenance standards be observed and that broken equipment be repaired immediately to protect the club's investment. Down time or the unavailability of needed equipment can hamper daily work or delay special projects. Equipment kept in good working order will be treated well, but workers forced to use damaged tools might harm the equipment even further.

Professional Associations: The Golf Course Superintendents Association of America is the professional association representing its members and is devoted to continuing education for its members. The association runs a certification program and most country club superintendents take great pride in receiving this certification. Most superintendents are Class A members of the GCSAA.

Golf Professional

Golf is a friendly, competitive game, requiring concentration, a degree of physical ability and stamina. A golfer scoring his best game experiences a real feeling of achievement, but very few golfers who play well, score well, and understand the game are self-taught.

The objective of the club's head golf professional is to manage the club's golf program to the members' satisfaction. Nearly everything the professional does relates to his members' playing ability or to their enjoyment of the sport. Most club professionals will be heavily engaged in:

1. Teaching.
2. Conducting member golf tournaments.
3. Managing the business interests of the golf shop.
4. Providing services and a friendly atmosphere for golf enjoyment.

Teaching

Club members expect excellence and proven teaching methods of a club professional. He probably uses one particular method more than others, but would not restrict his teaching exclusively to one method. The student's physical stature, ability, strength, and age are all factors the professional considers as he teaches. His methodology changes with the characteristics of the students, and even with the degree of student receptivity.

Conducting Tournaments: Administering club golf tournaments begins with determining the kind of tournament to be played. In addition to the prestigious Club Companionship, other tournaments may include Better-Ball Twosome, Best-Ball Foursome (with low net and low gross), Aggregate Low-Net Twosome, Beat the Club Pro, Father-Son, Father-Daughter, Mother-Son, Mother-Daughter, Guest-Day Invitational, and Holiday Tournaments (e.g., on July 4, Memorial Day, Labor Day).

The head golf professional sets up procedures for each event. His planning involves pairings (entering players with similar abilities on the same team) and determining the method to compute the winner. When the club officials and golf professionals have established all the details, the tournament director (a member of the professional's staff) is put in charge to implement the format agreed upon.

Assigning caddies to players, fastening bags to assigned golf carts, starting players on the tees at prescribed intervals, posting individual and team scores on the scoreboard, and recording scores in the official record books are administrative tasks often delegated to the professional's staff. Since the staff can handle these important and necessary duties, the professional is free for other responsibilities, such as refereeing the tournament.

As referee, the professional must be an expert on the rules of golf as approved by the United States Golf Association (USGA) and The Royal and Ancient Golf Club of St. Andrews, Scotland. (The USGA annually prints a booklet on the rules of golf. Copies are available in most golf shops or from the United States Golf Association, Golf House, Fairhills, N.J. 07931.)

Managing the Golf Shop: Managing the club golf shop is a very important part of the head golf professional's duties. Besides being the sales room for all golf-oriented merchandise, the shop is the hub of communication for all golf activity as well as being the golf professional's office.

The sale of golf merchandise requires the golf professional to be an entrepreneur. He must purchase merchandise for resale, price the merchandise properly, account for sales, control the inventory, file governmentally required reports (i.e., state sales and business income taxes), and keep the merchandise displayed attractively. In short, he is operating a retail golf store.

Golf shop staff must be trained to know the merchandise and to assist purchasers. As the golf professional's sales representatives, they must have a courteous, helpful manner and know about the day's activities as well as those scheduled for the future.

Some private clubs operate the golf shop rather than offer the risk and reward to their professional. In such an instance, the club becomes the retailer and operates the golf shop. The arrangement may be very attractive to a young, beginning golf professional lacking the capital to stock the inventory required for the club golf shop.

Member Relations: The head golf professional represents the club's golf program to members—he is constantly encouraging members to play and enjoy golf and he trains his staff to assure a friendly atmosphere in the golf shop. For its part, the staff reports constructive criticism to help strengthen the golf program and passes on suggestions to make golf more enjoyable for members.

One of the golf professional's greatest contributions to the game is his example as a gentleman and a golfer. Extending common courtesy to all people on the club staff, being strict but fair with the caddies, and following all the club rules are behavior patterns club members should see in their golf professional. He also educates the members by example—when he replaces divots, lifts ball marks on the greens, and rakes the traps.

The work of the golf professional and his staff consists of using their professional abilities to meet the needs of the playing members and to support the club's golf program. Since there are only a few all-male golf clubs, the programs of most golf or country clubs include events that encourage all family members to participate. For example, as consultant to club committees, the golf professional will recommend tourneys for the Sunday Mixed-Foursome Program. These events are held so that men and women can play golf together in tournaments and then enjoy whatever social function follows the game. This might be an informal dinner in the clubhouse, an outside barbecue, or simply cocktails while waiting for the field to finish and the winner to be determined.

Women's golf programs are varied in type of tournament play. A certain day of the week is designated Women's Day; only women may use the golf course on the morning of that day.

Junior golf is also encouraged as another part of the program. (A junior, for purposes of club events and rules, is a member's child under a certain age—usually eighteen years.) Clinics or group lessons are set up as needed, based on the number of club juniors. The golf professional and his assistants teach swing classes and golf/golf course etiquette and conduct junior tournaments. These tournaments provide competitive experience for juniors and require entrants to learn golf and tournament rules. Participation in these wholesome events has great appeal for juniors and is encouraged by their parents.

Professional Associations: Most golf professionals are members of the Professional Golfers' Association (PGA), which trains and certifies its members. The PGA certification program protects clubs and golfers using the services of a professional from incompetence. The PGA Class A professional has met rigid association requirements during a prescribed apprenticeship. All apprentices must pass PGA Business School I and II. Between the two courses the apprentices must take a playing ability test—a thirty-six hole exam that must be graded by a PGA Class A member—to be eligible to enroll in Business School II.

The golf professional is primarily concerned with activity at his club; most of his time is spent at the club, teaching and administering the golf program. However, he may play in local, state, or regional tournaments. A "touring professional" will have a retainer clause in his contract stipulating that he will be at the club a certain number of days per year; he spends the rest of his time on the professional tour, representing the name of his club. A "bench professional" is usually an older, retired club or touring professional who is basically a custom golf club maker. He designs and custom-makes clubs carrying his name. There are very few bench professionals left in North America.

Professional Interaction: The successful administration of a club's golf program demands cooperation, communication, and preplanning. In addition to carrying out their own responsibilities, the golf professional, golf course superintendent, and club manager should pass on to their colleagues the suggestions, constructive criticism, and comments from club members as well as their own observations.

The manager, the golf professional, and the golf course superintendent must have high regard for each other's professional expertise. An amicable relationship among the three will benefit the golf program as they work toward a common goal of membership satisfaction.

MANAGING THE TENNIS PROGRAM

A private club's tennis program is best designed after a study of its full membership profile. The ages of adult members as well as ages of the children are important planning factors. The tennis program is designed to help members learn the game and develop proper technique and to provide an activity involving social interaction.

A tennis professional keeps these elements in mind in designing a program for the total membership. Most private club tennis players play for fun and to enjoy the company of friends. For the most part, they want to play well, but they are not seeking to be world-class players.

Juniors

Junior tennis instruction is potentially the most rewarding, satisfying and challenging opportunity that a tennis professional has while managing a club tennis program. Additionally, it is considered the most important program in the eyes of the parents (club members). Therefore, it should be a priority for each professional.

The junior program should be planned on a twelve month basis and should offer classes to all levels of players from the beginner to the nationally ranked tournament player. Classes for beginners, advanced beginners and intermediate players should be offered on a continued basis throughout the year in a number of sessions. At the end of each session, a skill test can be given to enable students to advance as they improve. Each session serves to motivate the students as well as serve as a means of forming new groups for the next series of classes.

A ratio of four students per tennis professional or assistant professional is suggested. A mini-tennis class for youngsters up to age eight serves as an introductory program that teaches coordination, rules of the game, and court courtesy and responsibility. Group drills, group clinics, and private lessons improve individual skills and deepen interest. The junior program is designed to encourage participation. Challenge ladders offer the opportunity to measure the ability of individuals in a group. The club tournament is the culmination of the season's tennis activity.

Summer is an excellent time to offer complete beginner and advanced beginner classes since children are out of school and have more time to learn a new sport or simply brush up on techniques they previously developed. These classes should be geared primarily to the basics of serve and groundstrokes with emphasis on developing an interest in and enjoyment of the game.

These lessons should be in a series of clinics with four students per one tennis professional or assistant professional. A typical series would be three weeks long with each class meeting twice a week for one hour each lesson.

Summer tennis camp for the intermediate and advanced junior players should be a major part of the junior program. These lessons would also be conducted within a group format with the 4 to 1 student/professional ratio. A typical club day camp could run for a three-week period offering instruction two hours a day, Tuesday through Friday.

Tennis camp programs for intermediate and advanced junior players attract the more serious players as a general rule. Therefore, the instruction should not be limited to the basics of serve and groundstokes, but also provide instruction on volleys, overheads, lobs, dropshots, half-volleys, spins (topspin and backspin), singles and doubles strategy, etc. Though most instruction would be done in groups, the additional time allowed in a camp format provides more time towards individual attention.

It should be noted that the professional should be prepared and well versed in the use of advanced teaching aids such as ball machines and video equipment to complement all instructional programs. To foster further interest in tennis from the junior players, the professional should encourage competition at all levels with challenge ladders, leagues, round robins, and tournaments as often as possible.

It is also wise to involve adult club members in as many of the junior activities as possible in an effort to develop and provide support for the junior players. It is important to plan junior events well in advance to avoid conflicting schedules when they begin competing for limited court time.

The most sophisticated aspect of the overall junior program would be designing programs for junior tournament players and aspiring tournament players. As complex as the junior tournament system has become, maintaining a successful tournament players program is often considered a separate job in itself. It requires year-round attention to the players' training and tournament competition. It is not within the scope of this material to outline a complete program for developing junior champions. Therefore, it should suffice to say that qualified assistant professionals are required to carry on many of the aspects of such a program. A single club professional would not have enough time to handle this program separately and still deal with the other responsibilities as a director of tennis.

Junior tournaments are played in the following categories:

Boys	**Girls**
18 and under	*18 and under*
Winner	Winner
Runner-up	Runner-up
16 and under	16 and under
14 and under	14 and under
12 and under	12 and under
10 and under	10 and under

The winners should be recognized at an end-of-the-season awards dinner to which all club members should be invited. Trophies or medals are awarded to the winners of all tournaments. A "most improved player" award can also be given to honor the young person who has made a special effort to achieve excellence in skill and technique. The person receiving that award may or may not have been a tournament winner, but must have worked extremely hard to have earned it.

Another award that helps the professional promote discipline, good citizenship, and responsibility is one for sportsmanship. The criteria for the most-improved player and sportsmanship awards can be flexible and should be difficult but attainable; they should not be diluted to the level of a popularity contest.

Club members are particularly pleased to have their children enrolled in the club's tennis program. Besides helping achieve, improve, or maintain physical fitness, the tennis program offers daily practice in the more sophisticated skills of coordination, depth perception, judgement, and ability to get along with others.

Adults

In addition to the junior tennis program, an active adult program must be offered and encouraged. Programs should include ladies' day, ladies' leagues, ladies' group clinics, twilight mixed doubles, and men's group round robins. The adult tournaments will include:

Men's Singles
Women's Singles
Men's Doubles
Women's Doubles
Mixed Doubles
Father-Son Doubles
Mother-Daughter Doubles

The adult programs are generally not as complex as the junior programs at most clubs. Most lessons can still be handled successfully in a group setting with the 4 to 1 ratio, however, there is often a greater demand for private lessons from the adults than from the junior players.

A series of lessons should be offered for the various levels covering the different aspects of the game from stroke production to strategy. Summer clinics and camps may be successful with the adult players as well, provided the interest is high.

To create a keen interest is the most important side of adult programming. The development of competition beyond that of a social nature is vital to the ongoing success of a club program. This competition gives the adult player a reason to use the club tennis facilities to the maximum. The most simple means of creating this competitive spirit is with league play, both within the club and against other clubs. In addition, round robins, member-guest tournaments and club championship tournaments are also important to the adult players. These events, however, should be designed for more social play to balance out the club's tennis program.

The Tennis Professional

The committee that is assigned to select the club tennis professional should first determine the qualifications needed in their particular club's professional. For example, a club with many junior members will need a professional specially qualified to organize a junior program. Or it might need a professional with a lot of patience and skill to reach beginning swing classes. Teaching the strokes to develop coordination and body conditioning would not be as important in a club whose members had been playing tennis for several years. Therefore, the tennis committee should know the level of ability of the majority of the club members; whether there is a need for a strong junior program; and whether there is a need for superlative instruction.

The membership profile helps the committee analyze the data on the club's tennis needs. Each club has its own mixture of members: some with children, some without children—these members range in ages from young couples to older couples. The profile should guide the selection committee in seeking the tennis professional with the background skills needed by that particular club.

The tennis professional, like the other sports professionals, must be able to get along with others. He/she must deal fairly with club members and employees; as a disciplinarian, he/she must command respect; must practice professional ethics; and his/her character must be above reproach. The tennis professional's work is highly skilled; as indicated:

1. Supervises and gives tennis lessons to members during the summer. In a climate with cooler but not snowy winters, he/she supervises and instructs in the winter.
2. May administer and organize club tennis tournaments.
3. May formulate and enforce club tennis procedure for play on club courts.
4. Gives advice on proper selection and care of equipment.
5. May coach club tennis and platform tennis team.
6. Directs pro shop sales manager and salespersons who do the ordering, selling, and bookkeeping for tennis equipment and clothing.
7. May string tennis racquets and make other light equipment repairs.
8. Advises tennis court maintenance personnel on needs and care of courts.
9. May officiate at tournament play.

10. Should be responsible for supervising the maintenance, general appearance and cleanliness of the tennis courts, pro shop and tennis grounds.
11. Supervises lessons and develops lesson programs to include private, small group, semi-private, clinics, camps, junior development and tournament players' programs.
12. Is responsible for the complete operation of the tennis pro shop. Hires a shop manager and the attendants. Develops a budget for inventory and keeps complete records for the club.
13. Organizes and promotes club tournaments and social events i.e., develops formats, rules and schedules for social round robins, club championships, special events, leagues, professional tournaments, etc.
14. Assists in the layout and design of new courts and lights as requested by the general manager and board of directors.
15. Recruits, interviews and trains tennis instructors and additional personnel with the general manager's approval.
16. Serves as management's representative on the tennis committee. Assists said committee in efficient planning for and management of all tennis courts.
17. Contributes to monthly club newsletter when applicable.

Club tennis programs should be headed by a person who is a true professional in every sense of the word. In dealing with the club tennis patrol, the tennis professional is called on to serve in numerous capacities. The tennis professional must be dedicated and often sacrifice working long and irregular hours. Tennis professionals must always remain courteous and be as flexible as possible in lesson programs, tournaments and other club functions. An enthusiastic, self-motivated professional will promote as much activity among tennis players as possible.

A tennis professional must know the proper methods for maintaining the various surfaces of tennis courts. The tennis professional must be a competent player and instructor, and needs a practical business background to operate the tennis shop.

The USTA

The United States Tennis Association (USTA) estimates that there are 29 million players enjoying the game of tennis. Fewer than 1% are members of the association, but it affects all players because it establishes official game rules, sanctioned tournaments, provides data on all aspects of the game, and encourages play.

Tennis Pro Shop

The private club's tennis professional usually runs the tennis shop as an independent enterprise—with the agreement that the tennis equipment sold is at a profit which is the way he earns his income. The shop offers equipment such as wearing apparel, shoes, racquets, tennis balls, and other useful items and may also offer the service of racquet restringing.

The tennis pro shop should be attractive and offer as many amenities as feasible within a predetermined economic framework. It must include space for the professional staff; desk and telephone for accepting court reservation time, recording tournament results, and administering sales. Out-of-sight storage space is necessary so that the members' area will stay neat.

The members' area of the shop should include appropriate lounge furniture, a display of tennis merchandise, and a bulletin board for announcing future events and tournament results. A drinking fountain and restrooms should be nearby. A trophy case and plaques recording tournament winners make suitable wall decorations.

It is extremely important for the tennis shop to have dressing rooms if tennis apparel is offered for sale. Full-length mirrors stimulate clothing sales. Without dressing rooms, the members will simply shop elsewhere—where proper facilities are offered.

If there are not enough tennis-playing members to support the purchase of a soft goods inventory, it could be advantageous to have a local tennis shop supply apparel on a consignment basis. Thus, although his profit would be lower, the professional would avoid capital investment in inventory and would eliminate the risk of not selling the merchandise. The outside entrepreneur who owns the inventory should gain most of the gross income.

MANAGING WATER SPORTS

The club pool—with water so clear you can spot a dime in twelve feet of water, with clean-swept decks where lounge furniture abounds and is interspersed with flower-filled plants—is little more than ornamental unless used to capacity. An aggressive and ambitious water sports program will build club members' enthusiasm. Pool programs not only encourage club members to attend events in which their family members are participating, but also foster, in a natural sort of way, an interest in attending other functions and meeting other club families. Clubs should devote a portion of their water sports schedule to expanding and improving wholesome family affairs as part of their activities.

Swim Professional

The swim professional must be selected with great care. His responsibility is enormous because he is constantly dealing with members in situations where bad judgment or lack of training can end in tragedy. Good aquatic leadership demands a mature individual, professionally trained in physical education and possessing strong administrative abilities, superior water skills, aquatic knowledge, and above all, an irreproachable character. The swim professional should be enthusiastic in his approach to his water sports program. He should be friendly with all members but at the same time, command respect so that he can effectively enforce all rules as required.

The swim professional should select his guard staff in the same careful way he was selected. They are his assistants and representatives, and he must be certain that they are well trained and dependable.

The swim professional may be part-time or part of the full-time staff.

Pool Management

Certain attitudes toward his duties are required if the swim professional is to obtain the best results. He must always be aware that he is a professional and refrain from any actions that will cause criticism. He must take the attitude that he has a job to do and never give the impression of being on half vacation. He should stay active and self-sufficient in his supervision of the pool.

Dependability is an important quality in all pool employees. All tasks, however menial, are completed for the sake of the enjoyment, comfort, and safety of those using the pool. Dependable staff members work efficiently and complete their assignments within the time allotted. Slow days, from cool or rainy weather, afford the swim professional time to file reports, do extra cleaning (such as straightening up the filter room and scrubbing lounge furniture), inventory equipment and pool chemicals, and plan for coming events. Thus, extra time can be used wisely.

The swim professional should emphasize congeniality and courtesy in dealing with his staff and club members. The staff should be trained to be polite but firm when correcting a member or guest for a rule infraction. It is best to explain the rules in such cases; often the person being corrected will later help enforce the rules or regulations called to his attention. A reasonable degree of firmness is essential in dealing with youngsters, but this should not grow into unreasonable obstinacy.

Young members will imitate the treatment they receive from staff members. Thus, courtesy and control of temper in all staff actions set a good example and prevent minor, unpleasant incidents.

The entire pool staff should also have sound health habits. Good hygiene, proper nourishment, and necessary rest are essential. A tired guard is dangerous.

Lifesavers or Lifeguards—What's the Difference?

The lifesaver is trained to rescue people in distress. The lifeguard is trained to prevent people from being distressed. Therein lies the difference—and illustrates the need for training lifesavers to be lifeguards.

Guards should safeguard and regulate the conduct of swimmers in and out of the water to prevent accidents and drownings. Guards should be alert to observe any swimmers in distress and to make any necessary assists or rescues. Guards should avoid conversations while on duty and should be constantly prepared to take action necessary to prevent an incident from becoming a tragedy.

All swimming pool areas have some common hazards that an aquatic expert can readily identify. They must be identified to the entire pool staff, so that proper caution can be exercised by everyone—staff and members—around them.

Following is a suggested list of rules for the club's pool staff. (Individual clubs and swim professionals may add other items that apply to problems of their clubs.)

- Be prompt. Check in on time and in uniform.
- Never leave your assigned area except for a rescue or an assist. If you must leave the guarded area for any other reason, notify the person in charge.
- Protect individuals from their own weaknesses and inabilities.
- Do not teach diving or swimming while on duty.
- Wear the regulation uniform only when on duty. Keep your uniform neat and clean.
- Do not participate in or permit running, horseplay, or improper use of the springboard. Keep the diving areas free of swimmers.
- Be courteous when addressing members. When asking them to observe a regulation, explain the reason for that rule.

- Refrain from unnecessary conversation with members or other guards.
- Know the rules and regulations of the club. Enforce them without exception.
- Follow these four principles of lifeguarding: recognize trouble when you see it brewing; know trouble when you see it happening; know how to get the victim and how to bring him on to the deck; and know what to do with the victim when you have rescued him.
- Keep yourself in good physical condition by daily exercise, swimming, and skill conditioning.
- Get enough sleep.

Pool Discipline

Swimming pool areas should be managed so that children, teenagers, and adults of all ages can have fun, relax, and enjoy leisure or active hours at the pool. Members should be able to entertain guests at poolside without the embarrassment of misconduct. Maintaining necessary discipline is an integral part of the swim professional's regular job; he can't pass it off to anyone else.

It is not uncommon for country clubs to have an occasional sad experience from problems arising during pool activities. It is not uncommon for young people to "test" swim professionals to see how far they can go in "cutting up." Whether or not parents are partly at fault when children become unmanageable, swim professionals would have fewer problems if they themselves knew the rules and enforced them.

Included in the regular pool rules should be a clincher—not to be used as a threat, but to teach young people that, as a last resort, severe restrictions will be imposed on offenders and that it is considered a privilege to be able to use the pool. Indiscriminate use of such a rule diminishes its effectiveness as a form of discipline. Following is an example of such a rule:

> Parents are requested to caution their children and minor guests to observe all rules and to obey instructions of the swim professional and other employees. Any failure to comply with these pool rules shall be considered sufficient cause for immediate suspension of pool privileges for the offending individual for a period of from one to seven days.

Most disciplinary problems confronted by the swim professional are not serious—at least not in the beginning. However, with improper handling they can become an avalanche of trouble. The professional himself should be responsible for discipline, because having others handle it reveals an inability to deal effectively with young people. The pool with the best discipline generally has the fewest specific disciplinary problems.

The following guidelines for club managers and swim professionals who supervise children at pools may prevent some problems by helping to win and sustain the confidence and respect of the young people.

1. Get to know the young people by name. (Don't use nicknames that might be insulting or embarrassing to a child or adolescent.)
2. Take the initiative. Be friendly and show interest in the young people's progress in school, hobbies, or other activities.
3. Greet participants and make them feel at home. A warm attitude can encourage young people to play, work, learn new skills, and take part in pool programs.

4. Teach young members to take personal pride in their pool and its activities—this must be taught, not left to chance.
5. Listen to the ideas of participants for improving activities and program. Learn how to vary your program to keep it interesting.
6. Encourage everyone to take part in some activity. Misconduct usually comes from misdirected energy—energy that could just as well be spent constructively.
7. Try giving potential troublemakers some task with responsibility to provide them needed recognition. Many times this keeps them out of mischief. Look for the good qualities. All children have them.
8. Encourage participants to learn things or to help others, not just to look for fun from activities. Guide instead of dictating.
9. Give everyone an equal opportunity to take part in activities. Give special attention to shy or poorly adjusted children, but not in an obvious way.
10. Do not permit vulgar language, rough behavior, or unsportsmanlike conduct.
11. Avoid snapping at young people, nagging, and overdoing practical jokes.
12. Control your temper in order to keep self-respect as well as the respect of others.
13. Do not take out personal feelings and prejudices on the children, or judge conduct solely on how much it annoys you.
14. Bear in mind that where there is misbehavior, there is a cause—be it the professional himself, the activity, or some other influence.
15. Explain to an offender any discipline imposed, in order to prevent any misunderstanding. The young person should be brought to admit the need for correction and, whenever possible, cheerfully accept the penalty.
16. The most effective discipline closely follows the act that merits it. Discipline should be firm, suited to the offense, and adjusted to the offender.
17. Be sure the one being corrected is the real offender, disciplining the wrong child breeds future trouble and permits someone else to "get by."
18. Kindness and sympathy are the best treatment in most cases. A quiet, serious conference with the child—in which the swim professional asks well-directed questions that help the young person discover for himself the faults of his behavior—is the most effective way to correct a problem.
19. Deprive a youngster of privileges only when the offense is rather significant. A sense of disgrace as well as the sacrifice of privilege results.
20. Do not force expressions of regret for misconduct, for that violates the spirit of disciplinary procedure. There is no value in dictated apologies.

Pool Accidents and Pool Safety

In any type of recreation, accidents or emergencies can occur, requiring treatment of some kind by those responsible for the activity. Most country clubs have their swimming instructors make their own safety rules and regulations for the pool and enforce them. The instructors see that the diving zones are marked off, that the ladders are in good condition, and that pool depth markings are clear, among other things. But despite precautions, accidents still happen in and around pools.

Club pools have a special problem as a result of their type of clientele. The technique of caring for accident victims—no matter how minor the accident may be—is most important. Club members, their guests, and the club itself must be protected against possible improper treatment of injuries and resulting lawsuits. The instructor or staff member who handles an injury incompetently can cause severe criticism about the efficiency of the club and pool management. Members do not want to participate in activities unless the pool staff is competent and capable of rendering assistance efficiently. Improper care and necessary club insurance is discussed in the chapter about insurance.

Club pool personnel must give proper and prompt attention to all injuries. It is important for the club swimming pro to be well trained in first aid, for his position includes teaching, coaching, and guarding club members while they swim and dive; it also includes attending to injuries, no matter how great or small.

Most pool accidents are minor. Surveys have shown that running on pool decks causes more accidents than all other reasons combined. Slipping is second; horseplay is third. The most hazardous activity is diving: accidents can be caused by diving on someone, by horseplay or slipping on the board, and by board inexperience.

Prevention of accidents—by supervision and proper instruction—is a worthwhile "public health" program. Safety education requires the attention and direction of all pool managers. No pool environment can be considered safe unless members and their guests are willing to cooperate in preventing accidents. If a program of supervision is to be effective, members must be safety conscious, concerned not only about their own welfare, but about that of others as well. Members must be taught to observe the following rules:

1. *Walk* around the pool and locker rooms.
2. Use diving boards properly.
3. Minimize horseplay.
4. Refrain from interfering with anyone using the drinking fountain.
5. Conduct themselves safely.

A continuing safety education program should be carried on by personnel at all pools. Education accomplishes more than disciplinary action.

First Aid: The swim professional should be able to provide prompt and suitable first aid treatment for various types of injuries. The instructor does not, of course, take the place of a doctor, but he should be able to diagnose and treat minor cases sensibly and should refer the injured person to his or her family physician or possibly to a nearby club physician if necessary. In no case should the instructor's treatment be final. After receiving first aid (that is, first treatement) from club personnel, the *legal* responsibility for medical care rests with the parents or adults involved. Thorough training for the club instructor is essential.

The club first aid kit should be well stocked and kept close to the pool. A waterproof and rustproof cabinet will protect the contents; a portable cabinet that can be moved to the scene of a mishap is handiest. The cabinet should contain the various items recommended for any first aid kit; its contents should be handled only by employees trained in first aid, as far as practicable. The supplies should be inspected weekly during the busy swimming season.

Accident Reports: An accident report should be completed whenever the person in charge feels that an accident may result in repercussions, legal or otherwise, by the injured person or his or her guardians. If there is doubt, the form should be filled out as a protection for the club, for the staff, for the people involved, and for the insurance company that provides coverage for the club.

A procedure should be established to handle all accident cases; it should be faithfully followed whenever an accident occurs. An accident-reporting system should be established and accurate reports should be filed. Sometimes, months after a seemingly minor injury, an insurance investigation may inquire about the time or conditions of the incident. An accident record form on file in the club office will provide the information needed.

Swim Lesson Programs

The keys to a successful swim lesson program are good organization and quality of instruction. Also important is the instructor's ability to motivate the students.

Four main topics deserve special attention:

1. Class size.
2. Skill-level grouping.
3. Class period length and starting time.
4. Individual lesson organization.

Class Size

It is important to keep the number of students in each class to a financially feasible minimum. If class size cannot be kept to around seven to eight students per unit, then one should at least keep beginning classes reasonably small and place advanced students in larger groups. Younger children and beginning swimmers usually have shorter attention spans and require more individual attention. It is a good idea, however, to never exceed twelve students per instructor at any level.

Skill-Level Grouping

A lesson program should be based on a set of graduated skill levels. Several intermediate levels should also be included because they provide incentive for advancement. Each skill level could be named for a bird—for example, beginners could be sparrows. When the student adequately masters beginner skills such as bobbing, leveling off in waist-deep water, arm stroking and flutter kicking, he would move up to the robin level. Here more advanced skills—rhythmic breathing, crawl stroke, underwater swimming, and elementary diving—would be taught. Again, upon mastery of these skills, the student would move up to the next level, which could be called hawks. At this level, elementary backstroke, sidestroke, more advanced diving, and introduction to breaststroke whip-kicking should be the subject matter. Of course, improvement of previously learned skills would be emphasized throughout each course. The highest skill level could be called eagle. By that level, students should have mastered the freestyle (crawl) and rhythmic breathing, front running dives from a springboard, elementary backstroke, sidestroke, and treading water. In this course, backstroke, backcrawl, and survival swimming skills are taught. In addition, students refine previously learned skills to a high degree of proficiency, emphasizing endurance swimming. There would be sparrow, robin, hawk, and eagle awards for completing each course.

Length of Classes

One must consider the length of each swim lesson and class period from the aspect of labor versus profit. A good instructor is careful not to overload students with too much new information in a single class period. The class period should be relatively short, with a swim lesson sequence consisting of nine thirty-minute lessons and one testing period. One can realize a substantial profit from this type of program.

Lesson Organization

A good instructor is always well organized. Each class period should be thoroughly planned with regard to skills to be introduced, skills to be practiced, and time allotted for each topic. The hallmarks of a good instructor include confidence, enthusiasm, and, most important, patience. A swimming instructor should be both an excellent swimmer and lifesaver and should have mastered the four basic swimming strokes. He must be able to set an example of excellence and, in so doing, gain the respect of his students.

Mention should be made at this point of the American Red Cross (ARC). This organization trains swimming instructors, known as water safety instructors (WSIs), in addition to providing a whole range of swimming and lifesaving classes. The WSI course is a vigorous training session in which students learn how to organize and teach a swimming class as well as to master all the various swimming strokes. A good swim lesson program usually has a full staff of WSIs.

WSIs are trained to teach American Red Cross swim lessons (the familiar beginner, advanced beginner, intermediate, and swimmer courses) and are forbidden to accept money for that teaching. The curriculum mentioned earlier (sparrow, robin, hawk, and eagle courses) is a private program, not administered or sanctioned by the ARC and, therefore, a club can charge for these lessons and pay instructors for teaching them. According to the ARC, it is illegal to charge for lessons they administer, so giving their beginner, advanced beginner, intermediate, or swimmer awards at the completion of paid swimming lessons is illegal. Clubs may charge for swim lessons in order to pay for instructors and maintain the swim facility.

In conclusion, a successful swim lesson program is characterized by good, solid organization and high-quality instruction. A swim lesson program provides a service to the people participating in it, and its success is only measurable by the degree to which the participants (and parents) are satisfied.

Swimming Events for Young Members

Novelty Events: Novelty events should start off the swimmer's swimming competitions, because they provide a worthwhile experience for beginners who may not be ready for a speed-skill event.

Announce the event at least a week in advance, to create interest. To some extent, incidental practice can be promoted during a lesson or a free period when young people are around the pool. The physical condition of many participants is not good early in the season, so events should not be more than twenty-five yards in distance. If the club holds a second novelty meet later in the season, the events might be a little more difficult. Novelty prizes (each in a paper bag) or selected by chance from a grab bag make clever awards for first-place winners.

The events for a novelty meet might include categories such as the following:

- Boys fourteen years and under—egg and spoon race
- Boys fourteen and under—candle race
- Boys twelve and under—dry towel race
- Boys ten and under—balloon race
- Boys eight and under—tube-toy race (cross-pool)

Events for the girls would follow the same pattern and alternate with those for boys. A shallow-pool event can be planned for boys and girls six and under, with balloons for the little children.

When there are not many participants, a seven-year-old child, for example, could enter the ten-and-under event, as well as the event for those eight and under. However, if there is a large group, specific age restrictions should be observed.

Ribbon Races: The club can conduct ribbon races on several weekends before championship events. Ribbon races build interest in the championship medal events, provide experience, and encourage swimmers to work toward proficiency in the various strokes. The freestyle race would be held on the first weekend, the backstroke next, and so on, with the more difficult strokes scheduled for later in the season. Also, either backstroke or freestyle events can be arranged for younger swimmers when older swimmers are expected to compete in the more difficult strokes.

Most events—except those for the oldest teenagers—should be twenty-five yards in length. Ribbons are awarded for first, second, third, and fourth places, and are given out immediately after each event. Although the ribbons are inexpensive, they encourage the swimmers and make nice souvenirs.

Junior Championship: Qualifying heats should be conducted to find the fastest swimmers for each championship event. If a pool accommodates five lanes, the five fastest swimmers are selected. Those five might then choose by chance the lanes they will swim in during the following week's finals. Another common method of determining lanes, established by the American Athletic Union, gives the fastest swimmer the center lane; swimmers with the next best times have the lanes on either side of center, and swimmers with the poorest times have the outside lanes. The AAU method makes the race more exciting, because the fastest swimmers are closest together. It also gives the poorest swimmers the advantage of outside lanes.

Eliminations in diving are not often necessary. However, flight order can be chosen by the chance method.

After the trials, a mimeographed program is made up, listing names, lanes, events, and current records, and providing a place to record the three place winners and the winning times. For best possible attendance at the finals, this program should be mailed to the club membership as soon as possible.

The junior championships should be set up much the same way as the novelty and ribbon events. However, the question of age restrictions should be handled according to type of competition, as follows: in a club's junior championships, and in novice races, best-qualified swimmers should be permitted to compete in the finals regardless of age. The lower age group events are run off first, so a child does not jeopardize himself in his true age group. Then, if an eight-year-old beats a ten-year-old in the finals, he gets credit for such good performance. But, on the contrary in stiff league competition among clubs, the type of entry that imposes age restrictions is not desirable.

The rundown of events might be as follows:

- Girls ten and under, 50-yard free-style
- Girls twelve and under, 50-yard free-style
- Girls fourteen and under, 50-yard butterfly
- Girls fourteen and under, 50-yard backstroke
- Girls fourteen and under, 50-yard breaststroke
- Girls fourteen and under, fancy diving
- Girls fourteen and under, 100-yard freestyle

Here, too, events for boys and girls should alternate and be set up the same way.

Awards can be made on the basis of points, with five points required for a first-place gold medal, three for a second-place silver medal, and one point for a third-place bronze. A finalist program should be provided for members and guests attending the meet.

Novice Events: Novice events work into the schedule well just before senior championships begin. Novice events, which are good attendance-builders, should usually include fifteen-yard freestyle events for both girls and boys six years and under, and twenty-five yard freestyle event for girls and boys eight and under. Medals can be awarded to first-, second-, and third-place winners. Fourth- and fifth-place winners should receive ribbons.

Senior Championships

Senior championships follow novice events. In a senior meet, juniors fourteen years and under are limited to two events to keep seniors swimming and competing, and to avoid the need to conduct heats. Ranking juniors, determined by the junior championship results in any stroke specialty, should have the first opportunity to compete.

The order of events is similar to the junior championship rundown, but an additional 200 yard freestyle event is usually included for both men and women. Awards are made on the same point system.

As an added attraction, championship traveling trophies can be awarded to the woman and the man who receive the highest total points. Under this arrangement, winners keep the trophies a year and then return them to the club. Any person who has won three championships is given permanent possession of the trophy. If a traveling trophy is used, a smaller trophy is usually awarded for permanent possession.

Swimming Teams

Swimming meets with other teams need not follow a set pattern. (A certain time should, however, be set aside for team practice.) Whenever possible, meets should be scheduled for weekday evenings to keep the club calendar free on weekends for exclusively club events. Furthermore, parents are more likely to take part as spectators and to provide transportation to nearby pools during the early evening on weekdays than would be the case on weekends.

Clubs might want to consider joining an inter-club league. Dual meets on a home and away basis are enjoyable for youngsters and parents.

Many clubs are served by leagues that provide rules and meet schedules. However, swimming team activities can be detrimental at a country club pool. They can take an excessive amount of time and attention, sometimes with the result that young people are driven too hard to do better and, at the same time, adult participation is driven away, as are neophyte swimmers who need their share of instruction or attention.

A new club may do well to develop a pool program like the one outlined in this chapter. Then, in time, some of the more skilled swimmers might be selected and entered outside the club in competitive invitational meets. In that way, the more skilled will have an outlet to compete beyond the confines of the club program.

It should be mentioned, however, that some pool programs become neglected and do not meet the needs and desires of the general membership when the swim professional tries to make a name for himself by developing one or two outstanding swimmers. The pro should never neglect the general membership. Members generally must come *first.*

Annual Family Swimmers' Night

Family swimmers' night must be planned far in advance. A junior committee might be selected to decorate the dining room in an aquatic motif. Place cards should be used to seat the boys and girls of a certain age group together, parents sit together in a designated area of the dining room.

The club president or the swimming pool chairman can present the medals and trophies after the dinner. All the medal awards should be grouped together for each individual, with a summary card listing accomplishments. The trophies should be engraved. The usual procedure is to make the awards in order of age, with the youngest receiving their medals first.

Program Summary

The water sports program can be included in the club master list of events and in the membership yearbook.

Although a well-planned "core" program provides stability to pool activities and gives young members worthy goals, extra functions can add spice to the program. For example, featured events such as a fashion show at poolside, a water show, canoe tilting on the Fourth of July weekend, splash parties, and others can be planned and varied from year to year.

Conclusion

Appropriate pool services and safety procedures promote confidence in the pool manager and result in greater use of the club pool. Helpfulness has a positive effect on the attendance at and growth of the club swimming program, which, in turn, increases members' patronage of other club facilities and also increases the number of private lessons in swimming, diving, and lifesaving. It is most important to be a good aquatic teacher and supervisor, but an instructor will be even more effective and respected if he is knowledgeable and demonstrates the ability to deal effectively with emergencies.

EXHIBIT 9.1
Platform Tennis Layout

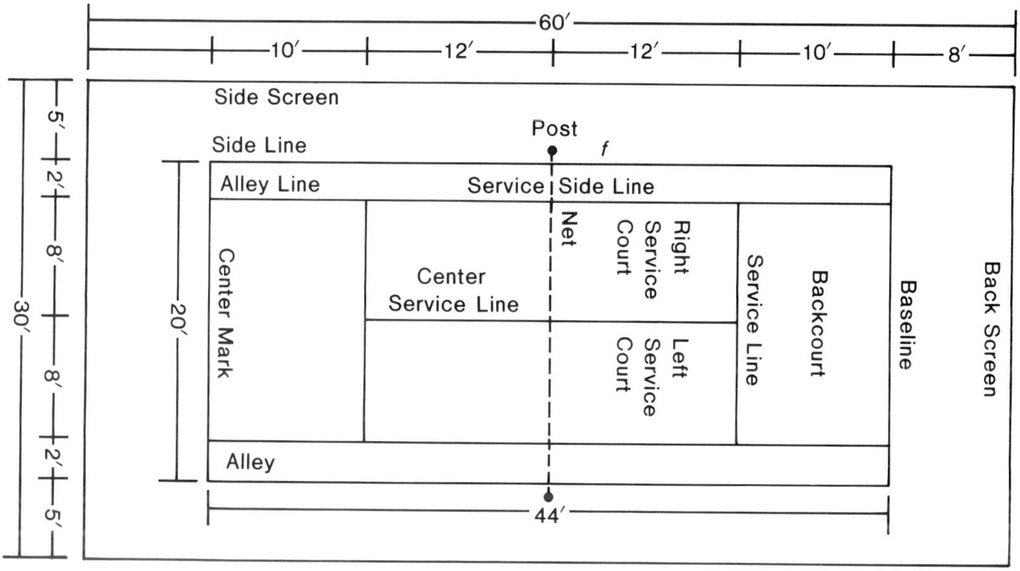

PLATFORM TENNIS

Platform tennis was invented in Scarsdale, N.Y., in 1928, by two tennis enthusiasts, Fessende S. Blanchard and James K. Cogswell, who were seeking outdoor winter exercise. From its modest beginning of two players, the sport grew until, as indicated in *Tennis Industry Magazine* (October 1978), the American Platform Tennis Association estimates that there are now 500,000 players.

Platform tennis is played with yellow American Platform Tennis Association (APTA) approved balls. The ball has less bounce than a tennis ball. The wooden paddle or racquet has a hole drilled through the head to decrease wind resistance. The short paddle handle makes it easy to hit the ball over the net.

The game is easy to learn, even without a background in racquet sports. In just a few weeks even novices can keep the ball in play for long, exciting points; thus it is an ideal family sport.

Platform tennis has had phenomenal growth since the early 1970s. As more and more Americans participate in sports, platform tennis is earning its share of devotees. It doesn't strain the pocketbook, since the cost of a ball and paddle is modest. It is a natural for country clubs because the courts take only a small space and the game offers just what its investors sought: healthy outdoor exercise, especially in the winter.

A few years ago, players came to the courts bundled up as if they were taking the family pet for a walk on a wintry day. Marketing experts from the sports equipment and apparel industry have now introduced sportswear that is fashionable and warm, but permits the player the desired freedom of movement. It is often sold at the tennis professional shop.

The game lends itself to sociability, and ladies' groups, men's groups, and mixed doubles are all popular. Although the game can be played by singles, doubles provides more excitement and fun with long rallies.

Many clubs have lighted courts, to permit play on dark days as well as in the evening. A system of reserving court time is recommended, with one or one-and-a-half-hour playing periods.

Platform tennis provides club members with the opportunity for outdoor fun, exercise, and comradery during the fall and winter months. Social activities such as steak night, or wine and cheese parties are appropriate after games. Doubles and mixed doubles make an enjoyable evening and also promote use of the club.

Court Maintenance

Maintenance of platform tennis courts is very important both to provide necessary conditions for safe play and to minimize deterioration. Wooden frames and decks exposed to the elements soon show signs of extreme wear and rotting wood. Maintenance, which includes replacing any bad decking, tightening the superstructure, and painting must be done in the off-season summer months. The high cost of maintaining wooden desks stimulated the search for more satisfactory building materials, and aluminum decks are becoming popular. Their initial cost is greater than for wood, but annual repairs and maintenance costs are lower.

INTRODUCTION TO FITNESS

Since the early sixties, people in this country have been taking a long hard look at their "state of fitness" and have realized something needed to be done to improve the situation. The club can render a great service to the total "wellness" of its members. Most physical educators agree that a complete fitness program should include strength conditioning, cardiovascular training along with adequate flexibility and stretching programs. Some specific components of a program you might want to consider are:

Nautilus

Nautilus is the name used to describe various machines used in strength training. These are most unique in that they meet all criteria for proper muscle development. Add to this the outstanding feature of giving your conditioning room a neat and orderly appearance. Information on nautilus machines may be obtained by writing: Nautilus Sports/Medical Industries, P.O. Box 1783, DeLand, Flordia 32730.

Aerobics

One of the most popular exercise programs of the past decade is aerobics. "Aerobics," a term first coined by Dr. Kenneth Cooper over two decades ago, can be most broadly defined as "any deliberate physical activity in which an individual's pulse rate is increased to 70 percent of its maximum level and maintained for at least 20 minutes." This amount and duration of physical activity (i.e., exercise) typically produces the correspondingly beneficial increased oxygen (aerobic) effect on the body.

Many clubs have instituted regular aerobic workout programs for their members. Jane Fonda's various workout programs, "jazzercise" and "dancercise" are three of the most popular.

Jogging

This is a sport that literally thousands participate in. Jogging is considered to be one of the best aerobic forms of exercise. That is, it conditions not only the skeletal muscles, it conditions the heart muscle itself. If space allows, a jogging trail on club property would be desirable. If space is a problem, then the next best thing would be suggesting various "runs" adjacent to the club location. If this program creates interest in running, the club might want to consider scheduling a "fun run" for the membership. Distances for runs can vary, but usually we are talking about a one-mile, five kilometer (3.1 mile) or a ten-kilometer (6.2 mile) run. These can be scheduled around certain holidays, i.e., Thanksgiving, Fourth of July, Labor Day, etc.

Squash

Squash, a racquetball sport, has been well entrenched along the eastern seaboard for a long time. More recently it has begun to spread throughout the country and is enjoying a steady growth. It appeals to a wide range of age groups, from teenagers to senior citizens, with the largest percentage being in the 30–34 age group.

The management of a private club offering squash is responsible for having the courts and necessary service facilities operating at optimum conditions at all times. An instructor or professional is needed to teach the game, manage the court time reservations, keep club tournament records, and encourage play.

Equipment and apparel should be offered as a service to squash players.

Interclub as well as intraclub tournaments encourage play and help members broaden their acquaintances in the community, especially as club interest in the game is developing.

Handball

Handball, like squash, badminton and racquetball, is more likely available in athletic or similar city clubs than in private country clubs.

Handball players must have a lot of stamina. The game is very fast and requires great agility and quick reflexes. It attracts players of all ages, although older players are generally veterans who have played for many years.

Club tournaments add to the overall recreational program, and they are often used to determine the club's entries to regional or state tournaments.

Racquetball

Racquetball is one of the fastest growing participatory racquet sports. This exciting, dynamic game is easier to play than tennis and, consequently, players are enthusiastic because they can play well soon after beginning.

Scheduling court use and initiating tournaments are all management duties. The athletic director, manager, and sports professional are all charged with keeping the facilities in excellent condition.

One of the big considerations with adding racquetball to your program would be the cost factor. IRSA, 132 Brookline Avenue, Boston, Massachusetts 02210, would be the source to consult with regarding court construction cost, how to initiate a viable racquetball program and even suggestions on arranging your racquetball pro shop. One way to help defray maintenance costs would be to make a nominal charge for court time. If you intend to make racquetball a big sport at your club, a racquetball professional would be a welcome addition to your staff.

Badminton

Badminton is a great game for men and women and can be played in singles, doubles, and mixed doubles. It is primarily a winter sport in city clubs with gymnasium facilities. Badminton can be played outdoors, but a breeze can blow the bird off course and diminish the fun of playing.

The athletic director must schedule all activities carefully for the time benefit of the participants and not infringe on the desires or rights of others. Optimally, the morning ladies' badminton league is finished and the net equipment changed before the noon businessmen's volleyball game is scheduled to begin.

In certain sections of the U.S. this sport enjoys exceptional popularity. As with tennis, squash, racquetball and handball, badminton has a governing body that can provide invaluable information covering clinics, tournaments and the like. The United States Badminton Association is the recognized authority on the sport.

Basketball

If your club has the facility for basketball but at present it is not part of your program, please reconsider. Intramural basketball at club level play can wind up being one of your most successful programs. By utilizing local officials one can keep play under control. To begin such a program, the athletic director or manager should select a commissioner to form the teams. Captains would then be chosen and in turn the teams are drafted. All of this takes place after the captains have had an opportunity to observe those interested in playing.

Court Maintenance: In their own way, athletic facilities seem to demand special attention; attention not only as to how activities are scheduled but to how facilities are maintained. Playing surfaces (hardwood floors) must be kept clean and dust free. Usually hardwood floors are renovated at least once a year. This helps maintain the color of the original surface plus it really cleans the floor well. Care should always be taken not to allow improper shoes on the playing surface.

Bowling

Bowling appeals to men, women, and junior members. To justify its expense and to have the bowling operation contribute residuals to the net food and beverage operation of a club, the bowling facility must be kept busy.

A bowling manager or instructor is needed to administer tournaments, manage the bowling staff, offer instruction, and promote club bowling. The bowling manager must know how to perform all the jobs in the operation. It would be a great asset if he knew how to keep the automatic pin-setting apparatus in proper repair.

Many bowlers enjoy a casual game, but most avid bowlers are members of a team or group that meets regularly. The bowling manager's delight is to have all his lanes busy. To promote interest he will set aside times for free open bowling, set up interclub tournaments, and have free bowling exhibitions.

Business hours and social mores of club members should be considered in setting up leagues. For example, if many club members leave their offices or places of business at 5:00 P.M., then a 5:30 P.M. league would be appropriate. Mixed doubles on another evening of the week bring out married couples for bowling. Most ladies' leagues play either in the morning or early afternoon.

A late morning ladies' league provides a gentle suggestion to stay for lunch. Junior instruction or league play is often scheduled for Sunday morning, so as not to interfere with school activities or adult bowling.

The bowling staff, like personnel in all other club sports departments, should strive to make participation easy and enjoyable. A friendly greeting, clean and well-maintained equipment, proper lighting and ventilation, and meeting published play schedules are all part of a well-organized, well-managed bowling operation.

In addition to the aforementioned programs, there are several other excellent activities that club members would enjoy:

Whitewater Rafting

Nothing beats the thrill and exhilaration of a whitewater trip. Again, with the emphasis on outdoor sports, one would have little difficulty in contacting a reliable outfitter to assist in arranging a trip for your members. Club members seem to enjoy this opportunity to meet other club members who have similar interests. For the more ambitious clubs, a trip down one of the Western rivers would be a highlight event.

Trail Hikes

You never realize the interest your members have in this activity until you ask. Most sections of the country have an established trail that has been marked, mapped and maintained by either local or federal agencies. Hiking is an activity that the entire family can enjoy and most trails usually add the opportunity to do camping. The Pacific Coast Trail on the west coast and the Appalachian Trail on the east coast are two of the more well-known trails. Local outfitters would be a good source to get information on what's available in your particular location.

Skiing

Ski trips would be a real plus to an active club program. These can be either single day trips or extended stays. Your club probably has a member in the travel business that could handle all the necessary arrangements. For the more daring or ambitious clubs, you might want to consider a European ski holiday. However, our East and West Coast areas offer magnificent skiing right here at home.

Shooting

Shooting is another activity that adds prestige to your club. Considering that arrangements can usually be made at a nearby gun club, there is really no capital outlay for this additional amenity. Many clubs find that in these various outdoor programs they form clubs within the club. This is not to be considered a negative factor. To the contrary, you are providing another program for your members' enjoyment.

Yachting and Boating

Many clubs have yachting and boating as an integral part of their particular club. This provides a whole array of social affairs, surrounding regattas, races, etc. that can actually be excellent revenue producers. As with all club facilities, the yacht basin should always be "ship shape".

SNOWMOBILES

Clubs located in areas that have heavy snow can offer snowmobiling. The club must first resolve the question of whether or not it wants to allow snowmobiles on its property and golf course.

The sport appeals to rugged individuals who enjoy the out of doors and the challenge of the elements, but snowmobiling is dangerous outdoor recreation and therefore needs proper regulation. (It also requires special insurance, discussed in the chapter on insurance.)

Snowmobile trails must be plainly marked by the golf course superintendent and a ranger representing the snowmobile enthusiasts. Care must be taken that trails do not cross, unless there is excellent visibility, and that trails are not close to hazards. Cross-country snowmobiling on a golf course could be disastrous if the machines ran across tees, greens, planting beds, or other fragile areas, or where the snowmobile and riders could be damaged or injured. Several inches of snow changes the appearance of topography, and it is very easy to forget just where rock outcroppings, stumps, water hydrants, and other immovable objects are located.

Rigid controls and rules for snowmobiling are necessary for the safety of participants, spectators, and personal property.

The following rules are required for the clubs' snowmobile program:

1. The names of all participants and the snowmobile number must be recorded before riders use the trails; particpants must sign out when finished.
2. Snowmobiles must refuel away from any outside warming fires.
3. All drivers must pass a test prescribed by the club's safety committee before operating a snowmobile on club property.
4. Speed limits in dangerous areas must be strictly enforced.
5. There must never be more than two persons on a snowmobile (a driver and one passenger only).
6. Snowmobiling on ponds, lakes, and streams should be prohibited unless a properly worded sign indicates permission and states the necessary conditions.

Daylight is safest for operating snowmobiles. Early evening or dusk—from 3:00 P.M. to 6:00 P.M.—with associated poor light conditions have the highest frequency of accidents. Evening snowmobiling (between 6:00 P.M. and 9:00 P.M.) has the next highest number of accidents.

As of this writing, no country club in Wisconsin, for example—which has ample snow—is known to encourage snowmobiling. Those clubs that did permit snowmobiling have completely stopped or diminished use to discourage the sport. Damage to tees and greens and the hazard of tort liability have made it unattractive to most clubs.

DUTIES OF THE GOLF COURSE SUPERINTENDENT

The success of the golf program at any private facility is the result of a cooperative effort among the club manager, the golf course superintendent, and the golf professional. These individuals working together with the various club committees can develop an attractive golf program that will satisfy membership expectations and provide the finest in sports recreation.

Managerial Roles and Relationships

With respect to club management, the role of the golf course superintendent may vary. At some clubs, the superintendent may report directly to the green committee, the board of directors or a general manager. At other clubs, the superintendent, the club manager and the golf professional will operate as a triumvirate—a management team. Under this system, these three parties are usually individually responsible for their own distinct departments or other defined areas of management and normally report to a higher executive level, such as a board of directors, chief operating officer or a general manager.

It is very important to the superintendent that the lines of authority be clearly drawn. This will eliminate any confusion between the different department heads and will allow for a smoother, more effective management effort.

At most private clubs, committees of members advise on policy as it pertains to each segment of the total facility operation. Committee involvement is crucial because this is the only way the club management personnel can receive input into their decision-making.

The green committee is typically a group of members who oversee the management of the golf course. Traditionally, the golf course superintendent has received advice and general guidance from that committee and reported directly to its chairman. This concept, however, is changing.

Many private clubs today are using a more business-oriented structure. This has become evident as clubs and other golf operations have increasingly delegated total operational responsibility for course management to their golf course superintendents. Golf course operations today are far too expensive and too complex to trust to anyone but a professionally trained superintendent who is held accountable for the "bottom line". The trend today is for green committees to assume an advisory role, and superintendents are more and more frequently reporting to a board of directors or a general manager.

It is very important for the general manager or the club manager to have a basic knowledge of golf course operations. Although the club manager who functions under the triumviral system of club management may not have direct responsibility for the golf course, it is still necessary for him to understand golf course management. Most club managers have the responsibility of integrating golf course operations into the overall club operations.

It is not necessary for the general manager or the club manager to be trained in agronomy. This is the responsibility of the golf course superintendent. However, a very basic knowledge of the science of turfgrass management is helpful to all involved. An understanding of the superintendent's qualifications, responsibilities and needs will result in greater insight into—and appreciation for—both the complexities of the game of golf and the increasingly ciritical importance of the superintendent's role in the game.

Understanding turfgrass management practices and why they are necessary can lead to better scheduling of golf events to avoid membership dissatisfaction. There is nothing more annoying to the golfer than to have to play a tournament just after greens have been aerified or some other essential procedure has been carried out, temporarily disrupting play. The club manager can be of invaluable assistance to the superintendent in communications between the members and the superintendent. The club manager can relay suggestions, constructive criticism and other comments from club members—as well as his own observations, which will be of help to the superintendent in managing his department.

Understanding golf course budgetary expenditures will allow for better departmental forecasting and how best to integrate it into the overall budget and long-range plans of the club. The communications process between the manager and the superintendent will be strengthened if the manager knows the needs of the superintendent and why certain requests are made.

In addition, golf course operations are subject to many governmental regulations. The club manager must know these regulations and how they affect the club's operations. The Environmental Protection Agency now requires all superintendents to be licensed to apply pesticides and, furthermore, there are strict regulations governing the use and disposal of pesticides. Adherence to these licensing and disposal laws is critical to the club to avoid penalties and lawsuits.

The Occupational Safety and Health Act (OSHA) of 1970 provides that each employer has the basic duty to furnish his employees a place of employment that is free from recognized hazards causing—or likely to cause—death or serious physical harm. It is crucial to the club that both the manager and the superintendent know and institute safety procedures that comply with the law.

In the areas of labor law, insurance, taxation, state and local regulations, plus personnel management, an understanding of how these disciplines affect golf course operations will immeasurably aid the manager in recognizing the needs of the superintendent in these areas.

In the final analysis, there must exist a mutual respect—and a high regard for respective professional abilities—on the part of the club manager, the superintendent and the golf professional. These three professionals, working in harmony, will ensure that the golf program is implemented in the most efficient and economical manner to the fullest enjoyment of the membership.

Qualifications for Superintendent Today

The science and technology of the turfgrass or golf course management profession have advanced to the point where formal training is mandatory for the superintendent. Furthermore, competition for the better golf course management positions has become intense. Thus, it is becoming increasingly important that young men and women aspiring to become superintendents prepare for the technical and managerial aspects of the profession by attending specialized programs offered at colleges and universities throughout the country. Many states now have at least one college or university offering curricula leading to an associate, bachelor or advanced degree in turfgrass management. Such programs provide a comprehensive education in the disciplines of agronomy, horticulture, entomology, soil science, plant pathology, landscape architecture, financial and business management, public relations, labor law, and personnel management.

The superintendent must know and understand the complexities and interrelationships of soils, irrigation, plant growth, plant diseases, insects, plant fertility and drainage. Superintendents must possess a thorough understanding of the safe use of chemicals—including herbicides, fungicides and insecticides—plus a general knowledge of a vast range of tools and equipment, ranging from simple hand implements to complex, hydraulically operated machinery.

In addition to the knowledge and skills needed in the culture of turfgrasses, the superintendent's duties require the use of skills in communications, computer technology, purchasing and financial management, as well as a thorough understanding of the game of golf. And the superintendent must have the knowledge required to deal with problems related to roadways, parking lots, trees, flowers, buildings, tennis courts, skeet ranges, swimming pools, golf car fleets and other facilities.

Finally, one of the most basic qualifications or skills a golf course superintendent must have is an inherent ability to get along with people. The superintendent must be able to effectively deal with and communicate with many different people, from unskilled laborers and the general public to industrialists and celebrities. Few other positions in business require interaction with such a diverse cast of people.

Given the preceding requirements, it becomes evident that continuing education is of nearly absolute importance to today's professional superintendent. Because the demands of managing a golf course are dynamic and changing, no individual can remain effective in meeting these demands without continually working to keep updated on current technology and proven innovations. A golf course superintendent has a professional obligation to do no less—and a golf operation should expect no less.

The Golf Course Superintendents Association of America (GCSAA) is the professional association representing today's superintendents and is devoted to their continuing education. Membership in this professional organization is invaluable to the superintendent because he or she can exchange experiences and practical, problem-solving techniques with other golf course management professionals.

GCSAA offers a yearly educational conference, plus many regional seminars on all the latest techniques of turfgrass management. Held concurrently with the annual educational conference is an industry trade show where the superintendent can see and make plans to purchase the latest in golf course products and equipment. GCSAA also offers numerous educational aids, including the monthly *Golf Course Management* magazine.

Professional Credentials

In 1971, GCSAA established a certification program (which has since been substantially restructured and improved) to identify progressive superintendents and to formulate standards of excellence in the golf course management profession. Certified status indicates the superintendent's desire to stay informed about his or her industry and profession. It says the individual will keep up with change.

The Superintendent's Responsibilities

The primary responsibility of the golf course superintendent is to provide the finest possible playing conditions for the game of golf. Local conditions and factors—ranging from the geographic-climatic location and the size of the golf course to the history and organizational arrangement of each course—must be considered whenever a superintendent's responsibilities are discussed. There are many areas of responsibility common to all superintendents, but there are also many localized aspects dependent on clientele, type of operation and the regional differences of nature.

Working with the forces of nature requires that superintendents be flexible in their planning and actions. Each superintendent knows full well that the best planning can easily be altered or reversed by natural phenomena such as drought, flood, insects, or disease—or by economic conditions, and he or she must be prepared to alter plans to accommodate these factors.

A typical job description for the superintendent would include the following responsibilities:

- Management of all golf playing areas plus surrounding areas, which may include swimming pools, tennis courts, skeet ranges, riding stables, roadways, and parking lots.
- Management of all landscaping around the clubhouse grounds and golf course to include all flowers, trees, shrubs, cacti, ponds, lakes and streams.
- Management of all golf course equipment and materials, including their purchasing, storing, repairing and inventory.
- Management of all golf course buildings and structures, which may include fences, bridges, shelters and other appurtenances.
- Management of golf course personnel, including their hiring, firing, training, retention and supervising.
- Financial management of the golf course budget, including its preparation, explanation, and implementation.
- Management of golf course records, including cost accounting, weather conditions, material application and inventories.
- Knowledge of golf, including that obtained by playing regularly and being familiar with rules and regulations.
- Adhering to all governmental laws and regulations—and staying current with all changes.
- Maintaining sound communications with the public, members, management, and employees.

In addition to all the preceding, for a superintendent to perform at full potential he or she needs to have the opportunities to assist and advise in the planning stages of major programs. A superintendent can accomplish many important improvements to help a golf course operation run efficiently and be of optimum service to its golfers, but changes to the course formulated without the input of the superintendent can result in tremendous waste—and in the ultimate dissatisfaction of golfers. Making the most of a superintendent's skills and knowledge has proven time and time again to be the most successful and effective manner of operating a golf course.

Another area where the superintendent's early involvement will prove to be advantageous to both the golf course and the superintendent is in the preparation of an agreed-upon, long-term golf course development program or master plan that provides for continuity. By establishing reasonable, time-related objectives for major course improvements—and by establishing a procedure that affords the superintendent the resources to implement the program—a definite pattern of improvement and performance can be fairly measured.

Finally, the golf course superintendent needs to be able to depend upon the cooperation of his or her employer in providing both time and reimbursement of expenses for continuing education and professional pursuits. The wise club will view such minor expense as an investment that will, in time, yield a multitude of returns—both in dollars and in golfers' satisfaction with the golf course.

REVIEW QUESTIONS

1. What are the general recreational management duties of a club manager?
2. Who runs and is financially responsible for pro shops?
3. Approximately how large is a 9-hole golf course? One with 18 holes?
4. Who certifies various sports professionals:
   Golf course superintendent?
   Golf pro?
   Pool manager?
5. What are the advantages to the club in hiring certified professionals?
6. Who establishes national rules of golf? tennis?
7. Describe a full club swim program. Should the club have a swim team? Why or why not?
8. What is characteristic of the role of the club manager in recreational management of (a) large clubs, (b) small clubs?
9. What are four objectives that the golf professional of a club will strive to achieve?
10. What is the most interesting fact about platform tennis?
11. Why have clubs discouraged the sport of snowmobiling?
12. It takes a cooperative effort from three people to make a successful golf program. Name them.
13. Why is it important that the lines of authority be clearly drawn for the golf course superintendent?
14. Explain how the responsibilities of the green committee have changed over the past few years?
15. Why is it necessary for a club manager to have basic knowledge of golf course operations?
16. What is agronomy?
17. What EPA regulations must a golf course superintendent adhere to?
18. What does OSHA stand for and when was it created?
19. In addition to the knowledge and skills needed in the culture of turfgrasses, what other duties are required of a golf course superintendent?
20. Why is continuing education for a golf course superintendent important?
21. What is the GCSAA?
22. Why is it important to have a long-term golf course development plan?

10

Insurance and Security Awareness

Pinehurst Country Club, North Carolina

A well-planned, well-managed, and frequently updated insurance program is vital to the continued success of any club. The primary rule of thumb is to insure anything you can't afford to lose.

This chapter explains the various types of insurance available to and required by clubs, including liability, property loss, automobile and employee coverages. The potential loss exposures are immense and risk management is essential. The material here should be supplemented by insurance textbooks and by a club's professional insurance adviser. How to select that person is discussed at the end of the chapter.

Too many people ask, "Is a loss likely to happen?" instead of "What will this loss cost if it does happen?" This standard of "likelihood" is a false one. The probability of a loss should be reflected in the rate charged for insurance; the cost of frequent, small losses will appear as increased premiums. The potential severity of a loss—probable or improbable—is the most important gauge as to whether a club should assume a risk or transfer that risk by paying an insurance company to assume it.

Like any business, clubs are exposed to risk; insurance protects the club from the consequences of those events that result in loss of or damage to club assets. Clubs must have a definite insurance-buying program for two reasons: they must operate within a budget and they are responsible for conserving club assets. Insurance is an economic tool. Hit-or-miss buying of anything is undesirable and, for insurance, it can cause embarrassment, criticism, and, perhaps, serious loss. Obviously it is impossible and impractical to maintain insurance covering every type of loss that could occur, but it is important to maintain a sound buying program.

The first step in planning an insurance-buying program is to analyze the losses to which a club is exposed and what these would cost. Many organizations, both commercial and non-profit, then try to draw some line and agree that they will not insure against contingencies for which the maximum possible loss would be below this line. Each club must determine for itself what this line or standard should be. A loss that would be bearable to a large club might cripple a small one. In any event, such a policy decision is fundamental to sound insurance programming.

One exception to the "large loss" standard applies when an insurance company can render important engineering and inspection services. Even though a club could withstand a financial loss without difficulty, its management is charged with a serious moral responsibility to prevent injury and loss of life. Thus, club management may purchase some kinds of insurance for the sake of engineering services alone.

The following types of insurance generally apply to club operations: coverage against fire and allied perils, including boiler and machinery; workers' compensation; public liability; automobile liability and physical damage; criminal loss; and various forms of umbrella protection. These kinds of policies are examined briefly in this chapter, as are risk management and self-insurance. Insurance textbooks devote substantial discussions to the various forms and an organization's need for them.

In applying the material here to a specific club, note that insurance policies change, as do state laws regulating them. This chapter provides a guide to kinds of insurance and policies now available or required. The information in this chapter should be adapted and updated to meet the needs of individual clubs.

A club should expect its insurance advisor, agent, broker, or consultant to analyze the club's loss exposures and its insurance protection. This person can recommend ways to improve protection and reduce costs wherever possible. A recommendation for additional protection should be accompanied by supporting data.

Any such analysis from the club's insurance advisor should include a definite plan to keep the club insurance program up-to-date in its operations and in the coverage and costs of insurance protection available.

Club management should also keep its insurance advisor informed of any change in its operations as those changes could have an affect on its insurance coverages. Communication is imperative.

FIRE AND ALLIED PERILS INSURANCE

Property loss exposures of any club include buildings and their contents, including furniture, fixtures, equipment, inventory, stock, mobile or grounds-keeping equipment, and valuable papers and records. Any loss or damage to that property would be a direct loss; but indirect losses should also be considered. Damage to the club's main building could result in business interruption, consequential damage, and loss of income, which could seriously affect the club's financial position. These exposures to loss must all be considered and reviewed in determining the adequacy and extent of an insurance program.

Insurable Value

Establishing accurate insurable values constitutes a real problem and should be given serious attention before a loss occurs. It is extremely difficult to determine values after a major fire; the result may be a complicated and unsatisfactory loss adjustment. Insurable value of buildings covered under a standard property insurance contract is generally arrived at by ascertaining the current replacement cost and making deduction for actual physical depreciation and, in some instances, obsolescence. The insurable value (value for insurance purposes) is this valuation, less any items not covered by the insurance contract. For buildings, the major items of value not usually covered are the cost of excavation, the foundations, and the utilities below the ground or lowest basement floor.

In the case of inventory, stock, or merchandise, "actual cash value" is the cost of replacing items with goods of similar kind and quality after deducting for depreciation, age, change of fashion, and saleability.

Actual cash value as applied to machinery, furniture, fixtures, and mobile equipment is generally interpreted as the net cash market cost of replacement, less depreciation for age, condition, and utility.

Insurable value as applied to papers and records is not only the cost of the paper but includes the labor, time, and research involved in their preparation or replacement.

It is important not to use "book" or "depreciated" values in determining insurance values. Book value normally reflects the maximum depreciation allowable for tax or other purposes and is generally lower than the true insurable value.

In determining the insurable value of buildings, do not rely on sales or market values, appraisal charts or indices, and square or cubic foot cost factors, because they can be misleading. Consult a competent appraisal firm periodically. Appraisals for insurance purposes usually show the current reproduction or replacement cost, the actual depreciation, and the actual cash value—all as of a given date.

An appraisal by a recognized appraisal firm is also recommended for personal property such as building contents, machinery, furniture, and fixtures. In lieu of any appraisal, all categories of personal property should be inventoried. The list should indicate original costs and acquisition dates. Such a list will help establish current values in the event of a loss. Keep the inventory in a safe place, away from the premises.

Co-Insurance Requirement

Most property insurance contracts contain a co-insurance clause. Under the terms of this clause, a club should insure property up to a certain percentage of its value. If the club fails to do so, it will not be fully reimbursed for a partial loss. The manner in which the co-insurance clause operates in event of loss is illustrated as follows:

Insurable Value	*Insurance Carried*	*Insurance Required*	*Amount Of Loss*	*Policy Pays*	*Insured Pays*
$500,000	$300,000	$400,000 (80%)	$100,000	$75,000	$25,000
$500,000	$300,000	$500,000 (100%)	$100,000	$60,000	$40,000

Thus, it is important for a club to carry sufficient insurance to meet the requirement of the co-insurance clause.

Most standard fire policies show the co-insurance percentage requirement in the policy declarations, for example, "80%." In other types of property insurance contracts, the co-insurance clause could appear in a different form. For example, one contract has this requirement:

> All covered property, except property in transit, must be insured for its total value as of the time of "loss" or you will incur a penalty.
>
> The penalty is that we will pay only the proportion of any "loss" that the limit of insurance shown in the declarations for all covered property at all locations bears to the total value of all property at all locations as of the time of "loss." This penalty will not apply to property in transit.

The quoted sentence is the equivalent of a 100 percent co-insurance requirement. The insurance company is liable for the same proportion (or dollar value) of a loss as the policyholder.

Agreed Amount Clause

An "Agreed Amount Clause" is desirable in property insurance because it abrogates the co-insurance clause. To implement the agreed amount clause, the insurance company usually requires the insured to periodically (usually annually) submit a statement of values that indicates the actual insurable value of the property insured. The company may also require that values be substantiated by an appraisal. Once the insurance company accepts a figure as the insurable value, it endorses the policy to provide the amount of insurance carried on the policy, subject to the agreed amount clause. The co-insurance clause is suspended, and any loss during the term of the agreed amount clause is adjusted without applying the co-insurance clause. An agreed amount clause usually expires on the anniversary date of the policy contract. A new statement of values is generally required and a new agreed amount endorsement must be issued. Failure to submit a new statement of values usually reinstates a co-insurance requirement.

In some policies offered by some insurance companies, the agreed amount clause is provided automatically in the body of the policy.

Replacement Cost Insurance

Most property coverage is written on an actual cash value basis, which generally means that, in the event of loss, the insured is paid on the basis of the present replacement cost, less actual use depreciation. Property insurance written on a "replacement cost" basis provides for repair or replacement without deduction for depreciation in the event of loss from any insured peril. Such coverage is readily available for buildings and may be available for other property, such as contents of buildings. A sound basis for determining replacement values may be required by the insurance company, and the amount of insurance carried must reflect true replacement values.

Special Form Insurance

Traditionally, buildings and personal property were insured against loss from specific hazards—fire, lightning, extended coverage (wind, hail, explosion, riot, vehicles, etc.), and vandalism. Today, most insurance buyers prefer the broader special form coverage instead of coverage against specified perils. Insurance buyers have generally changed to special form insurance for the following reasons:

1. It is impossible to predict which type of peril may cause serious loss.
2. Special form insurance is generally available.
3. Special form coverage has realistic premium costs.

Special form coverage protects the insured from any loss arising from a covered cause, other than those causes specifically excluded by the insurance contract. Special form insurance covers many perils excluded from the standard fire and extended coverage policy, such as water damage, freeze-up, and damage from weight of ice and snow.

Loss or damage from flood or earthquake is usually excluded under standard special form coverage, but a "difference in conditions" policy may include these. In some areas, the standard fire policy can be extended to cover loss or damage caused by earthquake, and flood insurance may be available through the federal flood insurance program.

Risk of loss protection is recommended. It can be provided by attaching the proper form to the policy or by a difference in conditions policy form.

Specific Versus Blanket Insurance

Property insurance for real and personal property may be written on a "specific" or a "blanket" basis. Under specific basis, a specified amount of insurance applies to each item insured, usually subject to an 80 percent co-insurance requirement. Under the blanket basis, insurance is provided under a single, all-inclusive item, usually subject to a 90 percent co-insurance requirement.

The blanket form is recommended because, with it, the insured does not have to maintain the exact amount of insurance needed for each item at all times; only the total values must be correct. In addition, blanket insurance coverage usually exceeds 100 percent of the values of any single building and its contents. Blanket insurance usually requires a statement of values, which lists all items insured. A club must take care to avoid overlooking significant property items.

Property Insured

Any club should insure all property of significant value which, if destroyed or damaged, would interfere with the use of the club by its membership and, thus, create financial loss. The list of such property is extensive and includes the building and contents values of the clubhouse; pro shops, refreshment, equipment, and storage buildings; garages; all sports facilities including their buildings; pumphouses; water towers; storm shelters; and bridges. Swimming pools are frequently not insured, although lightning or explosion can significantly damage them.

Some club property may be eligible for special insurance coverage, such as groundskeeping equipment or computer hardware. These items should not be included in the club's general property insurance.

Building Ordinances

Make sure that insurance on all significant club buildings conforms to local laws regulating building construction and repair. If a nonconforming building is seriously damaged, your club may have to demolish the remaining undamaged part of the building. Standard property insurance excludes (1) the undamaged part of a building that must be demolished, (2) the cost of the demolition, and (3) any increased cost of repair or construction. Insurance is available to cover this contingency and should be seriously considered if the exposure exists. Losses coud be substantial.

Property of Members

A club often has in its custody property of members and their guests, generally in locker rooms, cloakrooms, and pro shops. Insurance protection can be arranged to cover the club's liability for such property. Club rules may specifically state that the organization is not responsible for property of members and guests anywhere on the premises. In view of the rule, clubs may decide that it is not necessary to purchase liability insurance for members' and guests' property; but club management should rely on the opinion of legal counsel in this respect.

Consequential Damage

Property insurance that covers the contents of various buildings may not provide for loss due to "consequential" damage; that is, loss attributable to a fire or other insured peril even though the property damaged was not actually involved in the fire. For example, an exposure to consequential damage exists where perishable food is kept; if a fire disables a refrigerator, the food could spoil as a consequence. Club management should be aware of this potential loss and have their insurer advise them how it would interpret the coverage in event of a loss of this nature.

Deductibles

Deductibles are probably the most common form of "self insurance" and should be set at least at a level at which the costs of loss or damage can be handled "in-house" without too much difficulty.

The first rule in determining the amount of deductibles is to retain all predictable losses, and those up to a certain amount that occur so frequently as to be directly reflected in insurance premiums. However, losses for any individual club probably do not occur with any predictable frequency. Although a club may want to incorporate higher deductibles in its policies, no standard formula exists to determine the proper level. Keep in mind that smaller claims may cost more to present to the insurance company than they are worth.

Clubs should take care to avoid deductibles that apply separately to each insured item. A deductible applying to each occurrence is a better form.

Business Income Coverage

If a club's premises are damaged by fire or other insured peril, property insurance will reimburse the club for the actual physical damage to the property. The club could also sustain damages from a prolonged interruption of operations. Business income insurance reimburses a club for the loss of profit and for the continuing expenses of an idle club when normal operations are interrupted. This insurance is as important to a club as its insurance for direct physical damage.

Covered expenses include salaries that cannot be discontinued, expenses incurred under contract, taxes, mortgage payments on principal and interest, and generally all maintenance costs consistent with enforced idleness. "Profit" refers to the amount that would have been earned if operations had not ceased. In addition, business income insurance pays expenses incurred to continue operations insofar as they reduce the amount of loss from the interruption of the club's operations.

A club should also consider "extra expense" insurance. A club may want to make every effort to continue operations running as smoothly as possible after a serious loss, even though doing so entails great additional expense. Extra expense insurance is designed to meet this need.

It is important that business income or extra expense insurance be written with the same perils covered as those covered under the policies written on the buildings and personal property.

Fire Rate Schedule Analysis

A club's insurance broker, agent or property insurance representative should obtain all applicable fire rate schedules for all club buildings. Examination of these schedules may indicate that lower rates can be obtained by correcting some situations. Effective administration of a club's insurance program requires this type of analysis.

Accounts Receivable Insurance

If club accounts receivable records were destroyed or damaged to the point of illegibility, a club might be able to collect unpaid balances and outstanding accounts only to the extent that its members voluntarily paid them. Accounts receivable insurance indemnifies a club from direct losses resulting from its inability to collect money due from its members when the inability is directly due to loss or destruction of or damage to its records while the records are on the premises.

To the extent that duplicate accounts receivable records exist elsewhere, the need for this insurance diminishes. But when the only accounts receivable records are "chits" signed by members at various places on club premises or are allowed to accumulate in a club's accounting department until they are entered into the accounting system and the records duplicated, insurance protection is needed. If duplicate chits are temporarily held in a secure place until a club enters them into its accounting system, the club's exposure to loss of accounts receivable records is minimized. Then, maximal exposure occurs only when chits accumulate in an accounting department on a peak day.

Of course, duplication of all accounts receivable records eliminates need for accounts receivable insurance when the duplicate records are kept in another building. Further this exposure has been reduced with the affordability of and increased use of micro and mini-computer systems. These systems allow for easy back-up of data, which can and should be kept off-premises.

Valuable Papers and Records Insurance

"Valuable papers" means written, printed, or otherwise inscribed documents of records including books, maps, films, drawings, abstracts, deeds, mortgages, and manuscripts. Money and securities are not included. The progress of any club may depend on the availability of its valuable papers and records. Valuable paper coverage will reimburse for the loss or damage to such papers, not only for their "paper" value but also for the labor, time, and research involved in their preparation or replacement.

The valuable papers and records policy provides risk of direct physical loss coverage and there is no co-insurance requirement. The amount of insurance required is difficult to determine and may be based on management's best guess.

Mobile Equipment Floater

Country clubs have a considerable amount of mobile equipment, used on club premises for the care and upkeep of the golf courses and grounds. In addition, a club may own or be responsible for golf carts. Inland marine floater insurance is available to cover mobile equipment, wherever it might be located. Major equipment items are usually listed in a schedule attached to the policy with an insurance value indicated for each item.

There is usually a deductible clause, and it should be on a "per occurrence" rather than a "per item" basis.

Low-valued equipment should be carried under blanket insurance that covers its concentration in various buildings and takes note of its accelerated depreciation. Furthermore, smaller items are always being replaced and are thus difficult to maintain on a "scheduled" basis.

Inland marine contracts usually have a co-insurance requirement and coverage is almost always on an "actual cash value" basis (current cost to replace less actual use depreciation). When a club carries floater insurance on mobile equipment, it should be careful to exclude the equipment values from its other property insurance policies. Note that motor vehicles and boats are probably excluded from this coverage and must be protected by other forms of insurance.

Fine Arts and Trophy Insurance

Many clubs have valuable paintings and other works of art that should be specifically insured. In addition, most clubs exhibit trophies, frequently of substantial value. These should also be specifically insured.

Risk of loss coverage is usually readily available, although appraisal may be necessary to substantiate values. Note that the current cost of silver could increase club trophy values substantially above their actual acquisition cost.

Plate Glass

The typical clubhouse contains plate glass windows and doors; some may even have stained and leaded glass. Thus specific glass insurance, which covers the breakage of listed glass from any cause except fire or war, may be important.

Even if a club may not carry separate glass insurance it would not be entirely without coverage. Glass is usually included under standard property insurance forms for loss or damage from fire, lightning, windstorm, hail, aircraft, vehicles, explosion (except steam boiler explosion), riot, or civil commotion. Under standard property insurance contracts, glass breakage caused by vandalism is not covered. There may also be a limitation on the amount paid for loss of a single plate and to all plates in one occurrence under a standard property policy, a broad perils or a risk of loss policy.

To determine whether or not to purchase plate glass insurance, a glazier should prepare a schedule of all plate glass items and the cost to replace each item. With this schedule, club management can then determine whether any items should be specifically insured.

Boiler and Equipment

Standard fire and allied perils insurance contracts specify that insurance companies are not liable for explosions of steam boilers, steam pipes, steam turbines, or steam engines. Explosions of this equipment can be insured by a standard boiler and machinery insurance policy. Pressure vessels of all types are subject to serious explosion; even where explosion coverage is included under other property insurance, extension of the boiler and machinery policy coverage to include this equipment may be desirable.

It is essential that any club equipment specifically excluded under explosion coverage be insured elsewhere. A decision as to whether or not to carry boiler and machinery insurance on pressure equipment depends primarily on the possible bodily injury exposure and also on the property damage exposure. The insurance company will fully inspect the equipment to note faults and mechanical condition; it may require changes or repairs to avoid accidents before issuing or renewing a policy.

In addition to boilers and other pressure vessels, air conditioning and refrigeration equipment, motors, fans, blowers, and electrical switchboards may be insured under the boiler and machinery policy. Overloads, grounds, machine vibrations, oil-soaked insulation, and improper connections or lubrication often cause machinery to burn out or break down. Here again, the insurance company's inspection may note such faults and mechanical conditions. The repairs made as a result of these inspections increase the life of equipment and help avoid annoying interruptions. In deciding whether to buy boiler and machinery coverage on these kinds of equipment, a club should consider the equipment's value and whether the club's own staff can handle the inspection and maintenance.

For an accident involving an object insured under a boiler and machinery policy, the insured is reimbursed, up to the specified limit, for the cost of physical damage to all property (including the insured equipment) caused by the accident. Loss of business income insurance is also available under the boiler and machinery contract to cover the club against loss of profits and continuing or fixed expenses while a club is shut down wholly or partially due to the failure of insured equipment. Loss of business income on steam boilers may be essential to supplement a club's loss of business income coverage provided by other property policies.

A boiler insurance company should make a complete engineering survey. The survey should cover all equipment that can be insured under the boiler and machinery contract and should be presented to the club's management. The club will then be able to consider the recommendations of insurance company engineers and club engineering personnel and decide what it wants to insure.

Most equipment insured under a boiler and machinery policy carries no co-insurance requirement, but the limit of liability is the maximum amount available to cover damage to all club property. A low liability limit may not be adequate to cover property exposed to an accident. Business interruption loss exposures must be considered when a club establishes the amount of insurance required under loss of income coverage under the boiler and machinery policy. Under some forms covering loss of income there is a co-insurance requirement.

Repair and replacement coverage under a boiler and machinery policy eliminates depreciation as a factor in the event of loss. This coverage applies to all property of the insured damaged by an accident to insured equipment. This coverage is optional and available at additional cost.

Other Special Property Policy Forms

Property loss exposures discussed in the previous paragraphs are, for the most part, typical to all clubs. No list can include every type of property an individual club may own, and other property may require special insurance. Such property includes electronic data processing equipment and media; communication or water towers; animals; outdoor signs; visual and audio equipment; and rare property collections.

If the club rents or leases property, the rental agreement should be carefully reviewed to determine the club's legal liability for the equipment. Rental or lease agreements usually contain provisions covering the liability of the parties to the agreement and the responsibility for insuring the rented or leased property.

The following checklists can be used by any club to note what insurance is available to it, what it currently carries, and what coverage it needs to consider.

INSURANCE COVERAGE CHECKLIST

PROPERTY

Direct Damage Coverage

Has	Has Not	Needs		Has	Has Not	Needs	
___	___	___	Building(s)	___	___	___	Fire & vandalism & malicious mischief
___	___	___	Stock, materials and supplies	___	___	___	Extended coverages
___	___	___	Machinery and equipment	___	___	___	Broad perils
___	___	___	Furniture and fixtures	___	___	___	Risk of loss
___	___	___	Improvements and betterments	___	___	___	Sprinkler leakage
___	___	___	Building ordinances	___	___	___	Water damage
___	___	___	Replacement cost	___	___	___	Flood
___	___	___	Builders risk	___	___	___	Earthquake
___	___	___	Consequential loss	___	___	___	Deductible
___	___	___	Automatic cov. for newly acquired prop.	___	___	___	Fire dept. service
___	___	___	Mobile equipment (unlicensed)	___	___	___	Mortgagee/loss payee clause(s)
___	___	___	Outdoor communication equipment	___	___	___	Reporting form
___	___	___	Detached signs	___	___	___	Radioactive contamination
___	___	___	Property of others	___	___	___	Agreed amount
				___	___	___	Blanket or specific
				___	___	___	Sinkhole

Notes: ______________________________

Time Element Coverage

Has	Has Not	Needs		Has	Has Not	Needs	
___	___	___	Business income	___	___	___	Fire & vandalism & malicious mischief
___	___	___	Extra expense	___	___	___	Extended coverage
___	___	___	Contingent business income	___	___	___	Broad perils
___	___	___	Leasehold interest	___	___	___	Risk of loss
				___	___	___	Sprinkler leakage
				___	___	___	Water damage
				___	___	___	Flood
				___	___	___	Earthquake
				___	___	___	Radioactive contamination
				___	___	___	Off-premises power
				___	___	___	Agreed amount
				___	___	___	Valued form

Notes: ______________________________

INSURANCE COVERAGE CHECKLIST

BOILER AND MACHINERY

Has	Has Not	Needs	
			Limit per accident
			Boiler and fired pressure vessels
			Unfired pressure vessels
			Refrigeration and air conditioning
			Other machinery
			Electrical switch gear (MEA)
			Repair or replacement
			Water damage

Has	Has Not	Needs	
			Ammonia contamination
			Consequential
			Business income
			Valued
			Actual loss sustained
			Weekly indemnity
			Waiver of co-insurance
			Extra expense
			Deductible
			Comprehensive

RATING CREDITS

			Seasonal
			Reserve
			Unit rating of objects
			Proper object values
			Supplement to package

MARINE

			Vessels
			Outboard motors and boats
			Wharves, docks and piers
			Yachts

Notes: ____

____

INSURANCE COVERAGE CHECKLIST

INLAND MARINE

Has	Has Not	Needs		Has	Has Not	Needs	
___	___	___	Accounts receivable	___	___	___	Miscellaneous
___	___	___	Mobile equipment	___	___	___	Musical instruments
___	___	___	Air and truck shipments	___	___	___	Neon or other electrical signs
___	___	___	Antiques	___	___	___	Paraphenalia
___	___	___	Visual or audio equip.	___	___	___	Personal articles
___	___	___	Coins	___	___	___	Rifle or shotgun
___	___	___	Cold storage lockers	___	___	___	Silverware
___	___	___	Contractors equipment	___	___	___	Sporting equipment
___	___	___	Members' and guests' property	___	___	___	Tools floater
			Data processing	___	___	___	Communications towers and antennas
___	___	___	Hardware				
___	___	___	Media and data	___	___	___	Transportation
___	___	___	Extra expense	___	___	___	Valuable papers and records
___	___	___	Difference in conditions	___	___	___	Fine arts

COVERAGE

Has	Has Not	Needs		Has	Has Not	Needs	
___	___	___	Named perils	___	___	___	Reporting form
___	___	___	Risk of loss	___	___	___	Flat rate
___	___	___	Deductibles ($ ________)	___	___	___	Adjustable rate
___	___	___	Amended notice of cancellation (No. of days ________)	___	___	___	Delayed notice of accident
___	___	___	Notice of acquisition (No. of days ________)				

WORKERS' COMPENSATION INSURANCE

All states have a workers' compensation law. Insurance is probably essential for most clubs. Most jurisdictions require insurance or, in lieu of insurance, an employer's proof of financial ability to self-insure its own exposure. Some state laws do not cover specified classes of employees such as casual employees; a club should, therefore, cover all of its employees under its own insurance. The workers' compensation obligation can be met by commercial insurers in all but six states (Nevada, North Dakota, Ohio, Washington, West Virginia and Wyoming) and Puerto Rico where employers must obtain their insurance from the state fund.

The standard workers' compensation policy has two coverages. Coverage A is the statutory workers' compensation coverage. The insurance carrier pays all income replacement and medical benefits required by the state statute. Coverage B provides employers' liability to protect employers from exposure to damage suits arising from injury to employees.

Limit of Liability

Coverage A has no liability limit. The insurance company is required to pay on behalf of the employer an amount as required by the workers' compensation or other applicable laws.

Coverage B has a standard limit of liability of $100,000 for each accident for bodily injury, $100,000 for each employee for claim for occupational disease and $500,000 for all claims for occupational disease. In the absence of umbrella liability (discussed later in this chapter), the standard limit is inadequate. Without umbrella liability insurance, a limit of at least $1 million should be carried.

Premium

The workers' compensation premium is determined by payroll size and the premium is estimated at policy inception. After policy expiration the insurance company can audit the payroll account to determine the actual total amount expended for payroll during the policy period and adjusts the expired policy premium accordingly. Thus the estimated payroll must anticipate the actual payroll as closely as possible, to avoid paying an unusually large premium after a policy has expired. It is also important that payroll records be maintained to reflect any extra pay earned for overtime; workers' compensation rules permit the exclusion of overtime bonuses from the computation of premium.

Caddies

In some states workers' compensation rating rules provide that the actual remuneration of all caddies must be included with the payroll of regular club employees in computing the premiums. When the actual payroll is unavailable, the pay for caddies is based on $40 "per club member per 18 holes," subject to adjustment for larger or smaller courses, and also subject to adjustment if the club course is open to the public.

Employment of Minors

If a minor employee of a club is injured, the state's compensation commission could assess additional "punitive" damages, equal to or greater than the basic award, if the minor did not possess a work permit as required by state law. These punitive damages are not covered by workers' compensation insurance. Each club should review its list of present employees and examine future applicants carefully to make sure that it is in complete compliance with applicable state law.

Other States Covered

Most clubs have no operations in any state other than where they are located, but they might require an employee to travel into another state. The workers' compensation policy automatically provides the coverage, except in those states that have their own monopolistic funds. Most state compensation laws provide for coverage for an injury to an employee while temporarily outside of the state in which he or she is employed.

If the club has operations in more than one state, it is important that the workers' compensation policy reflect that in the declarations. Further, there are requirements for evidence that there is workers' compensation insurance in force for the employer. The insurance carrier provides the necessary filing and if it is not advised by the employer that it has employees in another state and an accident occurs, there could be fines or penalties assessed to the employer.

Rating Plans

Workers' compensation insurance may carry a substantial premium, and it is important that it is written under a rating plan likely to prove most economical for a club. In addition to the "guaranteed cost plan", retrospective rating plans are available. The success of a retrospective rating plan, which is based on actual claims experience, is directly related to an effective safety and loss control program. The guaranteed cost plan is probably the most effective for most clubs.

Participating Policy

Many insurers offer policies that allow an insured club to participate in the earnings of the insurance company. The extent and conditions of such participation are determined by the board of directors of the insurance company. Insurance companies offer various participating plans; some are based on a flat percentage of premium and others are based on the losses of the insured. A participating plan based on losses may be best for a club with a favorable claims history and a continuing effort at loss control.

Independent Contractors

Compensation laws require clubs to be responsible for workers' compensation for employees of any uninsured subcontractors. Consequently, the rules for determining premiums provide for employers to be charged for coverage of employees of subcontractors—unless the subcontractors have insured their compensation obligation and have furnished satisfactory evidence of that insurance. For its own protection, clubs should require certificates of insurance from all subcontractors working for them.

Many clubs' golf professionals and other professionals act as independent contractors. The golf professional may even operate the pro shop as a concession under personal contract and employ assistants to give lessons and perform other services specifically for him. It is important for a club to obtain a certificate of workers' compensation insurance from such a contractor to avoid being charged a premium under its own insurance plan for these same employees.

Extrastatutory Medical Coverage

Workers compensation insurance protects the club against liability and pays all medical benefits required in the state in which it operates. However, the medical benefits provided by a few states may not adequately provide for medical expenses incurred by an injured employee. In states where the benefits are limited by statute as to amount or time, a club can obtain coverage to pay additional medical benefits beyond those required by law.

Notice of Claim

Notice is required to be made to the appropriate state agency in the event an employee is injured while on the job. There is a time frame required for this notice to be given to the appropriate agency. Failure to do so could result in a fine or penalty. The club should have an adequate supply of the required form for reporting an accident (usually called Employers First Report of Injury) on hand. These forms usually state the time frame in which the claim must be reported. Some states also have a form which the employee must also complete. Your insurance agent, broker or representative can advise you of the requirements and should supply you with the forms.

Safety Engineering

Workers' compensation policies are standard for all companies and the rates are generally uniform, but standardization does not extend to engineering and conservation services, an important point for club managers to consider when determining where to place their insurance. Most insurance companies offer safety engineering services, but not all have built up real safety organizations. Safety engineering involves much more than making recommendations for safeguarding and eliminating obvious hazards. The real job of a safety engineering department is to assist its policyholders in selling the idea of safety to club management and employees alike. An effective safety program makes every employee aware of the importance of safe conditions and operations necessary to reduce accidents. A safety and loss control program will help reduce insurance costs.

PUBLIC LIABILITY INSURANCE

A club's liability exposures begin with club premises and operations and include the ownership, maintenance, and use of automobiles. (Automobile exposures are discussed later in this chapter.)

Whether a club purchases a separate liability policy or one combined with other insurance under a multiperil policy, commercial general liability including product coverage, must be included. A commercial general liability policy covers claims for bodily injury and property damage liability and provides all of the liability insurance necessary (except for automobiles) under a single contract, subject to a limited number of standard exclusions. It contains an automatic coverage feature so that, as new public liability exposures are created during the term of the policy—such as when the club acquires a new location or undertakes new operations—the club is automatically protected. The policy is subject to audit following expiration and the club is then charged a premium commensurate with its actual risks. A club's insurance advisor should carefully review the club's commercial general liability insurance to make sure that all exposures have been properly handled.

Adequate Liability Limits

High liability limits for both bodily injury and property damage are a necessity. Liability arising out of club premises and operations can involve a large number of members and their guests, and it is essential that any club's limits be adequate for present-day requirements. The trend of jury verdicts is toward ever-increasing amounts, and awards of several hundred thousand dollars or more are no longer unusual. In a catastrophic loss injuring or killing a number of persons, total judgments have been immense.

The latest commercial general liability policy has an aggregate limit applying to premises operations for all losses occurring during the policy term. Heretofore the aggregate limit only applied to product liability claims. It is important that your limits be reviewed and consideration be given to increasing the aggregate limit above the per occurrence limit of your policy.

The total liability limit under the commercial general liability policy should be supplemented by an umbrella liability policy. Further the latest editions of umbrella liability policies, like the primary commercial general liability policy, also have an annual aggregate limit applying to premises operations. Clubs should rely on their insurance advisors to arrange their total liability limits.

Umbrella Policy

An umbrella policy should be part of any club's liability insurance program. Not only does it provide excess liability coverage over existing policies, but it also covers some losses not covered by the underlying policies.

The umbrella liability policy usually supplements existing employers' liability, commercial general liability, and business automobile liability insurance. For example, a club's primary coverage could be $100,000 for employers' liability and $1 million for bodily injury and property damage liability under both its commercial general and business automobile liability policies. An umbrella policy of $4 million would provide additional insurance over this primary coverage. The umbrella policy for $4 million could apply for losses not covered by primary insurance, after the self-insured retention limit (usually $10,000 or $25,000) is exceeded.

Exclusion Endorsements

Club management should be aware that there are endorsements that may be attached to the commercial general liability that exclude liability arising out of certain activities. Further, the commercial general liability policy excludes liability arising out of professional services rendered. Services of masseurs, barbers, beauticians, or other professionals that could give rise to malpractice claims must also be covered by modifications to the policy. There are also "clubs endorsements" often attached to the commercial general liability policy. These endorsements exclude certain activities, depending on the kind of club.

Management should rely on competent insurance advice to review all exposures arising from the club activities. Other potential loss exposures are discussed in the following paragraphs.

Legal Liability of Club Members and Employees

Standard commercial general liability plans insure the personal liability of any executive officer, director, or stockholder acting within the scope of their duties. In addition, the policy includes employees as insureds. A club endorsement should be added which includes any member of the club as an insured, but only with respect to personal liability for club activities or activities performed by club members on behalf of the club (except while practicing for or participating in any game or sport).

It is possible that a judgement could be returned against a club member or an employee if a claimant's injuries could be attributed to any act of negligence on the part of the club member or an employee, whether the act was one of omission or commission. Furthermore, no law prohibits any person from suing any other person, so the possibility of a groundless suit against a club member or any employee also exists. Even though a suit may be groundless, a club member or employee could be subjected to considerable expense for an investigation and defense.

Personal Injury Liability

Club liability insurance should include "personal injury" liability. This coverage includes (1) false arrest, detention, or imprisonment and malicious prosecution; (2) libel, slander, defamation, or violation of right of privacy; (3) wrongful entry or eviction of a person from premises. Through the acts of club management or employees, it is entirely possible for a club to be subject to claims under one of these categories. The latest version of the commercial general liability policy includes this coverage and it should not be excluded by endorsement.

Liquor Liability

Operations at most clubs include selling or serving alcoholic beverages. A club could be held liable for claims arising from selling, serving, or giving any alcoholic beverage to a person already under the influence of alcohol or that causes or contributes to the intoxication of any person. Liability may be by statute or by common law. The standard commercial general liability policy excludes coverage for such claims. Clubs should obtain liquor liability insurance or have the commercial general liability endorsed to extend the policy or eliminate the exclusion.

If no formal policy exists on alcoholic beverage service at your club, one should certainly be formulated. The overall responsibility of the club manager is to provide a policy concise and consistent with the applicable state law on liquor liability that can be approved and adopted by the Board of Directors. The policy should then be communicated in the following ways:

1. Posting the policy in conspicuous areas throughout the club including bar service areas, communication boards, locker rooms, and employee areas.
2. Articles written in newsletters, communications from the Directors, and Manager's letters should state the policy, the reasons for its adoption, and the way in which the club will enforce the policy.
3. Training of all the staff and department heads in the club policy, the law and the methods to be used in the case of over-serving a member or guest.
4. Repeat communication every six months and retrain as needed for staff.

Sample Policy:

In accordance with the State Liquor Control Commission and the laws pertaining to the service of alcoholic beverages, the club has adopted the following policy: . . . .

Service is refused to minors or anyone who appears intoxicated.

Service is refused to anyone who may have imbibed sufficient alcohol to impair the ability to operate an automobile, even though they may not appear intoxicated. This is in line with court rulings that liability may exist even if intoxication isn't obvious. Absorption rates can vary drastically with the circumstances.

Transportation may be provided for any person who appears inebriated.

Obviously it is a sensitive matter for our employees to refuse service. We ask your help and understanding. Please remember that the staff has been asked to err on the side of caution.

The club cannot assume liability for loss or damage to any personal or group property brought into the club. This personal or group property is the sole responsibility of the individual or group. The group is responsible for the conduct of all of the guests, and for any damage incurred upon the club or its guests by persons associated with or representing the group's organization.

Aircraft

Commercial general liability insurance usually excludes aircraft. Consequently, if an aircraft used by a club for any purpose is involved in an accident, the club's liability for such an accident would not be covered. Thus, if a club uses aircraft, directly or indirectly, its management should consider insuring the club's liability.

Interests Insured

Insurance protection for golf and other professionals who operate as independent contractors or concessionaires is not provided by a club's public liability insurance. These individuals should be required to carry their own public liability insurance and to furnish an insurance certificate to the club. As discussed earlier in the chapter, the professionals should also carry workers' compensation insurance on their own employees and furnish a certificate to the club.

Property of Members and Guests

Commercial general liability insurance excludes damage to property of others in the care, custody or control of the club or for which the club is in any way exercising physical control. A club's commercial general liability insurance usually does not cover the property of members and guests while the property is on the club premises, including locker rooms, cloakrooms or guestrooms. As recommended earlier in the chapter, a club should rely on its legal counsel for advice concerning insuring property of members and their guests.

Products Liability

It is entirely possible that food served by a club to its guests or members could cause injury. Such claims actually materialize often and unexpectedly. Also the club may sell other products that could cause injury. Products liability coverage as part of the commercial general liability coverage is essential.

Fire Damage Liability

Every club should be aware of the possibility that it could be held liable for fire damage to any building or part of a building it is leasing. Liability from fire damage is similar to automobile or public liability, in that a club may be responsible to another party if, through negligence or the negligence of its employees, agents, the owner's property is damaged. The commercial general liability policy includes fire damage liability with a specific limit, usually $50,000. Negligence is involved in determining a fire liability loss, and a court and a jury usually have to establish such negligence. Fire damage liability insurance pays for these expenses and the judgement rendered (to the limit of the coverage), if a jury determines that such negligence did exist.

The club should seek the advice of its legal counsel in negotiating a lease and should have its insurance advisor review the lease prior to execution to determine what the club's liability is. It is sometimes possible to modify the lease to avoid the exposure to fire liability.

Stop-Gap Insurance

A club located in one of the states where workers' compensation insurance is provided by a state fund should consider stop-gap coverage to provide or add to its employers' liability protection. Standard workers' compensation insurance policies provide employers' liability coverage with a standard limit. This is usually supplemented by umbrella liability.

In lieu of a standard workers' compensation policy, stop-gap coverage can be added to the commercial general liability policy, and employers who participate in state fund operations may need stop-gap coverage.

Liability Coverages with One Company

All forms of liability insurance, including automobile and compensation, should be placed with the same insurance company. Commercial general liability insurance, for example, automatically covers certain types of mobile equipment for no additional premium; coverages for other mobile equipment must be provided by automobile insurance, and a specific charge is made. When these coverages are placed with different companies, disagreement can arise among them as to which is liable for a particular accident.

Similar reasons exist for having compensation and public liability insurance with the same company. Questions frequently arise as to whether an individual was an employee or member of the public at the time an injury was sustained. Such cases are much more easily resolved if both the compensation and the public liability coverage are with the same company. Liability insurance checklists are helpful to see what is available, what a club currently has, and what it needs to consider to properly round out its liability insurance program.

INSURANCE COVERAGE CHECKLIST
GENERAL LIABILITY
BASIC COVERAGES

Has	Has Not	Needs		Has	Has Not	Needs	
___	___	___	Commercial General Liability	___	___	___	Professional
___	___	___	Completed Operations	___	___	___	Errors & Omissions
___	___	___	Products Liability	___	___	___	Owners and Contractors Protective
___	___	___	Independent Contractors				
___	___	___	Medical Payments	___	___	___	B.I. & P.D. Limits $ ______

AUTOMOBILE LIABILITY

___	___	___	Uninsured Motorists	___	___	___	Comprehensive ACV Ded $ ______
___	___	___	Medical Payments				
___	___	___	Hired Automobiles	___	___	___	Comprehensive Stated Amount
___	___	___	Non-Owned Automobile				
___	___	___	Garage Insurance	___	___	___	Collision
___	___	___	Garage Keepers	___	___	___	Fire
___	___	___	Any Automobile	___	___	___	Theft
___	___	___	State Statutory Coverages	___	___	___	Combined Additional Coverage
___	___	___	Fellow Employee Exclusion Removed	___	___	___	Towing & Labor
				___	___	___	Employees as Insured (non-owned cars)

WORKERS' COMPENSATION

___	___	___	Workers' Compensation	___	___	___	Voluntary Compensation
___	___	___	Employers' Liability	___	___	___	Longshoremens Endorsement
___	___	___	Extra Legal Medical				
				___	___	___	Compensation Supplement

OTHER LIABILITY COVERAGES

Has	Has Not	Needs	
___	___	___	Umbrella Liability
___	___	___	Excess Liability
___	___	___	Excess Employers' Liability
___	___	___	Directors and Officers Liability
___	___	___	Aviation
___	___	___	Protection and Indemnity (Marine)

LIABILITY COVERAGE EXTENSIONS

Has	Has Not	Needs	
___	___	___	Employee Benefit
___	___	___	Fire Legal Liability Limit Increased
___	___	___	Personal Injury (Ex. Employees)
___	___	___	Personal Injury (Incl. Employees)
___	___	___	Broad Named Insured
___	___	___	Fellow Employee
___	___	___	Incidental Malpractice
___	___	___	Bodily Injury Deductible
___	___	___	Property Damage Deductible
___	___	___	Watercraft Exclusion Deleted
___	___	___	Liquor Liability Exclusion Deleted
___	___	___	Joint Venture or Partnership
___	___	___	Delayed Notice of Accident
___	___	___	Amended Notice of Cancellation
___	___	___	Severability of Interest
___	___	___	Waiver of Subrogation (between insured and members)
___	___	___	C.C.C. Exclusion Deleted

AUTOMOBILE INSURANCE

A club's loss exposure with regard to automobiles or trucks includes ownership, maintenance, and use of its own vehicles as well as loss or damage to vehicles owned by others that a club has in its care, custody or control.

Business Automobile Liability Coverage

Liability coverage under the business automobile policy should apply to "all automobiles" to give a club as much automatic protection as possible.

"All automobiles" includes all owned, nonowned and hired automobiles and trucks.

Automobile Physical Damage Coverage

It is customary for a club to insure its own vehicles for loss or damage caused by fire, theft, collision, etc., including any temporary substitute vehicles. If a club assumes liability for loss or damage to a non-owned or hired vehicle, it may have to make special arrangements for physical damage insurance.

Clubs are undoubtedly directly responsible for the automobiles of members and guests entrusted to their custody. In addition, many clubs maintain a parking valet service for members and guests and, accordingly, purchase Garage Keepers insurance to cover liability for loss or damage to those cars. Such vehicles can also be insured for loss or damage caused by fire, explosion, theft of an entire automobile, riot, civil commotion, vandalism and malicious mischief (named perils) or, essentially, for all risks of physical loss (comprehensive) coverage. Under either plan, collision or upset coverage is purchased separately.

Adequate Liability Limits

Because the club could be held responsible for an automobile accident causing bodily injury or property damage, a high liability limit is essential. As mentioned earlier in this chapter, the upward trend of jury verdicts requires that a club's liability limit be substantial. In addition, the public liability policy limits should be consistent with the limit provided in the automobile policy.

The total limit of liability under a club's automobile liability insurance must also be coordinated with an umbrella liability policy. Here again a club should rely on an experienced insurance advisor to arrange its total limits of liability between its primary and umbrella liability insurance coverage.

Kinds of Automobile Insurance

The following kinds of automobile insurance normally apply to a club's automobile loss exposures:

1. Liability insurance pays all sums for bodily injury or property damage caused by an accident and resulting from the ownership, maintenance or use of an automobile.
2. Physical damage insurance pays for loss to a covered auto. Comprehensive coverage (generally recommended) or specified perils and collision coverage are available. Towing and labor costs can be included for passenger autos.
3. Medical payments insurance provides payment of all reasonable and necessary medical, surgical, and dental expenses resulting from a bodily injury, sickness, or disease caused by an accident while anyone is occupying or getting into or out of an owned automobile. Employees operating club automobiles and trucks on club business are covered by workers' compensation insurance, so separate medical payments coverage may not be considered essential. The coverage may be necessary, however, for private passenger vehicles or vans or buses to cover members or guests, employees using a club's private passenger vehicle for personal business.
4. Uninsured motorist insurance pays damages the club is otherwise legally entitled to receive from an uninsured or hit-and-run motorist. This coverage also protects other persons occupying the owned auto at the time of accident. The basic limits are those required by a state's financial responsibility law. Higher limits may be purchased. In addition to providing adequate limits where no insurance exists, the higher limits of uninsured motorist coverage also apply to losses above the limits carried by the legally liable party.

5. Automobile nonownership liability insurance covers the club's liability for losses arising from the operation of vehicles the club neither owns nor hires. Hired automobile liability insurance covers the club's liability for losses arising from the use of hired or borrowed vehicles. A hired automobile is one used under contract on behalf of or lent to the club.

   Automobiles leased under long-term contract (twelve months or more) may be insured as if owned by the club; in fact, the lease will usually require this. Nonowned and hired automobile coverage is excess over any other available insurance and coverage is not provided to the owners of the nonowned or hired automobiles.
6. Garage Keeper's insurance pays all sums a club must legally pay as damages for loss to a covered automobile left in a club's care for parking or storage. Comprehensive or specified perils and collision coverage are available. As stated earlier, Garage Keepers insurance can be provided to pay for loss or damage even though a club may not be legally liable.
7. Personal injury protection is coverage mandated by law in some states. It can vary as to limit and scope of coverage, depending on the particular state.

Physical Damage Deductibles

"Comprehensive" physical damage insurance can be written on a full coverage basis; however, as a practical matter, most insurance companies will only provide the coverage with a minimum deductible of fifty dollars. Collision coverage is provided with a minimum deductible. A savings of premium can be realized if higher deductibles are assumed by the club. Individual club circumstances dictate the amount of deductibles.

CRIMINAL LOSS INSURANCE

A club requires several basic forms of criminal loss insurance, including protection from employee dishonesty, burglary, robbery, and depositor's forgery insurance. One policy can be issued to provide the required coverages. In any event it is important that coverage be coordinated with other property coverages in order to avoid duplication of coverages and gaps in coverage.

Employee Dishonesty Insurance

Just as vital to a club as fire or liability insurance is "employee dishonesty insurance." More money and property are embezzled annually by trusted employees than by all of organized crime. Dishonesty insurance takes three basic forms; individual fidelity bond (an individual employee named under the bond); schedule fidelity bond (several individuals or positions with the same or varying amounts in a single bond); and the blanket fidelity bond (all employees).

Blanket fidelity bonds are recommended because they have certain advantages over individual or schedule bonds. All employees of the club are bonded, so a club need not attempt to select the persons or positions from which a loss might occur. Moreover, a single uniform amount of coverage is applicable to all employees, and new employees are automatically covered. If a loss occurs and the person causing the loss cannot be identified, recovery can be made without identification, if proof is furnished that the loss was due to acts covered by the bond. In the event of loss, the amount of coverage is fully restored without additional premium, and no premium adjustments are made during the term of the bond except in case of merger or consolidation.

Amount of Coverage: The amount of coverage should be commensurate with the exposures, such as the value of current assets and the amount of annual receipts. The Surety Association of America has developed a formula to determine the amount of fidelity coverage a firm may need. It is endorsed by the American Institute of Certified Public Accountants. A club's insurance advisor should review this formula with the club's insurance committee and help it establish an adequate amount of coverage for employee fidelity.

Noncompensated Officers Endorsement: Standard employee dishonesty insurance covers loss of money, securities and other property "through any fraudulant or dishonest act or acts committed by any employee, acting alone or in collusion with others. Employees as defined in these policies usually exclude officers elected or selected from the membership. A club can purchase a noncompensated officers endorsement to amend the definition of employee to include officers by title, such as president or vice president. The club should also consider amending the definition to include chairmen and other members of a committee who might have control over money, securities or other property.

ERISA

The Employee Retirement Income Security Act of 1974 requires that all fiduciaries (trustees) of all employee benefits plans (pension, group medical, etc) be bonded. The act requires the bond's limit to be at least ten percent of the amount of funds handled annually. Clubs can usually meet this requirement by adding their employee benefit plans, by name, as insureds under their employee dishonesty insurance coverage. There should be no additional cost for this.

Theft, Disappearance, and Destruction of Money and Securities

The amount of coverage a club requires to protect its money and securities can be estimated by careful review and analysis of club operations. The average and maximum amounts of money on hand and checks from others form the basis for determining the amount of insurance to carry.

Depositors' Forgery Insurance

This policy covers a club against losses from the forgery or alteration of any check, draft, promissory note, bill of exchange, or similar instrument made or drawn on the club or its agent. A bank is generally responsible for payment of a forged check, but there are situations under which a depositor may be required to bear the loss.

To determine the amount of forgery coverage it requires, a club should recognize that the largest check the bank would cash without investigation does not limit the loss exposure. In many cases, forgery losses are composed of an accumulation of small losses that remain undiscovered for a considerable period of time.

Other Crime Coverages

There are several other forms of crime coverages that the club may need. They are listed as follows:

Robbery and Safe Burglary—There are two coverages under this form. One for robbery of a custodian inside the premises; the other for actual or attempted safe burglary inside the premises.

Coverage can be provided for robbery outside the premises. The coverage in its basic form only covers property other than money and securities. It can be endorsed to include money and/or securities.
Premises Burglary—This form provides coverage for burglary and robbery of a watchman inside the premises. The coverage applies to property other than money and securities.

These coverages are separate and distinct. The terms robbery, burglary, theft, premises and inside and outside have distinct meanings. Robbery is the taking of property from a person by one who causes or threatens bodily harm to that person. Burglary is the taking of property from inside a premises by a person unlawfully entering or leaving as evidenced by marks of forcible entry or exit. Theft constitutes any act of stealing. Premises is defined as the interior portion of any building that the club occupies in conducting its business.

Careful consideration of these forms of insurance should be made with other property coverages and criminal loss coverages to avoid duplication in coverage.

Package Criminal Loss Insurance

The Combination Crime policy is applicable to clubs. Plan 1 can provide coverage on employee dishonesty; forgery; theft, disappearance and destruction of money and securities; robbery and safe burglary. It can also include six other coverages. A separate limit applies to each coverage.

Plan 2 can be provided. The first four coverages enumerated in the above paragraph are mandatory with a single limit applying to all four coverages. The other six coverages can be included with a separate limit applying to each.

Records

Coverage under criminal loss insurance may be void unless records are maintained in such a manner that the insurance company can accurately determine the amount of loss. It is therefore of utmost importance to maintain an adequate set of records. Further, in event of most kinds of criminal loss, it is required that the loss be reported to the appropriate law enforcement authorities, or the loss will not be paid by the insurance company.

Criminal Loss Insurance—One Company

It is to the club's advantage to place all related kinds of insurance with the same insurance company. Doing so simplifies the reporting and handling of claims; further, if more than one kind of criminal loss coverage is involved in a claim, controversy is avoided as to which insurance company is liable for the loss.

A checklist of available criminal loss and other related policies follows:

INSURANCE COVERAGE CHECKLIST
CRIMINAL LOSS

Has	Has Not	Needs		Has	Has Not	Needs	
___	___	___	Blanket Fidelity Bond	___	___	___	Excess Bond
___	___	___	Position Schedule Bond	___	___	___	Credit Card Forgery
___	___	___	Individual Fidelity Bond	___	___	___	License Permit Bond
			Theft, Disappearance and Destructlon of Money and Securities	___	___	___	Notary Bond
___	___	___	Inside	___	___	___	Surety Bond
___	___	___	Outside				
___	___	___	Depositors Forgery				
			Robbery and Safe Burglary				
___	___	___	Inside				
___	___	___	Outside				

OTHER INSURANCE

Many insurance policies are regarded as "specialty" lines of insurance. Some of these can be especially important to a club.

Directors, Officers, and Trustees Liability Insurance

Club directors, officers, and trustees are exposed to loss involving liability from wrongful acts performed while carrying out the duties of their offices. In addition, the club itself has a similar loss exposure if it is required or permitted by law to indemnify its directors and officers. Dissatisfied members institute lawsuits for many reasons. Liability insurance protects the individual as well as the club from the possibility of financial loss and should supplement the noncompensated officers endorsement of the fidelity coverage.

Fiduciary Liability Insurance

The Employee Retirement Income Security Act of 1974 makes the individuals (fiduciaries) who are responsible for administering employee benefit plans personally liable for wrongful acts or omissions in their duties as fiduciaries.

Fiduciary liability insurance primarily covers this liability and supplements the ERISA bond requirement discussed earlier.

Unemployment Compensation Insurance

Nonprofit organizations may or may not have the option of paying unemployment tax applicable in their state or of reimbursing the government for any payments made to former employees. Although a club's employee turnover may be very low, a serious fire or similar event could suddenly put employees on unemployment rolls. If the club has used the "reimbursement option, unexpected demands could be made on club funds. Unemployment compensation insurance is available from a few companies to protect a club if its obligation to reimburse exceeds what it would have had to pay as its normal payroll tax.

License and Permit Bonds

States, counties, and municipalities usually have various requirements for license and permit bonds. The bonds may be needed to sell certain kinds of products such as liquor, cigarettes, or fuel, or for certain operations. Other lines of insurance could be required by some clubs.

As stated earlier, it is impossible to comment on every loss exposure a club faces or on every available kind of insurance. Clubs should rely on the advice of competent, experienced insurance and legal personnel.

Other Forms of Insurance

A number of other kinds of coverage may be applicable to clubs. In deciding whether or not to secure them, club management should consider the following points:

1. The total amount of the club's budget for insurance.
2. The premium or rate for the coverage.
3. The probability of the hazard.
4. Most importantly, the extent to which the club would suffer if it failed to obtain the insurance and then sustained a loss. Would the loss be serious or just inconvenient?

RISK MANAGEMENT

Self-Insurance

In the strictest sense, self-insurance means that an organization makes the financial plans necessary to meet its losses just as an insurance company would. In practice, self-insurance is the payment of insignificant losses that occur so regularly that they are considered ordinary expenses.

Theoretically, most clubs are not candidates for self-insurance. Self-insurance would essentially require an approach similar to that taken by an insurance carrier. No club should undertake any self-insurance program without expert outside assistance. Exposure to risk must be spread both numerically and geographically, to be cost efficient.

In practice, however, all clubs probably self-insure to some degree. Certainly the cost of replacing broken china and disappearing flatware are normal, expected expenses. To insure such losses with a professional insurer or under a formal self-insurance scheme is unnecessary.

Risk Management Procedures

Every club can use risk management to handle its loss exposures properly.

This approach involves identifying the values exposed to loss and their loss frequency and severity and following planned procedures to handle the exposures. Several plans can be used. They are:

1. Avoidance or Elimination. The club can avoid or eliminate the operation that creates the loss exposure—for example, cancel the annual Fourth of July fireworks display at the club.
2. Loss Control. The club can try to prevent or reduce losses. For example, hold the fireworks display in a restricted area where it cannot cause property damage or bodily injury (loss prevention) or maintain additional firefighting equipment and personnel at the display to handle the increased possibility of fire (loss reduction).
3. Risk Transference. The fireworks display company can contractually assume all liability (non-insurance transfer) or the club can arrange protection through its own insurance company (insurance transfer).
4. Retention. The club can retain the possible loss exposures that arise out of the display. This approach can prove costly.

The club may want to use more than one risk management procedure. Certainly in the fireworks example, loss prevention, reduction and risk transfer would be practical and partial retention (in the form of deductibles) may even be required.

Insurance is only one of several risk management tools. For a large organization, the use of insurance may be minimal compared to the use of other methods, but for most clubs, insurance is the major risk management tool. Effective use of other procedures could reduce insurance costs.

Loss Control

Loss control and risk transfer (insurance) are probably the two most important factors for most clubs. With proper loss control, the insurance transfer is facilitated. Inadequate loss control may make insurance more costly or even unavailable.

Every club needs its own active loss control program. Most clubs can look to their insurance carrier's engineering department to help establish the program. Company brokers, agents, or representatives will help coordinate the activities of all the parties involved.

Loss control measures can include sprinkler and automatic fire-extinguishing systems, improved housekeeping, guards, lightning protection systems in the main club building and golf-course shelters, which all prevent or minimize the possibility of bodily injury, death, substantial property damage. Although no two clubs are alike, their loss control procedures may generally be similar.

Safety engineering for the protection of members, employees, and guests is necessary as well as safety engineering for the protection of property (club and members' principally). Continuing attention to safety and loss control is required.

Fire prevention also merits continuing efforts of club management. Smoking, cooking, and cooking equipment, electrical faults, and heating equipment faults are the principal causes of fires at country clubs. Club fires usually originate in kitchens, heating equipment, or activity rooms.

INSURANCE MARKETS AND MARKETING

A number of different types of companies sell insurance. Moreover, insurance can be bought through several types of agents. What are the differences between stock and mutual insurance companies? Who are the insurance broker, independent agent, direct writer, and risk manager?

A stock insurance company is a profit-seeking corporation owned by its stockholders and operated by its officers.

A mutual insurance company is a corporation owned by its policyholders and operated by its officers, with any profits or savings going to the policyholder in the form of dividends (return or premiums).

Insurance brokers are agents of the insured customer (club), not the insurance company.

Independent agents represent one or more insurance companies, although their primary loyalty is usually to their clients. Both brokers and independent agents may deal with several companies. Agents have binding authority within limits specified by the company; brokers may not have such authority without company approval. Both negotiate with companies for their insureds for coverage and cost considerations and assist in settlement of losses. Both are compensated by commissions from the insurance companies.

Direct writers represent one insurance company and are usually required to place all of their clients' business with that carrier. The carrier may be very competitive in price and coverage; the direct writer is compensated by salary or commission.

Risk managers are responsible, wholly or in part, for developing, implementing, and monitoring a policyholder's risk management plan. The manager may be an employee of the club, its insurance consultant, its insurer or the insured's broker or agent. The average club probably does not have a full-time risk manager and looks to its insurance company, broker or agent for risk management services.

Most clubs should judge an insurance company on the basis of the various services offered that the club needs. These services can include loss control and safety engineering, claims, insurance coverages, capacity to handle a given type of business, and ancilary services such as property valuation assistance. As mentioned earlier, stock and mutual insurance companies both have advantages; these are discussed at length in insurance textbooks.

To select an insurance representative (usually an agent or broker), a club should judge the agent or broker along similar lines. In-house claim expertise, marketing and negotiating skills, experience with similar business organizations, reputation and references are important selection criteria. Some clubs' insurance committees include members who are active in the insurance business; an agent or broker who is not a club member may be responsible to the committee for the club's insurance program.

SUGGESTED PLAN OF INSURANCE SUPERVISION

A club must constantly supervise its insurance program. Insurance requirements change immediately if a club extends its operations; installs new facilities; invests additional money in equipment; acquires new buildings; enters into agreements, leases, or contracts involving assumption of liability; sells new products; contracts for building alterations or changes its methods of operation in any way.

Thus, even though an insurance program may be entirely in order and correct at a given time, insurance quickly becomes outdated unless a plan guarantees immediate adjustment due to changing conditions, either in club operations or the insurance business. Insurance programs need supervision, usually available from a competent agent, broker or insurance advisor. Such supervision should cover the following areas:

1. Review building values
   Annually consider the effect of appreciation or depreciation on building values and, thus, the appropriate changes required to the insurance.
2. Review equipment values
   Make an annual check to determine the effects of new purchases, depreciation, and obsolescence on equipment values and the insurance covering such property.
3. Review contents and supplies values
   Annually consider the value of furniture, fixtures, merchandise, and supplies and their insurance; make required adjustments.
4. Analyze fire rate
   Annually analyze fire insurance rates to determine whether any reduction is warranted by reason of changes in fire protective devices, business operations, adjacent exposures, or the tenancy of club properties.
5. Monitor rate changes
   Promptly notify the club of any rate reduction that might entitle the club to a refund or extension of coverage under existing policies.
6. Examine audits
   Inspect all audits in connection with workers' compensation and liability policies.
7. Provide claim adjustment service
   Personally supervise claims for losses, at any hour of the day or night. Represent and coordinate services when a claim arises, ensuring that a claim is adjusted promptly and in conformance with the contract.
8. Provide accident and loss prevention service
   Take active interest in loss prevention, studies of the club's accident problems, and closely cooperate with insurance companies' safety engineers. Even when adequate and proper insurance is carried, accidents cost money. Clubs lose the services of injured employees or are deprived of the use of damaged equipment; losses paid by insurance companies are ultimately reflected in higher rates. Consequently, loss prevention is as important as loss adjustment. Every insurance company offers loss prevention service, but the quality of this service and, thus, its value varies.
9. Check on policy warranties
   Periodically check that a club is meeting all warranties and conditions under the terms of its insurance policies.
10. Advise on new contracts
    Promptly notify a club whenever a new or improved form of insurance contract applicable to a club becomes available. New contracts appear frequently and, in many cases, provide broader protection than older versions.

11. Review new leases and contracts
    Review any new lease or contract, before it is executed, for insurance ramifications. This step does not reflect on the ability of legal counsel; rather, insurance advice supplements it. Routine contract language contains traditional insurance implications. A skilled insurance professional can frequently suggest another way to meet such obligations without the use or requirement of an insurance contract and should have the opportunity to do so at the time action can be taken. After a contract is executed, the insurance advisor can only react to the requirements; the opportunity to solve a problem in a more economically advantageous way may be lost.
12. Advise on new legislation
    Provide information concerning any changes in local, state, or national laws effecting insurance (i.e., automobile financial responsibility, compensation, and social security).
13. Examine policy
    Inspect all new and renewal policies and endorsements to see that they are properly written to fit the need for which they are purchased, and that the premiums are computed correctly.
14. Control insurance
    Establish a definite plan to permanently control the insurance program and yet require minimal club time. Review club requirements and notify the club of changes in insurance required by changes in its business. There is no other effective way to provide thorough, dependable continuing insurance supervision.

SECURITY AWARENESS

One dictionary defines the words *secure* and *security* as: "to render safe from danger, loss, attack; free from care, worry, fear". It goes further to sum up the definition by stating: "firmly fastened". Most club managers probably agree that "firmly fastened" would aptly be the solution to most security problems in our service-oriented business. An in-depth view of club security, however, shows that the area of security not only encompasses the protection of small asset items which tend to disappear, but also includes protection of all other club assets such as: building, equipment, supplies, funds, grounds, items entrusted into your care by others, and yes—even the protection of your employees, members, and their guests. What you do to protect and conserve these assets is your overall security program effort.

One main problem associated with club security is the total time span during the day and week that a facility or operation might be open. A full schedule of daily events normally opens a country club facility to early morning breakfast patrons and golfers, and continues for a period of 20 hours until it closes after the 2:00 A.M. party band has stopped playing and the room is reset for the next day's scheduled affair.

In this day of increased crime statistics, it becomes more and more important to implement various aspects of security in order to reduce exposure to theft, vandalism, etc. Managers should not concentrate their attention and efforts on "catching villains" as much as they should develop a program for the "prevention of villainous acts" at their facility.

Security can be discussed more clearly if grouped into divisions:

1. building and physical structures
2. controls, systems, and procedures
3. emergency measures
4. grounds
5. personnel and administration
6. equipment and apparatus

Building and Physical Structures

Most managers will not get the opportunity to participate in designing a new club facility. The designer of a new facility should recognize security requirements involved and insist that:

1. Outside night lighting is adequate in all areas involved with parking, walking, receiving, and building access points.
2. Cashier and valuable trophy display areas are not adjacent to the front door.
3. Employee exits do not open directly onto employee parking.
4. Employee dressing facilities are not immediately inside the employee entrance.
5. Food preparation areas are separate from central storeroom functions.
6. Employee egress through different operational departments is minimized.
7. Employee dining and lounging areas are provided away from production areas.

Other "Building and Physical Structure" considerations:

Hasps and Hinges—These items should be installed on doors and drawers so that the screw or bolt securing the device is covered when it is in the closed position. Hinges should have tamper-proof hinger pins to preclude removal of hinge pin and consequently the locked door. Old-type hinges can also be secured by removing one screw from one door hinge and replacing it with a sturdy nail driven into the hole by leaving 1/2 inch remaining exposed. Then—remove the opposite screw from the same hinge and the exposed nail head will act as a security pin for the door when it is closed.

Dutch Doors—Beneficially installed between operational areas and controlled merchandise areas. Half door permits communications and issues without personnel flow.

Employee Dressing Rooms—Rooms should be well lighted, bright, cheerful, with floor and wall surfaces that are durable and easy to clean. Lockers should have built-in combination locks of the type that a single core master key, controlled by management, can open. Signs should be posted indicating employee responsibility and club policy on maintaining alcohol, firearms, club property, etc., in the lockers. The tops of the lockers should be slanted so that items of club property cannot be placed on locker tops.

Lighting—Lighting has been described as the least expensive and most efficient of all security devices. Lights can be put on time clock or light controls for maximum efficiency. Specify low energy type ballasts and bulbs.

Controls, Systems, and Procedures

It behooves club managers to operate under clear, concise policies in securing the assets of the club membership.

These policies must then be converted into systems and procedures for their implementation. Subjects to be considered under this division are:

Internal Control—As far as practical, the arrangement of accounting records, methods, and general details of a fund should be diversified to insure that no part of a total procedure is under the absolute and independent control of any one person. All employees handling funds and responsible for storage of merchandise should be bonded. The insurance bonding company will screen those employees who are being bonded for reliability and the possibility of being involved in previous irregularities. Many internal and personnel problems can be diverted if a policy is made not to hire relatives of current employees. This question should be indicated on the application form.

Cashier—A daily cash verification should be made of each change fund and also between each shift of personnel. Too often, a shortage of funds without proper transfer of responsibility (acceptance of an uncounted change fund) has resulted in either loss of friendships, letter of reprimand, or termination of employment. "If a person doesn't have time to do it right—when will he have time to correct the wrong?" Adequate protection must be afforded each cashier: locked cash drawer; or locked cash box; or access to safe.

Checks—Checks received for payment should be stamped "for deposit only" so they become non-negotiable. Each check should be listed as received on a daily checklist in case a check is lost or stolen. Policy should be established on the cashing of employee checks. Blank, unused checks (payables, payroll, etc.) should be kept in locked containers until used. Management should be shown every check that is returned by the bank "for any reason" the same day it is received from the bank.

Deposits—Deposits should be made on a daily basis whenever possible in order to eliminate cash on hand and to maintain a constant audit flow.

Signatures—Dual signatures should be required on all club payable checks over a stated amount. Single signatures can be obtained on all payroll checks.

Purchasing—A policy statment sheet should be prepared and signed by all department heads and those responsible for procurement of any item, to the effect that: "It is the policy of the club to procure the best quality merchandise as specified by management without any favoritism and that any form of gift or remuneration will not be accepted from any vendor."

Nepotism—If permitted—employees who are members of the same family should work in different departments and should not have a direct relationship in dealing with each other (bartender—waitress; cook—waiter).

Trash—An interesting subject for security. Employees are normally restricted in the type of items and containers which they are permitted to remove from the building, but trash is not one of them. Therefore, trash boxes and garbage cans are prime places to hide nicely wrapped items of meat, produce, alcohol, supplies, etc., to transport to the rear of the club and into bushes or cars. In addition to the possibility of theft, garbage cans collect valuable silverware, glassware, coffee pots, and linens, that, without checking, go straight to the dump! The solution is the in-house inspection and dumping of one can into another—sort of a treasure hunt. This operation creates no added expense and can produce several thousand dollars of recoverables each year.

Seminar—Some clubs have found that security seminars conducted in-house at the club have greatly alleviated their overall security problems. Through these seminars, jointly conducted by local police and management personnel, the time and effort have resulted in: a safer work area; membership is gratified; theft infractions are reduced; each employee became a highly motivated security force within the club; and overall security was increased at no cost to the members.

Apprehension—The club board should establish in the official minutes, the policy they desire to pursue in the apprehension of members or non-member offenders who: wantonly damage club property or grounds; require forceful removal from club property for unbecoming behavior; break laws. The policy should instruct management so that his actions will be as directed by the club's governing body in case of legal dispute at a later date.

Emergency Procedures

One never needs an emergency procedure until he has an emergency! Are you ready for one?

Fire—A few club facilities are single story, concrete block buildings, with many exits, and located close to the fire station. Most are not. Management should check the fire requirements of the city and review the previous inspection reports for the past several years. Minimum fire prevention measures that should be considered are:

1. Instruct personnel in the proper use of fire extinguishers. The local fire department will bring equipment to your facility and conduct training.
2. Establish areas of responsibility for each employee in case of fire. Learn the location of extinguishers and type to be used.
3. Emergency numbers should be listed on the phones.

Robbery—It is not unusual for club receptionists and cashiers to be robbed even though clubs normally do not maintain large cash funds due to their charge sale transactions and payments being made in the form of non-negotiable checks.

Management should be alert to:

1. Maintain low cash funds.
2. Keep cash out of direct sight of members and employees when making transactions.
3. Install video cameras in the area.
4. Install finger and foot activated alarms at cashier locations.
5. Keep safes in locked position.
6. Develop procedures for cashier to follow in case of burglary (to include):
   a. Do not resist—stay as calm as possible.
   b. Move slowly in giving money—but give it up.
   c. Activate alarms or code signal.
   d. Remember assailants' clothes, height, weight, and description.
   e. Afterwards—write everything down immediately.

Bomb Threats—This category of emergency occurs more in some cities than others. Once started, they become a re-occurring menace to regular operations. Management is usually in a "no-win" situation—if you do evacuate the building with each "threat", then you are considered over-reacting and disrupting the social life of your guests. If you don't evacuate, then you are risking the property of the club and possibly the lives of your members.

It is best to have a plan that can immediately be placed into effect should a "bomb threat call" be received. The plan should include:

1. Police and fire notification.
2. Search of the entire building by employees.
3. Policy of the board as to evacuation and continuance of operation.

Employees are needed to search the areas because they are most familiar with the items that should be expected to be found in each area. If a suspicious item is found, then it should only be touched or opened by persons qualified in bomb detonation and control.

Club Grounds

It is estimated that half of the security problems encountered at a country club-type facility occur on the grounds surrounding the main club house or in the outside areas occupied by tennis courts, pool and golf course.

Fencing—Some type of fencing is desirable to completely enclose the club property. It may be various combinations of solid materials such as wood, chain link, hedges, brick, or stone. In those cases where home properties bound the club property perimeter, it may not be possible or even advisable to fence the club property. Some clubs have found the use of water-filled ditches and single strand wire cable accomplish an acceptable job of restricting vehicles from entering the property. Where chain link fencing is deemed unattractive, vegetation, such as ivy, can be grown to make it look acceptable.

Curfew—A good policy to be adopted by directors is the establishment of a nighttime golf course curfew as part of the grounds rules. The golf course grounds are then declared off-limits to pedestrian traffic, so if any member or dependent is observed on the course after dark, he is automatically infracting club rules and his membership is subject to discipline.

Rewards—One method of communicating the fact that your directors mean business when it comes to security or vandalism on the golf course, is to adopt and publish in the club bulletin and on bulletin boards—"A reward of up to $500 will be given for information leading to the arrest and conviction of persons vandalizing the club golf course."

Parking Lot—These areas should be well lighted and correctly marked. Employees should be instructed on the exact location in which they are to park. Friends of employees must wait in this same area for employees. Employees should also be instructed that they must leave the parking area when departing work.

Lighting—Lighting of building perimeters can serve both to aid security and also beautify structures, trees, shrubs, signs, and garden areas. Lights should be controlled by timers or light sensing devices.

Personnel and Administration

It is sometimes difficult for management to realize, but losses incurred directly from employee acts and employee untrustworthiness are far more frequent and usually larger in value than losses incurred from outside the organization. A most important aspect of security begins with the proper recruitment and hiring of prospective employees. Background investigations, to include contacting personal references and previous employers, is a must. One small bit of information gained during a check of references may be worth, ten fold, the time and effort you will spend eliminating your problems after an employee has been fired.

Employee Policies—Management should reduce to writing and make available to each employee the policies and rules under which the employee is to perform. A new employee normally desires to "be a good employee and do what the boss expects", but if the boss doesn't let the employee know the rules (parking, smoking, dress, removal of packages, where to eat, what to eat, etc.) then one can be certain that the employee will learn these subjects wrongly from the other emplyees and in the end, be detrimental to your operation.

Termination—Termination slips should be completed on each terminated employee by his supervisor. This slip will serve to remind you later as to the cause of termination. The slip should also be initialed by management, so that all terminations will come to his attention. Where terminations are not "for cause," it is recommended that a letter be sent to the terminated employee, asking for his reasons of termination. The return envelope should be addressed to and opened by the manager. If there is any security problem within the organization, this is one source of information.

Equipment and Apparatus

Safes—Safes should be of good quality. Local locksmiths can provide management with ratings on the fire and vulnerability of safes now being used. Safes containing funds should be welded or adequately secured to the building structure, have a three-position combination, and contain inner locked compartments, should more than one person need access. It is recommended that the combination be changed every six months or whenever a person knowing the combination no longer requires access to the safe. The local locksmith can train management in the correct method of changing the combination and also furnish the proper change key. Always try the new combination with the door in the open position (to preclude locking the door with a wrong combination). Dates of combination changes should be posted on the inside of the safe door.

Locks—Door locks should be of the "slide bolt" type. Where knob type locks are used they should be of the "tamper-proof" variety. Combination locks may be better suited to some conditions than key locks. Combination locks are also available of the style that can be reset with a combination set key. Care should be exercised when using the four tumbler bottom type combination lock to immediately remove (wind-off) the combination when the lock is opened; otherwise the correct tumbler combination remains for others to read when in the open position.

Keys—All operational keys should be correctly labeled. A master key should be kept on permanent file for every workable, useable lock in the facility. A locked master key cabinet should be maintained. All extra, loose, and unidentified keys should be grouped together by the identical type (master, Corbin, flat, etc.) tied, and put in the safe for future use. Should keys to a sensitive area be lost, then the lock core of that area should be changed and a new key made. It is advisable to put a padlock and hasp, in addition to the regular door lock, on areas such as bars, storerooms, and where items subject to pilferage are stored. This procedure acts both as a double lock and also provides the opportunity of changing the padlock immediately should a key get lost or change of access personnel be made.

Alarms—Various types of alarms should be installed on your facility. Alarms can be activated by pressure, heat, cold, water, smoke, sound, or motion. As in the case of insurance—put an alarm on "those things that you can't afford to lose". Smoke alarms located in the machinery room, dirty linen collection point, and kitchen can be automatically relayed to the local fire department. This type security alarm is very beneficial to those clubs which do not have 24-hour personnel guard protection for late evening and early morning periods when the building is unoccupied, and unprotected from fire. Some managers have installed inexpensive temperature alarm devices on the club's main chilled water pipe of the air conditioning system and also on the hot water pipe of the domestic hot water system. These two controls, attached to ceiling light sockets in the club main office and equipped with red light bulbs and small Christmas-type disc flashers in the sockets, provide management with a period of 15–45 minutes lead time to correct problems before complaints arrive from the members on high room temperatures and lack of hot water for showers. Alarm devices can also be placed on freezers, sump pump flooding, and other critical areas.

Camera Security—Remote security cameras are available for use in delivery areas, parking lots, kitchens, grounds, and other locations. These cameras can be installed with various type lens (regular, wide angle, telephoto) and the monitor screen placed where it will be attended.

Camera—Regular—Inexpensive, shirt pocket cameras are now available that can be issued to security personnel to assist in making "ready identification" of problem areas or personnel. This item can assist in identifying repeat offenders, slip and fall accidents, automobile identification, etc.

Engravers—Etchers—Vibrating or rotating engravers should be used to mark and identify small metal items of property which are used throughout the club and items that sometimes get in the hands of florists, decorators, and even members. A bottle of red finger nail polish and small bottle of white appliance touch-up paint can be kept on hand and used on the bottoms of porcelain, wood, and leather items to keep things from "walking."

Pictures—A permanent file of good quality 35mm wide angle pictures taken of each club area (from 4 directions) showing interior furnishings will suffice to prove loss in case of theft or fire. Make certain the pictures are dated and kept in a fire proof safe.

Pagers—Various companies now provide portable communication pagers that assist management in security and availability of personnel. Sophisticated two-way radios provide golf course grounds superintendents with direct communication with security guard personnel patrolling the course as well as instructional information to grounds maintenance crews. Small inexpensive rechargeable pocket pagers can be purchased which will receive one-way communications from anyone dialing a city telephone number. The pager is lightweight, can be carried during the day shift by one employee (mechanic, delivery driver, management, etc.) and then transferred during the evening to a security person. In those cases where a country club golf course is surrounded by homes owned by club members, the security guard "pocket pager telephone number" could be given to each home owner, should they observe reportable vandalism occurring on the course.

Cresting—The policy of having the club crest or logo engraved on new silver: trays, coffee pots, champagne coolers, candelabras, and other items of value, will reduce the chance of their disappearance. Once a local trophy company has made your club crest template, the engraving charge is small and well worth it. Cresting of tableware is beneficial since this act will usually result in the return of flatware from rental laundries (not resaleable), and employee misappropriation is not as great as when using plain patterns.

Mirrors and Windows—Convex, wall mounted security mirrors are available for locker room corners and aisles to provide attendants with a broader view of their area. One-way mirror glass can be placed in appropriate areas when behind-the-scenes surveillance is desired from time to time. Small slit type windows attractively placed in various room doors such as storeroom, party function, maintenance, and kitchen, provide several advantages.

1. Security personnel can observe personnel working.
2. Personnel hesitate to waste time in work areas.
3. Improves safety of entrance.

Managers desiring to procure new items of equipment and apparatus should contact other users of the equipment to determine the quality and application of the item to a given situation.

SUMMARY

To summarize, club security can be described as the total effort exerted to protect, conserve, and efficiently manage the assets and personnel of an operation. In addition to security subjects already covered in this section, total security of assets must include safeguards and controls previously mentioned in other chapters dealing with food and beverage preparation, storage and issue, purchasing, receiving, and accounting. Management must realize that the foundation of a good security system is based on the "awareness" of each person in recognizing security as being important and the fact that each member of the staff must be alerted, on a continuing basis, to the possibility of security incidents occurring within the operation in the future.

REVIEW QUESTIONS

1. Why does the author recommend blanket versus specific insurance?
2. What club-specific insurance coverages does the author mention?
3. What should a club consider when purchasing commercial general liability insurance?
4. Discuss the basic forms of criminal loss insurance.
5. What areas does competent insurance supervision cover?
6. What should be included in a total club security program?
7. Discuss suggested club emergency procedures.

11

Taxes and Regulations

Pinehurst Country Club, Denver, Colorado

TAXES AND REGULATIONS

Club managers must oversee the long-range tax and regulatory compliance of their clubs, as well as the day-to-day detail of club operations. Nonprofit clubs are exempt from federal income tax provisions if they meet certain requirements. Clubs are liable for other federal taxes (such as taxes on unrelated income) and state and local taxes on wages and other items. Profit-making clubs, of course, pay taxes on all net income.

In addition, clubs must comply with federal, state, and local regulations regarding such concerns as pesticides, fire hazards and prevention systems, and building codes. This chapter summarizes the federal requirements and highlights some of the important state and local regulations that may apply. Of course, state and local laws vary and each club must consult its own local tax and legal advisors.

Private social clubs are either proprietary (member-owned) or investor owned. Proprietary clubs, generally organized under the nonprofit corporate statutes of particular states, are generally eligible for federal and state income tax exemptions. Individual clubs may, however, fail to qualify for the exemptions or may choose to forego the exemption in the interest of greater operational flexibility.

Investor-owned clubs (distinguished from investor-owned facilities leased by a member-owned club) are almost always taxable, profit-oriented organizations, but whether a club is truly "private" does not necessarily affect its tax status. Many newer clubs have been organized to provide amenities (and consequent marketability) to adjacent residential or resort developments. Many of these clubs are owned by the developer at first, but are then acquired by members when the associated development nears maturity.

Under federal law, tax-exempt private social clubs must indeed be "private," "social" and "clubs" and they must primarily meet the needs and interests of their members. However, some amount of dealing with nonmembers does not necessarily jeopardize the club's tax exemption or its legal status as a private club for purposes of exemption from the public accommodations or employment practices provisions of the federal Civil Rights Act of 1964.

Clubs have been exempt from federal income tax since 1916, although recent attempts have been made to limit this exclusion. The tax-exempt status of clubs is determined by laws passed by Congress, regulations and rulings of the Treasury Department and the Internal Revenue Service and decisions handed down by various courts. Obviously, loss of federal income tax exemption is costly to a club; a manager must ensure that the club meets all legal requirements to maintain the exemption.

Federal Income Tax Exemption

Internal Revenue Code section 501(c)(7), sets five general criteria for tax exemption; a club must meet all five:

1. The organization must be a club.
2. The club must be organized for pleasure, recreation or other nonprofitable purposes.
3. Substantially all club activities must be for pleasurable, recreational or nonprofitable purposes.

4. No part of the net earning of a club may inure to the benefit of any private shareholder.
5. At no time during the tax year can the charter, bylaws or other governing instrument of the club contain a provision that discriminates against any person on the basis of race, color or religion. (Note that sex discrimination is not prohibited.)

Club managers must understand the five guidelines to understand why certain questions appear on the IRS annual information return Form 990; why certain questions are on the club's application for exemption (Form 1024) and why an IRS examiner probes certain documents during an audit.

1. Must be a club. The Internal Revenue Service has said that, to be a club, an organization must have the following:

a. a membership of individuals;
b. personal contacts;
c. fellowship; and,
d. commingling of members.

The requirement for *individual* membership derives from the requirement of personal contacts and fellowship between members. The IRS contends that although fellowship need not be present between each and every member of a club, it must constitute a material part of the organization's activities. Fellowship cannot play a material part where the club is composed of artificial entities. As a result, the Service ruled that gross receipts from corporate members will be a factor in determining whether a club qualifies as a social club. It is advisable, as a general rule, not to allow corporations as members. Note that under this rule a federation of clubs will not qualify for exemption.

The IRS has ruled that a social club does not jeopardize its exempt status by admitting corporation-*sponsored* individuals, if they have the same rights and privileges as regular individual members and are approved by the club's membership committee on the same basis as all other members. Caution should be used in accepting checks from members' employers. The Service has treated as unrelated business income, amounts paid to a social club by a corporation wholly-owned by members of the club for meals and other services provided to clients of the corporation. Clubs should attempt to obtain payment for large events directly from the individual member rather than his or her employer.

Personal contacts and fellowship must play a material part in the life of an organization for it to come within the meaning of the term "club." If an organization's only activity is to operate and maintain a television antenna system providing services to members in their homes, the group does not qualify as a "club" because those services do not afford an opportunity for personal contacts and fellowship among the members. National or statewide organizations made up of individuals, but broken down into local groups, satisfy the requirements for fellowship if fellowship constitutes a material part of the activities of each group.

A commingling of members must also play a material part in the activities of the organization for it to be a "club." An automobile club with the principal activity of rendering automobile services to its members, but with no significant social activities, does not qualify for exemption as a social club. An organization that conducts regular bowling tournaments for its members could qualify for exemption if its overall program is designed to promote a commingling of members for their pleasure and recreation.

Examples of the requirements for commingling are found in two IRS rulings involving flying clubs. The first ruling involved a club that was open to everyone interested in flying. The members did not join to participate in flying for recreation but rather to obtain economical flying facilities, suitable for their individual business or personal use. No expectation that members would form personal relationships with other members existed. Little commingling among members for social or recreational purposes occurred. The IRS said the club did not qualify for social club exemption.

Another flying club, however, did qualify for exemption. This group limited its members to those interested in flying as a hobby and members had to be approved by a two-thirds vote of the club members. The members of this club were in constant personal contact with each other at formal board and general membership meetings and at informal meetings to schedule the use of aircraft. There was a constant commingling to maintain and repair club-owned aircraft. In addition, the members flew together in the club's aircraft. The IRS ruled that this club met the commingling requirement.

2. Organized as a club. To be exempt from federal income tax, a club must be organized for the purposes set forth in the statute. The purposes of an organization are generally listed in its articles of incorporation, corporate charter or other instrument creating the group. Thus, the IRS requires that a club send a copy of such a document along with its application for federal tax exemption. Any changes in the instrument must be filed along with the organization's annual information tax return. Some court cases suggest that extrinsic evidence may be provided to show the real purpose of a club, but every effort should be made to properly set forth the purposes of a club in its organizing instruments.

Activities having a pleasure and recreation purpose are, in some instances, broader and more varied in concept than may be expected. For instance, a nonprofit organization formed to bring family members into closer association through social activities revolving around matters of common historical and genealogical interest to the members as a group was ruled by the IRS to be exempt. The IRS said that promoting closer ties among family members and providing social commingling among them were similar to providing pleasure and recreation for the members of a social club and that the organization therefore qualified for exemption under section 501(c)(7).

If a club is organized for business purposes rather than for pleasure, recreation or other nonprofit reasons, it is clear that the club is not exempt. The IRS looks at the facts and circumstances to see if profitmaking is a major purpose and to determine exemption.

3. Substantial Rule. Prior to 1976, statutes and regulations required exempt clubs to be organized and operated "exclusively" for pleasure, recreation and other nonprofitable purposes. Thus, a club couldn't run an untaxed, profitable business on the side to offset expenditures or help members avoid paying dues. Courts were reluctant to apply a literal meaning to "exclusively," and case law suggested that clubs could engage in some nonexempt activity and still retain their exemption.

The proper mix was generally a matter of "facts and circumstances," which had to be individually decided by courts. Unfortunately, courts frequently used conflicting sets of standards. Clubs with incidental profits that were either negligible or nonrecurring were generally able to maintain their exempt status. The 1976 modifications to the Code changed "exclusively" to "substantially," thus ending many of the interpretative problems. As a result, a club may now earn income from nonmember sources to a limited extent and may have a limited amount of investment income, without losing its exempt status.

In 1976, Congress concluded that a strict line of demarcation between the exempt and nonexempt activities of social clubs was no longer necessary. It then required a tax-exempt social club to be substantially devoted to pleasure, recreation and other nonprofitable purposes, but liberalized the extent to which an exempt club could obtain income from nonmembers and investment income. With the 1976 Act, Congress intended to make clear that a tax-exempt club may receive some outside income, without losing its exemption.

Whether substantially all of an organization's activities are related to its exempt purposes must be decided on the basis of all the facts and circumstances. However, the facts-and-circumstances approach applies only if the club earns more outside income than is permitted under the 1976 guidelines. If the outside income is less than the guidelines permit, the club's exempt status should not be challenged on *this* basis.

Under the 1976 guidelines, a tax-exempt club may receive up to 35 percent of its gross receipts including investment income, from sources outside of its membership. Within this 35 percent limit, no more than 15 percent of the gross receipts may come from use of a social club's facilities or services by the general public. If a social club permits nonmembers to use its club facilities and receives 15 percent of its gross receipts from these nonmember sources, the club then may receive no more than 20 percent of its gross receipts from investment income. If a club has outside income in excess of the 35 percent limit (or the 15 percent limit in the case of gross receipts derived from nonmember use of the club's facilities), all the facts and circumstances are taken into account to determine whether the club qualifies for exemption.

If a club loses its exempt status for that year, all of its income, even that received from its membership, is subject to tax for that year. In such a case, under the provisions of section 277 of the Internal Revenue Code, the income received from the club's members, but only this income, could be offset by the cost of services and goods furnished the members. A member loss cannot be offset against the club's other sources of income.

Social clubs are required to carry on activities traditionally carried on by exempt clubs. Even changes made in 1976, allowing additional unrelated business income, did not permit clubs to actively conduct a nontraditional business.

The Service has taken the position that the provision of personal services to members may constitute the active conduct of a business not traditionally carried on by exempt social clubs. A nontraditional business has been defined as any business which, if conducted on a membership basis, would not further the club's exempt purpose. In some insurances, the IRS has proposed that receipt of *any* gross receipts from a nontraditional activity might require revocation of the club's exempt status retroactively.

The line between acceptable and nonacceptable activities is a fine one. Providing hotel-type sleeping rooms on an occasional basis to members and the rental of mini-office space by half day or a day was permitted; however, when these activities become long-term arrangements, a questionable activity arises. The operation of a full-service barbershop was questionable. A parking garage used in connection with activities other than those at the club, the operation of a service station, a takeout food service and the operation of flower and gift shop or retail liquor store were deemed nontraditional.

Clubs cannot lease to others and simply use intermediaries to conduct clearly nontraditional activities according to the Internal Revenue Service. A rental of space must be at arms length and be for a fair value.

4. Inurement. Section 501(c)(7) says, ". . . no part of the earnings of which inures to the benefit of any private shareholder." The statute is generally interpreted to refer to members as well. Inurement, direct financial benefit to members, endangers a club's exempt status.

The IRS has held that a social club with active members who pay substantially lower dues and initiation fees than do associate members does not qualify for exemption under section 501(c)(7) of the Code, even though both classes of members may enjoy the same club rights and privileges. The IRS ruled, in effect, that the active members are being subsidized by the associate members and that this subsidy constitutes inurement.

A provision in a club's charter that its assets will, upon dissolution, be paid to the members or shareholders is not, in itself, sufficient to cause a club to lose its tax-exempt status. Every club could, eventually, disband or dissolve; the potential distribution of club assets is not sufficient for the club to lose its tax-exempt status.

As another example, a club purchased an office building and used part of it as a clubhouse. The part not used as a clubhouse was leased to commercial tenants. The club's gross rental income from the tenants amounted to approximately 75 percent of the club's total gross income. The club used the rental income to defray operating expenses of the building and to expand its facilities. The IRS ruled that the club was not exempt; one reason was that net income from the lease inured to club members in the form of improved and expanded facilities.

A "horse-and-trailer" riding club sponsored a rodeo for the pleasure and recreation of its members and the community; it charged outsiders for the cost of the rodeo. The U.S. Tax Court held that the enhancement of the club's facilities and retirement of its debt from the receipt did not constitute inurement.

A social club that regularly opens its golf course to the general public in exchange for payment of established green fees also runs into the problem of inurement. Such income from the public is considered inurement to the benefit of the club's members because it is used to maintain and improve club facilities.

Another example of inurement is the payment of sick, disability and death benefits by a club to its members or their families. The Tax Court has said that, when a club makes such payments, part of the club's net earnings inures to the benefit of members, thus jeopardizing the club's exempt status.

If the cost of a benefit is not significant, inurement may not be a factor. For instance, one court has said that sportcoats, bearing the emblem of the club and worn only at club functions, for which the total cost was $1,365.50, did not constitute inurement. The same court also held that sending flowers to sick members was not a financial benefit to the ailing person.

Clubs sometimes have tournaments in which their members compete for prizes. Awarding cash prizes to tournament winners from tournament entry fees also does not raise the question of inurement.

An incidental sale of property will not deprive the club of its exemption even if a substantial gain realized on the sale of club property exceeds the 35 percent threshold. A relief provision permits a club which receives significant income, such as from the sale of its clubhouse or similar facility, to exclude the amount from the 35 percent calculation.

The IRS has ruled that even though a profit is realized, the sale will not cause a club to lose its exemption if the sale is incidental; it is not a departure from the club's exempt purpose. If profit is the primary motivation, the sale will not be considered incidental. All the facts and circumstances of a sale will be considered in determining the club's primary purpose in making the sale, including: (1) the purpose of the club in purchasing the property; (2) the use the club makes of the property; (3) the reasons for the sale; and (4) the method used for making the sale.

When a club sold 10 acres of land that was originally acquired only because the original sellers refused to sell less than the entire tract to the club initially, the Service ruled the sale was incidental and would not adversely affect the tax exemption. The Service did note that the tract, used as a practice range and turf-grass nursery, had not been improved since its acquisition. Furthermore, the club had not intended to improve the land to enhance its value or prepare it for sale. The club was also allowed to sell the property in small parcels since an appraiser stated it was doubtful the property could be sold as a single tract within a reasonable time period. The IRS reached a similar conclusion where a club had planned to use a parcel of land as the site of a new clubhouse. After learning that the cost of the new facility would be prohibitive, and the intended use was in violation of local zoning ordinances, the club decided to sell the unimproved parcel and use the proceeds to make improvements to its existing facilities.

In contrast, however, where a club subdivided the land into building lots, made improvements, and marketed the properties over a period of years at substantial profits, the Service ruled that the sales were not incidental. The IRS concluded that the primary motivation for the subdivision and sales technique was to increase profits. Therefore, the club was not operated substantially for exempt purposes.

Although an incidental sale of club property will not be included in the 35 percent test when considering a club's exempt status, the gain is still taxable. Unrelated business taxable income (UBI) includes gross income (excluding any exempt function income) less allowable deductions directly connected with the production of the gross income. Capital gains and losses are not excluded from the computation of UBI *unless* they qualify for *nonrecognition* under special reinvestment provisions.

If property used directly in the club's exempt function is sold and other property is purchased and so used, gain will only be recognized to the extent that the sale price of the old property exceeds the cost of the new property. Tax is not imposed because the organization is merely reinvesting the funds formerly used for the benefit of its members in other types of assets to be used for the same period. The qualified reinvestment must be made during a four year period beginning one year before the date of sale and ending three years after.

When a club sold its facilities located on the front eight acres of a 16-acre tract and used the proceeds to construct new facilities on the back eight acres, no gain was recognized to the extent the proceeds were reinvested within the allotted three-year period.

Where a question exists whether the club used the property in its nonprofit activities, the Service has ruled that even if the organization had made no use of the land, the sale would qualify for nonrecognition treatment. The club had shown that the property was purchased as part of a single transaction, the property was to be used in the performance of exempt functions, and no evidence existed that the property was purchased for investment purposes.

A club which sells property used for club purposes and distributes the net sales proceeds to its members in dissoluton of the club, must recognize gain. Since the club did not purchase replacement property, the gain does not qualify for this relief.

This nonrecognition provision only applies to the gain from a club's sale of property not on income from an option on the sale of property. Any option premium is unrelated business taxable income to the club.

Procedures for accounting for this income are detailed in the chapter on club financing.

5. Discrimination. Until 1976, the tax law did not deal explicitly with the question of whether an income tax exemption for social clubs was incompatible with discrimination on account of race, color or religion. In 1972, in *McGlotten v. Connolly,* the U.S. District Court of the District of Columbia held that discrimination on account of race was not prohibited under the U.S. Constitution in the case of a club merely because of the club's exemption from federal income tax under section 501(c)(7).

In 1976, Congress took the view that it is inappropriate for a social club to be exempt from income taxation if its written policy is to discriminate on account of race, color or religion. Now, a club may lose its federal tax-exempt status for any tax year if, at any time during that year, the organization's charter, bylaws or other governing instrument or any other written policy statement, contains a provision that provides for discrimination against any person on the basis of race, color or religion. Although compelling constitutional arguments can be raised against this 1976 provision because it makes tax exemptions contingent on the forfeiture by club members of their rights of association and privacy, this requirement has not been challenged in court and remains part of the federal tax law.

A club may still be selective on a basis other than race, color or religion and maintain its exempt status under section 501(c)(7). For instance, a club may restrict its membership to the members of a particular political party or to homeowners in a particular housing development; such a restriction will not by itself cause a loss of exemption.

Exempt or Taxable?

Many exempt clubs may be considering a switch to a taxable status because of the many qualifications and limitations associated with maintaining their tax exemptions. Clubs should be aware of a whole set of limitations which apply when clubs relinquish their exempt status.

Any membership organization and specifically a social club operated primarily to furnish goods or services to its members, must still maintain a separate accounting of member and nonmember activities. All deductions attributable to member activities are allowed only against member income; any excess member deductions must be carried forward to offset member income in succeeding years. Taxable clubs still are denied a dividends-received deduction and are subject to the profit-motive requirement to deduct expenses against nonmember and investment income. Only expenses incurred in the conduct of a trade or business or for the production of income are allowable.

A club that is otherwise entitled to exemption will not lose its exempt status because it rasies revenues from its members other than by dues and assessments. The principal income of a club may derive from a bar or restaurant that only members and guests are permitted to use; the club's exemption will not be affected.

The fact that a club derived a principal part of its revenues from its recreational facilities does not affect its exempt status as long as the facilities are used only by the members and their guests. For instance, revenue from gaming devices does not affect a club's exempt status, although the gaming devices may be illegal under local law and raise other legal questions.

OTHER FEDERAL TAXES

Unrelated Business Income. Income not related to the purpose constituting the basis for the club's federal income tax exemption is "unrelated business income." It is taxable at regular corporate business rates; payment of this tax bears no relationship to a club's income tax exemption.

The unrelated business income of an exempt social club includes all gross income, less all allowable deductions directly connected to producing that income. "Gross income," for this purpose, does not include "exempt function income." Exempt function income is the club's gross income from dues, fees, charges, or similar amounts paid by members as consideration for providing goods, facilities, or services to the members, their dependents or guests in the course of serving the exempt purposes of the club.

Thus, a country club's gross income for unrelated business taxes does not include gross income from members for their use of the club's golf course. It does include such income from nonmembers.

Passive income, such as interest and dividends set aside for religious, charitable, scientific, literary or educational purposes or for the prevention of cruelty to children or animals, will generally not be subject to unrelated business income tax. Income set aside for these purposes is also exempt function income.

If club facilities or personnel serve to produce both exempt and gross income, expenses, depreciation and similar items must be reasonably allocated between the two uses.

The allocation of costs to reduce unrelated business income presents complex problems for clubs. The IRS has in several, but not all, cases been unwilling to accept use of the simplest allocation method—the "gross to gross" approach. However, in a 1985 Circuit Court case, a "gross to gross" allocation formula based on the ratio of nonmember sales to total sales was used and the IRS conceded that these indirect expenses were reasonably allocated.

In a particularly troublesome 1981 ruling, the IRS barred the allocation of costs if they were incurred in nonmember activities in which a club had no "profit motivation." An absence of profit motivation would apparently be indicated if a club lost money on the nonmember activity after indirect costs were computed.

Litigation has occurred over the presence of a profit motive. In *Northridge Country Club v. Commissioner,* the club argued that as long as nonmember activities generated revenue in excess of the direct costs of maintaining those activities a profit motive existed. The club would realize a double benefit: positive cash flow and partial defrayal of fixed, indirect costs which would have been incurred regardless of whether the nonmember activities were conducted.

The Tax Court looked at a profit motive as "an incremental increase in available funds" to the taxpayer rather than as taxable profit. The Court agreed that the club would incur various fixed costs such as depreciation and overhead regardless of whether the nonmember activities were conducted. It found that the club made a series of careful economic decisions regarding its nonmember activities. Therefore, each dollar earned over the direct costs of the activity served to benefit the taxpayer. After analyzing the nonmember activities, the Court found that a direct benefit inured to the club and rejected the IRS argument that there must be a taxable profit. Therefore, it concluded that a profit motive could exist where there would have been taxable profit in the absence of the allocation of fixed and indirect costs *and* where facts and circumstances showed consideration of economic factors in operating the nonmember activities.

The fact that gross nonmember sales receipts exceed direct expenses and losses result only after indirect costs are allocated to sales will not *by itself* prove profit motive. Economic decisions must underlay the operation of nonmember activities. Issues which should be carefully considered include:

1. Does the pricing structure cover direct costs?
2. Are market conditions considered in determining pricing, i.e., competition, advertising and market demands?
3. Are cost-cutting factors reviewed in scheduling, hiring and general operation of nonmember activities?
4. Are cost-sharing arrangements used with member activities to reduce operating expenses?

Until the Supreme Court rules on the issue, additional conflict between clubs and the IRS is expected. Clubs should become aware of the changes in the area and consult with their tax advisor as to the proper treatment of unrelated business income.

Nonmember Income. The IRS adopted guidelines in 1971 describing circumstances under which nonmembers who use a social club's facilities are assumed to be guests of members. The guidelines describe the records required when nonmembers use a club's facilities and the circumstances under which a host-guest relationship is assumed for purposes of complying with the exemption requirements and for computing exempt function income.

The guidelines provide that when a group of eight or fewer individuals, at least one of whom is a member, uses club facilities, it is assumed for audit purposes, that the nonmembers are the guests of the member. This rule applies only if the member or the member's employer pays the club directly for such use. If 75 percent or more of a group using club facilities are members, provided it is likewise assumed for audit purposes that the nonmembers in the group are guests of members, the same guidelines apply when one or more of the members or the member's employer pays the club directly for such use. Payment by a member's employer is assumed to be for a use that serves a direct business objective of the employee-member. In all other situations, a host-guest relationship is not assumed; it must be substantiated.

The club must maintain adequate records to substantiate that a group consisted of eight or fewer individuals, that at least one of them was a member and that payment was received by the club directly from members or their employers. If a member pays a club directly, the club is under no obligation to inquire about reimbursement the member might later receive.

The club must likewise maintain adequate records to substantiate that 75 percent or more of the persons in the groups larger than eight were, in fact, members of the club at the time of such use and that payment was received by the club directly from members or their employers. When a member pays a club directly, the club is under no obligation to inquire about reimbursement.

In the 1970s, the IRS said that amounts paid by members of one club that had a reciprocal agreement with another club would be treated as member income. However, the Service has reversed that position. Amounts paid to a social club by a visitor from another social club are considered nonmember income even if both clubs are similar in nature and the amounts paid are pursuant to a reciprocal agreement.

With respect to all other occasions involving nonmember use, the club must maintain books and records of the payment received. The record must contain the following information:

1. Date
2. Total number in party
3. Number of nonmembers in the party
4. Total charges
5. Charges attributable to nonmembers
6. Charges paid by nonmembers
7. When a member pays all or part of the charges attributable to nonmembers, the member must sign a statement indicating whether he has been or will be reimbursed for such nonmember use and, if so, the amount of the reimbursement.
8. If the member's employer reimburses the member or directly pays the club for charges attributable to nonmembers, the member must sign a statement indicating: the name of the employer; the amount of payment attributable to nonmember use; the nonmember's name and business or other relationship to the member; and the business, personal, or social purpose of the member served by the nonmember use.
9. When a nonmember pays the club or reimburses a member and claims that the amount was paid gratuitously for the benefit of a member, the member must sign a statement that indicates the donor's name and relationship to the member and contains information to substantiate the gratuitous nature of the payment or reimbursement.

Under the 1971 guidelines, failure to maintain records or make them available to IRS for examination precludes use of the audit assumptions set forth in the guidelines. See Exhibit 11.1 for a sample form which may be used as a record of a social function that may include nonmembers.

EXHIBIT 11.1

Sample Questionnaire for Group Party

MEMBER FUNCTION QUESTIONNAIRE

The provisions of the Tax Reform Act of 1969 require that the following information must be obtained for all functions of more than eight persons.

______________________ ______________ ______________

(Host Member's Name) (Acct. No.) (Date of Function)

Total Number in Group ______________ Total Charges $ ______________

Number of Nonmembers in Group ______________ Nonmember Charges $ ______________

The Following Questions Must Be Answered by the Host Member

	Yes	No
1. I have been or will be reimbursed for nonmember charges, or others will pay club directly. If yes, complete the following questions:	☐	☐
2. I will be reimbursed by nonmembers, other than my employer, or they will pay the club directly.	☐	☐

a. If yes, indicate amount paid by nonmembers $ ______________

b. If you claim a *gratuitous* payment for your benefit, indicate Donor's

Name ______________ and your relationship to Donor

____

	Yes	No
3. I will be reimbursed by my employer, or he will pay the club directly. If yes, complete the following:	☐	☐

a. Employer's name and address: ______________________________

b. Indicate the amount of the payment attributable to nonmember use. $ ______________

c. If a large number of nonmembers is involved and they are readily identifiable as a particular class of individuals, please indicate such class and the business or other relationship to the member.

Class of individuals ______________________________

Relationship to member ______________________________

(*OR* Use other side of this form to indicate *each* nonmember's name and business or other relationship to the member.)

d. Indicate your business, personal, or social purpose served by this nonmember use.

Member's position in company ______________________________

Purpose served ______________________________

Signature of member ______________________________ Date ______________

(Prepared by PANNELL KERR FORSTER)

TAX FORMS

Applications for Exempt Status. A social club seeking exemption must file an application on forms specifically prescribed by the Internal Revenue Service. Social clubs use Form 1024, Application for Recognition of Exemption Under Section 501(a) or for Determination Under Section 120. The application for tax-exempt status should be filed with the District Director of the IRS district in which the club is located.

Annual Information Return. Even though social clubs are exempt from federal income tax, they must file an annual information return, Form 990, Return of Organization Exempt from Income Tax. Clubs with gross receipts of less than $10,000 in each tax year do not have to file. The return is due on or before the 15th day of the fifth month after the end of the club's accounting period. If a club fails to file the form by the due date, or if it files an incomplete return, it can be required to pay $10 for each day after the due date until the return is filed (not exceeding $5,000), unless it can show reasonable cause for its failure to file. If the IRS demands that a delinquent return be filed, a similar $10 penalty for each day may be imposed on the person who fails to file the return for the club.

Tax on Unrelated Business Income. Clubs exempt from federal income taxation are subject to a tax on unrelated business income and must file Form 990-T, Exempt Organization Business Income Tax Return. Clubs with such income of $1,000 or more must file the return on or before the 15th day of the fifth month after the close of the club's tax year, the same as for Form 990, the annual information return. Exempt clubs are required to make quarterly payments of estimated tax on unrelated business income. Estimated tax payments must be made currently if a club reasonably expects its estimated tax for the year to equal $40 or more. Payments are to be made in the same manner as regular corporate estimated taxes, with underpayment penalties applicable.

STATE AND LOCAL TAXES

State and local taxes vary from state to state; only general highlights can be noted here. Club managers should check with their state and local taxing authorities to verify that their club complies with all applicable regulations.

In some instances, clubs may collect the tax and act as an agent of the state or local taxing authority to remit the fees. In other instances, the tax is imposed on the club and the club itself owes the tax.

Clubs should use extreme care when the law provides for them to act as an agent of the state or local government; under some statutes, failure to remit the tax amounts to embezzlement.

A club's exemption from federal income tax does not necessarily exempt that club from state or local taxes. Nor does the fact that the club is organized under state law as a nonprofit corporation automatically exempt it from taxation.

Some states have adopted the provisions of the federal income tax so that clubs exempt from federal income tax are also exempt from state income taxes. Such clubs exempt from state income taxation, however, may still be subject to tax on unrelated business income. Such states may also require clubs to file annual information returns.

Sales Taxes

Sales taxes are not applied uniformly from state to state, and local statutes, rules and regulations must be consulted. The manager of a social club should determine, with the club's attorney, whether the club is required under state and local law to pay the tax and whether it is required to collect the tax. Most states require a club both to collect sales taxes on sales of tangible personal property and to pay sales taxes on its purchases.

States frequently exempt charitable organizations, but a social club is not generally considered under most state laws to be a charitable organization, even though it may be organized as a nonprofit corporation. A social club's exemption from federal income tax does not automatically exempt the club from state and local taxation.

Clubs will probably have to collect taxes on meals and beverages sold to members. Some states require sales taxes to be paid on service charges. Tax laws of some jurisdictions also require sales taxes to be collected on rentals, including the rental of rooms and equipment. Country clubs, for instance, have to collect sales tax on the rental of golf carts, clubs and other such equipment and also on rooms and other accommodations rented to members and their guests.

States do not usually require sales tax to be collected on dues paid to organizations. However, where dues are not really dues but, rather, entitle a member to attend events sponsored by the organization, states may require payment of the tax.

If a club makes its facilities available to the public, there is an even greater probability that state or local jurisdictions impose a tax on sales to the public.

Most states with sales taxes require clubs to pay the tax on purchases of tangible personal property for use in the club. However, if clubs buy items for resale, the clubs do not generally pay taxes on purchases. Clubs are required to collect the tax when the items subsequently are sold. Some jurisdictions require clubs buying for resale to provide exemption certificates to those from whom they purchase the resale items.

Club executives should determine whether the laws of their jurisdiction specify how the tax must be stated on bills to members. Some state laws require sales tax to be stated separately.

As with all taxes collected by a club, proper records must be maintained and the tax fully remitted when due. Some state laws provide that sales taxes collected by retailers are held in trust until remitted to the state; failure to properly remit taxes constitutes embezzlement.

State and local sales tax laws can be very complex. Clubs should periodically inventory their sales and purchases and confirm, with their legal counsel, whether they are subject to sales taxation. A club should not rely on individuals or companies from whom purchases are made to advise the club of its tax liability.

REGULATIONS

Numerous federal laws and regulations apply to social clubs, as do those of states and local jurisdictions. State and county health departments license the operations of swimming pools and kitchens. Federal and state case law affects a club's membership policies; federal minimum wage law and immigration policies affect club employees: Land use is sometimes regulated by state "greenbelt legislation" and the National Environmental Protection Act. These and other regulations specifically applicable to clubs are discussed in this section.

State and County Licensing

Sound legal and local assistance is required to help clubs comply with various state and local licensing requirements and procedures. First, clubs must determine, under state and local law, what licenses are required to operate. For instance, a club with restaurant facilities will probably have to be licensed and meet certain minimum health standards regarding operation and equipment.

A club dispensing alcoholic beverages will usually have to obtain a liquor license. States generally have rigorous laws and regulations regarding alcoholic beverages. Age requirements, hours of serving, and provisions as to whether members may be served while standing at a bar are examples of such requirements. Violations can cause license revocation in some jurisdictions.

A club may be required to obtain a business occupancy permit. Before a permit is issued, the facilities of the club may be inspected to determine that state and local health, fire, and building codes are met and that the building is safe for occupancy. In the interest of protecting public safety, the local jurisdiction may also require a minimum amount of off-street parking before granting a permit.

License fees are required in some jurisdictions for the operation of swimming pools. Sometimes a fence of a certain height is required around a pool to prevent children from gaining uninvited entrance. Failure to meet such a local licensing standard may be used as evidence of negligence in a damage suit against the club by someone injured in the club's pool.

Health Department. Health departments in many communities provide a variety of information for clubs and their managers regarding state laws and local ordinances.

State and local health departments are responsible for sanitation in their jurisdictions and control the prevention and eradication of contagious and infectious diseases.

Most jurisdictions subject dining accommodations in clubs to the same regulations as restaurants. The state or local health department enforces regulations regarding cleanliness, water supply, sterilization of dishes, refrigeration, employee sanitary facilities, and ventilation. State and local laws generally provide health departments with police power to enter restaurants at reasonable hours to determine whether the laws relative to health and sanitary standards are being met. The health department is usually allowed to close a restaurant that is found in violation.

This same department may also be responsible for inspecting swimming pools to be sure that the club complies with all construction and maintenance regulations.

Membership Practices

Members of private clubs and other organizations have a constitutionally protected right to decide with whom they may or may not wish to associate in their clubs or organizations.

This right has its constitutional roots in the rights of association, privacy, and speech as derived from the First and Ninth Amendments to the Constitution.

The right of association has been recognized to have as its logical corollary the right to exclude from association. This was acknowledged by Justice Goldberg, in *Bell v. Maryland:*

> Prejudice and bigotry in any form are regrettable, but it is the constitutional right of every person to close his home or club to any person or choose his social intimates or business partners solely on the basis of personal prejudices, including race. These and other rights pertaining to privacy and private association are themselves constitutionally protected liberties. 378 U.S. 226, 313(1964).

Although dissenting on other grounds, Justice Douglas emphasized the same principle in *Moose Lodge No. 107 v. Irvis:*

> My view of the First Amendment and the related guarantees of the Bill of Rights is that they create a zone of privacy which precludes government from interferring with private clubs or groups. The associational rights which our system honors permit all white, all black, all brown, and all yellow clubs to be formed. They also permit all Catholic, all Jewish, all agnostic clubs to be established. Government may not tell a man or woman who his or her associates must be. The individual can be as selective as he desires. 407 U.S. 163, 179–180(1972).

There is no doubt that the membership policies and practices of private organizations are firmly anchored in constitutional principles. Individuals have rights of privacy and association that guarantee that those individuals, as members of private organizations, are free to decide entirely from themselves who their fellow members will be. Government is constitutionally prohibited from dictating or controlling such decisions. However, the Internal Revenue Code prohibits a club from discriminating on the basis of race, color or religion if it intends to maintain its tax-exempt status.

Despite the apparent acceptance by the courts of these constitutional principles, club managers should be aware that continued attempts will undoubtedly be made to force clubs to abandon selective membership policies through litigation, regulation, legislation, and public pressure.

Some efforts to bar discrimination in club membership have been brought under Section 1981 and 1982 of the Civil Rights Act of 1866. Section 1981 provides equal rights to all citizens in making and enforcing contracts. Section 1982 provides equal rights to all citizens with respect to the inheriting, buying, leasing, selling, holding, and conveying of property—both real and personal. Recent cases, however, have raised substantial questions concerning the applicability of these statutory provisions in the context of a bona fide, private social club.

Since its enactment, a principal defense against these and other attacks on alleged discriminatory club membership policies has been Title II of the Civil Rights Act of 1964. This statute contains a sweeping prohibition of discrimination on the grounds of race, color, religion, or national origin (but not sex), in specified places of public accommodation whose operations affect commerce.

However, Section 201(e) of Title II specifically exempts private clubs:

> The provision of this subchapter *shall not apply to a private club* or other establishment *not in fact open to the public,* except to the extent that the facilities of such establishment are made available to the customers or patrons of an establishment within the scope of subsection (b) of this section. (Emphasis added.)

This section exempts bona fide private clubs or other places not open to the public, except to the extent that such clubs or establishments make their facilities available to customers or patrons of a public establishment covered by the act.

A frequent tactic of those who would abolish selective membership policies is to maintain that the particular club in question is not a "truly private club." Proposals have been made to amend Title II of the 1964 Act to reclassify clubs as public accommodations if more than twenty percent of their revenue is received from members who are either reimbursed by their employers or who claim personal tax deductions for their club expenses. This same approach has been proposed in state and local bills that have been introduced but not passed.

Various other theories have been used to draw private clubs under statutes prohibiting discrimination. In California, Rotary International was ordered to reinstate the Duarte Club and was prohibited from enforcing gender requirements for membership under a state statute prohibiting discrimination in "all business establishments of every kind." The California Court of Appeals, *in a decision affirmed by the U.S. Supreme Court,* held that the Duarte Club and Rotary International were subject to the provisions of the state statute.

In 1984, New York City redefined private organizations so that larger clubs would be covered by laws prohibiting discrimination in public institutions or places. An association of private clubs and groups has unsuccessfully challenged this law at the local level. The U.S. Supreme Court ruled that the law was constitutional. A number of other cities have recently considered or passed similar laws.

Title II itself does not define a "private club". The statute only states that the establishment be "not in fact open to the public." During the congressional floor debates, Senator Hubert Humphrey, the Senate floor leader for the bill, stated:

> The test as to whether a private club is really a private club, or whether it is an establishment, really not open to the public, is a factual one. . . . It is not our intention to permit this section to be used to evade the prohibitions of the title by the creation of sham establishments. . . . We intend only to protect the genuine privacy of private clubs or other establishments whose membership is genuinely selective on some reasonable basis. 110 Cong. Rec. 1369 (1964) (Remarks of Senator Humphrey).

In the absence of a statutory definition, case law must be consulted to resolve the question of what constitutes a private club. Courts have considered a number of factors, including the following:

1. The selectiveness of the group in the admission of members.
2. The existence of formal membership procedures.
3. The degree of membership control over internal governance, particularly with regard to new members.
4. The history of the organization (for example, did it make substantial changes in its operation to avoid the impact of civil rights legislation?).
5. The use of club facilities by nonmembers.
6. The substantiality of dues.
7. Whether the organization advertises.
8. The predominance of a profit motive.

Membership policies play a crucial role in determining private club status. In *Wright v. The Cork Club,* 315 F. Supp. 1143 (S.D. Tex 1970), the court held:

> Selectivity is the essence of a private club. A private club must have some basis for its selectivity and must have machinery whereby applications for membership are screened by members. If there is no established criteria [sic] for selecting members, the courts are reluctant to accept the claim of private club status. . . . If there is no club machinery for screening membership applications, or if such machinery is ignored, . . . then private club status is not indicated. (Footnote omitted.)

Another favorite tactic in attacking selective membership policies is to attempt to revoke by statute specific governmental "benefits" for clubs with such policies, or for the members of those clubs. Targeted benefits have included tax exemptions and differentials (as in differential property tax assessments for golf clubs under greenbelt statutes), individual tax deductions for club expenses, and various permits and licenses (especially liquor licenses). This tactic is related to litigation based on the "state action" theory, which holds that essential involvement of a public authority with private discrimination removes the shield of privacy.

Effectively rebutting such arguments, however, are Supreme Court precedents holding that the provision of government services or benefits cannot be made contingent on an agreement not to exercise constitutionally protected rights such as speech, privacy, and association. Furthermore, although a private club may not receive direct financial assistance from the public sector without endangering some or all of its private status, it seems clear that normal state-furnished services, including such necessities of life as electricity, water, and police and fire protection will not be viewed as benefits triggering the state action theory. Neither will health permits, liquor licenses, or ground leases.

In summary, selective membership policies of private social clubs will continue to be under attack by private as well as governmental interests. Adversaries of those policies are both ingenious and determined. Club managers must be aware of the diversity of potential attacks and knowledgeable about the constitutional principles that are involved. Political sensitivity will also be essential at times. Although members of clubs have the right to adopt whatever membership policy they prefer, it is clear that this right must be defended and managers must be able to advise their clubs on the most appropriate arguments and strategies.

EMPLOYEES

Wage and Hour Division. The *Fair Labor Standards Act* (FSLA) establishes minimum wages, overtime pay, recordkeeping, and child labor standards. The act is administered by the Wage and Hour Division of the U.S. Department of Labor.

The act covers employees individually engaged in interstate commerce or the production of goods for interstate commerce. However, if only some of the club's employees are so engaged but the club has an annual gross dollar volume of $250,000 or more, the act covers *all* club employees. Note that excise taxes, imposed at the retail level and separately stated, are excluded from the $250,000.

The annual gross dollar volume includes initiation fees paid only once; direct charges for use of club facilities, including those for food and beverages; athletic or sporting rental fees; lodging and valet charges; membership dues and assessments paid as a condition of continued membership; and fees paid by members to club professionals for lessons (whether or not accounted for to the club).

Employees of a club are individually engaged in interstate commerce if they regularly handle interstate mail and telephone calls or receive merchandise from out-of-state shippers. These employees are individually covered for the weeks they engage in these activities, regardless of the annual dollar volume of the club.

As a rule, *all* clubs should regard themselves as covered by the FLSA. In 1988, workers covered by the FLSA are entitled to a minimum wage of not less than $3.35 an hour; overtime, at no less than one and one-half times the employee's regular rate, is due after 40 hours of work in the workweek.

The Fair Labor Standards Act allows credit for "noncash" payments, such as the reasonable cost of board and lodging, toward meeting this minimum hourly wage, if such payments meet three requirements. The payments must be:

1. furnished for the benefit of the employee;
2. voluntarily accepted by the employee;
3. of a type usually furnished by similar clubs.

These costs are not included to the extent they are excluded under an applicable bona fide collective bargaining agreement.

Meal credit may be taken against minimum wage for reasonable cost of meals furnished employees, provided the meals are furnished for the convenience of the employee and *not* for the convenience of the club. Only the cost of food and its preparation can be considered.

The cost of a unique uniform and its upkeep may be charged to the employee, providing the cost does not reduce pay below minimum wage.

"Tipped" employees are those who customarily and regularly receive more than $30 a month in tips. A club may consider tips to be applied toward the minimum wage amount, but this wage credit may not exceed 40 percent of the minimum wage. Clubs must inform tipped employees of this tip credit "allowance" before it uses the credit and employees must retain all of the tips individually or through a tip pooling or sharing agreement. Clubs must be able to show that employees receive at least the minimum wage when direct wages and the tip credit allowance are combined. Tip credit may be used on a straight-line basis for both regular and overtime hours. The credit can be applied for all hours an employee uses to set up a work station and prepare tables, as well as to clean up the work area at the end of a day's service. Members of the club who volunteer their services and do not expect to be paid are generally not considered to be employees. Neither are golf caddies engaged to serve the needs of players. Players generally pay caddies for their services, and clubs exert minimal control over them. No employer-employee relationship exists. If a caddy is engaged to perform other duties, an employment relationship is established and the caddy will come under the minimum FLSA's wage and overtime requirements.

Bona fide executive, administrative or professional employees are exempt from the minimum wage and overtime provisions of FLSA.

FLSA also regulates the employment of child labor. The provisions include named hazardous occupations, listed by the Secretary of Labor as being too dangerous for minors to perform. The basic minimum age for employment in private clubs is sixteen, except for those occupations declared hazardous by the Secretary of Labor. An eighteen-year minimum age applies in those instances.

Minors fourteen and fifteen years of age may be employed in a variety of nonmanufacturing and nonhazardous occupations, including office and clerical work and as telephone operators, bus boys, kitchen helpers (except cooking), waitresses, maids, bellhops, and attendants at snack bars.

Such employment must be confined to outside school hours and between the hours of 7:00 A.M. and 7:00 P.M. (except from June 1 through Labor Day when the closing hour is 9:00 P.M., not more than three hours on a school day, eighteen hours in a school week, eight hours on a nonschool day, forty hours in nonschool weeks.

In addition to the above occupations, minors sixteen and seventeen years of age may also operate a power mower or tractor, occasionally drive automobiles and trucks on the premises, act as switchboard operators and load and unload trucks. Minors under eighteen years of age may not be employed in any of the occupations listed by the Secretary as hazardous occupations unless such employment is in accordance with the exceptions provided in a particular order.

Various penalties apply for a failure to follow the requirements of FLSA. If both state and federal child labor standards apply, clubs must comply with the more stringent standard.

To protect itself from unwitting violations of the child labor provisions, a club should obtain employment or age certificates with reliable proof of age for the minors they employ.

Employers are required to keep records of wages, hours, and other items, as specified by Wage and Hour Division regulations. The information required is generally of the kind maintained by employers in ordinary business practice and in compliance with other laws and regulations. The records do not have to be kept in any particular form. The following records must be kept:

1. Personal information, including employee's name, home address, occupation, sex, and birth date (if under nineteen years of age).
2. Hour and day when workweek begins.
3. Total hours worked each workday and each workweek.
4. Total daily or weekly straight-time earnings.
5. Regular hourly pay rate for any week when overtime is worked.
6. Total overtime pay for workweek.
7. Deductions from or additions to wages.
8. Total wages paid each pay period.
9. Date of payment and pay period covered.

A poster that provides a brief outline of the basic FLSA requirements may be obtained from the Wage and Hour Division. Clubs covered by the act are required to display this poster where the club employees may readily see it.

Equal Pay for Equal Work

The Equal Pay Act of 1963 is enforced by the Equal Employment Opportunities Commission and provides that employers may not discriminate on the basis of sex by paying employees at a rate less than the rate at which they pay employees of the opposite sex for equal work on jobs requiring equal skill, effort, and responsibility, and which are performed under similar working conditions. An exception is made if the differences are based on a bona fide merit or seniority system, productivity, or any factor other than sex. Private clubs, however, are exempt from the equal employment provisions of Title VII of the Civil Rights Act of 1964.

Payroll Taxes

Social Security (FICA) taxes continue to rise in an attempt to improve the Social Security program and to ensure the stability of the system into the twenty-first century. The wage base, the amount on which the tax is applied, has increased from $22,900 in 1979 to $45,000 in 1988. This amount is indexed for inflation and will increase yearly. The same tax rate is applied to both the employer's and employee's contribution. This rate also changes frequently. (For 1988 it is 7.51 percent.)

The first $7,000 of wages is subject to Federal unemployment tax. The tax rate is 6.0 percent and is paid by the employer. A credit is allowed for unemployment insurance paid to a state. The maximum credit is 5.4 percent. Changes in rate and tax base are frequent so care should be used to determine the correct amount.

Clubs must also withhold income taxes from employees wages. The Federal payroll tax liability must be deposited according to a schedule based on the amount of outstanding liability.

State unemployment wage bases and deposit requirements for state and local payroll taxes may be different for each jurisdiction.

Immigration

The Immigration Reform and Control Act of 1986 added numerous requirements to ensure that employers do not hire illegal aliens. One premise behind the Act is that a key element in curbing illegal immigration would involve denying employment to illegal entrants. As a result, employers are required to play a key role.

Three key elements in the new legislation are (1) the employment eligibility verification procedure and the employer's duties in connection with it; (2) legislation procedures for certain illegal aliens; (3) increased enforcement measures. Details on the Immigration Reform and Control Act of 1986 are obtainable from the Immigration and Naturalization Service.

Greenbelt Legislation

Clubs with outdoor recreational lands and facilities are heavily affected by "greenbelt legislation." An historical perspective is needed to understand this concept.

Land use laws are principally a product of this century. Land use was not considered a problem in this country's early development; land was ample, and how it was to be used was generally left to the owner.

However, at the turn of this century, states began to see a need for zoning to restrict and regulate the use of land. As Justice Sutherland stated in *Euclid v. Ambler Realty Company,* 272 U.S. 365, 386–87, in 1926, in the first case of that court upholding a zoning law:

> Until recent years, urban life was comparatively simple; but with the great increase and concentration of population, problems have developed, and constantly are developing, which require additional restrictions in respect of the use and occupation of private lands in urban communities.

After World War II, new concerns in land use developed. Increases in population, a postwar building boom, and the relocation of large numbers of families from urban areas to the suburbs created problems. During the fifties, urban planning became an important function of local governments. Today, zoning is considered by the courts to be an exercise of the police power of government under the Constitution, and almost every urban community in the United States has some type of zoning requirements to regulate the use of land within its boundaries.

During the sixties, the concern began to develop that, as populations shifted to suburbs, America was sacrificing its quality of life and failing to preserve certain esthetic features of the land that the public and future generations had the right to enjoy. As a result, governments began to seek ways to retain and improve the quality of the air, land, and water resources. Among these concerns was the need to preserve and develop parkland and open spaces in communities. States began to enact laws designed to encourage the development of parkland and preservation of open spaces. These laws are referred to as "greenbelt legislation."

State and local governments can simply purchase lands outright for the development of parks and open spaces, or local governments can purchase the development rights and leave the owner with the right to retain the property. Development that would destroy its natural beauty is thus prohibited. This latter approach is generally very expensive.

A cheaper way to preserve greenspaces is to donate land to state or local governments or preservation of the natural state of the land by providing the owner with tax incentives. Property tax assessment laws that value land at its highest and best use often discourage the retention of the open space. For instance, a country club located in what has become an area of high-priced houses may find that valuation of its golf course for property tax purposes at the highest and best use would result in a prohibitive property tax bill. Recognizing that golf courses and other outdoor recreational facilities often help meet the needs of open spaces in communities and that such facilities frequently generate property tax revenues by adding value to surrounding properties, states have developed differential property tax laws as "greenbelt legislation."

Two types of differential property tax laws in the category of greenbelt legislation are generally used. The first and simpler approach is through a classification system that provides for a lower assessment of undeveloped parkland and open space property, including outdoor recreational property. The second method is to defer the payment of taxes, through lower assessments, for those who hold such property for a period of years and do not develop it. Under this method, some states contract with the owner of such property to lower the assessments; in return, the owners agree to retain the property in its natural state for a period of years. Thus, a reduced assessment is available to the owner for the specified period, and the development of the property before the end of that period results in a rollback of the property taxes along with penalties.

Greenbelt legislation is subject to frequent amendment; club managers should be familiar with the current greenbelt laws of their jurisdiction, and consult local legal advisors about any changes.

The Occupational Safety and Health Act

The Occupational Safety and Health Act was enacted in 1970 in response to congressional findings that personal injuries and illnesses arising out of work situations interfered with interstate commerce. The act is administered by the Occupational Safety and Health Administration (OSHA) of the U.S. Department of Labor.

The act covers every employer and all employees in the fifty states, the District of Columbia, Puerto Rico, the Virgin Islands, and all other territories under federal jurisdiction. An employer is defined as any person engaged in a business affecting commerce who has employees. The term employee is broadly interpreted under OSHA and includes part-time, temporary or limited service workers. The act extends to a broad spectrum of endeavors in fields as varied as construction, law, medicine, charity, disaster relief and certain secular activities of religious groups. Although some federal laws restrict their coverage of employers to those with a minimum number of employees, OSHA contains no such limitation. As stated in the applicable Labor Department regulation:

> The basic purpose of . . . Act is to improve working environments in the sense that they impair, or could impair, the lives and health of employees. Therefore, certain economic tests such as whether the employer's business is operated for the purpose of making a profit or has other economic ends, may not properly be used as tests for coverage of an employer's activity under the . . . Act. To permit such economic tests to serve as criteria for excluding certain employers, such as nonprofit and charitable organizations which employ one or more employees, would result in thousands of employees being left outside the protections of the . . . Act in disregard of the clear mandate of Congress to assure "every working man and woman in the Nation safe and healthful working conditions***." Therefore, any charitable or nonprofit organization which employs one or more employees is covered under the . . . Act and is required to comply with its provisions and the regulations issued thereunder.***

Thus, clubs, whether organized as nonprofit corporations or not, must comply with the act. Club managers should also consult safety and health regulations.

The act imposes general duties on both the employer and the employee. Primarily, it provides that an employer shall furnish each employee employment and a place of employment free from recognized hazards that cause or are likely to cause death or serious physical harm to the employee. The employer must comply with standards issued under the act as well as applicable rules and regulations.

OSHA is responsible for issuing legally enforceable safety and health standards and clubs must comply with all of those applicable. Under the act, however, employers may apply to OSHA for a temporary variance from a standard or regulation.

Exhibit 11-2 is a guide to the recordability of cases under OSHA.

The standards applicable to clubs are generally contained in the General Industry Standards and Interpretations. Some of the commonly applicable standards concern toilets and washing facilities, trash disposal, ladders, hand and portable power tools, compressed gases, pesticides, and miscellaneous chemical products, medical services and first aid, drinking water, and fire protection.

Employers of ten or more employees must maintain records of occupational illnesses and injuries as they occur. Also, employers selected by the Bureau of Labor Statistics to participate in periodic statistical surveys must keep such records. All work-related injuries and illnesses must be recorded if they result in death, loss of one or more workdays, restriction of work or motion, loss of consciousness, transfer to another job, or medical treatment other than first aid. Clubs may also seek variances from recordkeeping requirements from OSHA.

Employers must post certain materials designed to inform their employees about the Act, including a "Job Safety and Health Protection" poster, summaries of petitions for variances, copies of OSHA citations for violations of standards, and an annual summary of occupational injuries and illnesses.

EXHIBIT 11.2

Guide to Recordability of Cases under the Occupational Safety and Health Act

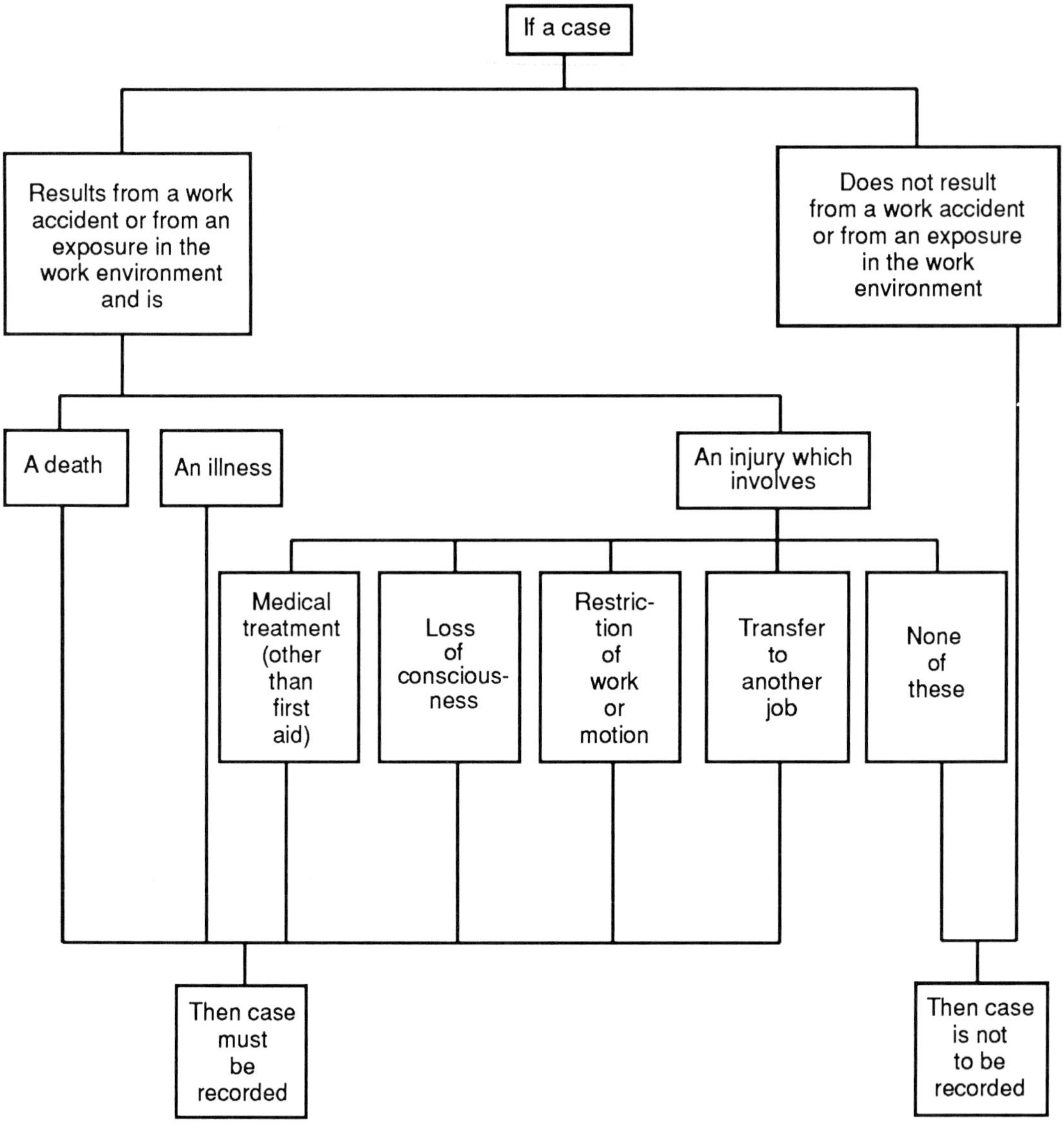

OSHA compliance safety and health officers enforce the act through inspections, or OSHA may permit a state to assume the responsibility for enforcement. Inspections may be triggered by employee complaints; the employer is prohibited from taking action or otherwise discriminating against such a complainant.

An employer who violates OSHA standards or requirements not only must correct the violation but may also be subjected to substantial fines and civil or criminal penalties, depending on the nature of the violation. Obviously, club managers should keep informed of developments in this area.

A summary of the types of records that the act requires employers to keep is contained in the appendix to this chapter.

Environmental Regulations

Pesticides. The Federal Insecticide, Fungicide, and Rodenticide Act (FIFRA) grants the Environmental Protection Agency (EPA) authority to regulate pesticides in interstate and intrastate commerce. Both civil and criminal penalties are provided for violation of FIFRA.

It is a violation of the act to use unregistered pesticides or registered pesticides in a manner inconsistent with their labeling. A club should ensure that its employees apply pesticides in its buildings and on its grounds in conformity with their labeling. Special licensing requirements exists for experimental use of pesticides. EPA may issue orders to stop the use of pesticides or devices, and the Act provides civil and criminal penalties for failure to obey those orders. If a club is notified to stop using a pesticide, it should do so immediately.

Under the Act, responsibility for prosecuting pesticide violations may be transferred to a state under a cooperative enforcement agreement. States may adopt additional restrictions on the use of pesticides provided the laws are not less stringent than FIFRA. Clubs should make sure they comply with state and local requirements, as well as federal ones, when they use pesticides.

Federal law requires that persons applying pesticides be licensed. Applicants must successfully pass a written test administered by the department of agriculture, trade, and consumer protection or its equivalent in the state in which the applicant is employed.

Sediment Control. Soil erosion is a major problem in the United States. It has been estimated that water washes 4 billion tons of sediment off the land each year. Wind erosion takes another 1 billion tons annually. In addition to the loss from soil erosion, pesticides and other pollutants are often washed off with sediment into rivers, streams, and ponds and create other problems.

Section 208 of the Federal Water Pollution Control Act Amendment of 1972, required states to develop water pollution control plans. This effort by Congress to clean up the nation's waterways has encouraged the states to become active developing their own programs.

Before undertaking any project that disturbs the land, a club must check with local governmental authorities to determine whether a grading and building permit is required. Such projects include constructing a building, developing a golf course, building a road, or other grading or earth changes. The local jurisdiction may require a grading and sediment control plan to be approved by the appropriate soil conservation district.

SUMMARY

Governmental rules and regulations affect nearly every aspect of the private club, including financial management, personnel supervision, and membership policies. Today's professional club manager must be constantly aware of what can and cannot be done under the plethora of laws. Both club members and club employees look to the manager for guidance. The manager in turn should fully utilize the advice and counsel of the club's attorney and accountant. Other sources of information and training on these matters are provided by the education programs and publications of the National Club Association and the Club Managers Association of America.

REVIEW QUESTIONS

1. Which clubs qualify for a federal income tax exemption?
2. Does a federal income tax exemption automatically provide a state income tax exemption?
3. Is income of a tax-exempt club taxable?
4. What credits can be applied to an employee's minimum wage? Under what circumstance and to what extent?
5. List three state or federal agencies that may inspect club facilities or records. Describe the purpose of each such inspection.

APPENDIX TO CHAPTER 11

Recordkeeping Requirements Under the Occupational Safety and Health Act of 1970

Public reporting burden for this collection of information is estimated to vary from 8 to 30 minutes per line entry, including time for reviewing instructions, searching existing data sources, gathering and maintaining the data needed, and completing and reviewing the collection of information. Send comments regarding the burden estimate or any other aspect of this collection of information, including suggestions for reducing this burden, to the Office of Information Management, Department of Labor, Room N-1301, 200 Constitution Avenue, NW, Washington, DC 20210; and to the Office of Information and Regulatory Affairs, Office of Management and Budget, Washington, DC 20503.

Instructions for OSHA No. 200

I. Log and Summary of Occupational Injuries and Illnesses

Each employer who is subject to the recordkeeping requirements of the Occupational Safety and Health Act of 1970 must maintain for each establishment a log of all recordable occupational injuries and illnesses. This form (OSHA No. 200) may be used for that purpose. A substitute for the OSHA No. 200 is acceptable if it is as detailed, easily readable, and understandable as the OSHA No. 200.

Enter each recordable case on the log within six (6) workdays after learning of its occurrence. Although other records must be maintained at the establishment to which they refer, it is possible to prepare and maintain the log at another location, using data processing equipment if desired. If the log is prepared elsewhere, a copy updated to within 45 calendar days must be present at all times in the establishment.

Logs must be maintained and retained for five (5) years following the end of the calendar year to which they relate. Logs must be available (normally at the establishment) for inspection and copying by representatives of the Department of Labor, or the Department of Health and Human Services, or States accorded jurisdiction under the Act. Access to the log is also provided to employees, former employees and their representatives.

II. Changes in Extent of or Outcome of Injury or Illness

If, during the 5-year period the log must be retained, there is a change in an extent and outcome of an injury or illness which affects entries in columns 1, 2, 6, 8, 9, or 13, the first entry should be lined out and a new entry made. For example, if an injured employee at first required only medical treatment but later lost workdays away from work, the check in column 6 should be lined out, and checks entered in columns 2 and 3 and the number of lost workdays entered in column 4.

In another example, if an employee with an occupational illness lost workdays, returned to work, and then died of the illness, any entries in columns 9 through 12 should be lined out and the date of death entered in column 8.

The entire entry for an injury or illness should be lined out if later found to be nonrecordable. For example, an injury which is later determined not to be work related, or which was initially thought to involve medical treatment but later was determined to have involved only first aid.

III. Posting Requirements

A copy of the totals and information following the fold line of the last page for the year must be posted at each establishment in the place or places where notices to employees are customarily posted. This copy must be posted no later than ***February 1 and must remain in place until March 1.***

Even though there were no injuries or illnesses during the year, zeros must be entered on the totals line, and the form posted.

The person responsible for the ***annual summary totals*** shall certify that the totals are true and complete by signing at the bottom of the form.

IV. Instructions for Completing Log and Summary of Occupational Injuries and Illnesses

Column A – CASE OR FILE NUMBER. Self-explanatory.

Column B – DATE OF INJURY OR ONSET OF ILLNESS.
For occupational injuries, enter the date of the work accident which resulted in injury. For occupational illnesses, enter the date of initial diagnosis of illness, or, if absence from work occurred before diagnosis, enter the first day of the absence attributable to the illness which was later diagnosed or recognized.

Columns C through F – Self-explanatory.

Columns 1 and 8 – INJURY OR ILLNESS-RELATED DEATHS.
Self-explanatory.

Columns 2 and 9 – INJURIES OR ILLNESSES WITH LOST WORKDAYS.
Self-explanatory.

Any injury which involves days away from work, or days of restricted work activity, or both must be recorded since it always involves one or more of the criteria for recordability.

Columns 3 and 10 – INJURIES OR ILLNESSES INVOLVING DAYS AWAY FROM WORK. Self-explanatory.

Columns 4 and 11 – LOST WORKDAYS––DAYS AWAY FROM WORK.
Enter the number of workdays (consecutive or not) on which the employee would have worked but could not because of occupational injury or illness. The number of lost workdays should not include the day of injury or onset of illness or any days on which the employee would not have worked even though able to work.
NOTE: For employees not having a regularly scheduled shift, such as certain truck drivers, construction workers, farm labor, casual labor, part-time employees, etc., it may be necessary to estimate the number of lost workdays. Estimates of lost workdays shall be based on prior work history of the employee AND days worked by employees, not ill or injured, working in the department and/or occupation of the ill or injured employee.

Columns 5 and 12 – LOST WORKDAYS––DAYS OF RESTRICTED WORK ACTIVITY.
Enter the number of workdays (consecutive or not) on which because of injury or illness:
(1) the employee was assigned to another job on a temporary basis, or
(2) the employee worked at a permanent job less than full time, or
(3) the employee worked at a permanently assigned job but could not perform all duties normally connected with it.

The number of lost workdays should not include the day of injury or onset of illness or any days on which the employee would not have worked even though able to work.

★U.S. Government Printing Office: 1988-202-080/85102

Columns
6 and 13 – INJURIES OR ILLNESSES WITHOUT LOST WORKDAYS. Self-explanatory.

Columns 7a
through 7g – TYPE OF ILLNESS.
Enter a check in only ***one*** column for each illness.

TERMINATION OR PERMANENT TRANSFER—Place an asterisk to the right of the entry in columns 7a through 7g (type of illness) which represented a termination of employment or permanent transfer.

V. **Totals**

Add number of entries in columns 1 and 8.
Add number of checks in columns 2, 3, 6, 7, 9, 10, and 13.
Add number of days in columns 4, 5, 11, and 12.
Yearly totals for each column (1-13) are required for posting. Running or page totals may be generated at the discretion of the employer.

If an employee's loss of workdays is continuing at the time the totals are summarized, estimate the number of future workdays the employee will lose and add that estimate to the workdays already lost and include this figure in the annual totals. No further entries are to be made with respect to such cases in the next year's log.

VI. Definitions

OCCUPATIONAL INJURY is any injury such as a cut, fracture, sprain, amputation, etc., which results from a work accident or from an exposure involving a single incident in the work environment.
NOTE: Conditions resulting from animal bites, such as insect or snake bites or from one-time exposure to chemicals, are considered to be injuries.

OCCUPATIONAL ILLNESS of an employee is any abnormal condition or disorder, other than one resulting from an occupational injury, caused by exposure to environmental factors associated with employment. It includes acute and chronic illnesses or diseases which may be caused by inhalation, absorption, ingestion, or direct contact.

The following listing gives the categories of occupational illnesses and disorders that will be utilized for the purpose of classifying recordable illnesses. For purposes of information, examples of each category are given. These are typical examples, however, and are not to be considered the complete listing of the types of illnesses and disorders that are to be counted under each category.

7a. **Occupational Skin Diseases or Disorders**
Examples: Contact dermatitis, eczema, or rash caused by primary irritants and sensitizers or poisonous plants; oil acne; chrome ulcers; chemical burns or inflammations; etc.

7b. **Dust Diseases of the Lungs (Pneumoconioses)**
Examples: Silicosis, asbestosis and other asbestos-related diseases, coal worker's pneumoconiosis, byssinosis, siderosis, and other pneumoconioses.

7c. **Respiratory Conditions Due to Toxic Agents**
Examples: Pneumonitis, pharyngitis, rhinitis or acute congestion due to chemicals, dusts, gases, or fumes; farmer's lung; etc.

7d. **Poisoning (Systemic Effect of Toxic Materials)**
Examples: Poisoning by lead, mercury, cadmium, arsenic, or other metals; poisoning by carbon monoxide, hydrogen sulfide, or other gases; poisoning by benzol, carbon tetrachloride, or other organic solvents; poisoning by insecticide sprays such as parathion, lead arsenate; poisoning by other chemicals such as formaldehyde, plastics, and resins; etc.

7e. **Disorders Due to Physical Agents (Other than Toxic Materials)**
Examples: Heatstroke, sunstroke, heat exhaustion, and other effects of environmental heat; freezing, frostbite, and effects of exposure to low temperatures; caisson disease; effects of ionizing radiation (isotopes, X-rays, radium); effects of nonionizing radiation (welding flash, ultraviolet rays, microwaves, sunburn); etc.

7f. **Disorders Associated With Repeated Trauma**
Examples: Noise-induced hearing loss; synovitis, tenosynovitis, and bursitis; Raynaud's phenomena; and other conditions due to repeated motion, vibration, or pressure.

7g. **All Other Occupational Illnesses**
Examples: Anthrax, brucellosis, infectious hepatitis, malignant and benign tumors, food poisoning, histoplasmosis, coccidioidomycosis, etc.

MEDICAL TREATMENT includes treatment (other than first aid) administered by a physician or by registered professional personnel under the standing orders of a physician. Medical treatment does NOT include first-aid treatment (one-time treatment and subsequent observation of minor scratches, cuts, burns, splinters, and so forth, which do not ordinarily require medical care) even though provided by a physician or registered professional personnel.

ESTABLISHMENT: A single physical location where business is conducted or where services or industrial operations are performed (for example: a factory, mill, store, hotel, restaurant, movie theater, farm, ranch, bank, sales office, warehouse, or central administrative office). Where distinctly separate activities are performed at a single physical location, such as construction activities operated from the same physical location as a lumber yard, each activity shall be treated as a separate establishment.

For firms engaged in activities which may be physically dispersed, such as agriculture; construction; transportation; communications; and electric, gas, and sanitary services, records may be maintained at a place to which employees report each day.

Records for personnel who do not primarily report or work at a single establishment, such as traveling salesmen, technicians, engineers, etc., shall be maintained at the location from which they are paid or the base from which personnel operate to carry out their activities.

WORK ENVIRONMENT is comprised of the physical location, equipment, materials processed or used, and the kinds of operations performed in the course of an employee's work, whether on or off the employer's premises.

Bureau of Labor Statistics
Log and Summary of Occupational
Injuries and Illnesses

NOTE:	**This form is required by Public Law 91-596 and must be kept in the establishment for *5 years*. Failure to maintain and post can result in the issuance of citations and assessment of penalties.** ***(See posting requirements on the other side of form.)***	**RECORDABLE CASES:** You are required to record information about every occupational **death**; every nonfatal occupational **illness**; and those nonfatal occupational **injuries** which involve one or more of the following: loss of consciousness, restriction of work or motion, transfer to another job, or medical treatment (other than first aid). ***(See definitions on the other side of form.)***

Case or File Number	**Date of Injury or Onset of Illness**	**Employee's Name**	**Occupation**	**Department**	**Description of Injury or Illness**
Enter a nonduplicating number which will facilitate comparisons with supplementary records.	Enter Mo./day.	Enter first name or initial, middle initial, last name.	Enter regular job title, not activity employee was performing when injured or at onset of illness. In the absence of a formal title, enter a brief description of the employee's duties.	Enter department in which the employee is regularly employed or a description of normal workplace to which employee is assigned, even though temporarily working in another department at the time of injury or illness.	Enter a brief description of the injury or illness and indicate the part or parts of body affected. Typical entries for this column might be: Amputation of 1st joint right forefinger; Strain of lower back; Contact dermatitis on both hands; Electrocution--body.
(A)	(B)	(C)	(D)	(E)	(F)
					PREVIOUS PAGE TOTALS →
					TOTALS (Instructions on other side of form.) →

OSHA No. 200

U.S. Department of Labor

For Calendar Year 19 ______ Page ___ of ___

Company Name

Establishment Name

Establishment Address

Form Approved
O.M.B. No. 1220-0029

Extent of and Outcome of INJURY						Type, Extent of, and Outcome of ILLNESS												
Fatalities	Nonfatal Injuries					Type of Illness							Fatalities	Nonfatal Illnesses				
Injury Related	Injuries With Lost Workdays				Injuries Without Lost Workdays	CHECK Only One Column for Each Illness *(See other side of form for terminations or permanent transfers.)*							Illness Related	Illnesses With Lost Workdays				Illnesses Without Lost Workdays
Enter **DATE** of death. Mo./day/yr.	Enter a CHECK if injury involves days away from work, or days of restricted work activity, or both.	Enter a **CHECK** if injury involves days away from work.	Enter number of **DAYS away from work.**	Enter number of **DAYS** of ***restricted work activity.***	Enter a **CHECK** if no entry was made in columns 1 or 2 but the injury is recordable as defined above.	Occupational skin diseases or disorders	Dust diseases of the lungs	Respiratory conditions due to toxic agents	Poisoning (systemic effects of toxic materials)	Disorders due to physical agents	Disorders associated with repeated trauma	All other occupational illnesses	Enter **DATE** of death. Mo./day/yr.	Enter a **CHECK** if illness involves days away from work, or days of restricted work activity, or both.	Enter a **CHECK** if illness involves days away from work.	Enter number of **DAYS away from work.**	Enter number of **DAYS** of ***restricted work activity.***	Enter a **CHECK** if no entry was made in columns 8 or 9.
(1)	(2)	(3)	(4)	(5)	(6)	(7) (a)	(b)	(c)	(d)	(e)	(f)	(g)	(8)	(9)	(10)	(11)	(12)	(13)

INJURIES

ILLNESSES

Certification of Annual Summary Totals By ______________ Title ______________ Date ______________

FOLD

OSHA No. 200

POST ONLY THIS PORTION OF THE LAST PAGE NO LATER THAN FEBRUARY 1.

Bureau of Labor Statistics
Supplementary Record of
Occupational Injuries and Illnesses

U.S. Department of Labor

This form is required by Public Law 91-596 and must be kept in the establishment for *5 years.* Failure to maintain can result in the issuance of citations and assessment of penalties.	Case or File No.	Form Approved O.M.B. No. 1220-0029

Employer

1. Name

2. Mail address *(No. and street, city or town, State, and zip code)*

3. Location, if different from mail address

Injured or Ill Employee

4. Name *(First, middle, and last)* — Social Security No.

5. Home address *(No. and street, city or town, State, and zip code)*

6. Age — 7. Sex: *(Check one)* Male ☐ Female ☐

8. Occupation *(Enter regular job title, not the specific activity he was performing at time of injury.)*

9. Department *(Enter name of department or division in which the injured person is regularly employed, even though he may have been temporarily working in another department at the time of injury.)*

The Accident or Exposure to Occupational Illness

If accident or exposure occurred on employer's premises, give address of plant or establishment in which it occurred. Do not indicate department or division within the plant or establishment. If accident occurred outside employer's premises at an identifiable address, give that address. If it occurred on a public highway or at any other place which cannot be identified by number and street, please provide place references locating the place of injury as accurately as possible.

10. Place of accident or exposure *(No. and street, city or town, State, and zip code)*

11. Was place of accident or exposure on employer's premises? Yes ☐ No ☐

12. What was the employee doing when injured? *(Be specific. If he was using tools or equipment or handling material, name them and tell what he was doing with them.)*

13. How did the accident occur? *(Describe fully the events which resulted in the injury or occupational illness. Tell what happened and how it happened. Name any objects or substances involved and tell how they were involved. Give full details on all factors which led or contributed to the accident. Use separate sheet for additional space.)*

Occupational Injury or Occupational Illness

14. Describe the injury or illness in detail and indicate the part of body affected. *(E.g., amputation of right index finger at second joint; fracture of ribs; lead poisoning; dermatitis of left hand, etc.)*

15. Name the object or substance which directly injured the employee. *(For example, the machine or thing he struck against or which struck him; the vapor or poison he inhaled or swallowed; the chemical or radiation which irriatated his skin; or in cases of strains, hernias, etc., the thing he was lifting, pulling, etc.)*

16. Date of injury or initial diagnosis of occupational illness — 17. Did employee die? *(Check one)* Yes ☐ No ☐

Other

18. Name and address of physician

19. If hospitalized, name and address of hospital

Date of report	Prepared by	Official position

OSHA No. 101 (Feb. 1981)

SUPPLEMENTARY RECORD OF OCCUPATIONAL INJURIES AND ILLNESSES

To supplement the Log and Summary of Occupational Injuries and Illnesses (OSHA No. 200), each establishment must maintain a record of each recordable occupational injury or illness. Worker's compensation, insurance, or other reports are acceptable as records if they contain all facts listed below or are supplemented to do so. If no suitable report is made for other purposes, this form (OSHA No. 101) may be used or the necessary facts can be listed on a separate plain sheet of paper. These records must also be available in the establishment without delay and at reasonable times for examination by representatives of the Department of Labor and the Department of Health and Human Services, and States accorded jurisdiction under the Act. The records must be maintained for a period of not less than five years following the end of the calendar year to which they relate.

Such records must contain at least the following facts:

1) *About the employer*—name, mail address, and location if different from mail address.

2) *About the injured or ill employee*—name, social security number, home address, age, sex, occupation, and department.

3) *About the accident or exposure to occupational illness*—place of accident or exposure, whether it was on employer's premises, what the employee was doing when injured, and how the accident occurred.

4) *About the occupational injury or illness*—description of the injury or illness, including part of body affected; name of the object or substance which directly injured the employee; and date of injury or diagnosis of illness.

5) *Other*—name and address of physician; if hospitalized, name and address of hospital; date of report; and name and position of person preparing the report.

SEE *DEFINITIONS* ON THE BACK OF OSHA FORM 200.

☆ U.S. GOVERNMENT PRINTING OFFICE: 1986 - 491-529 - 415/45773

12

Clubs and Computers

Fort Wayne Country Club, Fort Wayne, Indiana

During the past decade nothing has increased the professionalism or improved the productivity within the club management industry more than the computer. Computers have changed the ways in which managers plan, coordinate, control, and evaluate club operations. Club managers are no longer dependent upon an assortment of metal racks, a collection of mechanical equipment, volumes of sales journals, or a set of routine clerical procedures. From the moment a member enters a property through to eventual account settlement, a computer system is capable of monitoring, charting, and recording all member/club transactions. The nature of member services, degree of accounting controls, and evaluation of financial performance can be directly enhanced through the implementation of an information system.

INFORMATION SYSTEM CONCEPTS

Every business collects and analyzes data about its operations. While all businesses use some type of information system, a computerized system enables management to achieve its goals much more easily. A computer system can streamline the process of collecting and recording data and expand the ways in which information is organized and reported. In addition, a computer system enables management to speed up the process by which useful information is made available to decision makers.

How much does a club manager need to know about a computer to operate one? About as much as a motorist needs to know about auto mechanics to drive a car!

In order to use an automobile as an effective means of transportation, a motorist does not need to master the mechanical wonders of the internal combustion engine. A driver simply needs to learn how to instruct the machine: how to turn the ignition key; push the gas pedal; apply the brake; and so on. Sparks jump, cylinders explode, pistons pump, and gears turn, regardless of the driver's knowledge of mechanical engineering. However, if a motorist has some understanding of auto mechanics as well as basic auto maintenance skills, the car should perform even better and satisfy transportation needs for a longer period of time.

Similarly, in order to use a computer as an effective means of operating an information system, a club manager does not need to learn the intricacies of electronic circuitry etched on silicon chips. The manager simply needs to learn the commands by which to instruct the computer to carry out the desired functions. However, if a manager also has some basic knowledge about the essential operations of a computer system, he will be better equipped to use a computer as an effective tool in managing information needs.

A basic understanding of the way computer systems operate enables club managers to select computer systems which best meet the information needs of their operations, or to expand the data processing functions of their present computer systems.

Some knowledge of computer jargon (frequently termed "computerese") can be extremely helpful in identifying the functions desired from a computer system and in understanding the functioning of the system itself. This chapter introduces many basic computer terms while explaining the nature of electronic data processing and the essential hardware and software components found in club computer systems.

DATA PROCESSING

Data processing involves transforming raw facts and isolated figures into timely, accurate, and useful information. Every day, club managers are bombarded with facts and figures about the results of operations. However, these individual pieces of **data** are relatively meaningless until they undergo a **process** that organizes or manipulates them into useful **information.**

Information, the result of data processing, is clearly one of the most valuable resources of a business. Information can increase a manager's knowledge regarding members, services, labor, finance, and other areas of concern. For example, the results of a survey of members served in the dining room may provide food and beverage management personnel with important information about guest satisfaction, and also provide important feedback which may lead to more effective and efficient operations.

Information may reduce the uncertainty which club managers may experience in decision making situations. And, after decisions have been made, information can provide managers with important feedback on the effectiveness of their decisions and may even indicate new areas of concern which call for corrective action.

Data processing is not unique to the world of business; it is an important function that occurs in everyday life as well. Everyone processes data. For example, consider what may happen on a typical payday. After receiving a paycheck, a person may consider all of the items he or she would like to purchase, the cost of those items, and the difference between the amount of the paycheck and the total amount of the planned purchases. If the amount of the paycheck is greater than the amount of planned purchases, the person may decide to place the surplus amount in a savings account. If, on the other hand, the total amount of planned purchases is greater than the amount of the paycheck, the person may reconsider the purchase options or, perhaps, consider taking out a loan. In this example of data processing, a collection of data (the amount of the paycheck and the purchase options) is processed (totaled and compared) and, thus, transformed into information (surplus or deficit) useful in making decisions (what to buy).

The conversion of data into information is accomplished through a cycle of events identified as input, process, and output. Using this purchasing decision example, the paycheck and the purchase options are inputs; totaling the planned purchases and comparing that total with the amount of the paycheck is the processing; and the resulting surplus or deficit is the output. The sequence of input, process, and output is the basic **data processing cycle,** this cycle is illustrated in Figure 12.1.

FIGURE 12.1

Data Processing Cycle

INPUT ------> PROCESS ------> OUTPUT

During input, data are collected and organized to simplify subsequent processing functions. During processing, input data are mathematically manipulated or logically arranged to generate meaningful output. The output can be reported for immediate use or saved for future reference.

The data processing cycle is not new, nor is it limited to computer applications. For example, standard (food) recipes can be seen as data processing techniques which food service operations have used for a long time to convert raw ingredients into finished menu items. Viewed from the perspective of the data processing cycle, ingredients and their corresponding quantities are the inputs to recipe production; following the recipe's instructions is the process by which the desired recipe output (the number of standard portions) is produced.

Electronic Data Processing

The speed, accuracy, and efficiency required for an effective information system are often best achieved through electronic data processing. The difference between data processing (DP) and electronic data processing (EDP) lies in the automation of the process and the addition of a memory unit. *Figure 12.2* contains a simplistic diagram of an **electronic data processing cycle.**

FIGURE 12.2

Electronic Data Processing Cycle

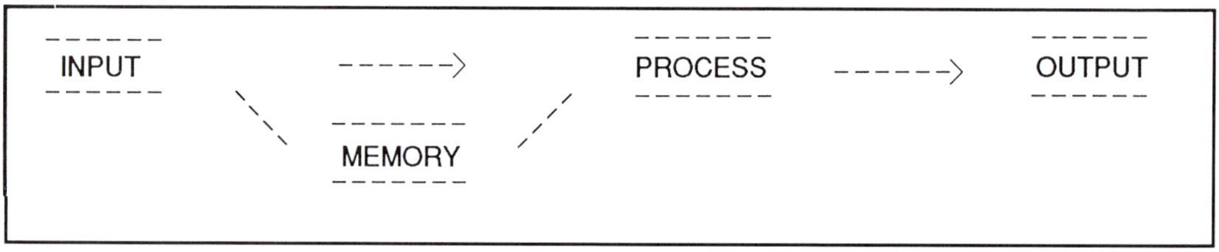

Electronic data processing employs a computer system. The automation of input, process, and output events within the basic data processing cycle results in faster and more efficient operation. Also, the addition of a memory unit allows for the storage of data and/or instructions for more reliable and thorough processing.

A **computer** is a managerial tool capable of processing large quantities of data much more quickly and accurately than any other data processing method. Computers can perform arithmetic operations such as addition, subtraction, multiplication, and division, and can perform logical functions as well, such as ranking, sorting, and assembling operations. In addition, computers are capable of storing and retrieving tremendous amounts of information and thereby allow managers to exercise control over procedures which might otherwise be overlooked.

Advantages of Electronic Data Processing

The primary function of all information systems, including computerized ones, is to transform data into timely, accurate, and useful information. Electronic data processing achieves this objective by: reducing turnaround time; streamlining output; and minimizing the handling of data.

Turnaround time refers to the time which elapses between data input and information output. An efficiently designed data processing system provides club managers with rapid access to the information they need in order to make timely and effective decisions. Inquiry and search procedures should be performed within an acceptable response time. For example, if an accounting clerk needs to know a club member's outstanding account balance, this information should be accessible quickly. Due to the nature of their architecture, computer systems are able to minimize turnaround time for almost all data processing tasks.

A frequent criticism of electronic data processing is that computer systems produce large volumes of irrelevant information. This criticism is misdirected. If a computer system overwhelms management with reams of useless information, it is not the fault of the computer—it is the fault of the computer system design. An efficiently designed electronic data processing system streamlines output. **Streamlining** the output of a computer means generating only those reports which are requested by those who will actually use the information.

Reducing the number of times that data must be handled enhances both the speed and the accuracy of data processing tasks. Consider the difference between a manual club accounting system and a computerized one. In a manual club system, the amounts of invoices which are received must first be recorded in a journal. The amounts are then carried over to a ledger. Amounts recorded in the ledger are then used to prepare financial statements. During each of these steps it is possible for a bookkeeper to make any number of mistakes such as recording the wrong number, writing a number's digits in the wrong order (transposing them), calculating a total incorrectly, and so on. The greater the number of times data must be handled, the greater the possibility for error.

In a computerized data processing system, the invoice amount is entered only once. The amount can then be accessed by the programs which prepare the journal, ledger, and financial statements. Therefore, when the amount of the invoice is entered correctly, all of the subsequent financial statements will be mathematically correct. If the amount is entered incorrectly, but the mistake is identified and corrected, the correction automatically flows from the journal through to the financial statements. With electronic data processing, there are fewer opportunities for error because it is not necessary to rehandle the same data at each step in the accounting process.

Types of Data

There are three distinct types of data. One type is called **alpha data** because it consists only of letters of the alphabet. For example, the names of club members, menu items, servers, and other employees are all types of alpha data. A second kind of data is called **numeric data** because it consists of only numbers. Member numbers, menu prices, guest check (chit) serial numbers, and food cost percentages are all forms of numeric data. The third type of data is termed **alphanumeric data** because it is made up of both letters and numbers. A club's street address, a menu item's description, and personnel records are all examples of alphanumeric data used in the club industry.

Classifying data by type can be very helpful when users are operating in a computerized environment. When a data processing system is programmed, each data element must be "introduced" to the computer so that the computer is aware of the type of data and the maximum number of **characters** (i.e., letters, numbers, or symbols) it may have. Once the computer is programmed with this information, the system will not allow users to input data which does not meet precise specifications. For example, if a membership system expects the telephone number of a member to have ten numeric characters, and a user mistakenly enters nine numbers and a single letter, the computer will refuse the data entry and thus inform the user that a mistake has been made. This feature reduces the potential number of data entry errors and enhances the reliability of the data entered into the electronic data processing system.

Type of Computers

Advances in computer technology have made it difficult to classify computers in terms of variables other than memory capacity. In the past, computers were relatively easy to classify in relation to such variables as: a. speed of operation, b. size of components, c. number of peripheral devices supported, d. number of simultaneous users, e. extent of software library, f. complexity of operation, and g. cost. These differences have since become somewhat blurred.

Recent advancements in computer design and technology have made it increasingly difficult to differentiate computers by any single variable. Given this situation, it is best to discuss the different types of computers from a historical perspective and define mainframe computers, minicomputers, and microcomputers in terms of their places in the evolution of computer technology.

Mainframe Computers

The term **mainframe computer** was originally used to describe the *main framework* of the central processor within a computer system. The first mainframe business computers appeared in the early 1950s and were made up of vacuum tubes for electronic circuitry. Punched cards were the main source of input, and magnetic drums were used for internal storage. First generation computers were slow, bulky, and generated extraordinary amounts of heat.

A second generation of mainframe computers evolved in the early 1960s as transistors and diodes became the main circuit components. Transistors were smaller, faster, and more reliable than the vacuum tubes which they replaced. Magnetic cores replaced magnetic drums as main storage and magnetic tape and disks became available for external data storage.

In the mid-1960s, transistor technology was replaced by solid-state logic in the form of silicon chips with integrated circuitry. **Silicon chips** are pieces of semiconductor material onto which electronic circuitry is etched. These chips are no larger than one's fingernail and can hold as much information as did hundreds of electronic tubes connected to the original mainframe computers. Along with the installation of silicon chips, computer storage shifted from magnetic cores to integrated circuit boards that provided expandable storage. The use of silicon chips produced gains in efficiency and also reduced the size and cost of computers.

Although newer mainframe computers may appear as large as their predecessors, they are each capable of processing more data than all of the original mainframe computers combined. In fact, some hand-held calculators offer virtually the same level of sophistication as early mainframe computers. Alternatively, many businesses may satisfy their data processing needs through the implementation of a minicomputer.

Minicomputers

The third generation of computers (early 1970s) produced the **minicomputer**—a slower, less powerful, but smaller and cheaper alternative to the mainframe computer. The exploitation of the computer's commercial potential really began with the appearance of these machines. Minicomputers possess the same components as larger mainframe computers but typically have reduced memory capability and slower processing abilities. Minicomputers also tend to allow fewer users to simultaneously interact, and support fewer peripheral devices (such as printers and display screens). Although the minicomputer is less powerful than a mainframe computer, it is generally more powerful than a microcomputer.

Microcomputers

The fourth generation of computers (mid-1970s) introduced the **microcomputer,** or "personal computer." This term is used to describe the smallest computers on the market. Despite their small size, microcomputers contain the same types of components as the larger machines and may also have additional options such as hard disks, color monitors, graphics capability, and others. A microcomputer is so compact that its central processing unit (CPU) is contained on a single silicon chip that is less than one quarter of an inch square and uses less energy than a 100-watt light bulb.

The CPU of a microcomputer is also known as a microprocessor. The **microprocessor** is an integrated circuit package containing a complete electronic circuit or group of circuits. Its circuits make up a central processing unit which controls the computer, carries out calculations, directs the flow of data, and performs many other functions as well.

Many hospitality businesses find that their data processing needs can be met by microcomputers. Club system vendors who had once relied on mainframes and minicomputers exclusively, now offer their clientele powerful microcomputer-based systems. Some microcomputers are designed to be portable and small enough to enable managers to take them with them while traveling.

COMPUTER HARDWARE

The physical equipment of a computer system is called **hardware.** Computer hardware is visible, movable, and easy to identify. Regardless of type, every computer system must have each of these three hardware components: an input/output (I/O) unit, a central processing unit (CPU), and an external storage device.

An **input/output unit** allows the user to interact with the computer system. The user can input data through a keyboard and receive output on a display screen and/or on paper through a printer. The most common I/O unit at work in the club industry is the CRT (acronym for cathode ray tube). The **CRT unit** is composed of a television-like video screen and a keyboard which is similar to a typewriter keyboard. Data entered through the keyboard can be displayed on the screen. The CRT operator can edit and verify the on-screen input prior to sending it for processing. Other types of club I/O equipment include keyboard and operator display units such as electronic cash registers and line-printing terminals.

One important difference among I/O units is the type of output they produce. A CRT unit displays output on a monitor for the user to examine; this type of output is referred to as **soft copy** because it cannot be handled by the operator or removed from the computer. Printers, however, generate a paper copy of the output which is called a **hard copy.** Many systems are designed so that they can produce both types of output. For example, a club's operator will have a CRT unit which an accounting clerk can use to view a soft copy of a member's statement of account between billing dates. However, when statements are to be distributed, a hard copy of the document will be generated at a printer for member review and use. Obviously, output displayed on a screen is much more temporary and its use more constricted than output printed on paper. Generally, club managers obtain essential reports in hard copy form, allowing storage outside the computer and providing a base for information backup.

The **central processing unit** (CPU) is the control center of the computer system. Inside are the circuits and mechanisms that process and store information and send instructions to the other components of the system. The computer is said to **read** when it takes data in for processing and to **write** when it sends processed data out as information. All input entering the computer system from any input device (such as a keyboard, disk drive, or other device) is processed by the CPU before it is sent to the internal memory or to an output device. Similarly, all output (sent to a display screen, printer, or other device) has first been processed by the CPU. There is no direct link between input and output devices. Whenever information is to be moved within the computer system, it must pass through the CPU.

An **external storage device** is a piece of equipment that retains data and/or programs that can be accessed by the CPU. Data and programs can be permanently stored on such external devices as magnetic tapes, floppy disks, and hard disks.

HARDWARE CONFIGURATIONS

Hardware configuration refers to the design and layout of the hardware components of a computer system. The size of a club operation and the number of departments needing access to the computer system are significant factors in selecting the appropriate configuration of hardware components.

A very small operation may find that a single microcomputer work station is sufficient to meet the needs of its limited number of users. This work station would be a complete system with input/output units, a single CPU, and external storage capability.

Other clubs may have a number of user groups from different departments that need access to the computer system. These properties can avoid spending unnecessary funds on computer equipment by selecting the particular configuration of hardware components which best meets the needs of their operations. In many cases, it is possible for users to share output devices (such as printers and external storage facilities) and/or the internal memory and processing capability of a central processing unit.

The advantages and disadvantages of each configuration should be considered before purchasing a computer system. The major differences among the various configurations are speed and cost. The CPU is the most expensive component in a computer system; therefore, the more CPUs a configuration requires, the greater its cost will be. The tradeoff in configuring a number of CPUs, however, is that the closer the CPU is to the I/O devices, and the fewer I/O devices making demands on the CPU, the faster the computer system will seem to operate.

The following sections discuss four basic configurations of hardware components: stand-alone configuration, distributed configuration, integrated configuration, and combined configuration.

Stand-Alone Configuration

A stand-alone configuration creates self-sufficient work stations, each with a complete set of the same hardware components. The presence of many individual computers at different locations limits communication to sharing data by exchanging external storage media (disks). The duplication of hardware components makes this a relatively expensive hardware configuration.

Distributed Configuration

The distributed configuration is an improvement over the stand-alone configuration. Each work station possesses a complete computer system. The presence of an I/O device, CPU, and external storage device at each location provides a multiprocessor environment.

What distinguishes this configuration from the stand-alone configuration discussed previously is that the work stations are cabled together. The cabling serves as a hardware interface which creates a **local area network** (LAN) of individual work stations. A local area network enables users to share data, programs, and output devices (such as printers). Data sharing facilitates system-wide communications, and program sharing enables users who are not in possession of a particular software program to benefit from its operation. From an economic perspective, device sharing is perhaps the most important benefit derived from networking. Expensive peripheral devices, such as high capacity storage devices and laser printers, can become available to all work stations cabled within the network.

Since each user group has its own computer, there is also more specialized application capability (use and storage). An additional benefit is that an individual system encountering operational problems does not affect the operation of the other systems in the network.

Integrated Configuration

An integrated configuration creates a number of work stations, all of which are dependent upon a single central processing unit and external storage device. While the I/O units may be distributed throughout the hospitality establishment, both the CPU and the external storage device are centrally located. Each I/O unit communicates with the CPU, and the CPU and external storage device work closely together. Since the integrated configuration is dependent on a single CPU and centralized storage device, power failures or system failures can render the entire computer system inoperable and/or result in a permanent loss of stored data.

Combined Configuration

A particular variation of a distributed configuration is a combined configuration which interfaces a microcomputer to an already established integrated configuration. While the microcomputer is stand-alone in nature (it possesses its own I/O unit, CPU, and external memory device), its connection to the integrated configuration allows for significant application flexibility not otherwise available. For example, the transfer of data files from the external storage device of the integrated configuration to the microcomputer allows detailed analysis on those files without affecting the ongoing workings of the integrated design.

The combined configuration is an important arrangement used in the club industry. For example, assume a club has an integrated electronic cash register system with a centralized processing unit and storage device. Connecting a microcomputer to this system will enable a user to transfer the day's sales from the register system to the microcomputer. The movement of this data allows for the production of analytical reports (within the microcomputer) without interference to the ongoing work of the club's cash register system.

The hardware of a computer system does nothing by itself. In order for hardware components to operate, there must be a set of instructions to follow. These instructions are referred to as software.

COMPUTER SOFTWARE

Instructions that command a computer system to perform useful tasks are called computer **programs.** A set of programs that instructs or controls the operation of the hardware components of a computer system is called **software.** Software programs tell the computer what to do, how to do it, and when to do it. This chapter briefly addresses the types of **programming languages** used to create software programs and then focuses on two fundamental types of computer software: applications software and systems software. Many people's first exposure to the power of computers is through applications software such as word processing packages, electronic spreadsheet programs, or database management systems. Persons in the club industry become involved with industry specific software which also tends to incorporate many of the characteristics of these generic applications. Experienced computer users are familiar with systems software which must be present for applications software to establish a connection with computer hardware components. Systems software focuses primarily on operating systems.

Programming Languages

Software applications are sets of computer programs. A computer program is a series of written instructions which guides the computer in carrying out a specific function. The particular language in which a program is written will affect the speed by which the computer responds to instructions, and the ease by which the program can be changed to meet new needs and requirements of users. Programming languages are usually characterized as either low-level languages or high-level languages.

All computers have **low-level languages** programmed into them because it is at this most basic level that their operations are carried out. Low-level languages are sometimes referred to as machine languages because the computer can directly understand their instructions. Machine languages typically vary from one computer manufacturer to another. Also, machine languages may vary among the different models offered by the same manufacturer. Initially, all computer programming was done in machine language. These programs were extremely cumbersome to write because basic instructions had to be written as long strings of binary digits. Programmers had to keep track of hundreds of thousands of zeros and ones; a single misplaced character could cause the computer to misunderstand an instruction and the entire program could malfunction. The tedious and laborious nature of programming in machine language also made it difficult to change a program once it had been written.

High-level languages are made up of familiar words and symbols. High-level languages are the most sophisticated programming languages because a relatively simple command instructs the computer to perform complex procedures that involve a number of different operations. For example, some computer languages recognize the word "SORT" and respond to this command by taking a list of separate items and arranging them in a predetermined fashion. Obviously, high-level languages are easy for a novice programmer to work with because they are similar to the user's own spoken language. While high-level languages draw closer to the user's own language, computers can only distinguish between positive and negative electrical charges. This means that a computer cannot understand the commands of a high-level language directly; these languages must first be translated into a form of machine language which can pose instructions which the computer will execute.

Applications Software

Applications software is a term for sets of computer programs designed for specific uses such as word processing, electronic spreadsheet analysis, and database management. Many of these types of applications are purchased separately from the hardware components of a computer system and are usually available at retail computer outlets or from vendors of club computer systems.

When a business plans to computerize its information system, the choice of applications software is always a decision which must be made before selecting computer hardware components. Management must determine what functions or tasks the computerized information system will be required to perform and then identify which applications software will best meet those needs. Only after these decisions have been made is management in a position to decide which kind of computer hardware components are needed to run the required software programs. Not all applications software is available for every computer brand, and the compatibility of software programs and hardware components is a critical factor in purchase decisions. By focusing first on which applications software will best meet the needs of the hospitality operation, managers can ensure that the computer system which is eventually purchased will be able to accomplish all of the desired tasks.

Some software programs are very application-specific while others can be used to perform a variety of different tasks. For example, a club manager can purchase a software package designed specifically to perform menu engineering. This type of software performs all of the necessary calculations involved in menu analysis and prints a series of reports. Because this software has one specific purpose, it is designed so that it requires no direct intervention by the user. The user simply inputs the appropriate data and the program does the rest.

Other types of applications software are less task-specific. For example, a spreadsheet program can be used for a number of different applications. Although the user must be able to create the appropriate spreadsheets which will accomplish the various tasks, spreadsheet software can be used for a variety of applications, including menu engineering. Such software is usually labeled as **generic software.** The most popular generic software applications are: word processing, electronic spreadsheet, and database management.

Word Processing Software

Word processing is an electronic means of writing, editing, storing, and printing textual material. A user inputs characters (letters, numbers, or symbols) from the keyboard of the computer system. The characters are then processed by the CPU, retained in the CPU's temporary memory (RAM), and appear immediately as output on the user's display screen. The flashing cursor on the display screen indicates where characters entered at the keyboard will appear.

The arrow keys found on the keyboard allow the user to move anywhere within the text appearing on the display screen. This makes it easy for the user to add, delete, correct, combine, and perform other basic editing tasks. Changes that are input at the keyboard are immediately made to the textual material which appears on the display screen. This edited version of the textual material replaces the original version in the CPU's temporary memory (RAM).

Special function keys and special combinations of keys permit the user to move words, phrases, paragraphs, pages, or even entire chapters of textual material from one point on the screen to another. Many word processing packages include special features which allow the user to design the appearance of the document to meet specific needs. For example, with a few key strokes: margins for the entire document, or for particular passages within the document, can be reset; columns of numbers can be aligned by decimal point; single-spaced textual material can be converted to double-spaced, triple-spaced, or whatever the user desires. These changes in the appearance of a document are executed in fractions of a second and are reflected in the output which appears on the user's display screen.

Electronic Spreadsheet Software

With a computerized accounting system, figures need to be entered only once into the accounting records. These entered amounts can then be accessed by programs which prepare mathematically correct journals, ledgers, and financial statements. This feature and others are made possible by electronic spreadsheet software.

An electronic spreadsheet program allows a user to input a model of the accountant's traditional worksheet in the temporary memory of the computer system and view it as output generated on a display screen. The electronic model is essentially a blank page of a worksheet which is divided into rows (usually numbered from top to bottom) and columns (usually lettered from left to right). The rows and columns intersect to form **cells.** The coordinates of a cell (the particular column letter and row number) identify what is typically called the **address** of a cell.

Cells can hold different types of data: alpha data, such as **labels** for the columns and rows; numeric data, such as dollar amounts; and **formulas,** which instruct the computer to carry out specific calculations, such as adding all numbers in a certain range of cells. The cells in which formulas are entered will display the results of the calculations. If any of the amounts entered in the range of cells change, a formula is able to immediately recalculate the amounts and place the new total in the same designated cell.

Electronic spreadsheet software is not limited to bookkeeping functions; it is capable of performing many different kinds of tasks which may be extremely useful to managers in the hospitality industry. The **recalculation** feature of electronic spreadsheet programs offers managers opportunities to explore "what if" possibilities. For example, an electronic spreadsheet could be created to indicate the effects that different member purchase decisions may have on a club's food and beverage operation, pro shop activity, golf course traffic, and other revenue-producing centers. Information which could take hours to calculate manually takes only seconds when calculated electronically.

The speed with which electronic spreadsheet software can generate information is an important factor that increases a manager's ability to make decisions. A manager is less likely to request certain kinds of information or reports when he or she knows that valuable personnel will be tied up for hours. With electronic spreadsheet software, a manager has all kinds of information and reports at his or her fingertips—and in a matter of seconds.

Most electronic spreadsheet software packages have graphics capability. That is, the programs are able to generate graphs (bar charts, line graphs, pie charts, etc.) from data entered in worksheets. This can be a valuable management tool for communicating information. However, in order for users to view the graphic designs which they are able to create, their display screens must have graphics capability. This is an important consideration when selecting computer hardware. Printers may have limited graphics capability as well. Just because a particular bar chart appears as soft copy on a display screen does not mean that the printer can produce hard copy of the chart. When selecting hardware components for a computer system, users must take care that the components fully support the capabilities of the software applications which they plan to run on the system.

Database Management Software

Database management software is a term for programs which allow users to catalog and store information about their businesses for future use. A **database** is a collection of related facts and figures designed to serve a specific purpose. The structure of the database provides a means of organizing related facts and figures and arranging them in ways that facilitate searching for data, updating data, and generating accurate, timely, and useful reports for management. Database management refers to the design and organization of databases as well as to the means by which data are handled within the computer system.

There is nothing mysterious about the function of a database management system. It is simply a computer program that permits the organization and storage of information in a central location. Since a database stores information like any other storage device, its overall function is similar to that of standard office filing systems.

A database is similar to a filing cabinet. The way information is organized within a filing cabinet will depend on the kind of information which is stored and the particular needs of the user. File cabinets have separate file drawers. Each file drawer contains separate file folders. The folders within each drawer contain similar records of related information. Each record within a folder contains specific facts and/or figures.

In the language of database management software, the file cabinet is called the **database,** the drawers of the cabinet are called **files,** the folders within the drawers are called **records,** and the detailed facts and/or figures in the records are called **fields.**

For example, an inventory database might be set up for inventory control. Assume that this database is made up of a single file. The file would contain one record for each inventory item, and each record would contain a number of fields, such as the item's name, number, cost, quantity on hand, reorder point, and so on. Different users of the computer system can access this database to perform any number of desired functions, such as: generate inventory checklists to assist managers and supervisors in taking physical inventory; perform variance analyses on the differences between actual quantities of items on hand versus the quantities projected (perpetual inventory) by the computer system, and calculate the total value of the items in inventory.

The value of a database management system can be enormous; especially in to the club industry. Not only does a database management system save storage space, but, more important, it limits the number of times that data must be handled and ensures that all applications using the database are working with the same information.

Currently, there are databases for all types of users. Many database packages involve a complex set of commands used to define fields and establish records, but an experienced (or patient) user can learn to efficiently organize large amounts of information.

Applications Software and User Concerns

After identifying the type of applications software that will meet the specific information needs of the hospitality operation, managers must research available software packages and eventually make a purchase decision. There are some general criteria which may guide managers in making purchase decisions. These criteria focus on fundamental user concerns. Such concerns as: user friendliness, integration of the software system, and completeness and usefulness of program output.

Some applications software packages are easier for new users to operate than others. Software that is menu-driven or designed with interactive programs is generally more user-friendly than packages without these features.

In order to operate many of the more sophisticated software packages, users must be familiar with dozens of keystrokes which are required to carry out specific operations. **Menu-driven** software packages provide on-screen information explaining which key strokes are required to carry out commonly used program commands. Users are generally able to access this on-screen information at any time while operating within the software program.

Many software packages provide users with a **keyboard template** which identifies common keystrokes. This template is usually placed directly on the keyboard and guides users as they operate the computer system.

Some user-friendly software packages provide **interactive programs,** which help users carry out specific operations by prompting them to respond to a predetermined sequence of inquiries. After the user responds to one prompt, the next inquiry in the series is presented. Interactive software is very popular among club systems because it is easy to use and helps ensure that all required information is collected and entered into the computer system. When club employees are required by the computer system to answer a series of prompts regarding member receivables, the property is able to generate complete and useful accounts receivable information. Interactive systems are usually able to generate reports at any time during computer operation. This provides an effective means of ensuring that data is processed and timely information is made available to decision-makers.

Batch programs are non-interactive computer operations. These programs do not provide the user with prompts or on-screen instructions on how to input data or keystroke commands. These programs assume the user is already well-informed about input procedures. Batch program execution is generally faster than interactive software because there is no time spent prompting the user in how to input data or carry out various operations. However, batch programs may often prevent on-line editing and may not have the ability to generate reports in as timely a fashion as interactive programs.

Integrated software allows several programs to use the same database. For example, data about the menu sales mix is essential to calculating both food service revenues and standard food costs. An electronic cash register (ECR) which has the ability to calculate and store menu counts can capture this data at the time of a sale. Since menu item prices are also normally stored in an ECR, a revenue report can be generated without any further data entry by the user. Similarly, an ECR with a recipe costing module can use the identical menu sales mix data to produce standard food cost reports.

However, if the club's dining room does not have such a system, menu sales mix data must be collected from an analysis of guest checks (chits) and then entered into an adding machine, or non-integrated computer program, to produce revenue information. Similarly, in order to calculate standard or ideal food costs without an ECR with the capabilities described previously, the standard recipe cost for each menu item must first be determined and then menu sales mix data entered for a second time into the adding machine or non-integrated computer program.

The advantages of integrated software over non-integrated software include speed and data integrity. Since pieces of data are handled only once, it is possible to update data for all applications at the same time.

Screen and report formats are important concerns to the users of an application program. While the issues of interactive versus non-interactive and integrated versus non-integrated software are important, the true value of a program lies in the completeness and usefulness of its output. Screen displays must allow for easy reading and eye comfort. Cluttered, jumbled, or unclear screens are more difficult to use than those with good spacing and legible information. In addition, display screens with color capabilities are often very helpful to inexperienced users whose eyes can readily follow the color differences.

SYSTEMS SOFTWARE

Hardware refers to the equipment within a computer system. Software refers to the instructions that direct the operations of the hardware. How do the hardware and software work together? How are priorities established within the system? Answers to these and related questions are explained by the functions performed by systems software.

The primary purpose of **systems software** is to control the interactions between hardware components of a computer system and software application programs. Although applications software instructs the computer how to manipulate data to yield desired results, each set of these programs depends on systems software for its instructions to be carried out correctly.

Read only memory (ROM) of the central processing unit stores a permanent control program installed by the computer manufacturer which enables the computer to read commands and instructions that program fundamental operations of the computer system. This control program is part of systems software; it instructs the computer how to interpret information received through a keyboard and other input devices, and how to output information to a display screen and other output devices.

Other portions of systems software, typically installed by the computer manufacturer, consist of programs which assist in the start-up process of the computer. The computer manufacturer may also provide diagnostic routines which are programs used to test the correct functioning of various hardware components. Some diagnostic routines are initiated by the user and are explained in the user's manual provided by the computer manufacturer. These routines should be carried out whenever a faulty hardware component is suspected.

The Operating System

Another portion of systems software is called the operating system. Like other types of systems software, the operating system controls interactions between hardware components of a computer system and applications software programs. An operating system is necesary for a computer system to be able to carry out instructions generated by applications software programs. The operating system manages routine computer functions while maintaining system priorities. In essence, the operating system mediates the interaction of application software with the hardware components of the computer system.

A computer system must have a control mechanism if it is to run applications software programs without constant intervention from the user. For example, when a user instructs a computer to save a program or data to an external storage device, something must happen within the computer system so that the entered command successfully initiates the proper sequence of operations for storing the program or data. The management of such routine functions is handled by the computer's operating system.

In simplest terms, the operating system is the program that controls the execution of other programs. Think of the operating system as the traffic controller of a busy metropolis, directing the flow of traffic by controlling the signals at every street corner. Like the traffic controller, the operating system is at the center of computer activity, directing the flow of data and instructions from applications software programs to the various hardware components of the computer system.

INFORMATION BACKUP PROCEDURES

Backup procedures should not be left to emergency situations. Information backup should be a standard operating procedure to ensure that data is not lost at any time. There are at least three ways to back up information: redundant copy, duplicate copy, and hard copy.

Redundant copy may not be a very popular backup technique in the club industry because it requires two storage devices working simultaneously. Assuming that a club's food service system employs a disk drive as a base for one external storage device, a second disk drive is required. As data is input, it is sent to both drives for storage on their respective disks. This can be an expensive hardware configuration and requires more attention than other backup methods. It is analogous to recording a theatrical performance on two tape recorders simultaneously. Many people feel it is more efficient to concentrate on producing one superior recording and duplicating it at a later point in time. Two recordings are still obtained, but through duplication, not redundancy.

Duplicate copy is the most popular and efficient means to accomplish information backup. The computer system writes to only one storage device so a second disk drive is not needed. A copy of the data on the single drive can be made later. It can be duplicated on the same device with a blank disk or can be placed onto magnetic tape. Because magnetic tape is comparatively inexpensive, but not as efficient as a workable storage device (due to its sequential access characteristics), some operators use it as duplicate copy. At the end of the day, the disk is duplicated onto magnetic tape for backup purposes. Since the backup tape is stored and used only in case of a disk error or failure, its sequential access method does not severely reduce the operation's ability to maintain efficient computer operations.

Hard copy (printouts from disk files) should only be used as a backup technique in conjunction with redundant or duplicate copy procedures. The user who relies solely on hard copy information backup will encounter an avalanche of work should data files need to be reconstructed. In this case, all information stored on hard copy must be manually re-entered to recreate the system's database. When used to supplement one of the other two approaches, hard copy backup provides a means for troubleshooting any missing or incorrect transactional recordings. Should a mishap occur that affects only a small section of a disk, that area of the disk can be compared with the most current hard copy to recover any information that may have been lost.

While many computer manufacturers advocate using more than just a single backup procedure, management must ensure that at least one procedure is used regularly.

SUMMARY

Information is one of the most valuable resources of the club industry. Information can increase a manager's knowledge of members, services, labor, finance, and other areas of concern. Information may also reduce the uncertainty which managers may experience in decision-making situations. And, after decisions have been made, information can provide managers with useful feedback.

Information is the result of data processing which transforms raw facts and isolated figures into timely, accurate, and useful reports. The conversion of data into information is accomplished through a cycle of events identified as input, process, and output. The primary objective of all information customs, including computerized ones, is to transform data into timely, accurate, and useful information. The speed, accuracy, and efficiency required for an effective information system by hospitality businesses are often best achieved through electronic data processing. The difference between data processing and electronic data processing lies in the automation of the process and the addition of a memory unit.

A computer is a managerial tool capable of processing large quantities of data much more quickly and accurately than any other data processing method. Three types of computers discussed in this chapter were mainframe computers, minicomputers, and microcomputers (also referred to as personal computers).

The physical equipment of a computer system is called hardware. Computer hardware is visible, movable, and easy to identify. In order to have a computer system, three hardware components are required: an input/output (I/O) unit, a central processing unit (CPU), and an external storage device.

There is no direct link between input and output devices. Whenever information is to be moved within the computer system, it must pass through the CPU. The CPU is the control center of the computer system and is the most important and most expensive individual hardware component found within a computer system. It is the "brain" of the system and is responsible for controlling all other system components.

An external component device is a piece of equipment that retains data and/or programs that can be accessed by the CPU. Data and programs can be permanently stored on such external devices as magnetic tapes, floppy disks, hard disks, and laser disks.

Hardware configuration refers to the design and layout of the hardware components of a computer system. The size of a club operation and the number of departments needing access to the computer system are significant factors in selecting the appropriate configuration of hardware components. This chapter discussed four basic configurations of hardware components: stand-alone configuration, distributed configuration, integrated configuration, and combined configuration.

A set of programs that instructs or controls the operation of the hardware components of a computer system is called software. Software programs tell the computer what to do, how to do it, and when to do it. Computer programs can be written in low-level or high-level programming languages. Low-level languages, also referred to as machine languages, can be directly understood by the computer. High-level languages are easier for programmers to use; however, programs written in high-level languages generally do not execute functions as quickly as do programs written in low-level languages.

Applications software refers to sets of computer programs which are designed for specific uses such as word processing, electronic spreadsheet analysis, and database management. When computerizing its information system, a club should:

1. Determine what functions or tasks the computer system will be required to perform.
2. Identify which applications software will best meet those needs.
3. Decide which computer hardware components are needed to run the required software programs.

Other user concerns in relation to applications software programs include user friendliness, integration of the software system, and the completeness and usefulness of program output.

Systems software programs control the interactions between hardware components of a computer system and software applications programs. Although applications software instructs the computer how to manipulate data in order to yield desired results, each set of these programs depends on systems software for its instructions to be carried out correctly. The operating system is part of systems software and must be present for a computer system to be able to carry out instructions generated by applications software programs.

To ensure that data is not lost at any time, information backup methods should be standard operating procedures. Information backup procedures include redundant copy, duplicate copy, and hard copy.

CLUB COMPUTER APPLICATIONS

Club computer applications focus primarily on membership demographics and financial accounting. Member demographic applications are designed to provide the club with varied data relevant to member type, personal data, account definition, and specialty interests. Membership receivables are, perhaps, the most important club application since collection of deferred payments, dues, fees, assessments, and the like are critical to the financial longevity of the club. Club financial accounting centers on accounts payable, inventory control, payroll, financial statement preparation, and financial management issues. Clubs may also implement a variety of related computer application software. Such packages as food and beverage cost control, function room scheduling, golf handicapping schemes, and the like are becoming familiar extensions of a club computer system.

Club Accounting

Club accounting is a systematic process of measuring and reporting various financial information for decision making, and operational reporting. Club accounting software should be **integrated** in design and **modular** in functionality. Integration involves data sharing and transference between component software and greatly simplifies the tedious manual procedures which would otherwise be needed. For example, the posting of a vendor invoice within the accounts payable module will lead to a simultaneous posting in the general ledger module. The fact that this second entry is automatically posted within the system eliminates the need for an additional, manual journal entry. An integrated computerization enables a double entry accounting system in which the user performs only the initial entry while the system performs subsequent, complementary entries. Similarly, the payroll module must be capable of automatically transferring data between itself, general ledger, and financial statements.

The degree of modularity within a club accounting package is an important factor to effective system utilization. By separating important application areas (e.g., accounts payable, receivable, payroll, etc.) the club is able to more easily identify the proper portion of the system with which to work. A club computer system that offers very few modules, for example, will necessitate that its user be more familiar with fundamental accounting relationships than one that has an array of specialized modular offerings.

The development of an accounting system is predicated on three important factors: a) to provide effective internal control, b) to produce accurate financial reports, and c) to enhance cash flow. The concept of **internal control** deals with protecting the club against dishonest employees, omissions in documentation, and inaccuracies incurred within the accounting process. A club accounting system must be capable of detecting these problems and of identifying the nature of their occurrence.

The production of **financial statements** is perhaps management's most important feedback information. A club accounting system must be designed so that accurate reports can be generated in a minimal timeframe. Reports that are not timely, or that are heavily biased, serve little purpose. It is important to note that although a club management system produces a multitude of reports for internal purposes, it may also be responsible for generating external reports as well (e.g., government and/or board of director reports). **Cash flow** is critical to the club's ability to meet its obligations to pay its employees and creditors. One of the most important considerations in any business is the ability to receive cash in order to meet expenditures and the tracking of cash is an essential objective of a club accounting system.

The **cash flow cycle** is that period of time from when goods or services are provided until the club receives cash payment for such purchases. Hence, cash flow is best described in terms of available cash. The club's ability to plan and project cash flows will enhance its ability to meet financial obligations on time. The firm's creditors and employees count on the club as a source of funds and the club, in turn, depends upon its membership payments for cash. Since a large percentage of club transactions are deferred through member account billings this leads to potential cash flow problems. The length of the cash flow cycle can be improved by speeding up collections, slowing down disbursements, or securing additional cash sources.

Club Accounting Applications Modules

Club accounting packages are typically separated into primary and secondary tier applications. In general, primary applications include: **membership (accounts receivable), accounts payable, payroll,** and **general ledger.** Membership receivables deal with monies owed the club; while accounts payable involve obligations to be paid by the club. Payroll includes employee time and attendance tracking, net pay computation, and governmental reporting. Most vendor systems maintain extensive payroll documentation and provide year-end analysis and tax reporting information. General ledger accounting centers on the club's chart of accounts and is responsible for tracking account balances leading to the production of financial reports (i.e., balance sheet and income statement).

Secondary applications include: **inventory control, purchase ordering, budgeting,** and **fixed asset accounting.**

Membership Receivable Module

The membership receivable module is primarily composed of deferred purchases, dues, fees, and assessments incurred by members. The ledger of member statements in the club's accounting office form the club's membership accounts receivable listing. These charges represent monies owed the club for financial debts incurred by its membership. Members are typically billed monthly and may be required to pay their outstanding balances in full. Typically receivable statements are automatically generated at the close of an accounting period. Regardless of data entry procedures, membership account billing and aging follow distribution of member statements. Figure 12.3 contains a summary of the component parts of a membership receivable module.

FIGURE 12.3
Membership Receivable Module

Member Receivable Module

- Member Ledger File
- Master Billing File
- Account Aging File

Accounts Payable Module

The accounts payable branch of a club computer system is used to track purchases, creditor positions, and the club's banking status. Accounts payable activities normally consist of posting invoices, determining amounts due vendors, and printing checks for payment. The entire process can become time consuming and tedious when several vendors, offering a variety of **discount terms,** are involved. Discount terms, consisting of a timeframe and percentage rate, enable the buyer to pay a reduced amount for payments made in a timely fashion. The monitoring of discount due dates, cash requirements to make payments, and control over check issuance are the focal point of an accounts payable module.

Accounts payable modules consist of at least three major subcomponent files. These files being: **vendor master file, invoice register file,** and **check register file.** A vendor master file normally contains an index of vendor name, address, telephone number, vendor code number, standard discount terms (time and percentage), and space for additional information. An invoice register is a complete list of outstanding invoices catalogued by vendor, invoice date, invoice number, and/or invoice due date. Inquiry modes normally provide data access by catalog fields. For example, a vendor inquiry will lead to a display of outstanding invoices for one specific vendor only. Listings by payment date will likewise generate output specific to the inquiry field. In other words, all invoices due by that payment date will be displayed. Invoice registers become especially important when management is desirous of taking advantage of vendor discount rates. The calculation and printing of bank checks for payment to vendors is monitored through the check register file. Check production and distribution is summarized into a payables report and reconciled through bank statement audit. Figure 12.4 contains a summary of an accounts payable component filing system.

FIGURE 12.4
Accounts Payable Module

Accounts Payable Module: Vendor Master File Invoice Register File Checks Register File

Accounts Payable Functions

1. **Automatic Check Writing**—club accounting systems should be capable of monitoring vendor accounts and tracking invoice due dates. This information is essential to the calculation and generation of vendor payments (checks) in a timely fashion to meet obligations. Automatic check writing eliminates the need for a person to monitor payment timetables and also provides the system with a data base by which to determine cash requirements.
2. **Cash Requirements Forecasting**—one of the most important features of an accounts payable module is its ability to forecast cash requirements, by date, based upon outstanding invoices, discount data, and payment due dates. Computation of amounts owed and cash specifications needed for settlement provides an important dimension of cash flow management not otherwise easily obtainable. Forecasts are presented in the form of a cash requirements report.
3. **Discount Payment Planning**—the best time to pay an invoice is often during its payment discount period. Most vendors extend customers a discount for payments made within a specified timeframe. An invoice that carries a 2/10 net 30 days term (interpreted as 2% discount if paid within 10 days but bill is due in 30 days), for example, enables the buyer to apply a two percent discount to the invoice amount if payment is made within ten days from its date of issue. Consider the club that receives an invoice for $626.47 with these same terms. This club would be able to deduct $12.52 so long as payment was made within the limitations of the discounted term (i.e., 2%/10 days). Taking advantage of such discount terms can lead to significant cost savings; savings sometimes large enough to help cost justify a club application package.
4. **Void Check Control**—the production of a check leads to changes in bank account balance. Cancellation or stop payment of a check previously issued automatically results in its being void. Voided checks need to be controlled so that all checks are accounted for and bank balance information is restored. Account payable modules enable an online update of relevant data at the time of voiding.

Payroll Module

The payroll module is aimed at tracking labor costs via calculations of gross and net pay. Payroll packages are also responsible for maintaining personnel records and extensive payroll documentation for period to date and year end analysis. Payroll modules must be flexible in definition of job codes, rates, employee's meals, tips, taxes, deductions, withholdings, and the like. In addition to the obvious payroll functions, such important data records as EEO, Workman's Compensation, sick pay, vacation tracking, and the like must be maintained. Critical variables in payroll accounting are: number of employees (hourly and salaried), staff turnover, length of payroll period, check production site, confidentiality of information, and withholding/deduction specification. Figure 12.5 contains a summary of payroll module files common to club payroll packages.

FIGURE 12.5
Payroll Accounting Module

Payroll Accounting Module: Personnel Master File Payroll Register File Gov't Reporting File

General Ledger/Financial Reporting Module

The general ledger accounting module is built upon the club's chart of accounts and is responsible for producing account balance, balance sheet, income statement and additional financial information. The general ledger module accepts automatic updates from other portions of the club computer package (e.g., accounts payable and payroll), direct journal entries (e.g., inventory and operating expenses), and data file transfers from membership components (e.g., accounts receivable and departmental revenues). A majority of club computer systems enable income reporting by operating department, responsibility center, division, and club-wide basis.

General ledger accounting involves the specification of a chart of accounts (listing of financial statement accounts and their account numbers) and a systematic approach to transaction recording. The implementation of a uniform system of accounts for clubs provides a logical approach to club accounting design. The general ledger must be capable of tracking member (accounts) receivable, accounts payable, cash, and adjusting entries. Some general ledger packages also offer a means for budget creation and comparative analyses. The general ledger module is a critical variable in the identification of an effective club management system.

The determination of bottom line profitability and fiscal well being of a club is found in the financial reporting module of an accounting application. Most systems are capable of producing flash reports as well as predetermined interval reports. Flash reports normally involve revenue statistics and general ledger (member receivables, cash balances, etc.) highlights. There can be differences, however, in report formats, user programmability, and compliance to industry standards. All financial packages should produce balance sheet and income statement reports. In addition, however, they may also possess the capability for analyzing cash flow, fixed assets, and disbursements. Club users are often more interested in being able to format financial data into a variety of reports. The degrees of freedom accorded the user varies from none to full system flexibility. The proper level of club input is a function of need and user competency.

General Ledger Functions

1. **Fiscal Period Definition**—the life cycle of the general ledger is divided into comparable accounting periods for the purpose of consolidation and reporting uniformity. The club's **fiscal year** can be segmented into twelve (coinciding to the 12 months) or thirteen (52 weeks divided into 13 four-week segments) periods. These divisions provide an equivalent timeframe for comparative analyses.
2. **Income Reporting**—classification of transactions according to a chart of accounts enable revenue and expense items to be sorted and evaluated through a variety of techniques and report formats. Income statements (revenues minus expenses) can then be presented for departments, divisions, or property on a daily, weekly, monthly, and year-to-date basis. In addition, general ledger software is also capable of presenting actual expenditures compared to previous period(s) and budget.
3. **Chart of Accounts**—throughout the club industry there is a standardization of accounts known as the uniform system of accounts for clubs. Although there are many important reasons for the uniformity in financial statement preparation, one of the most essential is to provide an industry-wide interpretation of financial results without regard to individual standardization. With a uniform accounts system club managers are able to evaluate their operations against national, regional, or local trends and averages. This system also helps clubs remain consistent in their own record keeping from year to year.
4. **Trial Balances**—since a club's accounting office package hinges on the accuracy of the general ledger, trial balance procedures are essential to an effective accounting system. A trial balance is a list of all accounts in the ledger having a debit balance as compared to the accounts with credit balances.

Figure 12.6 contains a summary of a typical general ledger module.

FIGURE 12.6
General Ledger Module

General Ledger Module:
Chart of Accounts
Posting Journal
Trial Balance

Balance Sheet

Assets, liabilities, and equity are the three major components of a balance sheet. Assets are items of value; they constitute the resources of the firm. Liabilities are the debts owed by the firm, while equities are interests in or claims upon assets. The balance sheet reflects the soundness of the club by presenting its statement of financial position, for a stated period of time. By equating the firm's valuable resources (assets) with its financial obligations (liabilities) and its sources of interest (equity), this report is simply a representation of the basic accounting equation: assets equal liabilities plus equity. This equality holds true since the sum of interests in assets can't be greater than the value of assets themselves. The balance sheet provides a detailed summary of the club's net worth and enables the calculation of some important financial ratios.

FIGURE 12.7
Balance Sheet Module

Balance Sheet Components:

- Assets
- Liabilities
- Equity

Income Statement

The purpose of the income statement is to report upon the financial profitability of the club for some period of time, usually a fiscal year. The statement is a summary of revenues received from the sale of goods and services and costs incurred by costs of goods sold and operating expenses. Although this document is also referred to as the profit and loss statement, or the earnings statement, the club industry has preferred the income statement heading. The net profit (or loss) of a club is found by simply matching revenues, dues, fees, and assessments against the respective expenditures incurred. If revenues exceed expenses, net earnings result; but should the reverse be true, then a net loss is determined.

FIGURE 12.8
Income Statement Module

Income Statement Components:

- Revenues
- Expenses
- Inventory Variance

Inventory Control Module

Inventory control is essential to efficient club management. The three most common inventory operations are: inventory status, inventory valuation, and inventory variance. Inventory status involves an accounting of how much of each item is in storage. Often times this information is combined with par stock (desired stock level) or minimax levels (order to maximum stock when minimum level reached) as an aid in replenishment and/or purchase ordering. Very sophisticated computer systems may go beyond this basic computation and determine the order quantity which is the most economical for the club to purchase given total inventory and project business cycles.

Inventory valuation deals with the extension of price against stock on hand. The critical factor here is in knowing which price is used. Club systems tend to employ either an inventory item's actual purchase price, a system computed average price, or a market replacement value for each item. The aggregation of price times stock yields an inventory valuation. The difference between a **perpetual inventory** tracking and a **physical inventory** is termed **inventory variance.** In other words, a beginning inventory level minus stock attributed to sales plus additional purchases will produce an estimate of stock available. A storeroom check (physical inventory) may not equate with the system's projected (perpetual inventory) inventory level. Variances should be investigated since they indicate a lack of **inventory control.**

FIGURE 12.9
Inventory Module

Inventory Module:

- Physical Inventory
- Perpetual Inventory
- Inventory Variance

Purchasing Module

A purchasing module permits managment to maintain control over purchase ordering, receiving, and storeroom inventories. Most purchasing programs are interrelated to an inventory module and are capable of generating purchase orders based upon inventory on hand and/or desired stock levels. Other systems are designed to use a zero based inventory level and produce a purchase order necessary to satisfy a projected volume of sales activities. In either case, the purchase order is logged in the system and used to verify receipt of all goods ordered. Upon receipt, items are placed into inventory.

FIGURE 12.10
Purchase Order Module

Purchase Order Module;

- Vendor File
- P. O. file
- Lead / Lag Time File

Budget Module

Budgeting modules provide a means for communicating planned or expected levels of financial performance. A budget is one of the best tools for achieving stated profits and established financial goals. Budgeting provides a detailed plan of accountability for achieving desired results. Although a budget can be developed for various planning horizons (short term, intermediate, or long term) and for variable levels of sales, its main utility lies in its ability to serve as a base for comparison with actual operating results. Hence, although preparation of a budget is important, its implementation and adherence is critical.

The most common forms of budgets are **operating budget, cash budget,** and **capital budget.** An operating budget details projected expenditures for the forthcoming accounting period based upon a forecasted level of sales. Since sales are the major premise upon which most allocations of expenditures are based, a dynamic budget is preferred to a static plan. Club accounting automation affords management the opportunity to forecast variable sales levels both quickly and easily. The operating budget, prepared in terms of revenues and expenses, can be translated into cash receipts and disbursements to produce a cash budget. A cash budget depicts anticipated sources and uses of cash and alerts management of potential cash shortages. Cash on hand, cash in the bank, and anticipated account receivable collections provide a sound basis for cash budget projections. A capital budget is concerned with planned charges in fixed assets. The addition of a member lounge, the remodeling of recreational space, or the refurbishing of a dining room are examples of capital expenditures that may require a capital budget. A capital budget is similar to an operating budget with the exception that it focuses on a specific project, not with an operating department.

FIGURE 12.11
Budgeting Module

Budgeting Module:

- Operating Budget
- Cash Budget
- Capital Budget

Fixed Asset Module

Another important club accounting application area is fixed asset accounting. Fixed assets include land, buildings, furniture, and fixtures. Fixed asset accounting is concerned with the computation and reflection of **depreciation** for property and equipment. Depreciation describes that portion of the cost of a tangible asset that is allocated to each period of the asset's life. Fixed assets are important to what clubs do and therefore must be properly monitored. Figure 12.12 captures the basic components involved in a fixed asset program.

FIGURE 12.12
Fixed Asset Module

Fixed Asset Module Asset / Inventory File Depreciation File

SUMMARY

The accounts payable portion of a club accounting system is used to track purchases, creditor positions, and the club's banking status. Accounts payable activities normally consist of posting purveyor invoices, determining amounts due, and printing checks for payment. Accounts payable modules are normally built upon three major files: vendor master file, invoice register file, and check register file. A vendor master file contains an index of vendor name, address, telephone number, vendor code number, standard discount terms (time and percentage), and space for additional information. An invoice register is a complete list of outstanding invoices cataloged by vendor, invoice date, invoice number, and/or invoice due date. Invoice registers become especially important when management is desirous of taking advantage of vendor discount rates. The calculation and printing of bank checks of payment to vendors is monitored through the check register file. Check production and distribution is summarized into a payables report and reconciled through bank statement audit.

Payroll accounting tends to be a major concern in a club computer application. The fact that club employees may qualify for unique benefits, rates, withholdings, deductions, and report requirements renders this a complex system function. Time and attendance recordation is needed for the computation of gross pay. Pay rates, job codes, employee's meals, uniform credits, tips, taxes, and the like are applied in the derivation of net pay. The unique nature of payroll data dictates that special care be exerted to maintain an accurate payroll register, to produce closely controlled payroll checks, and to protect the confidentiality and propriety of payroll data.

REVIEW QUESTIONS

1. What are some advantages of electronic data processing?
2. What are the advantages and disadvantages of the four types of computer system configurations?
3. What is computer software? Discuss each type.
4. What are the advantages of integrated software?

13

Effective Marketing Communications for Club Managers

Brookside Country Club, Canton, Ohio

MARKETING: AN OVERVIEW

Marketing is everything we do in a club to attract and satisfy members. Club managers and their staff frequently define marketing in vague terms that are loosely connected to their experiences as consumers and purchasers rather than as a system which they develop expressly molded to satisfy the needs of the club and its membership. Some managers equate marketing with advertising, some with sales, while the ultimate error is to think of marketing as the process which makes customers buy what they really don't want anyway. Marketing is none of these things, yet contains certain elements of all of them.

Marketing is a communication system which makes exchanges easier between the club and its members. Simply put, the club has something which the membership wants—products, services, and satisfaction; and the members have something which the club wants—money, time, and sponsorship of various club activities. There are three roles of marketing. They are to identify member needs, wants and desires through market research, to influence demand with persuasive communication, and to service demand by adapting club facilities and services to members of each specific club.

Marketing is like water; you can't survive very long without it. It is a necessary link between the club and its members. How well the club manager plans the marketing communication system will vitally affect how well the club meets its objectives and will determine if the club succeeds. Every marketing action the manager takes will either arouse enthusiasm, leave people indifferent, or provoke resentment. This is why marketing is such an important skill.

The principal tenet of marketing focuses on the customer and customer satisfaction. A marketing oriented club should indeed have an obsession with customer satisfaction and should continuously seek to meet or exceed club member expectations. In short, the concept of marketing essentially views "the customer (member) as king."

There are many types of clubs including city clubs, yacht clubs, country clubs, tennis clubs, golf clubs, fitness clubs, and social clubs. Why do individuals join these clubs? Certainly sailors enjoy memberships in yacht clubs, or a tennis buff is drawn to the tennis club or perhaps a country club with good tennis facilities. Though certain categories of clubs do exist, these kinds of differences are not really significant. From a marketing perspective, what the customer really wants goes well beyond tangibles such as fine food and wine, manicured greens, clay tennis courts or a slip for his yacht at the pier.

The club offers its members many intangibles such as personalized service, a retreat, a place to relax, entertain or be entertained and, most of all, prestige. It provides a home away from home and seclusion, a sense of belonging, the opportunity to identify and feel comfortable with other club members.

A club, like any formal organization, has a membership with common interests. And these common interests for clubs include the need for privacy, seclusion, a sense of belonging, as well as the need for tennis courts, docks and piers.

Effective management incorporates marketing as an integral part of its management philosophy. Any organization exists for its clientel but few enterprises serve such a limited universe as clubs. When a management loses sight of its members—what do they want, why are they here—you will lose sight of the purpose of the club's very existence.

Management that finds itself solely pre-occupied with food costs, green fees, insurance, taxes and such are indeed going to spend more time worrying about the bottom line instead of talking to their customers. The marketing concept simply means that through member satisfaction financial stability can be achieved.

Effective Marketing

When you, as a manager, formulate your marketing communications, you want to accomplish several goals:

1. Make certain you are providing the members something they want and that you can deliver.
2. You want to be understood but you must keep your message simple. This means communicating to someone exactly what you intended. You may want to provide information, persuade them to a certain point of view, or merely remind them of an activity or obligation. Members are usually busy people without motivation to read "stuff."
3. You want to be accepted. You want people to agree with you or at least recognize that *your* point of view is valid.
4. You want to accomplish something. You want to influence people to act in a certain way because *they understand* what *you* want done, and why, how, and when. This may involve helping them to change their attitude toward something by presenting it in a new way.
5. You want to understand others. By learning how others feel about you, your plans, a particular situation, or set of conditions will allow you to accomplish more and to serve the membership better. It is important to remember that marketing communications must flow two ways because only through judiciously adapting to feedback can member wants and needs be better satisfied.

There are only two absolute rules to keep in mind as you establish your marketing plans. First, all marketing communication has a single basic purpose of establishing or improving understanding between you and someone else. If you keep this in mind, you will avoid the most serious pitfalls. Second, the acceptance of your marketing communications will, in large part, be determined by the perception of your sincerity.

Here are some additional guidelines to consider as you plan your marketing communication effort.[1]

1. Determine what you want to say. You cannot make yourself clear to others unless it is already clear in your own mind.
2. Put the facts to be explained in a logical order.
3. Draw from your experience with the person(s) with whom you are communicating. Ask yourself this question, "What have I learned from my success or failure with them in the past that will help me to succeed this time?
4. Try to communicate with people when they are in a proper frame of mind. A person who is worried or angry won't hear you any better than if you were trying to communicate in the presence of a riveting machine. This applies to you, too. When you are disturbed or upset, effective communication is difficult.
5. It is important to arouse interest. To hold people's attention, you must motivate them and stimulate their interest just as you would if you wanted them to do anything else.
6. Find common ground. If you want people to agree with you or give you a sympathetic hearing, try to imagine how they feel about the topic and take their viewpoint into account.
7. Speak to people in their language. Don't confuse others by using unfamiliar words or jargon. Don't assume that others are comfortable with your ideas or that they have identical interests. Tailoring your language to suit others is important, but don't do it by stepping out of character or by being condescending.

8. Emotions mean as much as facts. People respond not only with their brains but with their whole personalities. Negative emotions such as fear, anger, or suspicion can be aroused by what you consider a simple statement of fact. Be aware that you are communicating on an emotional as well as a rational level at all times.
9. Discretion is an important part of communication. The good communicator keeps confidences and doesn't repeat anything that is heard unless all the possible effects are considered.
10. Too much information is bad; so is too little. Only a certain amount of information can be digested at any one time. If you have a lot to say, break it up into parts so that it can be understood.
11. Watch for responses. Find out if your message is getting through by seeing how others are reacting. If they look bored, irritated, or confused, or if their responses don't make sense, the approach should be changed. Attentive listening is important not only because of what you can learn but also because it means a great deal to the people with whom you are trying to communicate.

Planning the Marketing Effort

Planning is future-oriented.[2] It begins with the setting of objectives or goals. If objectives are to be effective, they must meet these tests:

1. *Congruency.* Objectives or goals of any department must be aligned with and contribute to the objectives or goals of the whole club. Thus, marketing objectives must take into account the club's goals of profit, growth, and perpetuity.
2. *Potential achieveability.* Objectives must be realizable in terms of the human and material resources available. There is no point in setting unrealizable objectives.
3. *Understandability.* Objectives must be understood not only by those who frame them, but equally important, by those who are expected to achieve them.
4. *Feasibility.* Objectives must appear to be workable and worth striving for if they are to have a favorable impact upon the staff and the governing bodies of the club.

Referring to Exhibit 13.1, note that for each objective there will be a *program,* a series of steps or events that must occur if the goal is to be achieved. The program should be formulated in terms that make each step *assignable* to appropriate staff for execution. Also, each step should flow into the next step with minimum backtracking. This is referred to as *sequentiality.* Obviously, too, the program in total and the separate steps must be *understood* not only by the people designing them but also by those who will be assigned the task of assuring their completion. As the program is formulated, it may be necessary to go back and refine or amend the related objective. An acid test of the feasibility of an objective is that a program can be designed for its achievement.

The third element, *contemplated execution,* involves thinking through in advance how each step of the program is to be carried out. Again referring to Exhibit 13.1, note that this involves such questions as: who will take care of each step in the program; what will be needed in the way of information, facilities, or materials to do this; how is the best way to do it; where is the best place for it to occur; and, by no means least, who else needs to be informed? As the contemplated execution phase is dealt with, it may be necessary to re-define some of the steps in the program to put them in a form that makes them more feasible as specific "jobs to be done."

EXHIBIT 13.1
Model for Marketing Planning

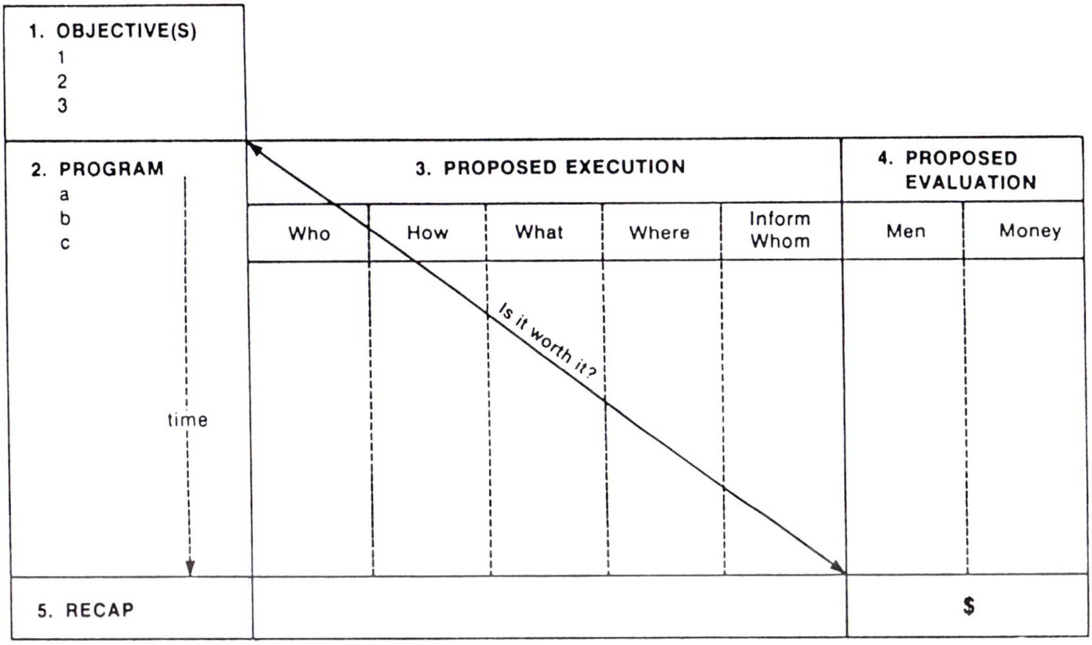

The fourth and last element, *contemplated evaluation*, is frequently omitted with disastrous results. This step taps the judgment of the club manager. The cost of each step in the program must be weighed. Finally, in recapping the total costs and looking at what is to be achieved, the question is asked, "Is it worth it?" It is bad to overcommit resources in achieving objectives, but perhaps even more dangerous to undercommit them.

Elements of the Communications Mix

The marketing communications mix consists of several elements. These include: advertising, merchandising, sales promotion, and public relations. While it is as true for clubs as for other organizations that these elements must be integrated and blended into a cohesive marketing effort, for each of the particular areas which follow we will see that one of the elements will tend to dominate. Exhibit 13.2 outlines this relationship.

EXHIBIT 13.2
The Marketing Communication Mix for Clubs

Activity	Dominant Element
Membership Growth	Enhancing
Food and Beverage	Merchandising
Special Functions	Sales Promotion
Building Goodwill	Public Relations

EXHIBIT 13.3
Bases for Member Selection

Socio-economic and Demographic Variables

Age
Sex
Family Size
Family Life Cycle
Social Class
Occupation
Home Ownership
Second Home Ownership
Ethnic Group
Education
Income

Service-related Variables

Recreation Activity
Equipment Type
Volume Usage
Benefit Expectations
Experience Preferences
Participation Patterns

Psychographic Variables

Personality Traits
Lifestyle
Attitudes, Interests, Opinions
Motivations
Life experiences

Geographic Variables

Region
Market Area
Urban Suburban, Rural
City Size
Population Density

MEMBERSHIP GROWTH

Membership Selection

The very first questions to be answered in the formulation of a marketing communication plan are: Who are our members? Who do we wish to have as members? The very definition of what a club is—a group of people associated, united, or combined for a common purpose—suggests that the club's membership will have certain common characteristics.

Nomination and selection are usually based on one or more of the characteristics suggested in Exhibit 13.3. However, selectivity must be exercised to assure that the club achieves an optimum mix in its membership. The club will want to maintain a compatible membership, but at the same time the membership base must not be so narrowly constructed as to make the club vulnerable during periods of membership erosion or during seasonal downturns in patronage.

The proper response to identifying members is frequently the responsibility of the Membership Committee. It is a part of its duties to rule on the admissibility of candidates. Within this function, it is particularly important for the committee to guard against racism, bigotry, and illegal procedures which would leave the club and/or its members open to poor publicity, public criticism, or legal entanglements.

Segmentation, Target Marketing, and Positioning

"Segmentation" is the act of dividing the total membership or potential membership into subgroups of people with similar interests, needs, wants and desires. Dimensions commonly used include demographic, geographic and behavioristic variables. Through the exercise of market segmentation we are better able to understand the profile of our members or potential members and better determine who our target markets should be.

Demographic variables include such items as income, occupation, age, and family status. For example, by examining the potential market in a university town we may want to consider university faculty and staff as one market segment and local professionals (such as bankers, realtors, lawyers, etc.) as another. However, occupation alone is not sufficient to identify a market segment with similar interests. Other demographic variables can help here such as income bracket, age, and family status. Continuing with the above example, we may find that income brackets do not vary significantly between university and non-university professionals but that age and family status do. We may even discover that family status turns out to be the best means by which to segment the market; i.e., families who want ample activities for young children and teenagers, compared to those who want to retreat from the kids.

Geographic boundaries may also be helpful for some clubs to discern who their potential markets are. A small town situated on one of the finger lakes in upstate New York recently discovered that the draw for their fledgling yacht club was much broader than the immediate area. (Many communities in this region do not have direct access to the lakes, and individuals were quite willing to drive several hours to "spend-a-day" at the club seeking water activities on the lakcshorc.)

Behavioristic dimensions for segmenting a market refer to the specific purpose for which one might utilize a club's facilities. Business or pleasure travel is a common segmentation scheme in the hospitality industry and is certainly applicable to club management. There may be one segment that uses the club heavily for business purposes, e.g., golf, dining. Another segment may be those who primarily use a club's facilities for pleasure, be it as a family on weekends or as a single looking to meet other single people.

Separating your market into "heavy users" versus "light users" is also a behavioristic approach to market segmentation. Heavy users may turn out to be the family pleasure market and light users the business-at-the-club market, or vice-versa.

A key aspect of segmentation is not which dimensions you use, but how thoroughly you analyze your market, incorporating several dimensions simultaneously. A common mistake is to rely solely on demographic variables for market segmentation. This tells us who the customer is, but not *why* they use or have potential to use the club facilities.

For this reason, a behavioristic approach is suggested as the bacic framework from which to analyze your market segments. (Other dimensions can then be added to help refine and/or more clearly define your market segments.) Understanding why individuals want to join your club or use your club on a regular basis often provides much more meaningful information than do the particular age, income, or home address of potential customers.

Once a satisfactory segmentation scheme has been developed, target markets need to be identified. "Target markets" are those markets that the club most wishes to attract. Common sense tells us we can't satisfy singles, families, empty nesters, sailors, golfers, and tennis buffs all at the same time in the same place. A conscious management decision needs to be made as to who the primary target market(s) of the club will be. From there, the "position" of the club can then be established.

"Positioning" essentially refers to the image you want to portray in the community. How do you intend the club to be perceived by club members, potential club members, and the community at large. Individuals will develop an image of your club whether you plan it or not. Thus, it is important to create and develop your own preferred image rather than just let it happen.

Images are largely based on the benefits offered and the club members it attracts. For example, you may want to position yourself as a family-oriented club offering benefits to all members of the family. Some clubs may prefer a more elite, upscale image for the more discriminating customer. Either one of these is appropriate assuming that (a) market segmentation has been well analyzed, (b) target markets have been clearly identified, and (c) the position/image will be positively received by the community.

Positioning is a pivotal point for the development of any marketing strategy. Indeed, it is the master strategy from which product, pricing and communication strategies are developed.

Once the prospective clientele segments have been identified, several other variables must be considered:

1. What are the expectations of the membership? For example, any club represents a means for individuals to make values manifest to others. Just as values are often reflected in a person's possessions, they can also be recognized by the places which are patronized and the people with whom a person associates. Some basic research can easily establish a profile of values for each key category of membership.
2. What level of membership is needed to maintain a stable financial base? Perhaps the club will find it necessary to achieve a minimum level of membership—a critical mass—to have the financial and human resources available to provide the services which the members desire. Conversely, it is possible that a smaller membership may be willing to bear the additional costs to maintain a certain exclusivity.
3. What is the demand on the current facilities? Several options are available: expand facilities and membership, expand one or the other, maintain the *status quo*. If facilities are underutilized, attracting new members is a means of more effectively using these resources. Consideration can also be given to expanding only those classifications of membership which will not result in placing a strain on a particular segment of the facilities. For example, if athletic equipment would be abused as a result of adding "regular" members, a special program to admit social members could be established.

Enhancing Cautions

Before proceeding, two warnings are necessary. First, as managers develop the means of attracting new members, it is important to remember that these messages are not produced in a vaccum. Current members will also be exposed to these messages. Each marketing communications "piece" should reinforce in the membership the idea that they have made a wise selection and should instill pride and a desire for continued support of the club and its mission. Second, some clubs maintain long waiting lists for membership. In these situations, communications to attract new members may not be necessary and may offend prospective members on the list. Keep in mind that such cases are the exception rather than the rule.

Enhancing Appeals

Marketing communication appeals (reasons to become a member) can be approached from two perspectives: that of the prospective member or that of the club. Those appeals from the prospective member viewpoint will emphasize the individual's physical and psychological needs. However, it is important to recognize that patronage motives are neither simplistic nor easily identified and they often overlap. It is often difficult to distinguish them from those messages which extol the virtues of membership from the club perspective.

The club also has several benefits which can be promoted through its marketing communications. These primarily include the facilities/services offered, the employees, and the desired image you wish to project.

For clubs, the facilities and/or services offered include a multiple number of decisions to be made. The club manager needs to determine whether to offer formal dining, informal dining, and/or snack bar facilities. Could your dining room present an informal atmosphere at lunchtime, with a more formal environment at dinner? Do you want to offer a standup bar, cocktail lounge, pool lounge, and/or club house approach for serving beverages? To what degree do you want to make available physical fitness facilities such as swimming pool (what size, how many), tennis courts (what types, how many, indoor/outdoor), golf facilities, nautilius/universal/exercise room, saunas/lockers/showers (how many, how big)? To what degree and how many professional instructors do you want to have for the various physical facilities? In other words, do you want to position yourself as a tennis club that has a swimming pool, or perhaps as a country club that has both.

Whether you are a new club, an established club, a club that desires to expand and/or reposition, or a new club manager, the above questions need to be addressed on a regular basis to insure the success and vitality of the existing operation. Answers to these questions can be gotten by reaching to the customer. It is too easy in any operation (clubs, hotels, restaurants) to fall into the habit of "board room" decisions. Constant and continuous communication with the club membership is essential and mandatory for the marketing-minded club manager.

Employees are very much an integral part of the product you offer. Once you have determined the profile and nature of your target markets, the employees need to be able to "relate" to this clientele. Are your employees sincere in their job to serve the customer in the manner they wish to be served; e.g., casual, formal, relaxed, discreet? The personality of your employee and style of service needs to adapt to the mood of your guests. The selection and training of employees, especially for clubs, is a critical component of the product offering.

In a recent article in *The Cornell Hotel and Restaurant Administration Quarterly,* Martin presents a helpful way to constructively analyze your staff's performance.[3] In essence, he suggests two categories from which to review your employees—procedural and convivial. Procedural factors include such items as timeliness of service, prompt greeting of guests in the dining room, and other

EXHIBIT 13.4
The Bundle Purchase Concept for Clubs

Attributes	Tangible	Explicit Intangible	Implicit Intangible
Benefits	Facilitating Good	Sensual Benefits	Psychological Benefits
Example A	Tennis Court	Condition of Court clay/asphalt/grass indoor/outdoor	Privacy Prestige Self-esteem Status
Example B	Steak for Dinner at Club	Quality of Steak Quality of Service Lighting Decor Noise Level Other Diners	Ambiance Seclusion Eliteness Aura

Source: Adapted from Sasser, Olsen, and Whyckoff, *Management of Service Operations,* 1978.

technical aspects of their jobs. Convivial factors focus more on the attitude, eye contact, body language, and responsiveness of employees when in contact with a guest. Using this approach for inquiry into the employee aspect of product quality may reveal, for example, that some employees show strength in the convivial sense yet are weak in the procedural aspects of the job. This procedural/convivial approach is a helpful suggestion of how you can examine the employee aspect of your product.

Club members or "patrons" of your club are also very much a part of your product offering. Why do people join clubs in the first place? To be with other people that seek the same kind of exclusivity and prestige that the club offers. This is why segmentation and target market selection needs to be done *prior* to product strategy decisions. Developing a product and then searching for customers is not marketing. Marketing looks at the customer first, determines what their needs are, then provides a solution to those needs. The solution is based on the particular needs of the target market selected for your club.

The bundle purchase concept is a useful tool to help analyze your product as a whole. Essentially, this concept (developed for service-oriented products) distinguishes between tangible, explicit intangible, and implicit intangible attributes of a service product.[4] Exhibit 13.4 summarizes by example how this approach can be applied to clubs. Tangible attributes refer to the basic facilitating good, such as the tennis court, a steak at dinner. Explicit intangibles refer to the sensual benefits derived from a product. This would include such items as condition of the tennis court, or lighting in the dining room and service style offered. Implicit intangibles are the psychological benefits the guest receives as a result of "purchasing" the product. These types of benefits, and probably the most important, include the privacy, prestige, ambiance, and/or security aspects of the product.

At the risk of sounding too academic, this conceptual approach to developing a product strategy can give excellent insight as to the focus you take when analyzing your product. You may discover, perhaps, that too much attention is given to the facilitating goods and implicit intangibles, and not enough effort given to the sensual benefits that your members are looking for. Rarely does the customer consciously scrutinize his or her needs in this manner, but the customer will indeed react if one or more of these product attributes is not consciously being received.

The key point for product strategy from a marketing perspective is that your customer is the person who determines what the product is or should be, not the operations side of the business. The job of operations (certainly no easy task!) is to make sure the product happens.

Communications Tools

The most powerful communications tool available is word-of-mouth. Nothing is as persuasive as a committed member espousing belief in a smoothly operating and well-organized club. This is why the "internal" marketing which a club does and the constant assurance of member satisfaction is so important. Enlist the help of your members. Provide them with incentives, if necessary. Gain their support and commitment.

Many clubs will produce descriptive brochures which will provide information on club facilities. The brochure can be given personally to a prospective member. It can also serve as a convenient reminder to the membership of facilities, services, and obligations. If this tool is used, it must be reproduced tastefully. Full color is recommended. Message content and illustrations must be monitored so that it doesn't become obsolete too quickly. For example, don't say, "The dining room was refurbished in 19xx", or include a picture of the current president of the club. These will quickly date the brochure. However, be sure to have enough printed to achieve appropriate economies of scale. Because producing a high quality descriptive brochure involves a substantial expenditure, serious consideration should be given to retaining professional services for its preparation.

FOOD AND BEVERAGE

Almost any discussion of marketing food and beverage concentrates heavily on such aspects as menu planning and development, pricing, and point-of-purchase displays. While these are important, the interested club manager can find the hows and the whys of these topics in almost any appropriate hospitality text. What is often lacking, however, is recognition of the importance that a personal merchandising effect can play in the creation and enhancement of an enjoyable experience by the member. It is this often-neglected facet of merchandising which is emphasized in the sale of food and beverage. Keep in mind that it is only one dimension of the marketing communications effort.

Merchandising: What is it?

Merchandising is influencing members' purchase decisions once in the club. It includes all of the promotional activities which you do after the member has entered one of your food service areas. It is important to remember that once members come in they have already decided to spend money. The questions now are: How much and for what? Therefore, merchandising has three purposes: (1) to sell the members more; (2) to influence them to purchase food and beverage; (3) to get them to return so that the first two purposes can be repeated; and (4) reenforce their decision to have chosen this club.

Merchandising is important for another reason. Consider this example. You have three ingredients—ice cream, canned peaches, and some brandy. You can make a peach parfait—food cost about 75 cents, selling price $2.00, gross margin $1.25. However, these same items can also be used to make a peche flambe—selling price $3.75, gross margin $3.00. Not only is the margin greater but you will probably sell more because you have made your operation distinctive and provided members with a memorable experience.

Pricing Strategy

Pricing is probably one of the most difficult decisions for a manager of any operation to make. As a result, price decisions often tend to be based on cost alone—an unfortunate oversight. Pricing is in large part a marketing decision, not solely an accounting decision. Costs certainly need to be covered, but, in concept, the cost of the product should be reviewed at the final stages of the pricing decision. And then, if necessary, the product should be modified accordingly.

Three key factors in the pricing decision include demand, competition and cost. Demand determines the highest amount you can charge for your services; i.e., "what the market is willing to bear." For clubs in particular, members are willing to pay a premium price for the basic desire of prestige in the first place. Yet there is a price-value relationship, too. In other words, there is a limit, or a "ceiling," for what they expect from a club relative to the price of its memberships dues and services.

The cost factor determines the lowest price you can charge. In the short run variable costs must be met. These are the costs of doing business, such as food and beverage consumption, labor. In the long run, fixed costs need to be covered which are the costs of being in business. These include such items as taxes, insurance, and liquor licenses. These costs are not necessarily recovered on a consumption per person basis. They may or may not be fully "collected" each time a club member uses the club.

For example, green fees should probably at least cover the variable costs associated with the operation of the golf course, and perhaps a portion of the fixed cost. The remaining portion of the fixed cost should be dispersed equitably among all club members, even if they don't play golf. It is only fair, and certainly reasonable, that all club members pay a portion of the total fixed costs to support the club's very existence.

A third key factor in a pricing decision is the competition. What alternatives are available to your club members? In addition to other clubs in the area, you also need to consider alternatives to your restaurant, pool, golf and tennis facilities. Restaurant pricing, for example, must take into account the prices of local restaurants that offer a similar product and service style to yours. Though club members are usually willing to pay a premium to "dine at the club," there is a point where the price will exceed the value of that privilege. Hence, a lost customer for dinner, but not necessarily a lost club membership.

There are obvious reasons why you want to retain that customer for dinner. The higher the patronage (and forecasts for patronage) the less you will have to incorporate a portion of the fixed costs into the price of each meal. Additionally, with higher and/or more stable patronage, food and labor costs can be better kept in line. Thirdly, and perhaps most importantly, no one likes to dine in an empty restaurant. As discussed earlier addressing product strategy, club members are very much a part of the actual product. People like to see and be seen, especially at a club.

Supply relative to demand is a primary force from which prices are determined. Should demand for your club exceed the membership quota, it is indeed tempting to raise the rates. Yet, caution is urged before membership dues, dining room prices, or green fees are increased arbitrarily. Pricing is a reflection of your positioning of the club. Excess demand could very well be the result of an excellent price/value relationship perceived by current and would-be club members. A dramatic shift in your pricing strategy will change that image. If all is going well, why rock the boat?

Basic Rules for Success

To avoid problems and improve profits, there are four fundamental rules that club managers must remember whenever an item is being merchandised.

1. Know your members. Providing an atmosphere of ultrasophistication in a coffee shop or pub is obviously inappropriate. Likewise, formality in decor and menu items is out of place in a family dining room. Even where the merchandising effort fits the operation, it may not fit the members.
2. Know your staff. The level of merchandising at which you operate must be compatible with the capabilities of your personnel. Keeping a salad bar fully stocked and maintaining its eye appeal takes a lot less skill than preparing flaming desserts. For special merchandising "events," be sure to select the employee with the right personality. For example, the flambe chef should be extroverted, even flamboyant. The people on the coffee cart should be tall and attractive (and properly costumed) so that they will be noticed from every table in the dining room.
3. Train, train, train. Professional attitudes and appearance are effective merchandising tools. Do not underestimate their value. An effective merchandising program puts your personnel in the spotlight. Therefore, they must be more aware of personal hygiene, proper dress, and good grooming and make-up. Proper instruction and rehearsal in the use of merchandising equipment and presentation of merchandising ideas to your membership will make your employees better sales people and your operation more profitable.
4. Food and service come first. No matter how much "zing" you add to your operation, it will never be a substitute for properly prepared and served food and beverages. In a recent consumer attitude survey by the National Restaurant Association, poor quality food and poor service ranked as the two most annoying factors in the dining experience. Other factors such as portion size, noise, and limited menus ranked much further down the list. The moral: an extra olive in a martini does not make up for a twenty-minute wait, and a broken sauce served in gleaming silverware is a sure means of driving away business.

Communications Strategy

From a textbook perspective, communication and/or promotional tools include advertising, direct selling, and public relations. For clubs, direct selling and public relations are probably the most effective.

Direct selling can be of both a personal or non-personal nature. Personal direct selling means that a club staff member has direct personal contact with a club member. For example, a major aspect of the waitperson's or bartender's job is direct selling to the customer. A waiter's or waitress' job is not only to serve the meal, but also to communicate with the guest on items such as suggested wines with certain menu items, specials being offered on a particular day, or perhaps suggesting a dessert that is particularily scrumptious and "loaded" with calories. Your waitstaff is your sales staff as well as part of your product. Good training on selling techniques is important for any of your staff in direct contact with the guest.

This form of direct selling is, as was previously discussed, often referred to as merchandising. However, merchandising can also be non-personal direct selling. Examples include tent cards suggesting exotic drinks in your cocktail lounge or dessert carts prominently displayed at the entrance of your dining room. Either form of merchandising—personal or non-personal direct selling—is an effective means to communicate to your members the many aspects of the product. In essence, merchandising is point-of-sale selling reminding the customer of particular items you have to offer. When well-planned and well-orchestrated it can only enhance customer satisfaction by communicating to club members options and alternatives available to them beyond the basic "facilitating good."

Direct personal selling is also a marketing tool that should be used for clubs that offer wedding, reception, and banquet accommodations. Whether you have separate facilities or perhaps close your main dining room on, say, Sunday nights to accommodate these types of requests, some member of your staff needs to directly communicate what you have to offer and finalize the details of the event. A member of your staff should be clearly designated as the person in charge for promoting, selling, and executing group functions. This individual could delegate certain responsibilities to other staff members such as appointing the chef to finalize the food and beverage details of a wedding reception. However, determining the time, date, price, billing procedure, flower arrangements, music, waitstaff scheduling etc., is probably *not* the job of your chef, nor should it be. Someone needs to be the "coordinator" for all aspects of the event and, thus, insure follow-up, follow-through, and a satisfied customer.

Public relations is an indirect selling technique and should be part of the marketing effort for any organization. Public relations essentially brings the club to the attention of the general public in a positive light. Community goodwill is an objective that can easily be achieved through well-planned public relations activities. A good example might be sponsoring a club tournament with the proceeds from entrance fees contributed to the local United Fund campaign. Or, perhaps an off-premise activity, such as club members volunteering to help plant trees in a local park on Arbor Day. Activities such as these are certain to capture the attention of your local newspaper, radio, and/or television stations and will promote a good posture for your club.

Through public relations two objectives can be reached; (1) a sense of goodwill and pride among your club members, and (2) a positive working relationship with your community. The club manager, with support of the board and club members, should in effect be the public relations "director." The job is too important to delegate.

Now, with a fundamental understanding of merchandising and of the key requirements to make it successful in implementation, you are ready to learn to survive in the communications jungle. The objective will be to simplify and condense the basic rules into an easily understood and workable format that can be remembered and practiced to enhance the effectiveness of your sales personnel and the profitability of the club's food and beverage operations. First, some background information is necessary so that you can see why it is important to put specific techniques to work. Second, concrete suggestions and actual examples will put the techniques into the context of club operations.

The Importance of Perception

Perception is important to the merchandising communication effort because every human being responds in a way that depends upon present circumstances and past experience. Mood, receptiveness, and needs all play a role. As a result, the message which we think we are sending to employees or members often is not received and interpreted as it was meant. Learning what to say to produce the effect you want is the important thing. It really is not difficult. All that is needed is the proper combination of "telling" and "selling." Remember, in conversations with dining patrons the service personnel are the authorities. The members are predisposed to accept the pearls of wisdom which are dropped.

The most important aspect of perception is selectivity. People see what they want to see and hear what they want to hear. For example, a husband and wife agree to go away on vacation. Although they think they have agreed, the word "vacation" means something different to each of them. The wife visualizes a posh hotel, sumptuous dining, and dancing—a time with no household worries. The husband sees a rustic cabin, trout fishing, and boating—and maybe a plentiful supply of his favorite brew. It is the same word "vacation" but the husband and wife understand it very differently. In club food service operations the possibilities for misunderstandings are many. Is your perception of a "king-size" steak the same as your customers'? Consider how many interpretations there are for "Polynesian cocktail."

A second aspect of perception which is closely allied to subjectivity is selectivity. Members and employees will pick out those parts of your communications efforts that they consider interesting, challenging, or of particular importance to them. They will tend to disregard and be unaware of those features of communication in which they have no emotional stake. For example, during your favorite television detective program, when the police interview victims or witnesses, each individual selects only those aspects of the case they consider important. How often have we heard the victim say, "I didn't notice what the thief was wearing; I only saw that big gun in my face." Club managers face similar problems when customers perceive selectively. Many members would not think of asking for a wine menu. Many are aware only of food prices and make no connection between price and the level of service. "Why is a hamburger at McDonald's only $1.75, but when I come to the club I have to pay $4.95?" Members will often remember special courtesies or minor slights to the exclusion of the rest of the dining experience.

The final aspect of perception to be considered is summation. This is the repetition of cues to bring conditions to our conscious mind. For example, as a motorist drives down the highway, the first two billboards for Howard Johnson's are not perceived. Suddenly, when the third billboard is reached, there is a realization that an ice cream cone would taste very good. In your club, the wine display at the front door, the self-serve wine bar, or the wine glass at each table may not individually make an impression, but together they "add up" to get members thinking on a track that will increase wine sales.

Each of these three aspects of perception should be kept in mind as we make concrete suggestions and give specific examples so that the effectiveness of the selling effort will be enhanced. The suggestions are simple and straightforward and with commitment on the part of managers, easy to apply.

Four Suggestions to Increase Member Utilization

The first recommendation is really common sense. *Be persuasive, suggest often*. The most effective suggestion approaches use phraseology which implies that the service person (and thus management and everyone connected with the club) is a knowledgeable merchant. For example, service personnel might suggest "a wonderful red California Cabernet wine. It would go well with your prime rib. May I bring you a bottle?" This approach has accomplished three things:

1. The member has been put at ease at the beginning of the suggestion, making him more receptive to what will follow. This was done through the use of the words "wonderful" and "California." Translation: the wine is good and probably not expensive.
2. The member knows that the wine goes with the meal.
3. We relieved him of possible embarrassment by saying the foreign-sounding word "Cabernet" for him. To order the wine, the member only has to say, "Yes, thank you."

Dining room personnel must be prepared to sell. They must be aware of combinations and be ready to suggest alternatives if a recommendation is rejected. If the member orders a hamburger, french fries are suggested. If this is rejected, the service room person suggests onion rings. If the member orders apple pie, ice cream is suggested. If this is rejected the service person suggests cheddar cheese. If the customer does not care for dessert, the sales person might suggest a liqueur. If the member is on a diet, a salad with low calorie dressing might be suggested in place of the starch that normally accompanies the main dish.

Another problem which we might encounter is the long-cooking item. Above all, be honest with the member. Tell how long preparation will take. You will be surprised at how much this courtesy is appreciated. This presents an ideal opportunity for the sale of an appetizer or cocktails.

The third recommendation is that you *use the "psychological box."* This simply means limiting the customers' choices to make their decisions easier. The use of the psychological box is a logical progression from category groupings on the menu, i.e., entrees, appetizers, desserts, etc., which are grouped to limit the choices and make meal selection easier. As an illustration, consider the service person who says to a member, "Would you care for a cocktail?" There are two possible responses: "yes" and "no." Only one of these responses results in a sale. But suppose the question were asked like this, "Would you care for a cocktail, or would a glass of wine be better?" The member can still refuse but positive suggestion has made that alternative more difficult. Either of the choices which the service person offers results in additional sales.

This can work the same way with items you are trying to "push." The service person might say, "The beef stroganoff is excellent but if you would care for something lighter, our special chicken with lemon sauce is delightful. I recommend either." Again, the choices are limiting. The member may select something else but we have effectively planted the seed to sell those items selected by management. Also, notice the positive phrasing in this illustration. It was never suggested that the beef was heavier, only that the chicken was lighter.

The final recommendation is to *phrase positively whenever possible*—tell your members that you have something good. "Would you like another drink" suggests that maybe the member is drinking too much. Instead say, "May I re-order for you?"—a positive suggestion. Never say,

"Would you care for dessert?" "May I suggest the chocolate torte?" is better. "Will that be all?" sounds like "I hope you are finished because I'm tired of serving you." "Is there anything else?" says "I'm anxious to serve you and you have been a wonderful customer."

In all of this there are certain implications. Artificiality and coercion will drive members away. A fine balance exists between being pleasantly persuasive and being "pushy." If your approaches are imaginative and your personnel are trained properly, then you can show members that you are truly interested in giving them a fine dining experience. Second, if there is special entertainment or if uniqueness is somehow accorded to the members, adding a significant percentage to the selling price of an item will not lower profits. Build into the price of every item not only its cost, but also the intangibles which members demand and are willing to pay for—ambience, affiliation, and recognition.

SPECIAL FUNCTIONS

Special functions by their very nature are "special." They represent a variety of activities which are characterized by a change of pace from the routine operating functions of the club. They might be one-time events (a reception for a visiting dignitary); events that are repeated at irregular intervals with modifications to suit a particular sponsor (a wedding reception); or events which take place infrequently but at regular intervals (the annual fourth of July picnic).

Functions of this nature will usually have promotional packages specifically designed for the occasion and this promotion will be of short duration. These promotional activities should stimulate interest, trial, or purchase by members. The distinguishing features are the custom design and single use of the promotional effort. Generally speaking, there are three aspects of promoting the club for special functions use: the environment of the club, employee contact, and printed material.

The Environment of the Club

Members will not want to use the facilities of the club to sponsor a special function or attend a special function that has been planned by management unless they are completely satisfied with their experiences with the club on a daily basis. In other words, the physical presentation of the club and the proper performance of assigned tasks by staff as well as the courtesies which are accorded to members will greatly complement the overt activities of marketing communication which managers use.

Additionally, there are some aspects of service over which the member is more likely to complain than compliment the club. Among these are: prices; availability of services; and availability of parking each appear on the complaint list but not on the compliment list. Because of their predisposition to have a negative impact, the club manager should give them special attention. High performance in these service areas will not enhance the members' perception of the club. However, if minimum expectations are not met in these areas, they will detract seriously from the members' impressions.

Alternately, members especially appreciate high performance in some service areas. Management should make special efforts to monitor the helpfulness and knowledge of employees, the neatness and cleanliness of the club, and the quality service level. It is interesting to note that items involving employee contact have the greatest potential for producing satisfaction or dissatisfaction among members.

Employee Contact

The cornerstone to the continuing sale of special functions is a member-oriented attitude on the part of all staff members. Managers can assure this by alerting employees to impending functions and special events and letting them know who the key persons are in each group. The more background that is furnished to employees, the more effectively they can relate to the members.

The astute club manager also will be aware of other ways of enhancing the member/employee relationship. These include:

1. Incorporating human relations topics into a continuing training program.
2. Establishing specific criteria related to personality and temperament to be applied during the initial selection process for employees. Criteria should be chosen that will translate into more effective interpersonal effectiveness with members.
3. Providing incentives for noteworthy efforts. These may range from awards for individual employees for particularly courteous service to group awards for departments which do an outstanding job.

Employees who have member contact can become effective sales personnel for the club, provided they are given sufficient training and the opportunity. Through attitudes and high performance level which promote member satisfaction, they lay the foundation for the use of a wider variety of club services as well as encouraging more frequent use of facilities. Through their conversations with members, employees cannot just provide information but actually take part in the selling process. It is both a selling tool and a service to members to remind guests of facilities on the premises, the excellence of the food, or the availability of special services at the club that can satisfy their needs. Obviously, the roles which employees are assigned should not be limited to job performance. They must be made aware that they have additional tasks, such as:

1. performing marketing intelligence
2. facilitating member activities
3. supporting positive feelings about the club
4. expediting the resolution of members' problems
5. maintaining a flexible and creative outlook
6. promoting facilities and services[5]

Printed Material

Every member must be aware of all of the services which the club offers on a regular basis as well as those special functions to which management would like to attract them. A variety of printed materials is available to promote the use of the club's facilities. Service directories, party brochures, banners and posters, table tents, and flyers and bulletins are a few of the devices commonly used. Each has a specific purpose for which it is best suited.

Service directories (similar to the informational brochure discussed earlier) include promotional material on all of the club's facilities in a single place. If used properly it will be your most important source of continuing business. Other printed matter is aimed at one-time or infrequently recurring functions. Service directories are much more versatile. Because they are selling devices that will be used to sell the club facilities on a daily basis as well as for special functions, they should be of a color and style consistent with the image which the manager wishes to maintain for the club. They constitute a ready reference and a reinforcing promotional tool for the direct selling and merchandising efforts of the staff.

Another form of non-personal direct selling is your club newsletter. It is probably one of the best ways to communicate directly with your club members. Through the newsletter you can tell your members about what is happening at the club, special events such as tournaments coming up soon, changes in the dining room hours, renovation plans, new lockers, whatever. You could also have a column about club members, such as who won the last tournament, Joe has improved his golf handicap, or Mary has recovered from surgery and is back on the court. You might even solicit letters from club members themselves. Specific content, of course, depends on what type of club you are and/or what your club members want the contents to be; maybe Joe doesn't want any one to know what his handicap is. What is important is that it be well-written, distributed on a regular basis, and specifically address the needs, wants and desires of your members.

Clubs may also have a brochure or package of materials specifically designed to sell function space and catering facilities for anniversaries, birthdays, receptions, celebrations, and special events planned by the club or its members. Its characteristics are similar to those used in the information brochure for prospective members but there are some important differences:

1. This brochure or package should have a readily identifiable color. This will make it difficult to misplace.
2. The "leave the driving to us" approach should be emphasized. The ease of entertaining as well as the willingness of the club to meet the members' needs should be featured.
3. Remember that the key function of the brochure is to serve as a reminder that the club is available, so the presentation need not be exceptionally detailed. Save detailed information for follow-up communications or for when the member comes to talk seriously about planning a function.

Banquet and party business is an important part of food and beverage sales. Many of the principles used in club dining facilities to increase sales also apply to the sale of function space and the activities which they incorporate:

1. Analyze your member market.
2. Determine how you can meet the needs of that market.
3. Set up a plan for solicitation.
4. Be willing to make adjustments to accommodate members.
5. Follow up activities with proper member relations, requests for repeat business, and the maintenance of complete and accurate records.

Local sources of substantial group business are the many civic and service organizations and business groups in your community to which members may belong. If you have members in any of these groups, direct personal contact and cultivation of your members can be helpful in obtaining such business, if that is desired, which often meets on a regular basis. It is important to make sure that members perceive these as "member functions" rather than as meeting of local organizations. This will reduce conflict between members. Also, each manager should have a policy statement on the use of function and meeting room space that has been approved by the Board of Directors.

An increasingly valuable source of business is the wedding reception, particularly as weddings are more and more elaborate. This complexity makes it imperative that the parents of the bride seek "expert" assistance in conducting this important affair. The all-inclusive wedding reception is a profitable business builder for many clubs and has an added bonus value in that it introduces your club to a wider group of people than it is likely to encounter during daily operations.

Signs, banners, and posters for the promotion of special functions should incorporate certain design characteristics which will make them more effective. To get the best results from these items, remember the following:

1. *Location*. Always pick spots that have heavy traffic flow so that the maximum number of members will see the message.
2. *Visibility*. There must be no obstructions to the view of your message, and the farther away that members can see it, the better.
3. *Brief, concise copy*. The message should concentrate on one point and should state the message in the fewest possible words. Remember that the people whom you want to read your message are on their way to someplace else and are just passing by.
4. *Simplicity of design*. For the same reasons that the copy must be brief, the design must be simple so that the entire illustration, layout, and message can be caught in a glance. If it is confused with several patterns in the design, it probably will not even receive the glance.
5. If possible, the piece should contain one large, bright picture or illustration and copy of ten words or less.[6]

Flyers and bulletins are usually a sheet which may provide information concerning a particular event or information about events covering a given time period. (Many clubs include monthly bulletins with each billing to members.) These are simple, quickly produced, and amazingly effective. They probably represent the most cost-effective means of disseminating information to the largest number of members.

GOODWILL

This final note is aimed more to the manager's personal development than to the development of the club. However, keep in mind that to many members, the manager is the club; they are one and inseparable. Therefore, as you build goodwill among your members for yourself, you also enhance the image of the club and the satisfaction of the members.

The club manager should consider goodwill to be as important a part of performance as cost control. Yet, somehow, it is an indefinable extra. Goodwill takes a considerable amount of time and hard work to create, yet it can be destroyed in an instant. It is a frequently overlooked and elusive element of marketing communications. This is because it can't be touched, packaged, or stored. Yet the goodwill of the members is one of the most precious assets of the manager and the club. Building goodwill is a full-time job.

A Member-Oriented Approach

For the excellent club manager, goodwill is achieved in three ways:

1. Putting the members' interests first. You must impress upon the members that you have their interests at heart. Because you are in a service occupation, your work hours are determined by member needs rather than by the clock. The member and the club must be constantly in your thoughts—during off hours as well as on the job.
2. Working with members.
3. Remembering to do the little things that make members think of you positively. Goodwill is more than doing favors for members. It's being thoughtful, considerate, and caring.

Don't talk with members as if the club were on fire. Even if you are in a rush, don't appear to be. Talk with members as if they were the most important thing in your professional life. They are. This is time well spent that frequently pays personal dividends. Let members know that, no matter what happens, you are always ready to serve them. Treat the occasional visitor with the same respect and deference as the member who visits regularly and spends freely. Goodwill is a quality that will precede the manager who practices it.

Confidences and Excuses

The club manager is truly the marketing director of a club and will need the support of the board of directors to successfully do his or her job. Marketing decisions are intrinsic to effective management and need to be explicitly addressed. These marketing decisions include identifying target markets, determining the position of the club, and developing product, pricing and communication strategies to support the positioning statement.

But most important is constant and continuous interaction with club members. Marketing objectives can not be achieved in the back office. "MBWATC" (management by walking around the club), supported by practitioners and academics alike, has its roots in the marketing concept.[7] Conscientiously applying MBWATC says that you are putting your customer first. In other words, you are making a point to find out what is really going on at your club and not relying solely on reports and financial statements for management decisions.

As noted earlier in this chapter, financial stability is obviously important to the vitality of the club. The philosophy of marketing is that it is *through* customer satisfaction from which financial stability can be achieved. "The customer is king" and will always be so.

Theodore Levitt, reknowned for his expertise in the field of marketing, has made the statement that "consumers are unpredictable, varied, fickle, stupid, shortsighted, stubborn, and generally bothersome."[8] I am sure there are many club managers who would agree with this statement(!) Albeit, the customer has needs and is the very reason for our existence. When we lose sight of the customer we have lost sight of what our job is all about—customer satisfaction.

The club manager also builds goodwill by respecting members' confidences, by being truthful, by displaying tact and courtesy in difficult situations, and by being an example of conduct that is above reproach at all times. If a manager exhibits these qualities, members will be more willing to share confidences, thus providing a basis for better service and greater member satisfaction.

Do not make phony excuses for jobs that are not performed well. If deadlines aren't met, if others do not perform as they should, admit your failing. You may upset some members, but more than likely you will command their respect and admiration for your honesty. Mistakes and accidents can happen and members know it, but they won't forgive someone who tries to weasel out of a bad situation with bad excuses.

Remember, selling the club and its services is only half the battle. The good manager follows through to make sure that promises are kept and that the members are entirely satisfied.

REVIEW QUESTIONS

1. Name several types of printed material that are available to effectively promote the use of a club's facilities. What are the advantages and disadvantages of each?
2. What are the three purposes of merchandising?
3. Consumer surveys made by the National Restaurant Association show that the two most annoying factors in a dining experience are:
4. How does marketing relate to merchandising?
5. What is the most powerful marketing communications tool available?

Answer the following statements TRUE or FALSE.

6. Marketing is a communication system which makes exchanges easier between the club and its members.
7. Marketing communications flow one way—from the club manager through his staff to the membership.
8. The single basic purpose of marketing communication is to establish or improve understanding between you and someone else.
9. In goal setting, shoot for the moon; don't hamper yourself in terms of human and material resources.
10. A person perceives in a way that depends upon present circumstances and past experience.
11. Every manager should have on file a policy statement approved by the club's board regarding the use of function and meeting room space.

ENDNOTES

1. Handout—US Air Force Open Mess Conference, Amherst, Massachusetts, pp. 4–5.
2. Material originally from W. J. E. Crissy, Robert J. Boewadt, and Dante Laudadio. *Marketing of Hospitality Services.*
3. William C. Martin, "Defining What Quality Service is for You," The *Cornell Hotel and Restaurant Administration Quarterly 26* (February 1986): 32–37.
4. W. Earl Sasser, R. Paul Olsen, D. Daryl Wyckoff, *Management of Service Operations* (Boston: Allyn and Bacon, 1987), p. 10.
5. Crissy, p. 162.
6. C. Dewitt Coffman, *Marketing for a Full House.* Helen J. Recknagel, editor, Cornell University, School of Hotel Administration, Ithaca, New York, p. 214.
7. Norman J. Spitzig, Jr., CCM. "Management By Wandering Around the Club" in *Perspectives on Club Management,* pp. 47–51.
8. Theodore Levitt, "Marketing Myopia," in *Strategic Marketing Planning in the Hospitality Industry,* ed. Robert L. Blomstrom (Educational Institute of AH & MA, 1983), p. 14.

14

Epilogue

Spessard Holland Golf Club, Melbourne Beach, Florida

This book dealt with club management—but there's another side to the story—the role these institutions play in our cultural, social, and recreational lives.

Clubs are basic to our social order. They have a special function and cater to definite groups of people. A. H. Maslow, a scholar of human behavior has identified and ranked people's needs as follows:

1. Basic physiological needs.
2. Safety and security needs.
3. Belonging and social activity needs.
4. Esteem and status needs.
5. Self-realization and fulfillment needs.

One club's charter provides that "the club is a nonprofit social and recreational membership club, organized under the laws of this state pertaining to nonprofit organizations. The club shall be operated exclusively for pleasure, recreation, and other nonprofitable purposes, no part of the net earnings of which inures to the benefit of any member."

Clubs provide food and shelter, so they serve some physiological needs. Members feel a sense of safety and security because clubs offer some protection from outside forces; thus, membership itself meets the belonging need. Every club satisfies social needs, both structured and unstructured. The free association with one's peers and social and business acquaintances offers the opportunity to meet esteem and status needs. Group participation in specific activities and the advancement of social, economic, and personal growth help meet the self-realization and fulfillment needs. Thus, clubs play a vital role in fulfilling the needs basic to human existence and will always be a major part of life in America—despite some forces working against them.

Social interaction is probably the basic function of most clubs—the other functions spin off from this idea. Brick, mortar, physical facilities, and real estate make beautiful edifices, but the real essence of a club is its people. Members make the club.

A club must have rules and regulations to lead an orderly existence. These govern use of the facilities and participation in club activities. The bylaws and various departmental rules provide this framework. Those members elected to serve the entire membership are responsible for administering the rules and regulations the people have agreed on collectively. This self-imposed discipline enables all members to use and enjoy the club to its fullest extent.

Recreation comes in many forms, ranging from golf to soccer and every other individual and team sport ever devised. Exercise facilities, steam baths, saunas, chess, cardplaying, and other rigorous and not-so-rigorous competitive activities all challenge the mental processes. Thus clubs improve health, both mental and physical.

Family life is the foundation of human existence; families are just as important to a community served by a club as to one that is not. Clubs reinforce family lifestyles and personal discipline. Children going from home to club participate on swim, golf, and tennis teams and behave in the same manner as they do at home.

The youngsters must abide by similar rules in both places because parents contribute to the rules and regulations of the club, thereby sustaining continuity in lifestyle, training, and personal growth for their children. In addition, club families interact with other families and form even stronger family bonds. The experiences and training gained from the home, school, church, and club mold an individual into the kind of adult that person will be forever.

A good club of whatever type—golf, country, city, yacht, or other—that is well-kept, well maintained, and well managed, not only creates pride in the community, it contributes substantially to a better environment and, in itself, helps keep property values up. Per square foot occupied, it uses fewer municipal services than do individual homeowners, apartment dwellers, and businesses. It requires fewer services from police, firefighters, schools, libraries, and other public facilities than does a residential or commercial development on a comparable piece of real estate. It also relieves the burden on public recreational facilities by providing these facilities for a large segment of the population. In addition, many clubs have reciprocity with community sports teams, including golf, swimming, tennis, and soccer, and host other social activities such as bridge, singing and dance groups, educational exchanges, and others.

As pointed out elsewhere in this book, clubs across the nation pay millions of dollars annually in taxes—real estate, utility, sales, unemployment, social security, and others. Approximately 10,000 of the 13,000 clubs operating in 1988 are "total facility" clubs. They have full-service clubhouses, facilities for food and beverage service, and, in most cases, some form of recreational facilities. Clubs employ well over 1,000,000 full- and part-time personnel, with a total annual payroll approaching six billion dollars. The total club membership approximates ten million; counting additional family members, membership approaches twice this number.

As clubs are different, so are their management needs. The Club Managers Association of America publication, *Job Descriptions for Club Operations,* describes several types of managerial positions: general manager; executive club manager; clubhouse manager; and, of course, those who assist them, such as an assistant manager and the catering manager or food and beverage manager.

There are variations to management roles, but the Association defines a general club manager as follows:

> The elected club officials (officers, directors, governors, or trustees) formulate policy and provide guidance for the general manager but do not involve themselves directly in the management of personnel or operations. The general manager is completely responsible for all phases of management and accountable to the governing authorities for performance of the entire management team and for all operating results.
>
> The relationship between the governing authorities and the general manager must be carefully defined. Both relationships are identical to those in any business corporation. The first is similar to the relationship between the board of directors and the company president or chief operating officer. Club committees should work with the general manager the same as subcommittees of a corporation board of directors work with the president or chief operating officer.
>
> Guidelines
>
> The general manager reports directly to the club's chief elected official, or his authorized representative. He also works in tandem with the full body of governing authorities.
>
> The general manager serves in the capacity of chief operating officer of the entire club and implements the policy established by the governing authorities.
>
> The general manager develops operational policies and is responsible for creation and implementation of standard operating procedures for all areas of the club.
>
> The general manager prepares the annual budget and, after board approval, manages and controls the operations to attain the desired results.
>
> The general manager supervises all department heads, including the club house manager, food and beverage manager, all professionals, golf course superintendent and the controller/auditor. The general manager coordinates all management functions of the club.

The manager sometimes has other unofficial responsibilities. He must frequently be a subtle and unobtrusive social moderator. He has to be an expert in psychology and a master in human relations. The demands placed upon him are enormous. He has to manage and inspire those who work under his direction so that they perform in exemplary fashion. Likewise, he must motivate and inspire those he serves to utilize the club and to participate in its activities. He has to walk a delicately balanced line—he must be friendly but not familiar; disciplined but not arrogant; firm but not authoritarian; wise but not almighty; and thoroughly competent in all the technical skills of managing a club efficiently.

According to a recent CMAA survey the average club manager has been a member of his professional organization for about 15 years; over 90 percent have attended at least one annual conference. The typical manager has attended in excess of 5 management workshops; 75 percent have attended at least one. More than half of CMAA's members hold at least one college degree. A club manager is in his mid 40s and has been at his present club for about 8 years; he has been a club manager for 15. His cash compensation varies from about $50,000 to $100,000 annually; CERTIFIED CLUB MANAGERS usually make more than do noncertified ones.

The future of clubs is tremendously important. It's important to club members and club officials because clubs serve basic human needs. The club gives members a great sense of satisfaction and pleasure; it stimulates the professional challenge to the club manager. It rewards him with a sense of pride and satisfaction in serving the needs of others and in doing a job well. It provides him with a livelihood and rewards him financially.

Club life in America has experienced something akin to a revolution in the last 30 years, and a whole new concept of club life has emerged. Clubs have changed from the playgrounds of the very rich to family centers for social interchange, recreation, and other healthful pursuits. Clubs have added all sorts of features—increased golfing activities for the entire family, more tennis in all its forms, and numerous programs and social and educational facilities.

There is a definite trend among younger people again to join clubs. Clubs are making it financially easier for younger people to join, and their interest is spurred by an ever-increasing sports- and exercise-conscious America.

Financially, clubs are no different from any other business in the American system of free enterprise. Clubs are, by and large, nonprofit organizations, but club managers are as concerned with the "bottom line" figures of a club's operating statement as any other corporate general manager. Even though clubs do not pay dividends to their stockholders, they must have incomes greater than their expenses in order to add to, improve, or maintain their facilities for the next generations of club members.

Inflation and economic adversity may take their toll. But those clubs that have a cadre of good members and that function under good management principles will survive. These clubs will continue to fulfill their responsibilities to their members, their communities, and the nation.

Yes, clubs are here to stay.

Index